HARD BARGAINS

Hard Bargains

MY LIFE ON THE LINE

Bob White

Canadian Cataloguing in Publication Data

White, Bob, 1935-
  Hard bargains

Includes index.
ISBN 0-7710-8836-1

1. White, Bob, 1935-   . 2. Trade-unions –
Automobile industry workers – Canada – Bibliography.
3. CAW-Canada – Biography. I. Title.

HD6525.W44A3 1987   331.88'1292'0924   C87-
093944-0

Printed and bound in Canada by union labour at
John Deyell Co.

McClelland and Stewart
The Canadian Publishers
481 University Avenue
Toronto, Ontario
M5G 2E9

To Mom and Dad,
who have loved each other
for almost sixty years,
and to my sister, Rachel,
who has spent so much of her life
taking care of them

Contents

ACKNOWLEDGEMENTS

The writing of this book was a new and interesting experience for me. I had previously read other autobiographies, but I had no idea of how important certain people, other than the author, are to the process of preparing a manuscript. Let me mention those who played an important part in the writing of my story.

I want to thank Jack McClelland, who wouldn't take no for an answer and without whose personal persuasion I would not have even started this book. Also June Callwood, a warm, intelligent, energetic, and supportive woman, who listened and asked questions as I talked into a tape recorder. She skillfully wrote the story on my behalf from those tapes. I would also like to thank the talented Dinah Forbes, my editor, who spent days taking out repetitive and uninteresting comments and making other important changes to make the story more concise and, I hope, more interesting. My thanks, too, to Wendy Cuthbertson for her encouragement and for her advice from start to finish.

INTRODUCTION

THIS BOOK IS dedicated to the men and women workers in plants, offices, and other work places, who are now members of CAW-Canada. All my adult life I have attempted to help them and their families achieve a better quality of life. Doing so has never seemed like work to me. It has been a privilege, a wonderful opportunity to broaden my education and horizons, and to make changes – changes in the work place, changes internally in our own union, changes in the labour movement, and changes in government policy and legislation, which have benefited hundreds of thousands of Canadians, many of whom are not even part of the labour movement.

I want to thank the men and women of the CAW and, especially, the local leadership, who helped make change possible and who encouraged the members to stand together even when it was unpopular to do so. One of those CAW members is one of my sons. I want to thank the staff, who work each day on important negotiations and problem-solving for workers and who get little credit.

Much of what I've done in my work and my personal life has been controversial. Change is always controversial and leadership demands risk-taking. It requires a measure of idealism and the courage to make those ideals happen.

Because of the men and women of the CAW, I have travelled this wonderful country. I have met and spoken with prime ministers, premiers, cabinet ministers, and other members of parliaments. I have talked with trade-union leaders, heads of churches and industry, publishers and journalists, and, most importantly, with workers and their families. Canadian trade unionists are part of a world-wide labour movement, so I have been fortunate to visit many countries and meet with other workers' representatives of all political persuasions.

When I was in Japan, I visited the museum that commemorates the tragic day when the atomic bomb was dropped on Hiroshima. I rededicated myself to speaking out, whenever and wherever I can, against nuclear-arms buildup and for dialogue between the superpowers in order to find a lasting world peace.

In recent years, I have turned down two proposals to do a book. Quite frankly, I couldn't understand what interest there would be. Also, most people write books after they retire, when they can afford to be candid, not while they are in the midst of a busy life. Many people I would have to mention are still active and have dealings with me. I was not sure, as well, that I wanted my personal life open to the public.

In early 1986, I had a visit from the very persuasive Jack McClelland with another request. The CAW director of communications, Wendy Cuthbertson, supported his idea, and the two of them convinced me to do this project. When I thought back over the major issues my union has faced, I realized that we've been in the forefront of a lot of developments that affect all Canadians. I realized, too, that there has never been a book that looks candidly at a union and its leader from the inside. Media portrayals of unions are seldom sympathetic, and people outside the labour movement often have only a vague idea of how unions work. I decided that if my story could help Canadians understand unions, then I would do it.

This book is not about the history of my union. I will leave that for someone else to write. It is about my life and how this great organization, now the CAW, has played such an important part in it. I have tried to be as factual as possible in my recollection of events, but I have never kept a journal so I was obliged to depend on my memory. I'm sure that, in some instances, I am not entirely correct.

If I was not candid in my recital of events, either in my personal or my working life, this would be a phony book. I've been candid. Let the chips fall where they may – including on me.

CHAPTER ONE

A New Canadian Union

THE FOUNDING CONVENTION of a new made-in-Canada union, UAW-TUA Canada, was held in Toronto the first week of September 1985. To look at us, you would think we had the world by the tail. The jubilant delegates knew they were making labour history. After years of unpleasant confrontations behind the scenes, Canadian auto workers were separating from one of the most respected and powerful unions in the world, the mighty United Auto Workers.

I moved around the convention hotel, shaking hands and grinning. This was the end of my seven years as director of the Canadian wing of the UAW and the start of leading a new union. After fighting the Detroit leadership of the UAW almost as often as we'd fought the corporations, we were about to take our destiny in our own hands as the sixth largest union in Canada.

We opened the convention two days after Labour Day on the afternoon of September 4, 1985. Early that morning I went alone into the hall and wandered around, watching people put the final touches to the simultaneous translation equipment and put out name cards. Behind the platform was a bright blue backdrop on which was blazened the white and silver UAW-TUA CANADA logo, with a red Canadian flag maple leaf between UAW and TUA. Looking up at it, I filled up.

The rows of tables in the convention hall were marked with the names of our 115 locals, including 222 mainly from the General Motors plant in Oshawa, which with 20,000 members is the largest union local in Canada; 444 in Windsor's Chrysler plant; 112 and 673 in de Havilland; 1163 in Ste. Thérèse, Quebec, where the Olds Cutlass, Grand Prix, and Pontiac Le Mans were assembled; 200 from Windsor, the oldest Ford unit in Canada; 240 of Ford office workers in Windsor; 1459 of Chrysler workers in Etobicoke; 720, which assembles Volvos in Halifax; 112 and 673 at Spar Aerospace, the plant and office workers who built the famous Canadarm used on the U.S. space shuttle; 1451, whose 1,500 members make up one of the largest locals in the auto-parts industry; 1905 in St. John, New Brunswick, a Northern Telecom plant making electronics; and 80 at Honeywell in Toronto, also in electronics.

The new union was starting life with 70,000 members in the auto industry, 30,000 in the auto parts industry, 10,000 in communications and electronics, and the rest, more than 30,000, scattered through the agricultural implement sector, the air lines, salt processing, pet food, candy bars, pharmaceuticals, and whisky.

Boxes containing policy statements and the stapled copies of the proposed constitution had been unloaded. Ballots were ready for the election of the new union's first executive board. In the area where excited delegates and guests were lined up to pick up their badges and folders, a dozen people were checking names off lists.

Plenty of Canadian unions have broken from their American parents, but none as large as ours. The automotive industry is Canada's largest manufacturer. More than 200,000 people have jobs directly or indirectly related to it, and the Canadian economy depends to a significant extent on the trade advantage we now enjoy over the United States through the Auto Pact.

Something about the spirit and toughness of the Canadian auto workers had caught the public's imagination. And the media had arrived in full force to record our celebration. But not everyone was celebrating. This year, 1985, marked the fiftieth anniversary of the UAW. The international union had been a pathfinder among trade unions for two generations. Now we were raining on its parade. Solidarity House in Detroit was so unhappy with us that the UAW president, Owen Bieber, had rejected our invitation to attend.

We were hoping to gloss over that absence and what it really meant to our union. Despite the mood of confidence and celebration at the convention, UAW-TUA Canada could not have been in worse trouble. Bieber was making our existence as difficult as possible. The $36 million promised us almost a year earlier for our strike fund and administrative costs had not yet been paid. Only the week before, Bieber had told me flatly that we couldn't use the name United Auto Workers. If we insisted on calling ourselves the Canadian UAW, he threatened, the parent union would leave us penniless.

I was dismayed at the meanness of his position and the danger we faced, but I had no choice but to carry on as if everything was fine. I couldn't allow our founding convention to be destroyed by bitterness and uncertainty. For the sake of the staff, the 350 excited delegates and hundreds of guests looking forward to three unforgettable days, and 140,000 Canadian members of our union, I had to assume that the dispute could be solved.

Much thought had been given to the order and placement of the some dozen people scheduled to address the founding convention. As president-designate of the new UAW-TUA Canada, I would lead off. The closing banquet speech, a convention highlight, was reserved for Victor Reuther, a legend in the labour movement. At seventy-two, Victor was a brother of Walter Reuther and the only surviving member of the Reuther family, who had founded the international UAW.

To the consternation of President Owen Bieber and other officers of the international UAW, Victor Reuther had been going around the United States applauding the move of Canadian workers to separate. Soon after the split was announced in December 1984, Reuther called the Canadian breakaway, "a laudable objective, a long time in the making." He suggested that the separation was inevitable. The Canadian part of the UAW, he said, had always shown "deep nationalistic feelings." He added sternly, "There does not have to be organic unity in order to have solidarity across international lines."

The convention was opened by Basil Hargrove, known as Buzz, one of my two administrative assistants. Buzz had been at my side through all the strikes, the all-night negotiations, the tough battles with corporations – and the internal disputes with the UAW. He introduced me, and as I walked to the podium, I got a hell of a reception from the delegates. As the standing ovation went on, I felt shivers go up my spine. My first words were, "If you don't think my adrenalin is flowing this afternoon, you've got another thought coming."

Using notes, because I don't like to read from a prepared speech, I spoke for about fifty minutes. I gave the historical background of the UAW in Canada, a parallel development with the UAW in the United States under the great leadership of Walter Reuther. We began as Region 7 of the UAW in 1937, with a few hundred members in our first local, 195, Kelsey Motor Wheel plant in Windsor, followed soon after by locals 222 in the General Motors plant in Oshawa and 199 in St. Catharines. Chrysler workers joined in 1943.

For most of those formative years, I said, the goals, objectives, and working conditions in the two countries were much alike and the union functioned as one body. Even so, there were stirrings of Canadian independence. More than twenty years ago, the Canadian director, George Burt, won a struggle with the union's headquarters, Solidarity House in Detroit, to change the name by which the Canadians were known in the UAW from Region 7 to "the Canadian Region."

Dennis McDermott, the Canadian Region's next director, took us further on that path. He succeeded in winning a constitutional change that gave Canada special recognition within the international union – from then on, the Canadian director was automatically made an international vice-president of the UAW. Nationalist feelings were stirred again in the late 1970s by the world-wide recession, which rocked the North American auto industry and shook the union. The Canadian dollar was devalued sharply against the American dollar. This factor, together with such economic differences as government support for health care and other social services in Canada, meant that Canadians were working cheaper than Americans and could develop different strategies at the bargaining tables. Since it was no longer possible for a pattern achieved in agreements in the States to fit Canadian workers, we began to bargain differently and get better settlements than the Americans could. This caused upheavals within the international union. In 1982, Canadian Chrysler workers, who for years had preferred to bargain jointly with American Chrysler workers, broke away and signed their own agreement. It was time to complete the transition to independence, I said.

I had to say that we still didn't have the $36 million we had been promised by Solidarity House. I was careful not to be critical. Instead, I treated the situation as a legal hitch, which would be resolved when the UAW had its next convention in June 1986.

I didn't mention my confrontation with Owen Bieber over using the name, United Auto Workers. I was afraid the delegates and media would seize on that symbolic issue and blow it up out of proportion. Rumours of the threat to cut off our money were around, but everyone was in such a good mood that few people paid much attention.

The convention went off without a hitch, thanks to months of intense, detailed work by our staff and local union leaders. We looked like a union that very much knew what it was doing and where it was going.

The crowning event was the final night when Victor Reuther addressed a thousand people at the closing banquet. When the old man rose to speak, some wondered if he could hold the room's attention. The bar was open again and a band was waiting to play for dancing.

Victor waited for the applause to die down, then pulled from his pocket a tiny piece of paper. He peered at about six lines of writing, lifted his head, and began to speak.

He spoke for about an hour and a quarter and the audience was as enthralled at the end as when he began. They were touched to the heart by Reuther, pioneer of the labour movement, veteran of strikes that changed the course of trade unionism. He told them of the early great days of the UAW and talked about where the union was going. He was critical of what the UAW was doing in the United States but said that Canada was "a breath of fresh air."

Victor honoured us by conducting the election of the first executive board, at which I was made president, and enjoyed himself hugely. He brought his wife, Sophie, one of the first organizers in the UAW, and they had such a good time that they stayed on the platform throughout the whole convention.

Just before the convention started, I received a telephone call from Detroit on a phone we had installed on the platform in case of an emergency. It was from Owen Bieber, president of the UAW.

"I just want to tell you I'm sorry that I can't make the convention," he said. "I've sent a statement by telegram to you and I'd like to read it."

"Just a minute, Owen," I said. "I'll get Helen Kramzyk [my secretary] to take it down in case it doesn't arrive. I think it's important that I read it to the delegates."

It was signed by both Bieber and Ramon Majerus, international secretary of the UAW. At some point in my opening speech, I paused and read it.

"On behalf of the International Executive Board of the international UAW, we send greetings and best wishes to members of your new Canadian union on the occasion of the founding convention. As you embark on the course of independent action we hope that the needs and desires of your members will be well served. While we wish you Godspeed, our greetings are tempered by a sense of sadness. For nearly fifty years we shared a common struggle and together we built a strong union. The brothers and sisters who built the UAW realized that multinational corporations knew no boundaries and neither should workers. From 1936, when workers on both sides of the border sat down to force General Motors to the bargaining table, until now, there has been more that united us than divided us. . . . Although we disagree with your decision to separate, we of course respect it. . . . We wish the members of the union success in the ongoing struggle for social and economic progress and justice."

I had hoped that he would have to use the name UAW Canada, but he avoided that by calling us the "new Canadian union." I'm sure lawyers helped draft that document. Bieber and the others couldn't have found it within themselves to be so generous.

John Duff, president of Local 439 in Massey Ferguson Toronto, is a very good friend and a loyal trade unionist, popular on both sides of the border.

He chaired the resolutions committee of the international UAW at three consecutive international conventions. His sentiments were with the international union and he had spoken many times, feelingly, against the split. Once the decision was made, however, he supported it.

His local was broke and not able to send delegates to the convention, but I just had to have John Duff a part of it. I asked him to be a sergeant-at-arms, with responsibility to check the credentials of the platform guests and swear in the new officers.

Duff, standing there in a white suit that made him look like a small version of Colonel Sanders, swore us in one by one. Halfway through, he interrupted the proceedings to read what he said was a telegram he had just received.

"Dear Bob," he read. "Come home. All is forgotten. Signed Owen."

Maybe it's one of those you-had-to-be-there lines, but it brought down the house.

CHAPTER TWO

Early Days

I DON'T THINK I'd ever known such misery as I felt when I first went to school in my new country, Canada. At the age of fourteen, after taking it for granted all my young life that I could manage any situation, I was suddenly uncertain and out of my depth.

In Ireland I had been an ordinary, fairly happy-go-lucky boy. I got average marks in school, never the top student and never the worst. I was as good at soccer or rugby as the best half-dozen of my age, but never the star athlete. My teachers sometimes found me a trial because I was a cut-up, maybe too quick with a joke, but I got along all right. I didn't back down from a fight, but I wasn't a belligerent kid. The only fights I picked were with bullies I'd caught pushing another kid around.

My parents had drilled habits of politeness and honesty into me; rudeness and lies just weren't tolerated. This served me well with adults.

About the only thing that set me apart from any other farm boy growing up poor in Northern Ireland was that my mother and father were among the sternest fundamentalist Protestants around. One thing they insisted on was that I couldn't play sports on Sundays. Like most kids, it made me uncomfortable to have parents whom my friends thought were a bit odd, but I didn't brood about it.

Although they were devout, they were free of the bigotry that has been identified with both faiths in Northern Ireland. They never shared the rabid Orange anti-Catholicism of some Irish Protestants. As children, we were aware of undefined barriers between Protestants and Catholics, but we were never taught hatred.

Up until 1949, when we emigrated to Canada, I was a confident kid. But when I started school that fall in Woodstock, a small city in southwestern Ontario, nothing about me was all right any more. I didn't speak like anyone else, my clothes were funny-looking, and other students in the high school treated me with indifference. Worse, I couldn't join in the games. I'd never even seen baseball, basketball, or football and I hadn't been on ice skates in my life. The last was the most serious; in Woodstock it seemed that every boy my age played hockey day and night. For the first time in my life, I was a complete misfit. It came as a shock.

I kept my feelings to myself. I was determined to be like the others, a process that started with getting rid of my Irish accent. As soon as I could skate, I turned out for hockey practice. By the time the next summer rolled around, I was playing baseball and football.

MY FATHER, Robert Johnson White, was born in 1901, one more of a huge brood of kids, ten children in all, three of whom died soon after their birth. This was a time when there wasn't much to go around, and from the age of three, my father was raised by his bachelor uncle. His uncle was relatively well-to-do, by the family's standards, and lived with his unmarried sister, Tillie, in a big farm house they shared with their parents, who owned the farm. The family decided this childless pair would need a boy to help them with the chores. In return, my father was expected to inherit the farm.

My father's siblings scattered as soon as they were old enough to escape from the poverty of their childhoods. Two brothers went to Canada, two sisters moved to Albany, New York, and there was a brother and a sister in London, England. Of the seven children, none stayed in Ireland.

The uncle who raised my father lived in The Vow, a place so small that it consisted of four corners. My father earned his keep. Though he was only a boy, he was obliged to do chores at the farm before going to school, to come home at noon to do more work, and, of course, work after school. My dad never talks about his childhood, but I know he dropped out of school when he was twelve to help on the farm.

At some point in what must have been a lonely youth, he became an avid reader, especially of the Bible, and he was drawn to an evangelical group known as the Faith Mission. He met my mother at a seaside resort in Ireland, Port Rush, where they were attending a religious conference.

He was twenty-nine and she was twenty-eight, both attractive, well-liked people. My mother says he approached her after the meeting. "I saw his blue eyes and fell in love with him," she explained to me not long ago. They married six months later, in 1930. They have had a wonderful marriage – I've never seen another like it. Religion has always been a solid bond between them. In 1986, they celebrated their fifty-sixth anniversary, still openly affectionate and deeply devoted to each other. I could count on the fingers of one hand the number of times I've heard them argue, and I've never known them to raise their voices to one another. Because of her, I think, he's been a happy man.

My mother is the educated, cultivated one, the child of warm, out-going people named Tumath. Her mother came from a farm not far from ours, and her father was the postmaster in Belfast, where she was born in 1902. She's the oldest of three children, all of them talented people. All three grew up with their parents' expectation that they would do well, and they, in turn, held the same attitude toward their own children.

After their wedding in Belfast, my parents went to live in the only home my dad knew, his uncle's house. I gather the aunt and uncle made life somewhat difficult for my mother in the beginning.

A year later, my brother Bill was born in the farmhouse. It was a difficult birth, achieved with forceps after a hard labour that lasted a day and a half. My mother suspects that Bill's brain was damaged during that harrowing time. He suffered from *petit mal* seizures throughout his childhood and seemed to have a learning disability.

His life has been hard. He married a Mennonite woman a few years after after we came to Canada and he and his wife moved to Victoria, British Columbia. There he worked in a forest mill and they raised their four children. One Sunday when he was out walking, he was hit by a truck. He suffered severe brain damage as well as other internal injuries and smashed bones. I flew out to Victoria and when I saw him lying in the hospital my first thought was that it might have been better if he hadn't survived. He has needed constant nursing care ever since.

His wife had a terrible time of it, with little money and four children to raise. For a while she lived on welfare, but about four years after the accident things started to look better. She went away to a religious retreat on her first holiday since the accident. Soon after she arrived, she had a massive heart-attack and died. A sister and brother-in-law, Stan and Vera Cressman, grain-farmers in Saskatchewan, became guardians of the children. Their own kids were almost grown, but they expanded their house and took Bill's four to live with them. Bill was transferred to Saskatchewan so he could be near them.

David Lewis, former head of the New Democratic Party, was a great help to our family at that time. He recommended a lawyer, John Laxer, a sympathetic and excellent person. We sued the people who owned the truck. Mr. Justice Tom Berger was on the bench and he made an award of $300,000 in damages, a substantial amount in those days. Unfortunately the people responsible later went bankrupt so the family received only about $85,000 in all.

I WAS BORN on April 28, 1935, about four years after my brother. This time my mother went to Ballymoney Hospital, the one nearest the farm, for the delivery. While I was still a nursing infant, I somehow got a serious kidney disorder and had to be rushed to hospital in Belfast for intensive care. Later in my life, doctors discovered that I had a congenital kidney malformation, a narrowing in the ureter, which might have been the cause of my problem as a baby.

My condition worsened and, at one point, my mother was told that I would die of kidney failure. I rallied slowly and, after two weeks, I was allowed home. I was still so weak that my mother had to rub oil on my body and keep me wrapped in cotton batting. My parents were frightened by all this, but the doctor told my father, "Don't worry about him. You'll see, he'll turn out to be the stronger of your two sons."

I was named Robert for my father, but until we moved to Canada everyone called me Robin. There were no more children until twelve years later, when my sister, Rachel, was born. She must have been a surprise. My mother was forty-six years old, my dad forty-seven.

I've never been really close to either my brother or sister. Though Bill is older than me, I always had the feeling that I had to look after him, rather than the other way around. One of my father's stories is about the first day I went to school. I was only four years old and Bill was eight, but as we left the house I said, "Don't worry about Bill. If anyone tries anything, I'll take care of him."

I started school early because I was showing some readiness to read, and because my brother could take me. We got along all right, quarrelling from time to time as brothers do, but I wasn't drawn to him. He was an edgy kind of person, easily upset, quick to flare up, moody. He suffered from terrible nightmares and would wake up screaming, which used to terrify me.

There was such an age gap between my sister and me that I never knew her very well. When she was small I took little interest in her. My own life was busy and I was out of the house. She hasn't married and still lives with our parents. She's the kind of person who puts her energy into caring for others and she is devoted to our parents. She takes after our family in that way. When we were growing up my mother used to say, "If there's soup for six, there's soup for seven." There always seemed to be somebody who needed a little help and my parents would share whatever we had.

My first memories are of the uncle's house in The Vow where my father was raised. It was an old brick house, two-storey, covered with ivy and surrounded by a stone fence. I can picture the outside better than the inside, maybe because I was an active kid, always tearing around.

My mother's father was fond of her and often came to visit. We kids liked him, though he was a disciplinarian. When we sat next to him in church, we didn't dare wriggle because he'd give us a sharp pinch on the arm.

My mother teases me about the afternoon grandpa was taking care of us while she and my dad were away. My brother and I devised a new game, grabbing the chickens by the legs, whirling them around and throwing them up on the garage roof. When my parents got home, the chickens were on the garage roof making a terrific fuss and my grandpa was running around below, trying to figure a way to get them down. The odd time we'd get a spanking from my dad and that was one of them.

My grandpa's name for me was "the artful dodger," because I always tried to get out of helping with the chores if I could. When it was time to do the dishes, I'd go to the bathroom and stay there as long as I could. He had a good eye for that kind of trick.

When I was about four, my parents got a shock. After a lifetime of working without wages because he expected to inherit the farm, my father learned the farm was so encumbered with debt that there was nothing in his legacy but bills. My uncle had spent everything he had, and more, and my parents were penniless.

My mother's father was visiting during this crisis and came to the rescue. Years before, secretly, he had taken out an insurance policy on my mother. If she wished, he said, she could cash it in. My father decided to buy a tractor with it and offer himself and his farm machinery to other farmers for rent. That providential insurance money, about £300, enabled him to become a contract farmer. My uncle still owned a small house at nearby Drumlee, with a bit of land around it, and it was decided that we would move there.

One evening in Drumlee, my grandpa visited us. My parents had tucked us into bed, as they always did and my dad stayed behind to say goodnight while my mom went downstairs. A minute later, I heard her call, "Come quick! Grandpa's dying!" My grandpa had drawn his last breath, sitting in a chair in the front room.

We had to stay in our bedroom while my father got a neighbour to help him carry grandpa upstairs to his bed, where my father washed him and dressed him for burial. He called the undertaker and said there was no reason to disturb himself until morning because everything was done. My father was used to that. He helped to prepare for burial his grandfather, his grandmother, his uncle, his aunt, and his own father, who died in his arms.

We raised a few chickens and sheep at Drumlee while my father launched his new career as a hired hand. I can remember the inside of that Drumlee house quite clearly. Upstairs there was one big room, a sort of playroom, where we kept our toys, among which were my treasures, a collection of Dinky cars and trucks.

It was obvious to me as a small child that my grandparents' homes were very different, and that they also were very different. I was young when my dad's parents died, but I remember that their house had a thatched roof and was heated by an open fireplace where they burned peat. They didn't have plumbing or electricity; they used oil lamps. That didn't seem strange to me; we lived the same.

My other grandparents, my mother's people, had a nice house in Belfast with a well-trimmed garden at the back and lots of interesting and attractive things around. My uncle, her brother, had a house in Londonderry that was a wonder to me. I loved going there because he had electricity and a gramophone and a telephone.

I was never envious that we didn't live in that style, except every now and then, like the time I wanted a toy sailboat that I saw. It was handmade of wood, a beautiful thing with proper sails, but too expensive. Bill and I knew that we couldn't have a lot of extras, but we could count on plenty of toys at Christmas, and we were never hungry or shabby.

My mother's nature is sunny and optimistic. In whatever situation she finds herself, she's unquenchable. My dad is much like her, warm and expressive, basically a contented man. It was my mother who instigated activities in our family, the picnic outings, the music lessons, that sort of thing. Also, she was the one who was keen about our education and made sure we did our homework. She bought books which she read to us when we were small.

Because my father had been raised by a bachelor uncle, he thought nothing of washing the supper dishes or cleaning floors. Even to this day, and he's had a stroke, he'll vacuum and dust. My brother and I grew up taking it for granted that boys did housework. My mother was very strict about it. Saturday mornings we weren't allowed to play until we'd done our chores, cleaning the silver, mopping floors, making the beds. Then she would inspect what we'd done to see if it was perfect before she'd let us go.

My parents were staunch observers of the Sabbath. On Sundays we weren't allowed to play sports, and work was forbidden, too. No matter how badly my dad was backed up on harvesting or seeding, or what needed doing around the house, it had to wait until Monday.

The Sunday ritual actually began on Saturday night with the bath. My mother would pump the water into a tub, which she'd heat on the stove, and then my brother and I would bathe. After that my dad would sit us on a board across the arms of a chair and he'd trim our hair. The next morning, dressed in our best, we went off to Sunday School before going to the church service. This was followed by Sunday dinner of roast beef, lots of vegetables, soda bread, and home-baked pies.

My mother supervised our table manners with a sharp eye. Sitting quietly, without squirming to be away and running, was always difficult for me. After an afternoon of reading or music, we spent the evening in the community gospel hall where my dad was the lay preacher and my mother played the autoharp and sang hymns.

My dad was a good speaker. His main theme, as I recall, was that we should be ready because the end of the world was coming. It sounded to me like it was maybe due next Friday. When your dad says that kind of thing, you figure there must be something to it. He wasn't a hellfire and brimstone preacher because he isn't that kind of man, but his faith runs deep. He used to read the Bible or some religious book every day, still does, in what he calls his "quiet time." When my parents were trying to make a decision about something like moving, they would get on their knees to pray. As a kid, I heard a lot of this or that mishap being "God's will." God was a real presence in our lives, a part of the family.

My parents were dead set against smoking or drinking, and would be outraged by a transgression like a lie or taking something that wasn't yours. Their rules of acceptable conduct were very clear to us. My mother, who had a proverb to suit almost any occasion, would lecture us with such adages as "Money can't buy you happiness." Not long ago when I heard her say that I told her, "No, but it can buy you the kind of misery you like."

Despite my parents' orthodox views, we had a lot of fun together, laughed a lot. My memories are of good times and warmth. We got our share of hugs, and my dad is still open in his affection for my mother, no matter who's around. He's quick to praise her, everything she does. We children always knew that there was a lot of love in our family.

As for sex, it simply didn't exist. I had to find out about that on my own because it would never occur to Bill or me to ask our parents about it. We used to go into the barn with our cousins and compare the stories we'd picked up about what men and women did to get babies. We'd show each other our genitals, but that wasn't a lot of help. We were all quite baffled.

The first school my brother and I attended was one-room. As we moved around, the schools we went to were larger. I was an active kid, something of a nuisance for the teachers, but I wasn't the class trouble-maker. I remember I suffered, as most small boys do, the pangs of secret crushes on girls who didn't know I existed. I was something of a loner. We moved around so much, I was always leaving friends behind. I haven't had an intimate friend at any time of my life, really.

The war didn't seem far off. At school each child had a gas mask and was drilled on what to do in air-raid alerts. We'd evacuate the school and run out to lie in the fields, wearing the gas masks. At night we heard planes overhead, and Belfast was a target for bombers several times. My mother and I went there after one raid to see if her relatives had been hurt, and when we got off the train we found the station had been hit. The roof was wrecked and there was debris everywhere. That was scary.

Maybe that's why as a kid I was afraid of the dark. My brother wasn't scared at all, but I begged my mother to let me sleep with the light on. She didn't think it was necessary, so I was never allowed one. It didn't help that the adults used to entertain one another with ghost stories when they came to visit. We were supposed to be asleep, but we'd eavesdrop, and I'd get back into bed more terrified than ever.

My mother was a comforting person, but she could be short on patience. If I protested about being sent to the store in the rain, she'd say briskly, "You're not sugar or salt. You won't melt. Just go."

One of the great treats of my childhood was an outing to the beach. In the summer after supper we'd drive to the coast, and I would walk along the shore during the long twilight hours, feeling a wonderful sense of peace. On one beach, called the Port Stewart Strand, you could drive your car for miles. I couldn't swim, none of us could, but my brother and I played in the surf in inner tubes and built sand castles.

Being on a beach still means something almost spiritual to me. To this day, when I can I'll walk for hours along the shore. I can really find myself quickly next to the ocean.

Some of the happiest times of my childhood were spent at Donegal in southern Ireland, where my aunt and uncle owned Shannon's Guest House. I would get bus-sick going there, but once I got my feet on the sand of the beach, I was in heaven. Even there my mother insisted that we work around the place, cleaning silver or something, but our afternoons were free. The beach was rugged, broken with coves and rocks, and I used to roam it for hours. Some days were misty, with everything looking soft and muted, and others so bright I'd get a sunburn to which my mother would apply lotions of buttermilk.

One day I saw a rainbow so vivid that I thought it surely must have a pot of gold at its end. It disappeared behind a hill, so I climbed up only to find that it was behind another hill. When I climbed that, the rainbow was still tantalizing me beyond the next hill. It was a while before I gave up thinking I'd find that pot of gold.

I told that story one time to a union colleague, who said it was the story of my life. "You're always chasing that rainbow," he said.

We lived in Drumlee for about two or three years and then, when I was seven or eight, we moved to Aghodewy into a house that had been converted from a pub. It was more modern, though it still didn't have electricity, and there was a big barn behind where my father stored his equipment. An army sergeant and his wife were billeted with us and made my brother and me a gift of two goats we called Gert and Daisy.

There were army camps nearby and we used to hitch rides on tanks, but what impressed me most was watching the paratroopers falling out of the sky. I decided that a big umbrella would work just as well as a parachute, so I climbed on the barn roof, opened the umbrella, and jumped. I usually talked Bill into trying these things first, but this time he wouldn't do it. The umbrella turned inside out and I came down in a hurry, but luckily I landed in some hay.

Aghodewy was a fair distance from Drumlee, so my brother and I had to change schools. I didn't mind much, I never minded moving around as long as I had my family around me.

When I was nine years old, we moved again, to a place called Upperlands. My father had been hired to manage farms for five brothers named Clark, who also owned cotton mills. It was a responsible job, hiring and supervising the staff, buying cattle, tending the crops. A big five-bedroom house went with it, the first we'd known with electriticy and grander than any we'd ever been in. There were big gates in front, and I was thrilled to have a room of my own.

Every now and then my dad would take me out of school and I'd go with him to buy cattle. I loved listening to the men driving a hard bargain. My dad was good at bartering, and I was proud to see how the others seemed to respect him. Those cattle men lived by a code of honour and never had to put anything on paper. When the deal was made, each man would spit on his right hand and then they'd slap their hands together with a crack, and that was it.

In 1945, when the war ended, we celebrated with fireworks and a massive bonfire. By that time my brother and I were in a secondary school such a distance away that we went by bus. The school required uniforms and was tough on discipline and decorum. Discipline was enforced by a cane, which the headmaster applied liberally to the backsides of the boys. I got it more than once and it hurt like hell. I had a little trouble with mathematics and needed extra coaching to pass. I did better in the athletic program, taking part in track and field events and making the school rugby team. I was a scrappy kid who liked contact sports.

My sister was born in 1947, when my brother was almost seventeen and I was almost twelve. One night my father woke us to say he was taking my mom to hospital and when he came back, he said we had a sister with black curly hair. Rachel was a pretty baby, easy to care for, and my brother and I were expected to help with her care, even changing her diapers.

About this time, I came privately to the conclusion that I'd had enough religion to last me the rest of my life. I said nothing about it then, but when I did break away a few years later I appreciated my parents' attitude. They didn't once reproach me. They felt that they had done their job of instilling in me certain fundamental beliefs, and they were sure those principles would stick.

TWO YEARS LATER, we were packing our belongings to move to Canada. My dad's brother, who lived in Toronto, had come home for a visit and talked a lot about this wonderful place. Unknown to us, my dad and mom had been thinking about emigrating. That's not unusual for the Irish, the country being poor and small and many families so big, but in the years right after the war there was a huge exodus.

My brother announced that he wanted to go with our uncle when he returned to Canada. My parents would not stand in his way, but they had long talks between themselves and prayed for guidance. Eventually they made up their minds that the family would not break up. Despite the fact that my father was doing well as a farm manager and they both had deep roots in Ireland, they decided that if Bill wanted to live in Canada, we would all live in Canada. My dad said simply, "If one goes, we all go."

He obtained a guarantee of a job as a farm manager in Ontario and we started to pack. One bleak day the auctioneer came to sell our furniture, massive tables and carved dressers that would fetch a high price now. Hordes of people passed through the house, touching our things and making comments. I felt a wave of misery.

Mom saved a few things she prized: a silver tray given her father for organizing a postmasters' association, her silver service in a cabinet, and some treasured dishes and linen. We loaded our things into tea chests and trunks. When my mother heard that we were not allowed to take more than a thousand pounds out of the country, she was amused. "That's no problem for us," she observed cheerfully. "We can't reach the maximum."

My parents wept as we left Ireland in April 1949, but I was too excited to feel sad. We sailed from Liverpool on the *Empress of France*, a 20,000-ton liner. Our first glimpse of Canada came a few days later when we entered the mouth of the St. Lawrence and sailed up the river, between the rocks and woods on either side. The first building we saw was the Château Frontenac in Quebec City, a castle hanging high on the cliff above us.

We docked in Montreal and made our way down the gangplank amid crowds of people excitedly greeting one another. I was struck forcibly by the fact there was no one to meet us. In Ireland, whenever we'd gone anywhere we were surrounded by relatives and friends who were glad to see us. I had a sense of apprehension and loss; something in the expression on my parents' faces told me that they felt the same.

To this day when I travel, I think it's neat to see people being met. I don't look for it for myself because I'm on the go so much, but I get a lift as I make my way through a mob of family and friends waiting for passengers to come through the gates.

We went directly from the customs shed at the dock to Windsor station and boarded a train for Toronto. It took a half a day to crawl along the northern shore of Lake Ontario, and we were stunned by the size of the country and the enormous fields. We were met in Toronto by my dad's brother and sister-in-law, who lived in Leaside and took us in for a week while we got our bearings.

I couldn't get over the bright lights of Toronto. After the austerity of Belfast, blacked-out for five years and slow to recover, Toronto's brilliant, blinking neon signs were a delight. We all stood rapt before a billboard sign for White Rose gas – a huge electric rose that opened and closed.

A week after our arrival in Toronto, we went to Union Station and boarded a train for Woodstock, where my father's employer would meet us and take us to the dairy farm that my father expected to manage. George Innes was waiting for us but with bad news – there was no farm-manager job. Instead, Innes told my dad he was hired to do farm labour for $100 a month, plus a house. My dad was nearly fifty, not a young man for that kind of life, but he had no choice and he didn't flinch.

Innes drove us along Highway 59 south of Woodstock and turned left into a narrow gravel road, the first road we'd ever seen that wasn't paved. He pointed out his land, on which he raised pure-bred Jerseys, which he showed at the Canadian National Exhibition. His farm seemed wild and huge to us after Ireland's tiny, well-groomed fields and stone fences. Finally, we turned into a rutted driveway leading to a sad little red-brick house, with an outdoor privvie at the back. We were home.

My mother wept. She'd never lived in a place as poor as this and she found the outdoor toilet particularly demeaning. Because the house hadn't been occupied for six months, it was deep in dust and mouse droppings. But in no time she was scrubbing the windows and floors and telling us brightly how homey the place would look with a bit of paint and fresh curtains at the windows. That was a long way off, because first we had to buy furniture. Until we had beds, ordered from Eaton's catalogue on credit, we slept on blankets piled on the floor.

She continued in that cheerful vein, assuring us stoutly that everything was wonderful. Her optimism was heroic in the face of the conditions she had to tolerate. A strong stench of cow manure permeated the house, there was no getting away from it. Because we didn't have a refrigerator, or even an ice box, she dug a hole in the earth and stored butter and milk there. She had to push my sister in a carriage for three miles along the shoulder of the highway to get to the nearest store in Woodstock. In the field next to our house, Innes kept his bull, a fierce-looking animal that terrified my mother.

My father started milking cows at six in the morning and then worked all day until it was time to milk them again in the evening. It was brutally hard work, but he never complained. I was having an easy time. I had just turned fourteen and I was supposed to be in school, but no one seemed to be concerned about that, which suited me fine. I hung around with Innes and his cronies, who liked to sit in the barn and talk. He found that I knew a store of Irish songs and sometimes he'd give me a quarter or two to sing for his friends.

One day that felt like spring, he mentioned to my dad that I seemed a capable kind of kid, could I handle the tractor? My father answered that I'd been around tractors all my life, and that I was a good worker. I was offered a job for a dollar a day and leaped at it. I worked literally from morning until night, ploughing, cleaning the barn, milking, driving tractors, and I loved it. I didn't like mucking out or helping pigs give birth, but the rest of it was great.

Soon after Labour Day, a truant officer arrived on our doorstep. Someone had spotted me in the fields and figured I should be in school. He explained to my parents that there was a law about fourteen-year-olds attending school, so I had to go.

Jimmy Innes, the son of our employer, was a grade ahead of me in the Woodstock high school. On the first day, I got a ride into Woodstock with him and he introduced me around. I felt so awkward I didn't know what to say. Nothing about me felt right. I couldn't overcome the barriers by joining in the games the other boys played, because I didn't know how. What bothered me most was the way I talked. I paid attention to the way Canadians pronounced words and I consciously worked, every waking moment, to get rid of my Irish accent. The misery of being a misfit lasted only six weeks, maybe two months, but it was so acute that I can still recall it with a pang.

I was placed in Grade Nine, since no one was sure how my education in Ireland would match with the curriculum in Canada. After a week I was moved to Grade Ten. That made me feel a little better, but not much.

Despite my initial discomfort at school, I never for a moment was homesick for Ireland or wished we hadn't come. There were many compensations in this new exciting country with its white roses in neon lights. Our first summer storm in Canada was thrilling – we had never before seen forked lightning. One morning, we looked out the farmhouse window while eating breakfast and saw two deer strolling across the field, a magical sight.

I saved my dollar-a-day earnings until I could purchase a brand-new, bright-red bicycle, which became the family's transportation. One evening my dad and I were riding it into town, with me on the cross-bar, when an old van came up from behind and hit us. I was only scratched and bruised, but my dad was dragged under the van and his leg was badly smashed. Someone called an ambulance. A few hours later, I was released from hospital and went home to try to calm my distraught mother.

My dad came home the next day with his leg heavily bandaged. The van owner's insurance company sent a man with a piece of paper waiving any future claim. He said if my dad signed it, he'd give him $100. That looked good to my dad, so he signed. I had a hunch that he'd made a mistake, but there was no one to give us any advice about it.

My dad could get around on his bad leg, but it was clear that he could no longer do the work on the farm. That meant we'd have to leave the house for the next employee. Because my brother Bill had a job in Woodstock at a woodworking factory, Hay & Co., we prepared to move into town.

CHAPTER THREE

Hay & Co.

BILL HATED FARMING, always had. Soon after we'd moved into the house on the Innes farm, he'd got a job at Hay & Co., a woodworking plant in Woodstock. My father decided to follow his example. Even without the injury to his leg, he was finding the twelve-hour days of a farm labourer more than he could take. But the factory was hard on him in a different way. After a lifetime of working in the open air, he was dismayed to be in a place where the air in some places was thick with wood dust and glue fumes that choked lungs and stung nostrils.

We rented a modest house at 9 Bexley Street, the last street in the west end of Woodstock, three miles across town from Hay & Co. The house wasn't in the best of shape, to say the least. The kitchen floor slanted so steeply a ball would roll away from you. A Quebec heater in the kitchen was the only source of heat for the entire house. It was fitted with an octopus of round pipes that were supposed to carry heat to other rooms but failed utterly. Mom, Dad, Rachel, and I slept upstairs, shivering in our beds, and Bill slept downstairs. One time, when a hotwater bottle fell out of Bill's bed in the night, he found it next morning, frozen solid.

Irish winters are damp and dreary – I've had enough of winter rain to last me all my life – but they're mild. The severity of the cold in Canada came as a shock to us all. Our clothes weren't warm enough and our bodies weren't prepared. My mother wore her winter coat in the house all day. She developed an ulcer and had to see a doctor regularly for treatment. She told me years later that when she returned home from those visits she was so sick, cold, and miserable from the long walk downtown and back that she would throw up. She never let us know about that at the time.

My father and Bill had to walk almost three miles to work, arriving many mornings with hands and feet near frozen. Though my mother and Rachel had to endure that icebox house all day, she bustled around as cheerfully as ever. With the walls painted and a lace cloth on the diningroom table, it didn't look at all bad.

My parents joined a Baptist church. Bill refused to go to church with us on Sundays, a decision my parents accepted with equanimity because he was grown and working, but Rachel and I had no choice in the matter. I went resentfully, impatient during the sermon and perfunctory in the prayers. Happily, my parents were quick to notice that few Baptists in Woodstock were strict about curbing activities on the Sabbath. They began to be more relaxed, and if I wanted to go skating on Sunday afternoons with the other kids, I could.

I had struck up a friendship with twin boys, Hugh and David Close, who lived nearby with their father and stepmother. Their father owned the grocery store where we used to shop, running a tab that we paid weekly on payday as most people in the neighbourhood did. Hugh and Dave used to deliver for their dad.

I had two other pals as well, Peter Moyer and Mike Kowalchuck, who said they would teach me to skate. I paid five bucks for a pair of used skates at Stubby's sports store and we went to a patch of ice close to South Side park. Peter and Mike howled at my first efforts and I was bruised from head to toe, but eventually I got the hang of it.

The more lenient attitude my parents were developing about Sundays didn't extend to chores. I was still expected to help around the house, and I still wasn't allowed out until my tasks were done to my mother's satisfaction. If she'd been born a generation or two later, I'm sure she would have been a feminist. I suspect she has some regrets that her intelligence and talents didn't have the outlets that women have today. With her logical approach to problems, her firmness of mind, her insistence on openness, and her clear principles, she set a high standard of conduct.

One struggle between us was over weekend mornings. My efforts to be allowed to sleep in went unrewarded. Mom was firmly opposed to people staying in bed unless they were at death's door. I'm not sure what she meant by death's door because I never seemed to be sick enough to qualify. Whenever I had a miserable cold, she'd scoff at my suggestion that I should stay in bed.

"What's a cold?" she would ask indignantly. "If you're *really* sick, that's one thing. But it's only a cold, so get to your chores."

I used to dream that when I grew up I'd sleep until noon on weekends, but you don't shake off those early habits so easily. Most mornings now I do a three-mile run before eight o'clock.

I was having trouble with the strange curriculum and the unfamiliar customs in my Canadian high school. Though I gave my subjects a serious try, I was only just getting by. I began to lose interest in academics, and school became just something to endure until I was old enough to leave and start earning a living. Meanwhile, I landed a part-time job in Loblaws after school and on Saturdays, cleaning vegetables in the basement of the store and loading them on a dumb waiter to be hoisted up to the produce department.

I was fifteen that April, and two months later, as school ended, I somehow passed Grade Ten. Greatly relieved, I was looking forward to a leisurely summer of baseball, rafting on the river and playing in the parks with my friends. My mother had other ideas.

"You're not going to sit around all summer," she informed me. "You've got to get a job."

She sat me down with the Woodstock newspaper, which happened that day to have an ad for a job in a restaurant.

"But I don't want to work in a restaurant," I protested.

"You'll go right down there and apply," she said firmly. "You've got to get a job, and that's a job."

The prospect of being a dishwasher all summer was so dismal that, to my great embarrassment, I cried. My mother wouldn't relent so I had no choice. With despair in my heart, I went downtown and applied for the job at the Foodrite restaurant and was hired. The Foodrite was owned by the Wong family, who offered a menu of plain Canadian fare and a selection of Chinese dishes.

Actually, the job turned out all right. The Wongs were nice people and good to me. I started every day by cleaning the washrooms and then I washed dishes until quitting time, except for sometimes helping to cook breakfast. My big ambition was to be promoted to work at the soda bar, where the kids my age gathered over ice cream. That never happened, though; all summer I was stuck in the kitchen at the back.

My modest wages at the Foodrite were turned over to my mother to help with household expenses. She gave me back some for spending money, but I didn't have much need of it. The girls I was meeting at the Baptist church didn't appeal to me and the popular girls at school were out of my reach. Mostly I hung out with boys, pleased that my Irish accent was almost gone and my ability to play Canadian sports was improving.

When I went back to school in the fall of 1950, I wasn't ready to settle down to books. Grade Eleven was a concentrated year, packed with heavy subjects, and I floundered. At Christmas my marks were so awful it was clear that I would fail. The guidance teacher made an appointment with me.

"What are your goals?" he asked. I replied frankly, "My goals are to wait until I'm sixteen and then quit school and go to work."

He had an interesting suggestion. "If you feel that way," he said, "you don't have to wait until you're sixteen. You can leave school now if you'll learn a trade."

That caught my attention. When he recommended that I become an apprentice printer, I agreed at once.

My dad was concerned when I told him my decision. "Have you thought this through?" he asked. "Are you sure this is what you want to do?"

I said I was certain.

"Well, it's your bed," he warned. "Remember, once you make it you'll have to lie in it."

That was fine with me.

I was interviewed for the job of apprentice printer at the *Ingersoll Tribune*, a small weekly in a town some distance from Woodstock. I spent the day watching various jobs then I asked the man how much the job paid.

"Eighteen dollars a week."

I was shaken.

"And how long does it take to become a printer?"

"Eight years."

I considered and then said, "I can't work that long for that kind of money."

My mother's response was predictable. "You're not going to sit around the house. If you're not going to school, you're going to work. Go get a job."

A few days later I went down to the factory where my dad and brother worked, Hay & Co., and was hired. It didn't seem to bother anyone that I was only fifteen. The workers were unionized by the United Auto Workers, which had a classification for "boys under eighteen," which is where I fit. The rate of pay for boys was forty-seven and a half cents an hour. Every two weeks, when we got our pay, I took out ten dollars for myself and gave my mother the rest.

Some people have an idea that the United Auto Workers only represents people who work in the automotive industry, but this is far from the truth. During the war, when an automotive parts plant in Woodstock was unionized by the UAW, people in nearby plants looked to the UAW to represent them, too. At about the same time as the union was certified at Hay & Co., it was also organizing a casting plant, a Massey-Ferguson plant, a dog-chow plant. That pattern happened all over Ontario. As long as the UAW wasn't in conflict with another union, it would take in whatever plant approached it.

My father had an Old Country suspicion about the labour movement. He warned me not to get mixed up with the UAW and declared that unions were "full of communists." I didn't know anything about unions, but the members in my factory seemed a good lot, always joking around and teasing one another. When the union steward, an old guy in my department, asked me to join, I wasn't sure what to do. I asked some of the other guys about it and learned they were all in. So I signed. My UAW membership card is dated February 1951, a matter of weeks after I first punched a time clock.

I didn't tell my father. My brother also had joined the union, and I don't think he mentioned it to my father either.

Hay & Co. was an old family company, run in paternalistic style by a respected Woodstock citizen, Tommy Hay. It occupied two buildings on Norwich Avenue. I worked in an old brick building with wooden floors and tall narrow windows covered with dusty grime. My father and Bill worked in the newer cement-block building directly across the street.

The noise was deafening in those parts of the plant where saws and sanding machines were located. We were always complaining about the poor lighting because, of course, people working with saws needed to see clearly.

At the end of the day, we'd clean off our clothes with an air hose, which only blew more dust into our lungs. In summer the plant was a sweat box. We'd drink from a cracked, ancient water fountain and swallow salt tablets. I noted management wasn't much interested in making working conditions safer, more sanitary, or more comfortable.

My father and brother worked in the plant where logs were peeled into veneer. In my building we made such articles as furniture and doors. The contract called for a forty-five-hour week, seven to five on weekdays and five hours of overtime on Saturdays. My job was to sweep the floor or take doors from the saw and pile them.

In June, less than six months after I started to work, the plant went on strike. The working conditions and the pay scale were so miserable that even my father joined the union and supported the strike. At ten o'clock one morning everyone in both plants put down their tools, turned off the machines, and in a holiday mood walked out into a fine summer day. The three Whites went on the picket line together, earning strike pay of five dollars a week each. I thought it was fun.

My mother had been scrimping to save a bit from the household money we gave her. One day, a few weeks before the strike, an ad in the paper caught her eye. It was for a used car that the dealer promised to sell at a price he would reduce by ten dollars every hour it remained unsold. She had strong nerves. She waited until it was down to $42.50 and bought it, a 1929 Dodge. My dad drove us to picket duty.

36

Our family couldn't survive long on strike pay of fifteen dollars a week, so we started to look for part-time work. We read that Woodstock was hosting an International Ploughing Match, so my dad and I got jobs parking cars for the entrants and spectators. When that finished, we joined a gang picking tomatoes; stoop labour is brutal work.

The weather was warm and on the picket lines we had nothing to do but walk back and forth with signs. We joked and kidded around and sipped free coffee and tea. Sometimes a UAW official would turn up from Windsor and we'd feel important. I enjoyed the strike. I wasn't behind in my rent or going into debt to buy food. My dad was the one who worried, wondering how we were going to survive.

The strike was settled in six weeks. The workers got a small increase in pay, but when the plant re-opened, some had lost their jobs and I was one of them. Somewhat shaken, I went to the unemployment insurance office and applied for benefits. I drew one cheque while looking for work before I landed a job in a slaughterhouse on the outskirts of town.

I was sixteen by then, and I had my driver's licence, so I was taken on as the driver of a pickup truck. Part of the job was picking up cattle for delivery to a slaughterhouse in Brantford or to my employer's abattoir. That was tough work for me; seeing cattle killed took some getting used to. It was my job to hold the rope halter secured through a ring in the floor while someone hit the animal on the head with a sledgehammer. Then its throat would be slit. The worst was killing pigs. They would be strung up by the hind leg while their throats were cut. The noise of their suffering and terror was unbearable. The only part of the job I enjoyed was driving the truck around town delivering meat, waving at my friends.

Some of my friends were starting to drink, but I wasn't interested. I didn't like the taste of beer, still don't, and I found I could have just as good a time without alcohol. We never had liquor in the house, and I didn't start having an occasional drink until I was about twenty-five or so. As for smoking, I'd tried stolen cigarettes with the rest of my friends when I was about eleven, but I'd hated it.

The following spring, I got called back to work at Hay & Co. and was glad to quit the job at the abattoir.

My dad couldn't stand being cooped up in the factory doing repetitive work. Soon after the strike was settled, he quit Hay & Co. and became a Fuller brush salesman, going door to door. He did very well at that for years, travelling all around Oxford county. My brother also quit the plant and moved to Toronto, where our uncle helped him get a job at Eaton's. Eaton's was a great place for hiring the Irish in those days. I was the only White left at Hay & Co., taking little pleasure in what essentially was drudgery.

ONE DAY a union committeeman in my plant, an old man known as Smitty, asked me, "Why don't you ever come to union meetings?"

I had started to rebel a bit in the plant. It riled me when certain foremen treated workers unfairly and, being a mouthy type, I was complaining a fair bit about management in general. Smitty told me the union was the answer for working people, so one evening I went along with him to a meeting of Local 636.

The meeting was very poorly attended and the spirit was listless. I wasn't much impressed. Smitty said, "I'm going to nominate you for steward in our department."

"I don't know anything about being a steward," I told him.

"Don't worry about it," he said airily. "There's not much to it. There won't be anyone running against you. When your name is called out, just say you'll stand."

My name was called out, I stood up and said I had agreed to run, and nominations were closed. No one else wanted the job. They gave me a steward button, and I went back in the plant the next day wearing it, feeling that I had the world by the ass. I was seventeen.

I changed from a kid whose curiosity had stopped growing in some ways, to someone who had responsibilities and a lot to learn. I realized if my badge was going to mean anything, I had to find out about unions and what was in the Hay & Co. contract – and what wasn't. Despite my youth, I was required to resolve disputes. Many of the complaints were about being passed over for promotion to a better classification. The foreman was a big stern man, but I had the badge and I was a chippy kid. I'd argue with him that the worker had seniority, he'd say the job belonged to someone else, I'd say that was bullshit. At first I got nowhere, but after a while, when I learned what was allowed in the contract, I began to win a few.

One of those small but significant victories concerned workers whose families lived in the Maritimes. On the day their vacations started, they would come to work with their cars already packed for the trip. They wanted to be allowed to leave early in the afternoon so they could get east of Toronto before the five o'clock traffic jams, saving themselves hours of driving time. Management wasn't sympathetic, but I hammered at them until they relented.

Another fight was to get Christmas Eve off. The company eventually allowed us to shut down the machines a couple of hours before five o'clock but wouldn't let us leave the plant. Of course, some people got into the booze. After a year or two of that, the company let us go a few hours earlier than quitting time on Christmas Eve – without pay, of course.

The plant had a number of women workers, all of whom were paid lower wages than the men. I remember the hot arguments I made to get the women the right to operate the tape machines. It took a long time before the company yielded on that point, but they never did pay the women a fair wage. I beefed about being clocked while we went to the washroom, about management taking the toilet doors off because they said the guys were smoking in the stalls, about the mirrors that were installed at one point to catch guys smoking in the washrooms. My style was chippy and I wasn't popular with the foremen, but we made small improvements here and there.

When you're doing repetitive work, day after unchanging day, the sheer monotony gets to you. Like most of the people in the plant, I was a clock-watcher, yearning for the five o'clock whistle so I could get the hell out of there. I don't think people who haven't worked in such jobs realize how deadening it is to have no say in your own work and where every day is the same.

Some of the older guys worried about my aggressiveness with management. They cautioned me against my habit of giving the foremen ultimatums about what would happen if they didn't shape up. Wiser heads pointed out to me that when I did that, I'd better be ready to produce.

I paid attention to advice when it made sense to me, but I didn't let up. It was heady stuff for me, a teenager, to see some improvement and to know that I had a hand in bringing it about. In my own way, I was putting into practice the principles my mother and father drilled into me about making things better for others. The deeper I got into the union, the more I came to believe that the labour movement is a great vehicle for social change, not just inside the plant but in the community as well.

I was gaining respect and recognition. My union work was interesting, even exciting. I was dealing with important and challenging issues and the union was gaining stature. I had developed a close friendship with a guy inside the plant, Tom Seymour, one of five sons in a family that suffered greatly. Two of his brothers had muscular dystrophy and died at an early age, and Tom was to die of a heart attack in his thirties. Tom and I used to date girls in Ingersoll, both of us convinced they were prettier and more friendly than Woodstock women. The two of us played hockey, about which he was keen. He was stick boy for the Woodstock Athletics, the town heroes.

At the same time I began attending UAW education classes, learning about the union movement and meeting people who worked in other UAW plants. I lapped up union shoptalk about contracts and bargaining tactics; I hung on every word when people talked union history. I couldn't get enough of it. I became an avid reader of books about the union movement and reports of legendary bargaining marathons and strikes.

The more I learned, the more excited I became. Headed by Walter Reuther since 1946, the UAW was founded in 1936 at a convention of auto and other workers in South Bend, Indiana. The new union made a commitment to go after higher wages, better working conditions, paid vacations, extra pay for overtime and night shifts, seniority and job security, a company-paid pension plan, and hospital-medical care programs – none of which the industry had ever seen.

As Reuther put it, the "nameless, faceless clock-card numbers with no rights, no privileges and no status as individual citizens . . . have won a new freedom in the factories, a sense of worth, a sense of belonging."

The UAW has a tradition of setting the pace for collective bargaining for the labour movement. In 1949 it obtained the first company-paid pensions, $100 a month including Social Security, and other unions followed suit. Walter Reuther's slogan for the campaign was, "Too old to work, too young to die." For years, workers only had one day off at Christmas to spend with their families, but the UAW negotiated for Boxing Day and then, gradually, the long Christmas shutdown until after New Year's.

Later, the UAW got the thirty-and-out pension so that a worker with thirty years on the line could retire with a full pension, whatever his age, of $500 a month. In 1955, the UAW tried to get the world's first guaranteed annual wage, a pioneering principle never before achieved by any industrial union. Auto workers were laid off every summer, for six or eight weeks at a time, while plants retooled for the new models. It imposed a severe hardship on workers and their families. When the line started to move again, it would take a worker about four months to get out of debt. The communities in which they lived were hurt, too, as automotive workers went through their seasonal poverty.

Reuther finally obtained the supplementary unemployment benefit fund, called SUB, in which employers paid so many cents an hour into the fund for every hour worked. This topped off unemployment insurance payments so the deprivation of layoffs wasn't so severe. We've built that up so that today a worker can get 95 per cent of his or her regular wages during layoff periods for a certain length of time.

The SUB was designed for short layoffs, because the fund would soon go broke if layoffs went on for a long time, but the arrangement had a good effect on the auto industry. Faced for the first time with having to pay employees during layoffs, the companies rationalized production and cut down the time that plants were idle.

The UAW got North America's first prescription drug plan, the first survivor-pension benefit paid by the company, the first major cost-of-living allowance provision, the first comprehensive health care program covering the worker's entire family and funded by the company. Other unions, like the steelworkers and electrical workers, picked up on what was happening in UAW contracts, but we always seemed to be first. We were one of the first unions that had a collective bargaining convention, for instance, where 2,500 delegates set goals for all our national bargaining units so that they don't go to the table catch-as-catch-can. I think that this, and our strong central leadership, made us the trend-setters in the labour movement. On top of that, the UAW had the economic clout to bargain hard because most of our members worked for the Big Three auto manufacturers. It helped that we were in an industry that was making enormous profits.

I found the UAW's history fascinating and inspiring. It was pioneering of the kind to stir a young man's imagination. Because I was so young, I think it pleased the older men that I was so enthusiastic, and they went out of their way to be helpful and encouraging. I was something of a phenomenon and this marked me for special attention. I had grabbed on to something I could put my heart into; that's a lucky thing to happen to anyone. I loved what I was doing, which was obvious to all, and I was getting better at it. I was seized with a single ambition – to obtain better conditions, better wages, and benefits at Hay & Co.

Sometime after I became a steward in charge of matters in one department, I was elected to the bargaining committee, which is the union's administrative body in a plant. As a committeeman, I was head of three or four departments with stewards under me. In 1956, just five years after I'd started at Hay & Co., I was elected chairman of the bargaining committee, which meant I was in charge of union matters in the whole plant.

In truth, my rapid promotion within the ranks wasn't too difficult. I was not only an obvious candidate because I was working so hard for the union, I was the only one. The man who held the job before me had been there a long, discouraging time and wanted out. There wasn't even a contest for his successor, so at the age of twenty-one I was elected plant chairman.

It didn't bother me that I hadn't advanced in the plant and was still doing the lowest-paid, unskilled jobs. For a while I ran a clipping machine, a long blade that cuts veneer, and another time I did sanding, but mostly my work was general labour.

A foreman once suggested to me that if I worked hard I could be a foreman some day. I wasn't in the least tempted by what he thought was a flattering suggestion. The only good part about going to work every day was what I could do there for the union. The union had become my whole life. I began a pattern, which has persisted, of having almost no spare time for anything else.

Because I wore the plant-chairman badge, I was entitled to drop what I was doing to settle disputes whenever the stewards needed me. I still had an aggressive style, but I was learning not to make as many rash threats. The path of wisdom and effectiveness, I'd discovered, was to mean what I said and back it up.

In the beginning I had to fight apathy. We had to think of gimmicks like raffles to get members out to union meetings. Once I had them there, I would talk about the UAW like a man in love. I showed them films of the great moments in UAW history, like the famous sit-in strike, and brought in speakers to describe what the union was all about. Getting back the respect of members for the union was a vital step. I'd learned from labour historians that you can't make any progress in negotiations if your workers aren't behind you. That word "solidarity" isn't rhetoric. For a union, it's everything.

Many of the UAW members at Hay & Co. were older people, close to retirement age, and my brashness made them nervous. To them I talked about a pension program. In other plants pension programs were beginning to be an important issue in contract negotiations. They were a long overdue benefit. The idea of a pension got the attention of older members.

ANY POSSIBILITY that I might have swerved from my path as a dedicated unionist vanished totally in the spring of 1957 when I went to Atlantic City as an official delegate to the UAW convention. I remember vividly how it happened. I was at home one night when the phone rang. A UAW staff member said, "Look, Bob, there's going to be an election to see who goes as the delegate from your plant to the convention. I think you should run for it."

By the UAW constitution, every plant with more than 250 members is entitled to send one delegate to the international convention. That meant that the amalgamated local in Woodstock, Number 636, could send five people, expenses paid, and our plant could choose one of them. The chance for a free trip to Atlantic City was quite a plum, but people at Hay & Co.

seemed to feel that I deserved to go. When they elected me as their delegate, I was the happiest man on earth.

On April 6, 1957, five of us representing the Woodstock local – myself, Frank Kenny, Clarence Chattington, George Burton, and Bill Elsey – left together for Atlantic City. The travel arrangements made by the financial secretary were quite peculiar. Early in the morning we took the train from Woodstock to Toronto, a bus from Union Station to Malton airport, a plane from Toronto to New York, a bus from LaGuardia airport to Grand Central Station, a train from Grand Central Station to Newark, New Jersey, and a commuter plane from Newark to the Atlantic City airport, where we caught a bus to the hotel, arriving very late at night. The financial secretary didn't know there was any other way to do it.

We stayed in an old hotel on the Boardwalk. The hotels were allotted in a draw and the Canadian director happened to draw a low number, which meant we had one of the poorest hotels in the poorest location. I didn't care. I was in Atlantic City for the first time in my life, I was on the famous Boardwalk, there was the ocean at my front door, and down the way Walter Reuther was going to give a speech.

I was spellbound. You couldn't have got me out of that convention hall if you'd paid me. Eleanor Roosevelt was there and brought down the house when she rose to speak. Walter Reuther talked at length, a rivetting man, who spoke with the aid of a few notes. He told us about the civil rights movement, which was just beginning then, and about the evils of segregation. He had a lot to say about international affairs, all of it news to me.

I soaked it up like a sponge. Reuther insisted that the UAW had to look outward as well as looking after the affairs of its members, that the labour movement had a responsibility to be informed and to take positions in national and world affairs. We'd done a bit of that in Woodstock, helping people sympathetic to labour get elected to city council, showing an interest in community organizations, but Reuther's vision included the whole world. The sense I had of the UAW from Reuther was that the union was at the heart of everything that mattered, that it was enormous, that it was involved in every issue that touched on people's lives.

The debates had me enthralled. Old union guys with big hard hands from working on the line all their lives would get up in the haze of cigarette smoke that hung over the hall and argue articulately and vehemently with Reuther. You'd think they had an unanswerable point, but he'd come back with an argument that would bring cheers. He thrived on that kind of bearpit. I paid close attention to how he brought people around to his point of view. His manner was persuasive, for one thing. He was a great orator, relaxed, confident, and funny. He could marshal facts, hammer them down one after another, and pull in past experiences dramatically to show how they related to one another and formed a pattern.

As most delegates do, I wanted to have my picture taken with Walter Reuther and he obliged. Later I bumped into him and his wife in an elevator and said hello. He asked in a friendly way what local I was from, nice to see you.

The whole experience in Atlantic City turned me on, cranked me up. I thought that the UAW was an incredible organization. I went home turned on as never before.

AROUND THIS TIME my friends were getting married and it was clear to me that it was time I did, too. I started dating a teenager, Carolynne Dickenson, who worked in a beauty parlour. I met her when I was coming out of the YMCA one day, after a weight-lifting session. She was on her way home from the Anglican church across the street, where she sang in the choir. We drifted into seeing one another. It started on a casual basis but it rapidly became serious. We'd been going together about a year when we set the date to be married in September 1957.

She was blonde and attractive, a talented soprano who had won awards during her years of studying voice at the Conservatory. Her family was having serious problems. Her mother was almost an alcoholic, so it was left to Carolynne to help with the four younger children. The environment at her home was so unhappy, she liked to spend time at my house, where she seemed to appreciate that we were a reasonably close, affectionate family.

My parents were uneasy about her unsettled background but said little to me about it, accepting it as my business. Carolynne was a nervous, tense person, but we were much in love and had good times together. She didn't talk much about her difficulties with her mother or how that made her feel. In retrospect, I can see we really didn't know much about one another. The idea of discussing our deepest feelings or what we wanted out of the marriage never occurred to either of us. I don't think we knew what marriage meant. All that was in my mind was that we had fun together and I was anxious to strike out on my own, independent of my parents. Carolynne was even more anxious to get out of her unhappy house.

CHAPTER FOUR

On Strike at Wellwood

I N THE LATE SPRING of 1957, a few months before Carolynne and I were married and not long after my twenty-second birthday, I led a strike that closed Hay & Co. for thirteen weeks. We asked for decent wages, improved working conditions, a benefit package that would include improved health care, reduction of the hours of work from forty-two and a half to forty a week, improvement of job classifications, changes in the collective agreement, and, most important of all, pensions.

Hay & Co. had been bought up by a giant multinational, Wellwood, which had headquarters in New York and plants all over North America. When it came time for a new contract, management refused to consider anything we were asking. We continued to bargain, but we got nowhere. Wellwood had adopted Tommy Hay's paternalistic attitude and argued that it knew better than the union what was good for workers.

As the strike deadline approached, Wellwood came up with the usual dirty tricks designed to frighten employees and turn them against the union. They claimed that the last strike at Hay & Co. had been a fruitless exercise, and they predicted that this one would be the same.

"People will lose wages they'll never get back," they warned employees. "In the end you'll have to settle with nothing gained."

The most frightening threat was one to close the plant. Wellwood had a new plant in Searchmont, north of Sault Ste. Marie in Northern Ontario, and management made sure the Woodstock employees knew that this plant was equipped to do the same work as we did, only cheaper. A company statement like that can create panic in a small community where jobs are scarce. The pressure to settle on management's terms comes not only from frightened union members but also from local merchants and politicians.

The Canadian UAW director, George Burt, came from Windsor to bolster spirits and made an impressive presentation at a packed membership meeting. He gave financial reports that showed Wellwood to be a highly profitable company and the Woodstock plant an integral part of the multinational's operation. We discovered that our wages were low in comparison with those in similar plants. Tommy Hay, when he owned the plant, had been noted as a tight-fisted employer, and Wellwood had inherited a bargain.

Much encouraged, we called for a strike vote and only one worker voted against. The workers were finished with backward conditions and poor pay. We'd become an aggressive local, despite the substantial number of older employees. In fact, we were somewhat more bumptious than the UAW staff member, Roy Brown.

Brown had replaced Jimmy Smith, the staff member who advised us when I first became chairman. Smith was a sickly looking man who had terrible asthma. I liked him, but he didn't seem to me to have leadership qualities. He used to come to meetings wearing an old baseball cap and windbreaker. When Walter Reuther sent him to Arizona for his health, he was replaced by Roy Brown. Brown introduced himself to me on the floor of the plant and I was impressed with him at first sight. He presented himself in a well-pressed suit, with a shirt and tie, and his shoes had a fresh shine.

He became a role-model for me. An articulate man who argued our case forcefully with Wellwood, he spent a lot of time with me after work and invited me to his home to talk about the UAW.

Brown wasn't as keen about the strike as we were, and soon there was tension between us. We shared responsibility at the bargaining table fairly evenly, but Brown felt he should be in charge, while I felt that the responsibility for the negotiations fell on me. I respected his superior experience, but I had a very clear idea of objectives and I didn't want anyone sidetracking us.

The strike began mid-morning. The stewards checked their watches and quietly said, "Let's go." Workers put down their tools, turned off the machines, picked up their lunch buckets, and left without punching the time clock. Outside, police were waiting to give us instructions on where we could picket and where we couldn't. We put on our placards and started the slow shuffle of picket duty.

To look at us, you'd think we didn't have a qualm that day, but workers always have mixed feelings when they strike. Most of the people near retirement were determined to get pensions, but they were apprehensive. People supporting a growing family had dread in their hearts that they would go into crippling debt before the damned thing was settled. The younger people acted like kids let out of school. They went straight to a bar to celebrate.

I wasn't worried. I didn't have enough experience to be frightened at the decision we had made. All I could see was that our cause was just and the workers were with us. The strike pay was low, however, $15 a week for single workers and $25 a week for workers with a family. I knew we couldn't take a long strike, but I was confident that we would get a good contract quickly.

A sage unionist and friend, Frank Moroz, once said to me, "Bob, the only way you can handle things is to do your best. As long as you can get up in the morning and look yourself in the eye and say you've done your best, you've made your decision based on what you thought was the right way to go, then don't worry about it. Whatever happens after that, you can't change it."

That's helped me through some times of terrible stress. I make decisions based on the best information I can get and I don't second-guess myself much. I can be wrong, and I have been wrong, but I've learned not to guilt myself afterwards.

I know now that what I hoped to accomplish in the Wellwood strike was unrealistic. We aimed for too much, a judgment I blame on my youth and cockiness. It resulted in a near-disaster – we almost lost.

A strike is a peculiar time in a working person's life. After the initial euphoria and enthusiasm wear off, anxiety about the future is never far from anyone's mind. The fears they share bring people together. Even though they have worked together for years, workers rarely confide in one another what's really going on with them. But walking the picket lines side by side, having coffee together in the trailer, freed of the necessity of chasing a production piece on the assembly line all day, they form friendships and become philosophers.

If the strike is a long one, financial and family problems develop. Strikers then start to count on one another for understanding and support. For some of them, it's the first time they've ever really talked from the heart about private matters. A camaraderie develops that later will make them almost wistful for the strike days, as soldiers are after a war.

This intimate solidarity is particularly marked when the strikers are women. In the bitter Fleck and Blue Cross strikes, and in the Bank of Commerce strike, women who started as near strangers developed a real sisterhood. These were long and exceedingly difficult strikes, but the women gave one another extraordinary emotional support.

Tommy McLean, longtime assistant director to George Burt in the Canadian Region, used to say that the only way to build a union in a plant is to have a strike. He came from the old school, which believed that people have to struggle together in order to understand unionism. I don't necessarily agree, but in certain cases, in small plants especially, the bond between strikers can turn into loyalty to the union.

The time strikers spend together can also turn sour. If fear of losing their jobs builds beyond the point that workers can bear, panic seizes the picket lines like an epidemic and contaminates even the optimists. Nerves can get ragged, especially as bills mount, and some families start to resent the union.

About six weeks after the strike started, I went to a leadership meeting of the Canadian Council at the UAW's education centre in Port Elgin. I wasn't one of the 150 delegates, but I was allowed time on the program, as usually happens when someone has a strike going, to make an appeal for funds for the Woodstock strike.

The evening before the meeting there was a social gathering at the centre. The star of the occasion was the international UAW secretary-treasurer, Emil Mazey, one of Walter Reuther's closest associates. I was introduced to him and as he shook my hand he asked how my strike was going. I was stunned that a top official of a union with 1,200,000 members would know, and care, about a few hundred people on strike in Woodstock.

The next day I got my chance to make my pitch. For the first time in my life I was facing an audience that wasn't made up of people I knew. The men I'd been reading about – Emil Mazey, George Burt, and Cliff Pilkey, president of the Canadian UAW council – were all there. My legs were jelly. Though I had made extensive notes, my hands were shaking so much I couldn't read them.

Despite my terror, apparently I made a barn-burner of a speech. Cliff Pilkey told me years later that a man next to him turned and said, "You better watch that young sonovabitch. He's going to go some place."

The strike was now in its second month. The workers were hurting. We went to the hydro and telephone companies to beg them not to cut services. We talked to landlords and banks to get them to hold off reprisals for unpaid bills. I tried to get involved in the work of a welfare committee looking into hardship cases but the UAW man from Detroit who was coordinating it told me, "You can't have these personal and financial problems on your mind. Pick some people you trust to do this, and then stay out of it. Your role is to lead the strike."

In those days it was considered a sign of weakness to call the company and say you wanted to talk about a settlement. Similarly, management couldn't make the call because it didn't want us to get the impression that they were desperate. So both of us were stuck.

It was a war of nerves, and ours were shredding. A few strikers were beginning to grumble, and Woodstock was full of rumours that Wellwood was going to pull out. The mayor called us and offered to convene a meeting of management and union. I thanked her, but said I thought we'd better leave that kind of negotiation to the experts in the provincial labour department.

The UAW meanwhile had organized a car cavalcade to drive from Windsor to Ottawa to protest widespread unemployment in the auto industry. Someone in the head office prevailed on the organizers to have the cavalcade detour through Woodstock and join our picket line.

I was ecstatic that these seasoned trade unionists, the president of Local 200, the president of Local 444, would be stopping to support my strike. When they got out of the cars, shook our hands, picked up our placards for a few minutes, and gave us a few speeches, I was exhilarated.

We'd been out for three months, with no resolution in sight, when the provincial Department of Labour finally intervened, to my relief. Meetings were called in the government offices in Toronto with the government's conciliator, a man named Bradley. He met first with us. We had the top men in the Canadian UAW there, the Canadian director George Burt and his assistant, Tommy McLean, a man who was to play a significant role in my life, and John Eldon, a key staff member on whom Burt relied.

At the raw age of twenty-two, I was impressed to be in such company but tried not to show it. Bradley asked us to lay out the issues, and Burt laid them out. Then Bradley met with the Wellwood representatives and asked the same question.

While that was going on, Tommy McLean took me aside, his face all smiles like a kindly uncle. "You're a bright young guy," he said, "and we've all heard a lot about you. You've done very well. You've got a good strike going. You've had them out for almost thirteen weeks." I listened, pleased and wearing a modest expression. He went on gruffly, "I just want you to know that any dumb sonovabitch can take them out. The test is: Can you put them back? I think it's time you started to find a solution."

That was a crucial lesson for me as a union leader. If you're prepared to lead them out, you also have to lead them back, and that means you've got to find a settlement.

Bradley started to negotiate. His word to us was that Wellwood had moved a little but there was no way we could achieve what we were after. "You'll have to make compromises," he said. "There's no way I can get most of what you want." Bradley then recommended a contract we didn't much like.

To our consternation, Burt and McLean agreed with him. When we withdrew to hash it out in committee caucus, they pushed us to accept Bradley's recommendation.

"This isn't nearly as good as you expected it to be," Tommy McLean told us, "but you can't stay out forever. You'd better take the goddamned thing, otherwise this is going to be a disaster for you."

I felt we could do better, but I had to be realistic; I had to respect their view. McLean was the most politically astute man in the Canadian office. People said he was the power behind George Burt, the one who went around to all the locals and did the director's dirty work. His sense of the membership was uncanny, but I was to learn that there was no mystery, it was the result of sheer hard work. He made it his business to know everyone, especially promising newcomers, and find out what each key person was like. He was one of the handful of Canadians who sometimes spoke against the UAW administrators in the United States. He had both integrity and a strong political instinct, so when McLean said we should settle, we listened.

Still, it was a bitter pill to swallow. For two days and two nights, the bargaining committee wrestled with the unhappy decision. We couldn't agree on what to do. Two people thought that if we held out another two or three weeks, the company might yield. We argued every possibility and finally concluded that we'd have to trust Burt's opinion that our objectives were impossible. The strike had gone on for too long, and we had to end it.

It was late when we reached our gloomy conclusion, so we stayed overnight in Toronto, eating in some crummy restaurant. The next day we drove back to Woodstock to face the music with the membership. It wasn't easy, but I knew I had to level with them. I went through the bargaining session step by step, explaining what Bradley had done and what McLean and Burt had said. The bargaining team, I reported, could see no advantage in staying out any longer. I was sorry that we didn't get what we set out to get, but we were recommending that they accept what we did get.

Despite my disappointment with it, the settlement wasn't a bad one and the membership accepted that we had done our best. Some members had recriminations that we had called the strike in the first place and two or three militants were all for continuing the strike, but when we called for a vote, a good majority supported our decision.

To my relief, the settlement didn't tear the union apart. Surprisingly, there was little criticism of my leadership. In fact, when I ran for president of the local soon after, Wellwood workers turned out in huge numbers to vote for me.

Carolynne and I were married in September 1957, a few weeks after the strike was settled. I was twenty-two and she was only eighteen. She was under a great deal of stress at the time. Her mother had left the family home and her five children, and didn't come to the wedding. Her father had just learned that he had terminal cancer, and it was obvious that he had little time left.

Despite all this anguish, or maybe because of it, we went ahead with our plans. It was quite a big wedding in St. Paul's Anglican Church, Carolynne's church, in Woodstock. My parents were there, my brother Bill, and my sister. Bill had left Eaton's by that time and was working as an orderly at the Ontario Hospital in Woodstock. My mother had a job, too, helping with a retarded teenager who lived a few blocks from us.

I bought a new black suit for the occasion. The Close twins, my brother, and my buddy from the plant, Tom Seymour, stood up with me.

Carolynne's father died soon after the wedding, and we had to decide what to do about the younger children. It was agreed that Carolynne's seventeen-year-old sister Mary would take two of them and we would raise Anne, the youngest, who was only five.

I was making $1.62 an hour, not a lot to support three people. We moved into a tiny two-bedroom apartment over a cigar store, for which we paid $49.50 a month rent.

Carolynne already knew that I wasn't going to be kind of husband who gets home every night for dinner. I think I'd been living on doughnuts and sandwiches in the union hall for the whole summer of the strike. I didn't think much about it being hard on her that I was rarely home.

That marriage lasted nineteen years. Some people tell me that the marriage failed because I was so preoccupied with the union, but I know the marriage failed because we were the wrong people for one another. For most of the time we only coexisted.

We had good times on motor trips with the boys and in a summer cottage we rented by a lake. Like other couples our age, we had friends over and went places together. We believed that everything was fine because we thought that all marriages were like ours.

Right after the wedding, Tommy McLean gave me some advice about being happily married, which, on reflection, may have been the only truly bad advice he ever gave me. He said that I should never take my work home. I learned too late that he was wrong. I should have been sharing what I was doing with Carolynne. It might have relieved her isolation. Perhaps it would have made no difference to the outcome of the marriage, but she would have had a better appreciation of why I was so wrapped up in the labour movement.

THE UAW LOCAL IN WOODSTOCK was what is called an amalgamated local because the 1,500 members were scattered in twelve plants. Our local joined with other unions from the area in the Oxford and District Labour Council. Besides the UAW, the Council had representatives from the textile workers, the firefighters, and so on. These labour councils can be active or passive in the community. The Oxford and District Labour Council was pretty passive. It was a struggle to get any unionists to take it seriously, but I thought it had potential to make an impact. I had no difficulty becoming president of it in 1956. Later on, in 1959, I was elected as president of my local.

Earl Carnegie had been president of the local for years, and the general feeling was that it was time for him to move out. He was a careful, methodical type, and his thoughtful ways did the Woodstock local a lot of good. One of his notable achievements was his insistence that we purchase a union hall. When we inspected the premises he had selected, we were appalled. It was an old Weston's bakery stable, one half of which had accommodated horses and still stank of manure. We couldn't see the possibilities in it, but he had enough sense to persevere until we came around to his way of thinking. We fixed it up with offices and a hall equipped with plywood stacking chairs and an adjoining kitchen that had a hatch through which women volunteers passed out coffee and snacks. It turned out to be a great home for the local union.

In other ways Carnegie was less effective. He wasn't bold in bargaining and he didn't present the union forcefully in the community. When he stepped down, I decided to go for it.

I was seeing a lot of Tommy McLean at the time, very flattered that he was taking such a keen interest me. He was a genial man, a stout, strong-looking Scotsman with a ruddy face who loved to talk. Sipping draft beer in a pub while I nursed a ginger ale and hung on his words, he spent hours talking to me about union principles, and how important teamwork was. He was one of the first people in whom I confided that I was running for the presidency of the Woodstock local against Don Morton of Eureka Foundry.

His eyebrows shot up. "What do you mean *you're* going to run?" he asked scathingly. "You can't run as one person. You've got to put a few people together to run as a slate. You haven't been paying attention to a goddamned thing I've been saying."

He convinced me to sit down with a few of the people who had been urging me to run for president. Between us we decided who would run for each of the available positions on the executive – president, vice-president, secretary-treasurer, recording secretary, and so on. We put some money in the pot and had our names printed on a card, making sure it carried the union bug.

There had never been a slate in the UAW in Woodstock, though it happened in the big locals all the time. In plants like General Motors in Oshawa, the candidates organize themselves into slates along ideological lines. There was no ideological split in the Woodstock local, but there were clear differences of style. Our slate was the ginger group. The previous leadership had run the local with caution and conservatism.

Some of the older members resented the slate approach. They rose at union meetings to complain about the introduction of "politics." That was a laugh. There had always been politics in union elections. The difference was that the politics had been controlled by a certain group, and now we were pushing in.

Frank Kenny, who was not on our slate, ran for the vice-presidency. He was from the Standard Tube plant, which was accustomed to dominating the local because it had the most members. Kenny is a good unionist and he later joined my staff, but during that election there was little love between us. He was furious about the slate and tore into it, and me, every chance he got. He demanded to know where we'd got the money for the cards. That was easy to answer – we'd paid for them with our own money. Others said a slate was out of line because it had never happened before. We explained that there was nothing in union regulations to forbid presenting a slate.

My age was never really an issue. I was only twenty-five, but Woodstock unionists were used to me by then and didn't hold my youth against me. Our campaign argument was that Standard Tube had been running the local for a long time and had done a good job, but it was time for a change.

The union hall was packed for the election. When I went down from Wellwood to vote, I had to grin. There was a long lineup of people waiting for their turn to vote and almost all of them were holding the little card on which the slate's names were printed.

We waited nervously while the election committee counted the ballots. People on the slate were scattered through the crowd, trying to keep a low profile. A lot of people thought that Frank Kenny and his Standard Tube group would win simply because they always had, but the slate swept almost every position. I was the new president of the local.

The position of local president wasn't salaried, of course, but it did come with some benefits. For one, Wellwood was contractually obliged to give me a leave of absence, without pay, whenever I visited other plants on union business. Sometimes they'd refuse to let me go, and I'd raise hell about it. The UAW takes the position that the company should pay for the union's administration of the agreement, since it is the union that does most of that work. In the big plants, the company pays for a union office with full-time staff, telephones, and so on right on the premises. In a big plant like General Motors at Oshawa, with 17,000 people, the union has several offices with dozens of elected or appointed union committee people to deal with grievances, health and safety issues, and benefits.

It took the UAW years to get that concession from management, pushing it up gradually from one hour a day for a steward to two hours a day, and so on. Today, in some of the biggest plants, this is a full-time job. It's an important victory. I don't know how we'd function without that in our agreements. We're now keeping our eye on a problem of it going too far, making sure that union leaders spend time on the shop floor and don't sit around the office all day.

Wellwood didn't yield gracefully on this point, but towards the end of my time as president I was spending about 50 per cent of every working day on union business.

That didn't mean I went to work dressed up. Though I always liked to be neat and clean, I still wore work pants and a T-shirt. Like everyone else, I brought a lunch bucket and punched the time clock.

Some of the tasks of the president were similar to the responsibilities I'd known as union chairman at Wellwood, but on a larger scale. There were the same problems of getting members out to meetings and keeping up morale but also new ones, such as deciding whether we'd participate in a labour conference and how many delegates we would send. I learned how to chair executive meetings, write reports to membership meetings, monitor union finances, and organize educational sessions.

For the first time I was expanding my role as a union person by venturing into the community. We allowed the union hall to be used by such local groups as the Woodstock branch of the Canadian Red Cross for its blood donor clinic, and in other ways tried to move the UAW into involvement in community activities.

I recommended some changes in structure, one of which was to set up a screening process to separate those grievances that were significant enough to take to arbitration from those that could be resolved some other way. Locals would soon go broke if they took every grievance to arbitration.

It was a stimulating time for me, full of growth. Roy Brown was ill for a time, so the UAW assigned another representative, Frank Moroz, to service the Woodstock area. Frank and I became great friends. He was from the Studebaker plant in Hamilton, where he'd played quarterback for the Hamilton Wildcats. A much younger man than Brown, he was full of energy. He and I went knocking on doors at night, trying to organize workers in non-union plants to join the UAW.

I put a lot of time into encouraging workers to get more involved in the union. I'd learned at the Wellwood strike that as the leader of a union, you have to have the members with you, and you can't get them with you if they don't know what you're doing or why you're doing it. Whenever I found someone who seemed keen on the union, I'd push that person to participate.

A sizable anti-Bob White faction existed, of course, consisting in good part of defeated Standard Tube people and their supporters. They turned out faithfully to membership meetings to criticize what I was doing. Within the UAW no one can escape, by reason of high office, being criticized during the regular membership meetings and called to account. Some union members criticize simply because it is their nature to go against any authority, whether management or union, but others bring complaints that have considerable thought behind them. As president, I had to have answers ready and good reasons for making my decisions and recommendations.

I don't enjoy being attacked, but it's a sign of a healthy organization when leaders have to take the heat. Some unions penalize members who criticize the entrenched leaders or try to run against them in elections. That's not the UAW way. When a UAW leader makes a mistake, he or she has to face the membership and admit it. I got a good lesson on that point soon after I started working fulltime for the union. I was sent back to the Woodstock local to be the UAW representative for a few months while the regular rep was sick. At a meeting I passed out some information about equal pay for equal work, and the next day I had a phone call from headquarters. My information was completely wrong, I was told.

"I'm sorry about that," I said. "I thought I had it right."

"Go back and correct it," he said. "Go back and call another goddamned membership meeting like the one where you gave them all the good news. Give them the bad news. Tell them you didn't know what you were talking about. You've got to learn that when you give people the wrong information, you've got to go back and tell them you made a mistake."

I did as I was instructed. It was a humiliating experience, but educational. The members took it all right. People usually understand if you level with them.

In my early years as a unionist, I bought the conventional wisdom that a union leader shouldn't go alone to talk to management. People would grumble, "No wonder he didn't get anywhere. He went by himself." Eventually I came to think that it didn't make sense and I rebelled. I pointed out that union stewards talk to shop foremen every day by themselves, so there was no difference if a union president wanted to talk to a company president by himself. To my mind, anything else suggests a mood of mistrust.

The agreement we had signed with Wellwood after the strike came up for renegotiation in the spring of 1960. The bargaining committee consisted of Roy Brown, William and Helen Ryckman, Dick Jones, Charlie Rockett, Vaughn Rhindress, and Al Seymour, brother of Tom Seymour, who had been best man at my wedding. This time Wellwood yielded on some of the things we hadn't been able to get in the last agreement. There was no need to strike, and the workers at Hay & Co. were happy with their gains.

CHAPTER FIVE

The Youngest Staffer
in the Union

TOMMY MCLEAN HAD become my mentor. He was in the habit of spotting people who seemed to be keen on the union movement and ready to learn. He'd spend time with them, giving advice, telling them what the UAW was all about, encouraging them to move into leadership. Most often, the relationship faded. The worker wasn't as keen as Tommy wanted him to be, or pulled in another direction.

I wasn't exceptional in the beginning, just another of Tommy McLean's protégés, but something in our chemistry worked and I became known as his star pupil. Possibly I responded more than some of the others he had tried to bring along. Certainly, I had the enthusiasm and the willingness to work my head off that McLean liked to see. For whatever reason, McLean became my teacher, father, critic, and friend.

He started to seek me out after the Wellwood strike. He made detours to come to Woodstock as often as he could, and in between visits he called me frequently to talk about what I was doing. He was watching for an opening to move me up. When it came in the summer of 1960, I almost blew it.

That year I rented a cabin at Wasaga Beach so that Carolynne and I, her sister Anne and her brother Tom could have a week's vacation. I told the financial secretary of the local where I was going but not where the cabin was located. That same week George Burt decided the union needed to hire an organizer for three months to work in Barrie, and McLean talked him into offering me the job.

Their decision startled a good many in the UAW. I was twenty-five that summer, which made me the youngest employee in the union in either the U.S.A. or Canada. Almost everyone else on staff was a seasoned trade unionist at least fifteen years older than I. McLean wanted to surprise me with the job offer, so he drove from Windsor to Woodstock, where he learned that I was in Wasaga. Thinking it wouldn't be hard to find me in such a small place, he went on to Wasaga. I later learned that he drove up and down the beach for hours, getting madder and madder, fuming about what a stupid son of a bitch I was.

When I returned home there was a note under the front door from the financial secretary. He said Tommy McLean wanted to talk to me on an urgent matter. I reached Tommy at the Windsor headquarters of the Canadian Region and he chewed me out for not leaving instructions on how to be found in an emergency. That done, he said, "How would you like to go on the UAW staff for three months? We've got an opening on a temporary basis for an organizer in Barrie."

"Yes," I said, as soon as I could speak.

No one from Woodstock had ever been been taken on the UAW staff, so it was quite an honour. That temporary job has stretched into twenty-seven years with the union. Since that summer day in 1960, I've never had a morning that I didn't get out of bed glad to be going to work. That makes me a very lucky man.

Tommy McLean filled me in on why I was being hired. The UAW was in serious trouble with what were called runaway plants. In places like Windsor, Brantford, and Wallaceburg, unionized automotive parts factories were being closed down. The companies were moving to smaller centres like Barrie, Lindsay, and Peterborough where they could re-open without a union and pay less than union wages and benefits. The UAW had to sign up those workers.

The Canadian Region had no full-time organizers on staff, so Burt and McLean decided to switch some staff people from what they were doing and hire temporary help, of which I was one, to meet the emergency.

I had little experience at organizing, and I was nervous about the job. All I'd done was knock on doors in Woodstock a few times with Frank Moroz to see if we could sign up someone who didn't have a union card. McLean dismissed my concern impatiently.

"There's nothing to organizing," he said. "Go tell them why you joined the goddamned union. The same reasons that made you join the union apply to them. We're sending you to Barrie."

Universal Cooler, a UAW plant, had closed its operation in Brantford and relocated in Barrie, throwing a lot of people out of work. I was assigned to make Universal Cooler a UAW plant again. A staff man originally from Wallaceburg, Jack Pawson, was already in Barrie trying to organize another runaway plant there, DeVilbiss, and we were to work together.

The vice-president of Local 636, Jack Bryson, took over my responsibilities as president of the Woodstock local and I worked out a three-month leave of absence from Wellwood. It wasn't difficult to get permission because we had a clause in our contract stipulating that employees who are appointed to carry out full-time duties for the union on a temporary basis are entitled to a leave of absence without pay. Giving up my Hay & Co. paycheque was no problem. Though I had been working there for almost ten years, I was still only earning $1.62 an hour. That gave me $110, after deductions, every two weeks. The UAW salary was a decided improvement over that.

As it turned out, Carolynne and I had to move. She was pregnant and so it was urgent that we find a roomier place to live. We rented a small house in Woodstock, 34 Aileen Drive.

I was supposed to start on a Monday morning, so I left Woodstock on Sunday. In Toronto, the radiator of my used Ford sprung a leak, putting me in a panic that it couldn't be fixed in time. To my relief I got it patched up a few hours later and drove on to Barr's, a small motel on the highway outside Barrie. It was a dingy place – a gravelled parking lot, small, bleak rooms with tacky furniture – but I didn't care.

Jack Pawson came over the next morning. Pawson was a little guy who talked a mile a minute. We went to a doughnut shop for breakfast while he filled me on what had to be done and what Barrie was like. We were on our own. What we did, and how we did it, was up to us. According to Ontario labour legislation, the union had to get 55 per cent of employees to sign membership cards before the UAW would be recognized as the official bargaining agent.

Our first task was to figure out how many people worked in the plants. That wasn't as easy as it sounds because employees are always being hired and laid off, shifts come and go, and there are part-time workers. Once we knew the numbers, we had to go out and get the requisite cards signed.

Neither of us knew a soul in Barrie so we started from scratch. We stood outside the plant gates at quitting time looking at the workers coming out, trying to pick out a likely one. Then we'd follow that person home, hoping we weren't too obvious about it, and make a note of the address. After giving the worker time to have dinner, we would go back at night and knock on the door. We said we were from the UAW and we'd like to talk for a few minutes, if it was convenient. Once inside, we'd make our pitch. Talking enthusiastically about the UAW wasn't difficult for me. I loved the union and it showed.

Then we'd do the same thing for the night shift – follow workers home when they left the gates at dawn, give them time to sleep, and knock on doors in the afternoons. Saturdays and Sundays, we worked like hell.

Pawson went with me the first night. A lot of people weren't home to our knock, but the ones we found were receptive. The UAW had a good reputation as a well-run, strong, and democratic union, so that helped the cause, as did the fact that conditions at Universal Cooler were far from ideal.

The next night I went by myself. The first two people invited me in. One signed and one didn't, but the one who refused was polite. I was thinking this was easy work as I knocked on the third door. A big, tough-looking man answered. I told him who I was and said I'd like to talk to him.

"You lazy, no-good, communist sonovabitch!" he yelled. "I'm going to count to ten. You'd better be off my fucking verandah or I'm going to throw you off."

"There's no reason to act like that . . . ," I began.

"No reason my ass," he roared. "I'm not interested in a goddamned union run by creeps who don't work for a living. Guys like you are ruining the country!"

One thing I'd been told about organizing was not to antagonize people. I said, "Okay, if that's the way you feel about it, I'll leave." I went back to my car, devastated. For a while I just drove around, unable to get the courage to make the next call. Finally I made myself stop the car, get out, and knock on another door. Luckily it was answered by someone who was friendly. I don't know if I could have handled another reception like that one.

On many nights the results were discouraging. Some people slammed the door as soon as I said the word "union." Others would invite me in, listen for two hours, and then tell me they didn't want to join. Sometimes I'd go back five times, talking my head off about the UAW and what it could do for the workers at Universal Cooler, and I still wouldn't get a card signed.

Sometimes I'd make six calls at night and only find three people home, none of them receptive. Some nights I'd get one card signed, other nights none at all.

It wasn't always a total loss, even when people didn't sign. Some who weren't willing to join would still give names and addresses of other people in the plant who were more likely prospects.

As the weeks passed, Pawson and I started to make progress. We were building up a cadre of people in each plant who not only had signed cards themselves but also were keen to help us organize from within. They would give us names of people to approach but, more importantly, they became volunteer organizers within the plant. We gave them blank union cards and they went to work to sign up members.

Though Pawson and I rarely saw one another while we were working, me at

Universal Cooler and him at DeVilbiss, there was a lot of comfort in having him around. When it got too late to make any more night calls, we'd meet in some diner for a late meal to compare our successes and laugh about the crazy things that happened.

We didn't have money to throw around on good restaurants because the UAW paid us only eight dollars a day for expenses. Pawson cut costs that summer by renting a cheap cottage by the lake for his family. When schools opened and his wife and kids went back to Wallaceburg, the UAW said it wouldn't cover two motel rooms. We would have to live together.

We hunted around and found a motel outside Barrie, Wonder Valley. It was a small place with only eight or ten rooms, but more pleasant than Barr's. We took a room with two double beds and made it the union's Barrie office.

I was seeing Carolynne only every other weekend, going to Woodstock on Saturdays and back to Barrie again on Sundays, a long drive on a two-lane road that went through every town and village on the way.

Tommy McLean came to Barrie frequently to see how we were doing. He had taken over responsibility for organizing the runaway plants. He spent hours with us, talking about organizing mostly but also yarning about the strikes he'd seen, the legendary confrontations he'd witnessed, the famous political struggles within the union. He talked about the 1936 strike at General Motors, where Walter and Roy Reuther had worked out the strategy of the Flint sitdown strike which launched the UAW.

He had stories about the 1937 Ford strike, when the company sent hoodlums to beat the workers in what was called "the Battle of the Overpass." The company held out against the UAW for four bloody years before yielding. A few years after that, in April 1948, there was an assassination attempt on Walter Reuther. Shot in the kitchen of his home, his right arm was shattered and he was in hospital for three months. A second attempt on his life a year later resulted in the loss of his brother Victor's right eye.

McLean was teaching me more than labour history. He was anxious that I understand that the UAW stood for the ideal of accountable democracy. I learned that in 1957, when a number of unions were facing federal investigation for unsavoury activities, Reuther got the UAW convention to approve the establishment of an independent body, the Public Review Board, to monitor the union's internal practices.

Another important principle that Tommy drummed into me was loyalty to the leader. It was one thing, McLean told me, to have an internal fight over policy, but quite another to undermine the leadership once the position was taken.

His relationship with George Burt was a perfect example. Though he was Burt's strongest supporter at election time and Burt leaned heavily on McLean's judgment, they didn't always agree. Both were big, powerful men, and when they argued they tended to shout. People said that the walls would shake in the Windsor office when Burt and McLean tangled, but when the argument was over, McLean was absolutely loyal to Burt and carried out the decision whether or not he liked it.

"It doesn't matter if you hate the sonovabitch," he told me sternly. "The membership elected him leader, so you do what he wants done."

One time when McLean and I were alone, I told him that my dream was to work for the UAW as the service representative in Woodstock after Roy Brown left. McLean was shocked.

"You mean your vision is so limited that all you want is to go back to your goddamned home town and be the rep?" he asked incredulously. "Is that all you want to contribute to this union? Don't you want to do something? Don't you want to move around and learn something?"

He explained that the union didn't believe in putting people back in their own areas because they wouldn't grow. They'd become an extension of what they had been before, a committee person. That made sense right away to me, and it still does. If workers stay in their own communities after being taken on staff, they usually get stuck in the politics of the local scene instead of representing the broader responsibilities of the union.

Eventually, Pawson and I decided we had enough cards in the two Barrie plants to ask the Ontario Labour Relations Board (the OLRB) to certify the UAW in both. The companies got wind of what was happening and swung into action. Their first salvo was a petition against the union that circulated in the plants. Universal Cooler told its employees that it had moved from Brantford to Barrie to get away from the union, and if the UAW succeeded in being certified, it would move again. Rumours started up about Communists in the UAW and union bosses who live in luxury off the sweat of honest working people. "Why do you want your money to go to Detroit?" the company would ask.

People got fired, ostensibly because they weren't needed or they were inefficient, but really because they were recruiting for the union. We'd fight to get them their jobs back, but even if we succeeded, the damage was done. The man would have lost wages for a month or six weeks, and other workers were intimidated. Many times, we couldn't win. The man was out, permanently, and he might find it tough to get another job because personnel people in other companies would be watching out for a union troublemaker.

There was not much industry in Barrie. Consequently, there weren't many people in the town who knew much about unions. The rubber workers and the electrical workers had organized, but I think that was about all. The general feeling started to run against us, especially after the company threatened to move.

With men in the plants growing more nervous, it wasn't difficult for the company to get workers to sign their petitions. Even people with union cards were signing the damned things, trying to protect their jobs. Soon after we went to the OLRB to say we had 60 per cent of employees signed up at a dollar a card, the board received a petition also signed by 60 per cent, who said they didn't want a union.

The OLRB had to check both lists and remove from our membership rolls any names that appeared on the petition. That meant our count dropped below the necessary 55 per cent needed for automatic certification. Instead, a vote was ordered. Companies love to force a vote because it gives them time to work on employees to change their minds.

I was convinced that we could beat the petition at Universal Cooler on the grounds that it wasn't a genuine expression of the employees' feelings but had been engineered by the company. We had witnesses who had seen the petition in the office of foremen. If we could prove that management was behind the petition, the OLRB would throw it out.

The UAW had an older man working out of the Toronto, Fred Brooks, a well-read person, active in amateur theatre, who always wore a bow tie. He was representing the UAW at the labour board hearings. Our group from Barrie took rooms in the old Prince George Hotel and spent most of the night going over our testimony.

The next morning we met with Fred Brooks.

"I don't think we should argue about the petition," he advised us. "I think we should let it go to the vote."

I think he simply wanted to avoid a conflict. He was a courteous kind of man who liked the easy, gentlemanly way. I stared at him aghast. He'd been around the UAW for years and here was I, only twenty-five years old, with no seniority on the staff, but I was mad as hell.

"We've got to fight this!" I yelled.

"There's no point in doing that," he told me in a pained way.

I had to accept it, but I was in a rage. As Pawson and I drove back to Barrie, my fury at Brooks only increased.

"Goddamn it," I said, "I'm going to call McLean."

I called Windsor the minute I got back to the motel and told McLean what had happened.

He was calm. "There's a staff meeting coming up," he informed me in a friendly way. "You can raise it there."

The UAW staff meeting, the first I had ever attended, was in the Prince George Hotel. I got up and hotly criticized Fred Brooks. The response was not what I expected. Brooks's colleagues descended on me in full force, while McLean sat there smiling. He'd set me up for a humbling experience, knowing goddamned well that everyone would take Brooks's side against me. The fact that I had some justification didn't matter. Experienced UAW people there couldn't get excited about fighting a petition. They had all been through votes before, for them it was no big deal.

Pawson and I had to get back those people who had signed both the petition and union cards. I arranged for an open meeting and invited George Burt to speak.

The Barrie newspaper ran a story about Burt's impending arrival. As head of the Canadian Region of the UAW, he merited attention. The paper printed a picture of Burt that looked about twenty years out of date. When I happened to be talking to him on the phone about arrangements, I mentioned the picture.

"It looks like it was taken about thirty-five years ago," I told him genially.

George Burt was never a nice man. He was a good negotiator and a good administrator, but he had a harsh edge. He showed it now.

"Who the hell do you think you are, talking to me like that?" he roared. He went on to tear me apart. I learned that he treated his secretaries the same way, but I thought then that I must be an exceptionally stupid person to have brought such a tirade on myself. That was another lesson, not to kid George Burt about his age.

Burt gave a good account of the union at the meeting. When the votes were taken at Universal Cooler and DeVilbiss, the UAW won both by a squeaker. Pawson and I were overjoyed. But the story doesn't end happily. Universal Cooler and DeVilbiss refused to accept our first contracts, so the plants went on a strike that lasted about a year. In the end, the UAW lost both strikes.

I wasn't around for that. My first three-month employment period had been extended for another three months. I ended up working as temporary staff for two and a half years, taking one three-month extension after another, because the crisis in runaway plants didn't stop.

After the first extension, I had to resign as president of the Woodstock local, turning over the post to Jack Bryson. My leave of absence from Well-wood continued. The plant is closed now, but technically, if it was in operation, I could go back tomorrow and start sweeping sawdust again. That's in the contract. Dennis McDermott was on a leave of absence from Massey-Ferguson the whole time he was head of the Canadian Region of the UAW and, later, leader of the Canadian Labour Congress.

Pawson stayed in Barrie for the ill-fated contract negotiations with the two plants, but I was assigned to Niagara Falls to organize the new Ford glass plant there. Some of the workers there were former UAW members out of the Ford plant in Windsor, whose jobs were lost when Ford moved from Windsor to Oakville. Because so many people were hurt by that move, Ford had agreed to hire some of the Windsor workers in its new Niagara Falls plant.

These former UAW members gave me contacts inside the plant, making Niagara Falls a much easier organizing job than Barrie had been. Ford knew we'd be coming after those workers and didn't resist the campaign very strenuously. My main problem was that a rival union had also sent organizers. As soon as I spotted a car with an Ohio licence plate parked near the plant, I knew the glassworkers were in town.

I moved into a tiny motel on Lundy's Lane and threw myself into organizing, the pattern now familiar. I started at dawn, distributing leaflets outside the plant gates, and finished only when it was too late to knock on any more doors. I was eating irregularly and getting little sleep, but I was young, I didn't drink alcohol at all, rarely drank coffee, and didn't smoke, so I could handle the long hours. Also, I was living circumspectly, for a young man away from his wife so much. For one thing, I was too busy to tear after women, and for another, there was Tommy McLean. He had impressed on me that there are a thousand ways to go wrong in the organizer's job, and only one way to go right. That one way, he said, was to conduct myself so as not to bring disrepute in the community on myself or on the union.

McLean was even fussy about the way UAW staff people dressed. He was like a drill sergeant, insisting that we be neat, wearing clean shirts and ties, our pants well-pressed and shoes shined.

When I first got to Niagara Falls, I was drawn by that thundering river. For days I hung around the gorge, staring at the falls, reluctant to tear myself away. Around the end of the week, I'd had enough.

"I'm not going to look at that goddamned water again," I announced, "unless it starts flowing *up*."

I worked closely with two men inside the glass plant. Both had been Ford employees in Windsor and neither had moved their families. They lived in a motel in Chippawa, close to Niagara Falls, where they led a sparse existence, cooking their meals on a hot plate in the room. I went over there most evenings to talk about the organizing campaign and share some laughs. They commuted to their homes every Friday night, a long, punishing drive.

Occasionally McLean and Burt would send a seasoned staff member to help me. One of them was a round-faced, white-haired man, Harry Ford, from Chatham. He spent a couple of weeks making housecalls with me. The two of us were in Welland one night, making a call on a house where the people had a lot of cats. The cats went straight to Harry, who fondly took them on his lap, stroking their backs and scratching them behind their ears. When we got out of there, he was almost shaking. "I hate cats," he complained bitterly. "I wouldn't have a cat around my goddamned place if you paid me." He picked cat hairs off his clothes for the rest of the night, steadily cursing all the cats in the universe. A good union man.

The organizers for the glassworkers were doing the same. When the UAW is in competition with another union, we never run down the opposition. We don't ever mention their name. Instead, we put forward positive material about our union and let the glassworkers, or anyone else, do whatever they want to do. Our tactic sounds noble, but it's also smart. It doesn't pay to say shitty things about the opposition. Workers are sensible people. If they see an organization that's constantly cutting up someone else, they assume that there's something wrong with the organization that's doing the cutting.

In June 1961, after a campaign of less than three months, the UAW was certified in that Niagara Falls Ford plant and we weren't even pushed to a vote.

My next assignment was in Welland, where the union wanted to take another try at organizing the John Deere plant there. Because the company paid its employees wages and benefits that matched levels in the United States, we'd never been able to organize it.

Jack Pawson joined me and we saved on expenses again by living in a motel room in Welland, a plain but clean cement block building painted an unfortunate yellow inside and out. We worked hard, but it was hopeless. That Deere plant still isn't organized.

MCLEAN SWITCHED US OVER to St.Catharines. A big auto-parts plant there, Thompson Products, had no real union, only a shop association, called the Thompson Products Employees Association, which was basically a social club. The dues started at about twenty-five cents a month compared with

UAW dues of five dollars a month. The contract was a good one because the UAW was in the General Motors plant next door, and Thompson wanted to keep us out of their plant.

For years the UAW had heard rumblings that Thompson workers were dissatisfied. Several times the union had responded by putting an organizer at the plant gates, but every time the effort had failed. Thompson simply was too big: Some twelve to fifteen hundred people worked in the plant.

The president of the Thompson shop union was Charlie Stevens. Surprisingly, he was pro-UAW and wanted to help us organize. We accepted his help gratefully.

The Thompson campaign was fascinating. Not only was there fierce loyalty to the plant association, but the company itself was strong. It was part of a group of plants in the United States who had fought the UAW many times and knew some tricks.

One tactic the company used against us was to say that if the UAW got in, the popular savings plan they had would be taken away. We immediately put out a pamphlet listing the plants where the UAW had been certified and got contracts that retained the savings plan. The company had to think up something else.

There had to be a vote at Thompson because the shop association had a contract. Under new legislation, the vote had to be taken immediately on application, and all that we needed was 45 per cent of employees signed up. That quick vote was important for us because it meant the company didn't have time to pressure the workers who had signed cards.

We applied to the OLRB, feeling sure we had the requisite 45 per cent, but we couldn't be absolutely certain even though we had counted time-clock cards in each department. The OLRB sent an examiner, a fussy man named Edwards, to compare our cards against the company's payroll records.

"You don't have forty-five," he announced. "You're below the forty-five per cent."

I was devastated. Pawson and I couldn't believe it. We knew enthusiasm for the union was building. We were still signing cards in the plant, though they didn't count because they came after the application. We decided to stall, hoping a solution would emerge. We told Edwards we didn't believe the company's list. We didn't know what else to do.

We discovered that Edwards wrote down every challenge in longhand, slowly and laboriously. Much encouraged by the slowness of the process, we challenged names left and right. Each challenge meant that the worker had to be brought from the plant to show that he was real, or a supervisor would have to testify that the person existed and was working on the day of the application. We also protested that the company list included lead hands, who should be ineligible because they really were foremen.

Many of our challenges were bullshit, but they ate up time while we frantically thought of ways to get out of the situation. Our friend Charlie Stevens, head of the company union, started to behave in a way that troubled me. I had a hunch he was drifting away from us.

I placed a call to Toronto to Tim Armstrong, a young lawyer in David Lewis' office. Lewis, who later became leader of the federal New Democratic Party, was then in private practice as a labour lawyer and did work for the UAW. I explained to Armstrong the mess we were in and asked for his help.

Armstrong researched the legislation and called me back with good news. He said there was nothing in the rules to prohibit us from withdrawing the application and submitting a new one the next day. The board wouldn't like it, he warned, but we could do it.

We announced we were through challenging the decision and the weary Edwards gathered up his papers. As he was leaving the building, we piled into a car and beat him to Toronto, where we withdrew the application before he got back to his office with word that we hadn't signed up 45 per cent. The next day, we submitted a new application, which included members who had signed after the first application. We had an easy 45 per cent of the workers.

As Armstrong had warned, the board wasn't too pleased with us. The government quickly passed an amendment to the legislation which closed that loophole forever.

Jack Pawson and I had been working on the Thompson campaign for almost a year, so we had a lot invested in winning the vote. I was worried. Stevens had gone back to the company's side, as I suspected he would. I never knew why he changed his mind. His support was a serious loss to our credibility because he was telling workers that he had thought it over, he'd seen what we were like, and he'd changed his mind.

Remembering how effective George Burt had been in the Barrie organizing campaign, I invited him to speak at an open meeting of Thompson workers.

Tommy McLean had been in and out of St. Catharines throughout the whole campaign, encouraging and advising us. He arrived a couple days before the Sunday afternoon we had set for Burt to speak. We had decided we didn't want Tommy on the program. McLean was a loud, aggressive speaker, who went over well in union halls but would be too thunderous for the non-union, undecideds we were expecting. In such a forum, Burt, a more reasoned man, was better.

It fell to me, as McLean's fair-haired boy, to tell him we didn't want him to speak.

"We don't want a lot of speakers," I explained to him in an attempt at tact. "We think it's enough to have me open it up and introduce George."

Tommy was furious and blamed me. George Burt spoke well but the outcome didn't change. We lost the Thompson vote by a margin of sixty to forty. That was a tough one.

McLean paid me back for keeping him off the platform that day by assigning me next to a dead-ass job trying to organize Otis Elevator in Hamilton by myself. Everyone knew you couldn't organize Otis. The steelworkers had tried it, the electrical workers had tried it, we had tried it, year after year, with no results. For three or four months I worked until I was ready to drop, but I got a mere eighteen people signed up out of 900 employees. McLean knew that would happen.

CHAPTER SIX

Thirty-five Thousand
More Members

Our FIRST SON, Robert Todd, was born in 1961, and I was counting Thompson votes in St. Catharines in March 1963 when our second son, David Shawn, arrived. Both were big babies, weighing about nine pounds at birth, and we were delighted to have them. I got home more often now I was working in the Hamilton and the Niagara region, but still it was infrequent and for short periods. Carolynne was left to raise the boys without much help from me. Her sister Anne was of school-age and a big help with the babies, though neither boy was much trouble.

After Todd was born, I bought Carolynne a nearly new Ford stationwagon so she could get around more easily with the baby, but she was left to her own resources much of the time.

We could both see that there were problems in the marriage, but we weren't facing them. I think we survived as a couple as long as we did because we were apart so much.

Todd and Shawn played a lot of sports. Every winter after we moved to Burlington in 1964, I made a rink in our backyard and fitted it with lights so they had a place to play hockey with the neighbourhood kids. I found time to coach house-league hockey teams on which the boys played, on one occasion fitting bargaining sessions around a playoff.

I never pushed the boys in sports. "I don't care what games you play, or whether you win," I told them. "Just make sure that it's worth doing, that you're having fun at it." But, remembering how I had felt left out because I couldn't swim, I insisted that they learn.

Towards the end of 1963, McLean decided to end my punishment at Otis Elevator. He pulled me off and gave me a major project, organizing de Havilland Aircraft in Malton. With the cancellation of the Avro Arrow, a Canadian-designed military aircraft that was ahead of its time, A.V. Roe sold the plant to de Havilland. That raised some problems. The union in A.V. Roe had been the International Association of Machinists (IAM), but the union in de Havilland at Downsview was the UAW, Local 112. We took the position that our union should be the bargaining agent in both plants; the IAM, not surprisingly, didn't agree.

Several OLRB hearings had already been held to decide the issue, and the labour board eventually ruled the UAW properly represented the 3,500 Malton workers. That infuriated the machinists, of course. Because the two unions worked closely in the States, the IAM raised hell with Walter Reuther about what the Canadians were doing. They persuaded him to allow them to campaign to get their members back. This was raiding, but he agreed in the interest of good relations. He knew this was an important campaign and said he'd come up if we needed him.

The machinists had to meet the 45 per cent rule to get a vote. I was assigned the critical task of trying to hold our membership, many of whom were former IAM members still loyal to the machinists.

Dennis McDermott, then a sub-regional director for that area, rented us a small office as campaign headquarters over Able's corner drug store in Malton.

"You're in charge of the campaign," McLean told me. "Make sure the local guys do what you want done."

This was the big-time for me, and I was still just on temporary staff. I moved into a motel near the airport, the Aero Inn, and prepared for my first meeting with the de Havilland workers.

The president of the UAW at de Havilland was an Irishman, Johnny Firth. He was a handful, a rebellious man who was always at odds with UAW staff. Unaware of his reputation, I laid out my strategy for the campaign. Firth and the others tore my ass off. They told me they were running things, and they didn't like anything I had proposed.

I called McLean the next morning. "Christ," I said, "what have you got me into here?"

He laughed. "Those are local union guys," he told me. "They've got a right to have their say. What do you think you are, a dictator?"

That was McLean's way of telling me to respect process. I went back to the Local 112 guys and eventually worked out a good relationship with Johnny Firth. I told him I didn't care about his fights with other UAW staff. My job was to keep the de Havilland plant in the UAW and that's what I intended to do. He gave me a hard time for a while longer, but by the end of the campaign, we were getting along fine.

The IAM conducted itself well. Their organizers worked hard and had good leaflets, but so did we. It was a duel of wits, of matching leaflets, of offsetting one union's big meeting and speech-makers with the other union's mass meeting and orators. After a while, Jimmy Hogan arrived from the UAW regional headquarters in Windsor to organize office workers in the area, so I wasn't completely alone.

Jimmy Hogan and I became close personal friends. A former Ford office worker and member of Local 240, he was a tough trade unionist with a lovely round face and a great sense of humour. But, even with Jimmy's help, I had a lot of trouble. The IAM poured a lot of organizers into the campaign and greatly outnumbered us. For a while, we knew everything they were planning because the IAM people were also staying in the Aero Inn. A woman who worked there used to call me when they went into the coffee shop for breakfast and save me a table nearby. I used to sit next to them, ostensibly reading a newspaper, but listening to them talk about their strategy. Eventually, they caught on to who I was and that source of inside information dried up.

By the time the campaign finished, all the UAW's leaders, including Walter Reuther, had come to Malton to speak to de Havilland employees. Leonard Woodcock, a UAW vice-president, came from Detroit on May 26, 1964, and Reuther flew to Malton on June 17, 1964, to address a rally. I met Reuther at the airport to drive him to Crang Plaza where the rally was being held. He and George Burt sat in the back of my car talking about the coming auto-trade pact between Canada and the United States and how it had to include wage parity for Canadian and American workers.

"My policy on this one is simple," Burt told Reuther. "I'm going to fight to the last drop of American blood to get Canadians the same wages as the Americans get. I hope you feel as strongly about this as I do because we need your help to win it."

Reuther gave him assurances that he agreed. Americans were as anxious to get wage parity as we were. If Canadians worked for lower wages, jobs would be siphoned out of the States into Canada.

Reuther was spellbinding at that rally in the Crang plaza. I have a picture of him standing in front of a banner with the slogan I created "UAW – Canada's Trail-Blazing Union." Afterwards Reuther wrote me a note which I treasure. It said, in part, "I was very pleased to have had the opportunity of being with you and I am delighted to know that the results of the meeting were most favorable. Kindest personal regards, Fraternally, Walter Reuther."

De Havilland presented a curious situation for organizers. Usually our job is to teach non-union people about the labour movement, but at de Havilland the workers were already committed to unionism. They were being asked to make a choice between two big unions. We used to meet in debate, which I relished. UAW is hard to beat. Our bargaining program was better than the IAM's, we had a more democratic structure, and the contract we had with de Havilland at Downsview was better than the old IAM contract at Malton.

Both unions ran clean, intelligent campaigns from which I learned a lot. The task of covering the plant gates, every shift, with people to distribute leaflets was a scheduling headache in itself. I also had to coordinate all the work inside the plant, where UAW committeemen were talking to old IAM members. In the end, we won. The machinists signed maybe 35 per cent but they couldn't get the rest.

DISCUSSIONS ABOUT the proposed Canada-U.S. Auto Pact were well advanced that year, 1964. At that time, the Canadian car industry was protected by a 17.5 per cent tariff and had become so inefficient that Canadian-made cars cost more in Canada than imports. In order to rationalize the industry, General Motors, Ford, and Chrysler wanted to treat their plants and suppliers as a free-trade entity. The Big Three automotive companies had lobbied the U.S. Congress to make the deal with Canada.

Canada was willing to go along with the Auto Pact providing there were guarantees in it to ensure Canadian content. The fear was that otherwise all the work would be done in American plants. The safeguards that Canada wanted, and eventually got, were expected to create an estimated forty thousand new jobs in this country.

It was interesting in 1986 to hear Prime Minister Brian Mulroney declare that the same people who oppose free trade now are the people who opposed the Auto Pact, an obvious reference to the UAW. A correct version of what occurred in 1964 is that the UAW supported the Auto Pact and was instrumental in getting the safeguards, and the Conservative Party was opposed.

The UAW was gearing up for the tremendous expansion of the auto industry in Canada that would result from the Auto Pact. We knew that the new plants would open without a union. Solidarity House, the union's headquarters in Detroit, decided to move organizing into high gear. A UAW vice-president, Pat Greathouse, was assigned the responsibility of supervising the organizing staffs in both Canada and the States. He talked to George Burt about putting a team together in Canada, Burt talked to McLean, and I was their choice to head it. That was my reward for the success of the de Havilland campaign.

Burt and McLean put together the team, picking out men straight from the local unions, and I had no choice in their selection. The first one assigned was Carl Anderson, president of a local in Hamilton. He was a tall, handsome man, who wore his hair in a brushcut. Aged forty-four, he was a veteran of the raid on Dieppe and the Normandy landings on D-Day and a long-time socialist active in the CCF. Next was Bruce Lee, forty-eight, president of Local 252 in Toronto, who had been around the union for years.

Jack Pawson, who was thirty-seven then, came on team as did Malcolm Smith, brother of Smitty in Woodstock, president of Local 222 in Oshawa. His handicap for organizing was that he'd never driven a car in his life. Someone had to teach him to drive.

Tom Green also came out of Local 222, a good union man who came off the line at the Duplate plant. He wasn't cut out to be an organizer, but he worked at it. Later we hired Les Rudrum and Albert Seymour, who had worked with me at Wellwood in Woodstock. Al was the last one hired on the team. I got him just before Dennis McDermott became director, knowing that Dennis would never hire him.

By that time, I was on the permanent staff myself. Someone finally decided that three years of being on a temporary basis was enough. The success of the organizing team drew some criticism from detractors. I heard that some people were saying, "All White's trying to do is build an empire."

When Al Seymour turned up in the tiny, battered, crowded office, I grinned, "Well, you finally made the empire, eh?"

Some saw us as troublemakers because the plants we organized came into the UAW with high expectations, which put pressure on the headquarters staff to deliver. The newly recruited tended to be critical if things didn't move quickly, to the great annoyance of some staff.

"Don't worry about that kind of bullshit," I advised the guys when they heard we were being called names. "Let's just keep going." I've always believed that the best strategy is to work hard and to produce. If you stop and argue about every little criticism, you can't get the job done.

The organizing team got lucky with its office staff of one. Helen Kramzyk came to work for us, a funny, dedicated, smart, highly efficient woman. She is still my secretary. Helen will work all kinds of hours without complaining. I'm a demanding person to work for, I know. I expect people around me to put in a lot of hours, but no more than I'm willing to do myself.

Helen is much more than a secretary. She's also a good friend. Over the years we have shared our personal problems. She's a vital part of the close-knit team in our office and sometimes receives little credit.

Helen was recommended by Jimmy Hogan. He spotted her when he was organizing in Brantford and she was a keen young secretary in a plant office there.

Soon after Seymour joined our team, I was asked to pinch-hit for Dennis McDermott as the service representative at de Havilland because Dennis was needed elsewhere. On Monday, September 28, 1964, I was thrust abruptly into the first arbitration hearing I'd ever handled in my life, a discharge dispute before Bora Laskin, later Chief Justice of the Supreme Court of Canada. I was nervous and my arguments weren't polished, but they worked: Laskin reinstated the worker.

Carolynne and I decided it made no sense for her and the boys to stay in Woodstock. We purchased a pleasant three-bedroom, split-level house in Burlington, an easy commute from Malton. It cost $18,500, most of which was mortgage. Anne was in school all day and Todd was in kindgarten, so Carolynne had more time for herself. She did hairdressing at home and took part in amateur musicals.

Despite the move, I still rarely got home for dinner at night and I worked most weekends. As often as I could, I spent Sunday afternoons prowling in rubber boots through the woods with the boys, digging up toads and examining the things that grow in wetlands. I was travelling a lot to Windsor, Kingston, Winnipeg, all over. I was also handling the union's dealings with the Ontario Labour Relations Board and critical organizing work in Barrie.

In the plants we were organizing, we didn't hear many comments any more about the UAW being "full of Commies." Instead there were complaints that we were in bed with the socialists, the CCF. We avoided making a strong defence of the CCF as we didn't want to get sidetracked by a debate about party politics. There's no point trying to recruit someone into a social democratic party, or talk about those broader issues, when you haven't even got him or her in the union yet.

"Each local is free to make its own decision," I'd explain. "Some have affiliated with the CCF and some haven't. But first of all let's talk about the union."

The criticism we heard most often was that the UAW only wanted to fatten its own purse; that we were only out to get union dues to make the union richer.

"Look," I'd say. "We're required by law to collect a dollar when you sign a union card, but you don't pay any dues until after we negotiate a collective agreement. We're not asking you to pay until you vote to ratify the agreement we get for you. The dollar is an investment you make. All the expenses incurred while we negotiate for you are handled by the international union."

One company argument is that it will give workers good benefits, so why lose money from your paycheques in dues to a union? Those same companies take deducations off paycheques for these benefits, so the workers are paying for medical drug coverage anyway. But management doesn't see the illogic of their argument.

Another issue that always came up was that dues paid by Canadians went to Detroit. My reply was that it wasn't true. Most of the dues raised in Canada were reinvested in Canada and went to support the activities of the UAW in this country.

A big concern we often heard was the fear of being forced to go on strike. Some non-union people have the idea that if there is a strike at GM, all the workers in parts plants have to strike, too. That's not the case. The only way there can be a strike in a plant is when the workers directly involved vote to strike by secret ballot.

We learned to be forthright about these prickly issues. The best tactic is to get those issues about dues and strikes out in the open at the beginning. At the back of everyone's mind is the fear of being fired if the company finds out that he or she is supporting the union. Companies almost always threaten that with great effect. All we can say is that we'll keep the names of people who sign as confidential as we can, and that if the employer discharges the worker for joining the union, we'll take the case before the labour relations board.

The UAW had a lot to offer. Because it had the North American automotive industry sewn up, it had been able to pioneer clauses in contracts that afterwards became standard in all union contracts. The union was known to be democratic, with the leadership accountable to the workers, and free of corruption.

I felt then, and do now, that organizing is the backbone of the union. You can't grow if you don't bring in new members; you grow stale. If I heard that workers in a plant in Kingston were interested in a union, I'd have an organizer in the car and on his way to Kingston that same day.

I thrived on the work; we all did. We felt on top of the world and we had fun together, though we worked our heads off. We knew we were the UAW's hot shots. We were signing up more members, per man, than any other UAW organizing team in North America. To be fair to the Americans, organizing is easier under Canadian law than it is in the United States.

Some time in 1967, I got a recurrence of kidney pain. It hadn't bothered me since I was a teenager working at Wellwood. At that time, a Woodstock doctor talked of removing the kidney, but my father wouldn't hear of it. The bouts of pain had disappeared and I thought no more about it until they came back when I was thirty-two. I would get periodic attacks of extreme pain in my groin. The doctor thought it was a kidney stone, so he gave me some pain-killers and advised me to drink beer to flush it out.

One night early in 1968, I had to attend an organizing coordinators meeting in Detroit and I forgot to bring the pain-killers with me. That night, just after the last plane left for Toronto, I got a pain in the kidney like a horse had kicked me. I was in agony, but there was nothing to do but sweat it out for what seemed a long night.

Bruce Lee met my plane the next morning and drove me to the Burlington hospital. After a day or two, a urologist informed me that my ureter was completely blocked. One of my kidneys was scarcely functioning.

A young surgeon said he would do a resection, but the operation would have to wait a week because he was going to a medical meeting in Montreal. He said my condition had stabilized so I could leave the hospital. The delay suited me fine. Dennis McDermott had just become director of the Canadian Region, and he had arranged a staff meeting at Honey Harbour that weekend. It was the first time the Canadian staff had ever gathered to look at the future of the UAW, and I wanted to be in it.

I was feeling terrible, but I made the meeting and a week later went back to hospital. The surgery took four and a half hours and I was in hospital a month recovering. I was weak for a long while after, but I haven't had a major health problem since.

I went back to the cheerful, jam-packed offices in Malton. The team was having a great time. We were organizing everything from the big Northern Electric Telecom plant in London and the Ford Talbotville plant in St. Thomas, to plants in the auto-parts industry like Budd Frame in Kitchener.

Northern Telecom was a huge undertaking. It had been successful for years in keeping a union out because it had a shop association, almost like a company union. The United Electrical Workers had tried to organize many times without success. Banking on our good reputation in neighbouring plants, where our collective agreements were the best around, we put on a good campaign headed by Carl Anderson. We won. Workers at Northern Telecom joined the UAW.

The victory at Northern Telecom in London gave us the foothold in the company we needed, so we went after their plant in Belleville, and then the one in Kingston, and next we signed up white-collar workers in Northern Telecom offices. It's now the fourth largest section of the CAW.

My function in most of those campaigns was supervisory. I'd take part in meetings and I'd stand at the plant gates at six in the morning giving out leaflets whenever I was in the area, but mostly my role was to be a consultant to the organizers on the scene. I'd sit down with them to thrash out such problems as what to put in the leaflets, many of which I was writing, and how to respond to whatever opposition we were getting.

Working out of that sardine-can office over the drug store in Malton, a handful of us recruited some thirty-five thousand people into the UAW in five years.

IN 1968 GEORGE BURT would turn sixty-five, retirement age. He'd been director of the Canadian Region for almost thirty years. The jostling for power had begun between the two obvious candidates as his successor and those who wanted to be close to the eventual winner. As we were a success story in the UAW our choice for the new director carried some weight. I was seen as influential, and found myself getting a lot of attention from the headquarters staff.

Tommy McLean wasn't yet sixty-five, but he announced that he would pack it in at the same time that Burt left. He had been Burt's assistant all those years and I knew, because he confided in me, that he would have loved to be director of the region for one term. Tempting as that was, and I don't think the union would have denied him that, he decided it wasn't right.

"It has to be a new team," he told me sadly. "When Burt goes, we should get a fresh new team. That's what's best for the union."

His decision was principled and, for the most part, he kept a noble silence about what he was really thinking, but alone with me he bitched. Burt should have left a lot sooner, Tommy thought, to give him a few terms as director. He felt he had deserved that.

George's greatest problem was that he was a person with what I call "I-itis." Everything with him was "I did this," and "I did that." He never gave Tommy or his staff credit for their success. It fell to Tommy to do most of the legwork and all the dirty work, all the difficult political deals, to help maintain George's power and prestige. It was a thankless task. The UAW is famous for its internal power struggles but equally famous for keeping its act together, always coming together solidly when the squabbling is done. A lot of that reconciliation and that philosophy of loyalty came from Tommy McLean's fierce dedication to solidarity. Burt owed him, but Burt never acknowledged publicly what Tommy did for him and for the UAW.

Now all that Tommy could do as a final hurrah before he departed was to help put together the team that would succeed Burt. He threw himself into the battles ahead, and I was right behind him.

78

The Windsor office of the Canadian Region was seething with rumours and plots as people jockeyed to be in a good position. It settled down eventually as an even-bet race between Herb Kelly and Dennis McDermott. Herb Kelly was the former president of Local 200 in Windsor, a new member of the staff and a basic, down-to-earth, veteran trade unionist. He was about fifty years old and very popular with the rank and file. In UAW terms, he was on the left. He never shirked from challenging UAW leadership, even Reuther himself, if he thought something was wrong, and he was a strong advocate of workers' rights.

He was McLean's man, and mine. I liked Kelly's honesty, his firmness, his ability to speak forcefully and convincingly, his willingness to wade in and help if a worker had a problem. McLean and I were sure that unionists would work well with Kelly, that he knew the ropes and would keep the Canadian part of the UAW strong and spunky. When the organizing staff got behind Kelly, it caused quite a stir.

The other contender, Dennis McDermott, at forty-five, was a slightly younger man than Kelly and more controversial. A lot of people didn't like his style, which seemed brash and trendy, or his reputation for being lazy. George Burt, however, was promoting Dennis. That made my organizing team nervous. If Dennis got in despite our hard work for Kelly, we might be on the firing line. Our insurance was Pat Greathouse, an international vice-president of the UAW who was responsible for our organizing team. He was high on us, so I had a measure of confidence that I could take a chance and oppose Burt. To complicate matters, though, the word was out that Walter Reuther preferred Dennis.

Joe Mooney, one of the Detroit staff people, was the person in charge of the Canadian organizers for Pat Greathouse. Mooney and I were friends, so he'd pass along bits of news from Solidarity House in Detroit. My conspicuous support for Kelly made him uneasy, and he used to caution me when he thought I was leaving myself unprotected.

I didn't like Dennis. I thought he was lightweight and superficial, a man not nearly enthusiastic enough about hard work. His manner hadn't endeared him to a lot of people. Dennis doesn't suffer fools gladly and is impatient with small talk; he's high-handed, even imperious, with people who bore him. He was never one to sit around shooting the breeze with local union guys in order to know them better. During a negotiation that didn't particularly interest him, he'd retire to a corner and read a book.

But Dennis was very good in negotiations and an excellent representative for the union in arbitration hearings. He was the match for any lawyer the corporations could put against him. His indifference to others, however, counted heavily against him. Dennis was disliked and distrusted by some in the union. The criticism I heard always had to do with surface things such as, "He never speaks to me," or "He won't shake hands."

One day I was driving George Burt to the King Edward Hotel in Toronto for a bargaining session when he started to berate me for supporting Kelly. At that point, the Canadian staff hadn't made its decision. We hadn't yet held a caucus meeting and thrashed the options over until we came to an agreement. So, I thought I was free to pick my candidate and work for him.

"You've got no goddamned right supporting Kelly," Burt yelled at me.

"What do you mean?" I protested indignantly. "The staff hasn't made its decision yet. I've got as much goddamned right to support Kelly as someone else has to support McDermott."

"I'll go to Pat Greathouse and you'll find out if you've got a right or not," George shouted, getting madder and madder.

"George, you go wherever the hell you like. As far as I'm concerned, until we make a decision, I'm supporting Herb Kelly."

Burt was tough. We got to the hotel and I stopped, leaving the motor running as a hint for him to get out. He wasn't half finished with me and made several more threats that I would lose my job if I didn't support McDermott. I thought he was out of line and told him so.

"You think you've got protection in Pat Greathouse," Burt roared. "I'll show you how much protection you've got."

Trade union politics are not Boy Scout stuff. They can be very intimidating. I wasn't feeling very safe as Burt got out of the car and slammed the door.

Later Burt reported to McDermott, "I had the young sonovabitch in a car in front of the King Edward Hotel in Toronto and I jawboned him so long that the car ran out of gas, but I still couldn't move him."

CHAPTER SEVEN

New Leaders and
Old Heroes

ERB KELLY HAD a slight heart problem early in his life, which he appeared to have overcome. It was far from our minds as we gathered at the King Edward Hotel in Toronto for the regular District Council meeting. I was returning to the meeting room after lunch when someone seized my arm. "Did you hear? Something's wrong with Herb Kelly."

I found Herb on the bed in his hotel room with Tommy McLean bending over him. Herb was taking nitroglycerine pills, his face pale and sweaty. He gasped that he thought he was having a heart attack.

When the pain subsided, he said he was sure he could get to the hospital without an ambulance. With Tommy on one side of him and me on the other, he walked through the lobby and along a few blocks to St. Michael's Hospital. Nurses put him into a wheelchair and took him away for tests, leaving Tommy and me in the waitingroom. We didn't speak.

After a while, Tommy turned to me. His steely eyes were glittering.

"You know what this means, don't you?" he asked.

"I think I do," I nodded slowly.

"If we put this guy in as director, we'll kill him," Tommy said roughly. "Herb can't be director."

I had reached the same conclusion but I said, "Let's wait a bit. We'll see how he comes out of this. . . ."

Tommy snapped my head off. "What do you mean 'let's see'?" he said. "He's had a goddamned heart attack. He can't do it."

I protested weakly but I knew he was right. When word of Herb's condition got around the locals, McDermott supporters would use the issue of his health against him. Herb would be put on the defensive while trying to recover from what appeared to be a serious heart attack.

We reached the unhappy conclusion that, in the best interests of both Kelly and the UAW, we couldn't continue to support Kelly for director. The job would kill him. Tommy and I cobbled together a compromise, which was to persuade McDermott to make Kelly his assistant director. That would be some consolation for Herb but, more importantly, it would mend the split in the Canadian Region.

The first problem would be to persuade Kelly to give up his dream of becoming director and accept a secondary role. The bigger hurdle was McDermott, who already had decided to appoint George Specht as his assistant. Specht was from London, an older, solid union man who was a long-time associate of McDermott's.

Tommy was too much the consummate strategist to reveal the game plan. Cautiously, planting a word here and a word there, he worked his contacts, convincing them the McDermott-Kelly ticket was good.

While McLean quietly worked the back rooms, campaigning continued as if the heart attack hadn't happened. Union business was beginning to suffer from the bad feeling between staff people in the opposing McDermott-Kelly camps. Early in the spring of 1968, we arranged for the entire Canadian Region staff to gather in Windsor and end the rancour by deciding which man would be our choice. We didn't have a vote at the convention, of course, but at least we'd end the divisiveness. We were aware of the danger that the even split in the staff gave an opportunity for a third candidate, possibly one from the Communist Party faction of the union, to slip in and win.

The meeting began with a lot of bitching about underhanded tactics, about people being uncooperative, about back-stabbing. Blowing off steam was the top of the agenda. With about forty-five full-time trade unionists in one smokey room, and all of them experienced debaters, there was both heat and noise.

No one mentioned Kelly's heart problem. It was too sensitive an issue to be touched and none of us was ready to admit that he was a non-candidate. I spoke in support of Herb just as if nothing had changed. McDermott supporters argued back forcefully that it was time for fresh ideas. The wrangling went on for several hours. It was time to make the decision, and the vote went to McDermott. Though I knew it would happen and thought I had accepted it, I had an unexpected sense of loss. I didn't think McDermott was half the man for the UAW that Herb Kelly was.

I know now that I was wrong. McDermott proved to be a man of deep intellect who infused the Canadian Region with his ideals about labour's role in social change. His grasp of where the Canadian Region should go was far more visionary than anything Herb Kelly, for all his sterling qualities, could have contributed.

Kelly was a bread-and-butter trade union man, part of the old George Burt-Tommy McLean tradition. He was great in a bargaining session, a man of camaraderie and good sense, but he wasn't much interested in protests at City Hall or peace marches. Kelly would never have given the union the public profile that McDermott did. It was time for the Canadian Region to grow, and McDermott was exactly the right man at the right time to do it.

McDermott was fascinated with that world outside the union. He was interested in civil rights, in farmworkers in California, in the peace movement, in the egalitarian theories that the hippies were talking. To the dismay of many UAW members, McDermott was even starting to look like a hippie. His hair was getting longer, his sideburns extended down his cheeks, and he had bought a Nehru suit, which he wore with a peace medallion around his neck.

Ironically, it was Dennis McDermott, Walter Reuther's man, who had the courage to make substantive changes in the relationship between the Canadians and UAW international headquarters. With Reuther's backing, McDermott was able to persuade the UAW executive to recognize that Canada was not just another region, that the Canadian Region should have special status.

At the time, however, I didn't have much use for McDermott and he didn't care for me either. We were civil enough and sometimes he'd joke about us both being Irish, an exaggeration on his part because he was born in England. He served in destroyers in the Royal Navy during the war, no piece of cake, and when he came to Canada, he went to work on the line at Massey-Ferguson and joined the UAW. Like me, he loved the union. He went the usual route through all the levels of elected positions until he was taken on staff.

At one point he had been selected to attend the UAW's Franklin Delano Roosevelt education centre in Port Huron, Michigan. That's where he caught the Reuther fire about the UAW taking an active role in civil rights and the peace movement. McDermott was one of the founders of the first Fair Employment Practices Committee in Canada, along with Dan and Donna Hill (Dan later became Ontario's Ombudsman), Eamon Park, and Kalmon Kaplansky.

Now the staff was united behind McDermott, there was little doubt he'd be elected the Canadian director. Dennis was known to be sensitive to criticism, so people wondered what he would do to Kelly supporters, who had made his candidacy so difficult. Though I was one of the most conspicuous of these, I wasn't worried that Dennis would take revenge on me. I knew I was doing a good job and I knew Dennis was sensible enough to know that he would need good people. He might not like me, but I was sure he wouldn't dump me.

I was slow to realize that McDermott was good for the union because I didn't have much contact with him. We avoided one another whenever we decently could and that wasn't difficult because he had no responsibility for the organizing team in Malton. Working directly under Pat Greathouse, as we did, we were in an unusual position. Technically, we were attached to the Canadian Region and obliged to do whatever Burt or McLean or McDermott wanted, but we had a lot of independence because we were supervised from Detroit.

THE UAW's 21st International Convention was in June 1968, in Atlantic City. Some 2,500 delegates gathered at the biennial event in a mood to celebrate. We had assets valued at $63 million and, as Walter Reuther told the cheering delegates, the membership gained nearly $5 billion in the 1967 and 1968 negotiations, more than the workers had gained in the 1955, 1958, and 1961 negotiations combined.

Reuther was in fine form, holding that huge gathering in the palm of his hand. He spoke of standing by the coffin of Martin Luther King Jr., and what he felt about the civil rights movement. He tied it in, as he always did, with the UAW's responsibility to be active in the community.

"We need to ask ourselves," he said, "What good is a large wage increase if the world is reduced to atomic ash? What good is a guaranteed annual wage if your city and neighbourhood are burning? What good is a longer vacation if the air you breath is poisoned and the water is polluted and the highways so strangled with traffic you can't move? We must demonstrate that the kind of a world we are committed to build is a world in which people can have both bread and freedom."

I was enthralled once again by Reuther, but the convention hype, the balloons and bands and placards, struck me as childish, inappropriate for an organization with such a serious purpose. I couldn't see the point of grown people marching around in flashy satin jackets and funny hats.

At the mid-point of every UAW convention there is an election for the leadership and every delegate votes. There was no move to throw the Walter Reuther team out, but in theory that could have happened. He and Emil Mazey, Leonard Woodcock, and Pat Greathouse were standing for re-election, and the convention was happy to give it to them.

Even so, the formalities were observed. Nominations were called. After a decent pause, it was announced that nominations were closed and Walter Reuther was elected by acclamation. Horns blew, the band played, people cheered, balloons were released and streamers filled the air and fell on heads. The *entire* convention then lined up to shake Walter's hand. The same thing happened when nominations were called for secretary-treasurer. Emil Mazey was acclaimed and everyone lined up again to shake *his* hand. The whole thing was repeated for Greathouse and Woodcock, the vice-presidents. It took all morning to acclaim them.

In the afternoon, each of the seventeen regions of the UAW met separately to choose their regional directors. For almost thirty years George Burt had been elected head of the Canadian Region, usually without a challenger. Once Cliff Pilkey ran against him, which meant a voice roll-call vote though its outcome was never in doubt. Tommy McLean always knew exactly how strong the opposition was and rarely was out by more than a few votes.

It isn't one man one vote. Delegates from small locals, such as I was when I represented Wellwood, carry three votes each. Delegates from the large locals can have as many as eight votes, but that's the limit, a rule which ensures that the big locals like GM in Oshawa and Ford in Oakville don't control the union.

A roll-call vote is an open way of electing a director. We take pride in the fact that any member can get up in the caucus and vote against the director. There's nothing wrong with members letting everyone know where they stand, so long as they close ranks afterwards. We see competitive elections and disputatious meetings as a sign of health.

In this case, however, everyone knew McDermott already had full caucus support. His selection was unanimous. Dennis kept his promise to McLean. He immediately announced he was appointing Herb Kelly as his assistant.

Each region reported to the full convention the name of its director. Those seventeen directors automatically became members of the twenty-five-member International Executive Board, along with the officers who had been elected that morning. Dennis McDermott, like George Burt before him, was the only Canadian on the executive, but as McDermott was close to Reuther, we were sure our interests would not be overlooked.

Dennis prepared for his first test as the new director, which was a District Council meeting in the fall of 1968. The District Council, a UAW invention, is made up of 250 to 300 delegates elected by locals in each region. In Canada they met every three months to hear a report from the regional director and state their views on what the leadership was doing. The original idea of the District Councils had been to allow delegates a forum to report what was happening in their locals, but George Burt had turned that around to make the director more accountable to the members. They can criticize and demand explanations. If they don't like what they hear, they can go back to their locals and start working to replace the director.

Burt used to face heavy attack from some old Communist Party types in the union. He loved to take them on. I used to suspect that his reports were designed so they would challenge him and he could demolish them. Some of these people put their heads together before McDermott's first District Council meeting to decide how to handle the newcomer. Should they give him a rough ride to test his mettle? They decided to hold their fire and let him have the first one out of the barn. It was the biggest mistake they could have made. McDermott got up and seized control, never to let it go. He positioned himself five steps ahead of everyone in the room and stayed there.

Dennis is a fine orator, articulate and confident. Though he touched on union business and showed a good grasp of labour issues, the most compelling part of his report dealt with his outside interests and his intention to put the union at the center of social change. He spoke of the UAW playing a role in such issues as the civil-rights movement in the American South, the grape boycott in California, world disarmament, Canadian civil liberties, Pierre Trudeau's "Just Society," and the Vietnam war.

Walter Reuther talked the same way, so Dennis couldn't be dismissed as a crazy. While the rank and file of our membership didn't always agree with such stands as opposition to the American war in Vietnam, Reuther had established the principle and our members took a certain pride in seeing a Reuther kind of person as Canadian director.

I loved the direction McDermott was taking us. McDermott and Reuther were right. Workers have an important perspective to bring to issues of social justice, and I firmly believe that we belong in the forefront of these struggles.

Not everyone shared my enthusiasm for what Dennis was doing. People grumbled that he was an egotist and thought he was only out to get attention. He knew that people thought him a showboat, but he didn't care. He put his picture on the cover of his report, for instance, indifferent to the outrage it provoked. Next, he ordered carpet for his office and Kelly's office in the Windsor headquarters. I heard a lot about those rugs, and how true unionists shouldn't have rugs, but I couldn't see what was wrong with making the office more comfortable.

Dennis went right ahead as if his critics didn't exist. About a year after he became director, he announced that the Canadian headquarters would be moved from Windsor to Toronto. That was a gutsy decision. No one had ever before questioned why the Canadian Region was being run from Windsor when the majority of members were centered around Toronto. It was accepted that Windsor should be the headquarters because it was handy to Detroit and Solidarity House.

Dennis later described his difficulties in Windsor. He said, "All I did was arrive at my office in the morning and head for the tunnel. Everything was over there."

If Canada was to grow, he reasoned, it had to get out from under the shadow of the American eagle. Living so close to Detroit, the Canadians in the UAW had no opportunity to establish an identity of their own. When the Canadian Region had an announcement to make, the media here paid little attention. The press looked instead to Detroit to provide information about UAW activities in Canada. Dennis saw that the UAW in Canada would never be seen as distinct and different until we moved.

The main opposition to the move came, naturally, from Windsor local leaders. Dennis spent hours talking to them until most conceded that he was right.

Early in 1970, Dennis rented the seventh floor of the MCA building at Victoria Park and Highway 401 and made preparations to move. It made sense that he would consolidate the region's operations so I wasn't surprised when he notified me he was closing the organizing office over the drug store in Malton and moving us into the new headquarters.

Many organizers on the team were alarmed. The old fear that Dennis would want blood for my support of Kelly was revived. I was uneasy about being under McDermott's thumb after years of comparative autonomy, but I could see the logic of everything being under one roof. Anyway, I would still be working directly under Pat Greathouse. Dennis would have to sort it out with Pat if he wanted to change my duties.

I was bothered most about the lack of walls in the new offices. Dennis liked the sixties fad for open-plan offices and open-plan classrooms. He had the crackpot idea that the absence of walls would inspire collegiality. Even his own office had no walls, just a few plants and low dividers to mark the territory.

I took one look at the layout and decided it would be a disaster, and it was. Privacy was impossible; everyone could see what everyone else was doing and hear what everyone else was saying. People trying for a quiet word with the Canadian director found the rest of the staff watching them. Arguments or conferences on strategy were overheard by all, and the constant noise of typewriters, conversations, and phones made it impossible to concentrate. Dennis loved it.

Happily, the office space assigned to the organizing team was in a corner diagonally across from McDermott's office, somewhat shielded from his view by the elevators. But, despite the gloomy prophesies, McDermott paid little attention to us anyway. We soon were humming away as usual, organizing in Orangeville, Collingwood, Toronto, Chatham, Wallaceburg, Windsor – all over the place.

Dennis and Herb Kelly proved to be a good team. Kelly was a hard, diligent worker who took care of details leaving McDermott, who hated mundane duties, free to tackle the broader issues that didn't interest Herb at all. Dennis built up the education section, an area that Burt had allowed to slip. He believed, as Reuther did, that the way to maintain enthusiasm in the membership is to provide opportunities for trade unionists to learn labour history, the political process, labour legislation, human rights, and collective bargaining.

One of his most important decisions came two years after he became Canadian director. He got Reuther's support for a change in the UAW constitution that made the Canadian director automatically an international vice-president of the union. He argued that the Canadian Region was not like any other region in the UAW. It was a different country with different labour legislation, different attitudes, different health benefits, different history.

Reuther, Mazey and Greathouse, Bannon, and Woodcock – the vice-presidents – always met the day before the regional directors came together to review the agenda and agree on their positions. Dennis wanted the Canadian director to be included in that session. It wasn't enough that the Canadian director sat on the International Executive Board, Dennis said. He maintained, and he was right, that Canada's input didn't count for much when it came after the officers had conferred and made up their minds. The decisions of the officers were discussed and had to be approved by the regional directors, but new input at that point rarely made any difference.

Reuther accepted Dennis' reasoning. At the 1970 convention in Atlantic City, the UAW voted to recognize the special status of Canada and established that the Canadian Region director would automatically be a vice-president.

The Canadian Region took on new stature. A few Canadians complained that Dennis was acting out of vanity again, but most were proud. It was a good, farsighted move for which McDermott and Reuther deserve great credit. The concern some felt for McDermott's ability to cope with an increased work load, however, was justified. Dennis was no workaholic. He came in late and juggled his responsibilities casually. Stories of a backlog of unanswered mail were all too true.

But he was drawing a lot of attention to the UAW, by appearing at various rallies and peace marches. The Toronto media fell upon him gratefully because he was an articulate, handsome, provocative, colourful man, accessible and quick with a trenchant comment. Dennis McDermott of the UAW was becoming a familiar face on television and front pages. His voice was heard on radio open-line shows, his presence was guaranteed whenever a controversial issue was being discussed. As a consequence, the Canadian wing of the UAW moved into the public eye and the labour movement acquired an articulate spokesman. Politicians sat up and took notice of this brash newcomer on the scene.

Being at the centre of issues was Reuther's style of leadership, and it very much suited McDermott. It was good for the UAW, good for the image of unionism, and good support for those issues.

McDermott also moved the UAW to take a more active role in the Canadian Labour Congress. At the next CLC convention, Dennis was elected vice-president of the Congress. That was more or less automatic because when George Burt was the UAW director, he also was made a CLC vice-president.

The Canadian Labour Congress is a collection of most national and international unions in Canada. The only unions outside the CLC are the teamsters, who left in a flurry of charges of unethical practices, those nationalist unions affiliated with the Confederation of National Trade Unions, and the building trades, who withdrew years ago because they wanted the CLC to be less democratic. The CLC is unique among the national labour coalitions in the world. The American equivalent, the AFL-CIO, for instance, has only union staff and full-time executives represented at its conventions. At CLC conventions, the delegates are elected by union members, their numbers determined by the size of the unions they represent.

As the public sector unions grew in size in Canada, the building trade unions objected to their growing influence in CLC decisions. They proposed that the CLC should vote as the AFL-CIO does, with the head of the union casting all the votes of his or her membership. That's not how the CLC operates. We have one person, one vote. It means that a large union can outvote a small one because the large union will have more delegates, but the system is democratic and it works. We decided to keep the Canadian style, and the building trades departed in disgust. They had another grievance as well – they objected to the CLC's involvement in political issues, particularly its affiliation with the New Democratic Party.

The structure of the CLC is layered. CLC policy on such matters as free trade has to reach down to the grassroots if it is to be effective. The president can talk about labour's opposition to free trade, but the work of campaigning against free trade falls on the CLC's affiliated unions, on the provincial federations of labour, on the municipal labour councils, and finally on local members themselves.

The CLC is an interesting, interlocking organization. At the head are the officers, a president, a secretary-treasurer and two vice-presidents, all elected and full-time. Then there is an executive committee made up of the four officers and heads of the eight largest unions in the CLC. There's also an executive council, elected at the biennial CLC convention, usually made up of area directors of some of the larger unions and the twelve presidents of the provincial federations of labour.

Complex as that is, the CLC also maintains a balance of men and women in leadership, a balance of national and international unions, and a balance of public-sector and private-sector unions. That's what holds the organization together, plus a lot of goodwill. It's a good representation of the labour movement in the country, and its success depends on the willingness of the affiliates to carry out its policy.

Dennis had always been active in party politics, first in the old CCF, now known as the New Democratic Party. He tried to draw the UAW closer to involvement in the NDP. The membership was divided, some felt that he was trying to tell them how to vote, others opposed the NDP because they thought it was too left, some opposed because it wasn't left enough.

Dennis replied to critics in his usual flaming rhetorical style. His point was that there was a natural alliance between trade unionism and democratic socialism. He knew that labour doesn't always vote that way, but to his mind and mine the two are inseparable. McDermott settled for union leaders and staff taking an active role in the NDP, and hoped that the membership would follow.

ON MAY 9, 1970, there was a District Council meeting in Windsor. A bunch of us were sitting around the motel, shooting the breeze. A bang on the door interrupted us. It was a delegate from Local 636 in Woodstock.

"Jesus Christ, Bob," he said, "Walter Reuther's been killed."

I couldn't take it in. "What are you talking about?" I asked angrily.

"Turn on your television," he said. "There's a report that Reuther has been killed in a plane crash."

The delegates piled out of their rooms, pulling on their clothes. We sat in silence, too stunned to talk, watching the television screen and waiting for bulletins. The phones rang constantly as people tried to reach one another to see if anyone had more information.

I called Herb Kelly. He'd been in touch with Dennis, who confirmed that Reuther and his wife, May, had been in the crash. They were flying in a UAW-chartered Lear jet to visit the UAW's Family Education Center, which was under construction at Black Lake in northern Michigan. Approaching the Emmet County airport an hour after sunset, the plane struck a tree, crashed, and burst into flames.

Six people were killed, Walter Reuther, his wife, May, Oskar Stonorov, architect of the centre, and a young Reuther aide, William Wolfman, as well as the pilot and co-pilot.

Walter Reuther *was* the UAW for many people. He had been president since March 1946, and it was his brilliant leadership that put the UAW in the forefront of the labour movement in North America. The Reuther family put its unique stamp on the union, making it both a pathfinder for all unions and a thoroughly democratic organization, whose integrity was unquestioned. It was Reuther's vision that made the UAW a voice for social change and civil rights.

Sickened and grieving, we wondered if we were seeing the end of the UAW years of influence. Four dozen newspaper editors had rated Walter Reuther as America's "greatest living labour leader." The *Wall Street Journal* the next day called Walter Reuther "a symbol of enlightened unionism and social activism," and the *Des Moines Register* wrote, "The death of Walter Reuther has silenced one of the most compassionate and creative voices of our time."

We should have realized that Reuther's loss couldn't destroy the union because he'd built it too carefully. He had surrounded himself with good people who could carry on in his tradition, as we were to see, but that night, as we waited for news, we were shaken by doubts.

The next morning, Dennis McDermott emerged from his room wearing sunglasses. I guessed he had been weeping. He and Reuther had been very close. The last time I had seen Reuther alive was at the UAW convention and Dennis was at his elbow. I said what was uppermost in all our minds. "Dennis, how the hell are we going to carry on?"

"We have to, that's all," he said curtly.

Dennis made a brief statement about Walter Reuther to the District Council meeting, bringing tears to many eyes, and we adjourned. He was needed in Detroit, where the UAW executive was holding an emergency meeting to work out arrangements for Reuther's funeral.

Emil Mazey was acting as president, but it was obvious we would have to make a permanent arrangement quickly. An organization like the UAW can't be seen as leaderless, especially not in 1970, a major bargaining year for the union. Our contracts with the Big Three auto companies were coming up for renewal, and the union had ambitious plans for better agreements.

Dennis was almost overcome by Reuther's death. Reuther not only was Dennis's role model and idol, but had become his patron. They worked together on such causes as the support for Cesar Chavez in the boycott of California grapes. Reuther was opening doors for Dennis, who was seen as one of Reuther's most promising protégés. Undoubtedly, Dennis was counting on Walter's backing for the further changes he wanted in the Canadian Region. Without Reuther, Dennis knew it would be more difficult.

A few days later, I went across the river to Detroit to the Veterans Memorial Building in Detroit to join the slowly moving line of mourners who had come to pay their final respects to the Reuthers. Two closed coffins containing the bodies of Walter and May were placed side by side. People were weeping openly, and I was struck by how many in the long, sad line were black.

As we waited our turn to pass by the coffins, we kept mumbling the same things, that there were too many deaths of fine people. That was the period which saw the deaths of John F. Kennedy, Martin Luther King, and Bobby Kennedy. I had a crazy idea that there was a conspiracy at work to destroy every good person in America who was advocating social justice, who had a vision of a better world for the poor and for blacks.

Both Kennedys had been friends of Reuther and warm supporters of the UAW. John Kennedy came to a UAW international convention soon after entering the White House. The ovation for him was deafening. When it subsided enough for him to be heard, he said, grinning from ear to ear, "Yesterday I addressed the American Medical Association and I wondered how I got elected president of the United States. Today I know how I got elected."

Right after Reuther's funeral, the International Executive Board of the UAW met to pick a successor. The two obvious candidates were Leonard Woodcock and Doug Fraser.

Woodcock was a serious, intellectual man, but he didn't have a very engaging personality and wasn't a good speaker. Doug Fraser was a warmer person and was widely believed to be Reuther's choice as successor. Dennis favoured Fraser, but Woodcock won the presidency by a vote of thirteen to twelve. Irv Bluestone was elected as vice-president to replace Woodcock.

It is a great tribute to our union that once the decision was made, the UAW closed ranks behind Woodcock. To make sure that everyone in the union knew that the team was together, and that the union was in the same good hands, Woodcock, Fraser, Mazey, Bluestone, and Greathouse travelled together to every region. It was imperative that these leaders healed their wounds after this struggle. It's one thing to give leadership when times are easy, but it matters more in tough times. Pursuit of personal power by any of the group who had surrounded Walter Reuther would have been shattering. A wave of relief went through the locals when workers saw that the top was holding, that nothing had changed in any important way with Reuther's death.

CHAPTER EIGHT

The Art of Bargaining

L EONARD WOODCOCK HAD been head of the UAW's General Motors department for a number of years, which meant he represented 450,000 UAW members. Next to the presidency, his was the top job in the UAW. Because GM was his specialty, people were laying bets that the UAW's target during contract negotiations with the Big Three in 1970 would be GM.

The UAW's three-year contracts with the Big Three automakers usually expire at the same time in mid-September. The advantage for the union is that it allows us to hold bargaining conventions where we can fine-tune the objectives we'll be hoping to achieve in the industry and present the Big Three with a consistent approach.

Bargaining with all three companies simultaneously presents a tempting opportunity to shut down the entire industry if the talks go badly. Reuther cautioned against that. He said it would never be necessary. Though the Big Three talk about holding the line together, they can't seem to resist taking advantage of each other when one of them is hit by a strike. In short order, the two still in production start trying to take over the market, which puts pressure on the target company to settle with the UAW in order to protect its share.

Bargaining begins almost simultaneously with all three companies. While the UAW has a focus for each round of bargaining talks, we also give negotiators flexibility to move. We may have decided to go after better pensions, but we don't want a gain in that area to be made at the expense of everything else.

By having three-year contracts, we avoid bumping into a strike deadline every year and companies can make long-range plans. The union needs the breather too. We have hundreds of other collective agreements to negotiate, as well as servicing our locals, and tending to education matters, to organizing, and to political lobbying on domestic and international issues.

The opening of the simultaneous talks with the Big Three is really an exploration to decide which company will be the target. Each negotiating team sets out the union's position and watches the companies' reactions. Afterwards the three UAW vice-presidents in charge of the three sets of negotiations will compare notes with each other and the president. Then the president decides which company to go against, the one that makes the most sense strategically or appears to be the most reasonable. Some think we go for the weakest, most vulnerable company but that isn't necessarily true. We try to select the one where we think we have the best chance of achieving our goals. It used to be said around the UAW that if you wanted money you went to General Motors, if you wanted a breakthrough on a principle, such as a new kind of benefit, you went to Ford.

Well before the September deadline, when the contracts expire and the union is in a legal position to strike, the target company is selected. The next step is a report to the International Executive Board, after which all three companies are notified of the decision.

At that point talks come to a standstill at two of the companies while everything the UAW can muster, from economic analysis to gut instinct, swings behind the team that is bargaining with the target company. The president heads that team, which meets in caucus and goes over every inch of the territory to be covered. A strike deadline of approximately three weeks is set and after that the pressure is on.

The Big Three have mixed feelings about being picked as the target. They don't mind as much as you might think because there are advantages in being the pace-setter. The others have to live with whatever pattern is decided in the negotiations with the target. It's established practice in the industry that the contract signed with the target company will become the standard for the other two. The other two, accordingly, worry that the company under the gun will cave in and give away the store.

The Big Three don't like this tradition, but they have accepted it. They agree that our reasoning is sound. It is in the best interest of both the union and the companies to maintain somewhat similar cost structures in terms of wages and benefits.

The pattern we set in negotiations with the Big Three carries into all other negotiations that follow. That's one of the reasons the UAW has been such a successful union. When we get something we like with the Big Three, a certain benefit or something like voluntary overtime, we carry that into our round of talks with the auto-parts industry, and then the agricultural-implements industry, the aerospace industry, and so on. There might be some differences in detail, but the general thrust is the one set with the auto companies. The standard established in the Big Three talks permeates our whole union and raises the sights of other unions.

We can't get a whole package accepted in smaller plants, of course, but we try for a piece of it: better pensions or health care paid by the company, that sort of thing. We're conscious of our leadership role in the labour movement. We were the first union to have a central strike fund, which we built by voting to increase our dues. Reuther argued that a good strike fund was a clear message to the corporations that the union was ready to support workers who chose to go on strike. Labour historians agree that the UAW has pioneered more collective bargaining firsts in both Canada and the United States than any other union.

Those who figured in 1970 that Woodcock would make General Motors his first target company were right. The objective was to get the cap off the cost of living allowance (COLA) because if the COLA didn't keep pace with inflation, workers' incomes would decrease in real value by the end of the contract.

The background to it was an unfortunate concession Reuther made in the 1967 negotiations. In what proved to be a mistake, the UAW accepted the auto companies' insistence that there should be a limit of eight cents an hour on the cost of living allowance. Even though inflation went through the ceiling, the companies didn't have to pay more for the duration of that contract.

The UAW membership, therefore, hated the cap on the COLA. The mandate that came out of the bargaining convention in the spring of 1970 was to remove the limit and permit cost of living allowances to keep up with inflation.

The UAW executive met in late summer to consider the target company for this objective. Woodcock said the union should go after General Motors. After consultation with McDermott and some of the GM Canada bargaining committee, he proposed that for the first time in UAW history, Canadian and American GM workers should go out together. That was gutsy of him because it meant a terrible drain on the strike fund if the talks failed. His reasoning was sound, however. For years the target company had been either Ford or Chrysler. If we didn't confront GM soon we risked giving the impression we were afraid of the giant and anxious to hang on to the strike fund. The last thing Woodcock wanted was to give the Big Three the impression that he was a faint-hearted leader.

In September 1970, the UAW struck GM. We totally shut down that huge enterprise all over North America. The slogan was, "Out together, in together."

Afterwards some wondered if Walter Reuther would have taken on that fight in the way that Woodcock did. Those comparisons between Reuther and Leonard Woodcock were inevitable, especially in the months of grieving right after Walter's death. When Leonard spoke at his first international convention a few weeks after becoming president, the contrast between his style and Reuther's was painful. Reuther used to hold that unruly audience so still so that you could hear a pin drop, but when Woodcock spoke there was such bedlam that every window in the place could have shattered and no one would have noticed.

That long strike against General Motors is part of union history now. It lasted two months and it crippled the UAW for a long time after.

We had hoped it wouldn't be a long strike, but GM is tough. They used their size against us, gauging our resources fairly accurately. Though strike pay was low, some $40 a week at that time, our reserve of close to $200 million couldn't last. We were wiped out in eight weeks, after which we started mortgaging our property.

Woodcock had prepared for the worst. He told us in the beginning, "If this goes more than a few weeks, we'll be laying people off. You'd better think about it right now and figure out where we can make the first cuts in staff."

Leonard Woodcock set the example of sacrifice as soon as the strike began by taking himself off the payroll. Reuther always did that, as did the directors of the UAW departments of the target company. All went on the same strike pay as the workers.

A week or so later, the whole UAW staff in Canada and the United States went on half pay. We couldn't isolate ourselves from the sacrifices the strikers were making.

A month later, the organizing staff in the States was slashed. The union couldn't reduce service staff because providing backup to the locals is a first priority, so the most vulnerable jobs were in organizing and education. Because the Canadian organizing team was so productive at getting new members, we were left almost untouched. I think we lost only one person. But, as the weeks wore on, we figured our days were numbered. Because of the strike, we weren't signing up members at anything like our old pace. Grim stories about the hardships that strikers and their families were suffering discouraged recruitment. It didn't help either that the media were critical of the UAW. Editorials declared that the union was seeking to destroy the economy. We were all fearful as we waited for the axe to fall.

97

The UAW can't spend more than it takes in – it's as simple as that. Not only were the strike fund and our reserves gone, but the UAW had lost the substantial dues income from our 450,000 members at GM.

Staff in the States was hit hard but the Canadian Region weathered the cutbacks remarkably well. The Canadians had always run a thrifty, tight ship. George Burt set a standard of penny-pinching and Dennis, despite the complaints about his carpet and potted plants, had not been lavish either. The Canadian Region had the lowest staff ratio in the entire UAW. That meant we all carried a much heavier workload than the Americans did, but we were so accustomed to it that we thought long days were normal. The Canadian office had so little fat in it that the only major job position lost in Canada during that entire strike was one researcher.

The feeling of solidarity in those days was magnificent. UAW locals all over the continent took up collections and sent generous amounts to the strikers. Despite the hardship, it proved to be a good time for the UAW. It helped heal the pain of Reuther's death because we felt he would have been proud of us. He was gone, but even General Motors couldn't push the UAW around and destroy what Reuther had built.

We were conscious that we were proving something important about the UAW to the rest of the labour movement. The GM strike finished all talk of the UAW hoarding its strike fund in order to enjoy the interest. We laid everything we had on the line, risking ruin for an important principle. Even when we ran out of money, we didn't quit. We just found ways to raise more.

The younger workers at GM were cocky about taking on the multinational colossus, one of the biggest companies in the world, but veteran trade unionists didn't swagger. They knew that anyone who takes on GM is in for a helluva fight. GM management was tough and the issue was critical to them. They knew to the minute when the strike fund would be wiped out. To Woodcock's credit, he surprised them. With nothing in the bank, he still stuck to the position that the cap had to come off the COLA.

In the end he won. GM yielded and the cap was lifted. That was an important victory psychologically and in substance. In that bitter autumn of 1970, the UAW matured a lot.

"Out together, in together," proved a mockery. In the United States GM settled after seven or eight weeks and workers went back, despite that Canadian GM workers were still on the picket lines. In Canada GM held out over some other issues that had to be settled before we could get back in.

During those extra weeks when our members were still out, Dennis took the heat for what was seen as a betrayal by Woodcock and Solidarity House.

There was a lot of bad feeling about the UAW head office in particular and American workers in general. Finally, five weeks after the strike had ended in the States, GM settled in Canada and our people returned to the plants.

I didn't join in the criticism of the Americans for going back in ahead of us. I couldn't see the point of keeping the American workers out because it wouldn't have changed the situation in Canada. Actually it helped us that they returned to the plants because it ended the financial crisis and allowed the UAW to concentrate its resources on solving the issues in Canada. Leonard Woodcock himself came to Toronto to lead the the Canadian negotiations and his prestige and expertise helped to break the impasse.

The prolonged strike left the UAW and GM battered but more respectful of one another. The truce that resulted held for fourteen years. We didn't strike GM Canada again until 1984.

The union bounced back remarkably quickly. For a while we had to watch expenditures carefully. An organizer would think twice about making a long-distance telephone call from Toronto to Kingston or about ordering leaflets.

Our Canadian organizing team got a boost from the outcome of the GM strike. Our reputation as a tough, aggressive, smart organization soared with the victory over General Motors and workers were delighted to sign UAW cards again.

OUR WORK WAS BACK TO NORMAL and I was watching with interest Dennis's activities outside the UAW. In 1971 he headed a group from the UAW and some churches that went to California in support of the grape boycott.

"What's he doing running off to California?" people complained.

I said, "That's good stuff. That's what the UAW is supposed to do. We've got to look around and keep up with what's happening."

In March 1972, I was in Kingston to distribute leaflets and see how our campaign was going at Northern Electric, a new cable plant we were trying to organize. Carl Anderson, an easy-going, confident man and a natural organizer, was assigned to head that operation. He and I had finished a chilly hour or so of passing out leaflets at dawn at the plant gates and were back in my motel on a Monday morning, March 20, when Helen Kramzyk, the organizing team's secretary, called me from Toronto.

"I've got some real bad news," she said. "Herb Kelly's dead."

Herb had been in negotiations with a plant near what is now called Cambridge. When the session wound up on Friday he returned to his motel and died of a heart attack there some time during the night. His wife telephoned him from their home in Windsor and, receiving no answer after many tries, raised an alarm. Al Seymour and Ken Simpson, two organizers who were working nearby in Kitchener, went to the motel and found him dead.

I got a call Monday afternoon from a UAW staff man, Ted Oana, a great friend of both Herb and mine.

"You've got to call McDermott right away and tell him you want to replace Herb as his assistant," he said.

"I won't do that," I told him. "As far as I'm concerned, Dennis can make that decision himself. I'm not going after it."

Herb's funeral was on Thursday, March 23, in Windsor. Until then I stayed in Kingston working out organizing strategy with Carl Anderson. I was told that the Toronto headquarters of the Canadian Region was buzzing with speculation about who would succeed Herb as assistant director. A jockeying for position had started and I wanted no part of it. Though many raised the subject with me, I refused even to talk about it.

The funeral brought together everyone on staff. All the contenders for Herb's job were present and so were their supporters. My name was one of the ones heard frequently and I wanted the job, but I kept out of it. I felt a sense of emptiness over our loss of another good person.

I have a fixed opinion anyway that staff people shouldn't lobby for that kind of job. I learned from Tommy McLean that the director is entitled to pick whomever he wants as his assistant. McDermott had yielded to pressure to accept Herb Kelly as his assistant and he was owed the opportunity to make this choice himself. Anyway, Dennis was very much his own man in such matters. Dennis made decisions on his own, and no one had a string on him. I knew enough about him to stay out of the jockeying. He wouldn't want advice about an assistant this time.

When talk about Herb's successor came out in the open after the funeral, there was speculation that McDermott would turn to George Specht, the old friend he had passed over for Kelly. Another contender was Frank Fairchild, a staunch, dependable UAW staff person. Others said I deserved it, though I was only thirty-seven, because I had worked so hard. I was dedicated to the UAW, loyal to the leadership, and I got along with rank and file members. Hearing this, I began to think I had a good shot at it.

Then rumours started flying that Dennis was thinking of two administrative assistants instead of one because of his heavy responsibilities as a UAW vice-president. If there were two jobs open, I knew I'd have a chance at one of them.

The biennial UAW convention in Atlantic City was only weeks away. It had always been the assistant director's job to handle the complex details of housing delegates and putting schedules together. Even though Dennis badly needed an assistant for those chores, it appeared that he had no intention of being rushed. Instead, he parcelled out the chores among half a dozen people, including myself. The position, or positions, remained vacant.

Dennis and I never referred to the opening. When we met, we talked affably about what was happening in organizing or generally about the union. The relationship between Dennis and the organizers was straightforward and sharp. Whatever he wanted us to do, we did. Over the four years since his election as director, he had come to have confidence in us. We had floated a few rumours around to test the system and locate the gossips, but he soon realized that we weren't up to anything underhand. Eventually that trust was so solid that if someone reported to him that we were up to some mischief, Dennis simply didn't believe it.

The 1972 convention opened April 21, and I had scheduled a week's vacation right after it. Carolynne and I were going to Mexico with Al Seymour and his wife. I went around the office saying goodbyes. Hoping Dennis would tell me what he was planning to do, I made a point of seeing him.

"I don't know if you know that I'm headed for Acapulco for a week," I said.

"No I didn't," he responded. "Have a good vacation."

"I'll see you when I get back," I said, reluctant to end the conversation.

"Fine," he nodded, turning to some papers on his desk.

I left the number of my Mexican hotel with Helen, explaining that this was "in case anyone wants to get hold of me."

Helen looked at me knowingly. "Thanks Bob," she said. "If anyone needs you in a hurry, if there's *any news*, I'll let you know."

I was back in the office Monday, May 8, 1972. Dennis was there ahead of me, something highly unusual for him. I could see him busy at his desk across the floor. He beckoned me over and sat down on one of his two chesterfields in a corner, indicating that I should sit on the other.

"I guess you know that I've been thinking about my assistant," he began. "I've decided to do it differently than in the past. I'm going to have two administrative assistants and I'd like you to be one of them."

I had been thinking about what I would say if I got the offer, but now that it had happened, the words didn't come easily.

"How do you feel about it?" he asked.

"I feel great," I replied carefully. "But you know me well enough to know that I've got to have some input. I can't be an ass-kisser."

"I don't want an ass-kisser," he said quickly. "I'm not asking for that."

I wanted to make sure he knew what I meant. "I have to have my say about what the union is doing," I explained. "If your decision isn't what I want it to be, you know I'll carry it out anyway. You can be sure I will go with whatever decision you make, but you have to let me give you my views before you make it."

"I don't have any problems about that," Dennis assured me. "But there'll be a lot of goddamned work to do. You'll have to put in a lot of hours."

I grinned. "When do you want me to start?"

"Right away. Get your stuff and move over here."

I started to get up, but he stopped me. "There's one more thing," he said. "About the other administrative assistant. Who do you think it should be? Think it over and let's talk about it tomorrow."

I thought it over right then. "If you look at the politics of the union," I said slowly, "if you look at what's been happening these past four years, I don't think you have any choice. You've got to give it to George Specht."

Dennis studied me. He's got a poker face when he wants one.

"The rumour was that you once had a commitment to make George Specht your assistant," I went on. "I'm not asking you if that was true. But George Specht is an older man who has been around the union for a long time. He's got some finesse and some experience I don't have. If he's your other assistant, I know I'll have to carry a hell of a load but I don't mind doing that. I think George is entitled to it, and I think appointing him would keep the Canadian Region well knit."

Dennis smiled but made no comment. Later that day I heard he had appointed George Specht his other assistant.

The appointments went down well, though some were flabbergasted that I got the job, knowing how McDermott and I felt about each other. Many thought it was a good idea for him to appoint me because I was part of the Herb Kelly faction of the region. Also, it appealed to everyone's sense of justice that George Specht, who got shut out the first time in the interest of union solidarity, should have his chance this time. He was reasonably close to retirement age so it couldn't wait much longer.

There was disappointment among the two or three people who had been close to Dennis before he became director. They had entertained the hope that he might reward them at last and were annoyed when that didn't happen. George Specht was an appointment that pleased them, however, so their chagrin over my appointment was somewhat lessened.

It was hard to leave organizing after so many happy battles on the team but I'd already thought of my replacement, Carl Anderson. As I moved across the floor I felt a wave of fear. I was taking on a heavy responsibility that would include speaking to the local unions, supervising staff, taking care of administration, and playing a key role in collective bargaining sessions. Some of that was familiar territory but the idea of collective bargaining made me nervous. I hadn't been around a bargaining table for a long time.

I admitted my concern to Dennis.

"You'll do fine," he assured me. "Just get your feet wet and you'll see. You'll be all right."

Cliff Pilkey said the same. "Don't worry about a goddamned thing. You've got the ability. It'll just take time. Besides, everywhere you go, there'll be a staff guy with you."

I've always been very grateful for the help of Cliff Pilkey and the staff who saw me through those early bargaining sessions. With their support I learned on the job what bargaining is all about. You have to know the strengths and weaknesses of the company across the table and the individuals representing that company. You have to listen carefully to what is being said, and most carefully to what isn't said. You have to be prepared to be patient, willing to talk issues through, listening to the same objections over and over.

I've never thought that a good bargainer had to be a financial wizard. Profit and loss statements are fluid, and the picture they give is temporary. The main thing is to keep the goals firmly in mind, to be aware of the mood of the membership, and to have the priorities right. Some of the contract objectives will be achievable but maybe not all of them. You have to be willing to swallow some disappointment. Bargaining requires flexibility, of course, but you have to make it clear that there are some issues that you won't move back from.

Strong leadership counts at the bargaining table. If I feel insecure, I make damned sure that no one knows it. I always use a lot of humour because I truly enjoy the camaraderie of bargaining. I guess that harkens back to the good feeling at the cattle sales in Ireland where I used to watch my father making a hand-spit deal to buy a cow. Besides, laughter helps relieve the tension, not least my own.

I didn't have to bargain alone. Along with experienced staff men, there were members of the bargaining team from whatever local was involved. These people were old hands at collective bargaining, canny and observant trade unionists who taught me a lot.

Because I was McDermott's assistant and his representative, I was the leader of the bargaining team whenever he wasn't present. I watched the others carefully and picked up the techniques as we went along. I was supposed to be there to support people like Cliff Pilkey, Frank Moroz, Bill Marshall, and Dominic DeAngelis, but they helped me more than I helped them.

My first lesson – one that Tommy McLean had drilled into me – was not to go in a direction that the shop-floor workers didn't like. Veteran trade unionists have minds of their own, and I could see that they weren't impressed by McDermott's hotshot young assistant. It wasn't at all unusual for me to come in, lay out for them what I thought should happen, and be told very clearly that they had no intention of doing it that way. Unless I could come up with good arguments, I'd have to back off.

The saying in the labour movement is that the union goes into bargaining with a little water in the pail. In the early days when bargaining focused on increased pay, there was a fair amount of water in the pail. In other words, we asked for a good deal more than we thought we could settle for. We learned over the years that this didn't make sense. While bargaining, you may want to win a new benefit which means settling for a smaller wage increase. But if you tell the members they're going to get a dollar an hour, and you come out with fifty cents, it causes a lot of problems. You can explain till you're blue in the face that they've got a better holiday package or whatever, but what they see is that you've come up fifty cents short.

I guess I'm now considered a good bargainer, with fourteen years of it under my belt, and I know now why McDermott and Pilkey didn't try to teach me how to bargain when I asked. You can't teach bargaining. It's a matter of individual style. What works for me wouldn't suit someone else. All I know for sure is that a bargainer has to have two things: strength and integrity.

It's vital that the person across the table knows that your word is good. When you give your word, the other person has to know that you won't let anything fall apart behind that promise. Both sides will do a lot of bluffing, of course, because that's part of bargaining, but that's not what I'm talking about. When I say that we've got a deal, that's it: we've got a deal.

When I am involved in major auto or aerospace negotiations, most of the publicity focuses on my comments about the state of negotiations. This leaves many people with the impression that I make all the decisions, which is far from the case. Few people outside the labour movement understand the decisive role the bargaining committee plays. Committee members are all elected by their workplace colleagues and, in most cases, know the issues well. They join me and the staff in articulating our position to our counterparts in the company.

Some of the toughest arguments in bargaining are in our committee caucus as we try to reach a consensus. I and my staff make strong recommendations on whether to accept or reject a company proposal, but we do not make that decision. The only people who vote on that are the elected committee members.

We had seven or eight strikes running in the auto-parts industry in 1972 when I became McDermott's assistant. There was no time to be nervous about it, I had to plunge in and take the reins. One was a bitter strike against Lanark Manufacturing in Dunnville, a multinational which was a terrible employer. The wages were appalling, the working conditions were dreadful, and there were a lot of women in the plant who were all paid lower wages than the men.

This company played psychological warfare to the extreme. It threatened to move the plant, and boarded the place up as soon as the strike started. It ran as many as thirty trucks a day through the picket line. We discovered the trucks were empty, sent through just to scare us. Next they put a padlock on the gates and a For Sale sign on the lawn. We weren't asking much, but we were getting nowhere.

Bill Marshall was our staff member on that strike. He warned me that this company had a notorious reputation in the U.S. and Canada for breaking unions. We had a meeting in Toronto under the auspices of the Department of Labour. There, I met Frank Galucci, who headed the multinational's labour relations staff. He was a soft-spoken, well-muscled guy, so confident of himself that he came into the meeting alone without a briefcase and took no notes. He began by taking out an American penny, which he put on the table between us.

"There's a cent," he told me. "I want you to know that you're not even going to get that. Never mind what you're asking for, twenty-five cents an hour or whatever. You're not getting even that one cent."

I replied with a few heated comments, but we still had to find a way to solve the strike. After several meetings, we did. We got a small raise, not much but more than the penny.

Collective bargaining, I was discovering, isn't a science. There's no book on it. You learn as you go along and every situation is different. You've got to have some guts and you've got to take some chances, but you also have to be able to read the situation to know when enough is enough, when you can get no more.

One strike that hurt us was at Acme Screw and Gear. The company had been demanding wage cuts. The guys gave in once, then Acme asked for more cuts and the workers gave in again, but the company wanted still more. We called a strike, but the company closed the plant and all the workers lost their jobs.

THE FIRST MAJOR bargaining session I had to deal with was Massey-Ferguson, which had been Dennis McDermott's job before he became director. Herb Kelly followed Dennis as the UAW's man at Massey-Ferguson, and after Herb's death Cliff Pilkey took it over.

Massey-Ferguson had a stong bargaining team. There were two UAW locals in their plants, Local 458 in Brantford and Local 439 in Toronto, with a great deal of friendly rivalry between the two. We were trying to get a settlement to avoid a strike and we thought we were close. On Saturday morning we finally reached agreement on a settlement that we thought the membership of the two locals would accept. We were to meet that afternoon with the steward body of 439 in Toronto. They were a tough, ornery group of workers we referred to privately as Camp Runamok. Local 439's steward body was at such odds with its own members that people said if the steward body rejected the agreement the membership automatically would go for it.

Cliff and I hadn't had a decent dinner for days. We'd been eating greasy junk food whenever we had time for it. On the way to the meeting with 439 we laid plans to finish our work in Toronto, drive to Brantford to present the agreement to the Local 458 steward body, and then relax over a fine meal and a bottle of wine. We were a pleased pair of men as we went into what we expected to be the first of two quick meetings.

The steward body of 439 cut us to ribbons. They used words like "sellout" and rejected the agreement almost unanimously. We were despondent on the drive to Brantford, where a meeting in the union hall had been scheduled for six o'clock that evening. Brantford is a quiet city. Unionists there are not particularly belligerent, so we didn't anticipate the same reception as we'd received from 439 in Toronto. We had failed to take into consideration, however, the fact that the bar in the union hall had been open since one o'clock. When we walked in the door, the members were flying.

The steward body of 458 hated the agreement as much as 439 had. Every one of them, it seemed, wanted to tell us at length what a mess we'd made of things. When they got tired of yelling and took a vote, they, too, rejected the agreement almost unanimously.

Cliff and I got out of there, shaken, at about ten-thirty that night and we wound up eating in a hamburger joint on the highway, two exhausted men.

That night we checked into the Holiday Inn in Brantford and went to our rooms. As soon as I was by myself, the pressure got to me and I started to shake and sweat. I called Pilkey that I wasn't feeling well and he came at once. He placed a chair at the end of my bed and sat down, his feet crossed on the bed, looking relaxed in his undershirt and slacks.

"I'll just hang around," he explained.

He stayed there, a comforting presence, talking about inconsequentials until I fell asleep.

The first ratification vote was scheduled the next day in Brantford in the Capitol Theatre. The second one would be held Sunday afternoon in a theatre on St. Clair Avenue in Toronto. When I walked out on the stage of the theatre in Brantford, I was greeted by boos that shook the room. That was before I'd opened my mouth, so I knew we were in trouble.

Cliff and I and the committee presented the agreement and explained why we thought it was a good one. A few good speakers rose from the floor to tell us to stick it in our ear, they weren't going back to work. In Toronto we got basically the same kind of reception. In both places the vote against us was about two to one.

We talked to McDermott.

"Did you see the votes counted?" he asked.

"Well, no," I admitted.

"You've got to see the goddamned votes counted," he snapped. "Those guys could have stolen some votes on you. Your rep card as my assistant gets you in any place. You've got to watch those goddamned ballots being counted."

We went back to bargain, but Massey-Ferguson would give nothing more. The company said it didn't have the money. Then Dennis got involved in the talks. He got the company to cough up a few pennies and he was able to change the package around a little, so we were ready to go back to the membership with what looked like a different settlement.

This time we got a slightly better reception at Brantford, though there was still plenty of opposition. The ballots were to be counted together, so we saw the boxes sealed and took them to Toronto. This time we were meeting the 439 membership in the Queen Elizabeth building at the Canadian National Exhibition. That meeting was a rough, but a decided improvement on the previous one.

It was time to count the ballots. The election committee started ordering everyone out of the hall. I told them that I was staying. I wanted to watch them count the ballots and I was entitled to do that by virtue of my office.

A huge man stood in front of me. I'm five ten, weigh about 160 pounds, but he had a hundred pounds and several inches on me.

"A coupla deaf sons of bitches here, I think," he observed coldly. "I said everyone out of the goddamned hall. We're going to count the ballots."

I said, "We aren't going any place. We're staying while you count the ballots."

"You are, eh?" he responded. "Then you're going to be here a long fucking time because we aren't counting them while you're here."

One of the men on the twelve-member election committee had an artificial leg. I leaned over to Pilkey.

"Cliff, I said, "I think I can take the guy with the artificial leg if you think you can handle the other eleven. If not, we're going to get the hell out of here."

There was a pay phone outside the building. I put in a dime and called McDermott.

I told him, "I just found someplace that the card doesn't get you in."

"Where's that?"

I told him. He laughed his head off.

We cooled our heels outside until the ballots were counted. To our great relief, the membership of the two Massey-Ferguson locals voted to ratify the agreement this time, though they still weren't too pleased with us.

I often thought of Tommy McLean's derisive comment that any damn fool can take them out, but the test is whether you can negotiate a good settlement and get the workers back in. Now I was in the same position as he had been when George Burt was director. It was up me to do what McLean had excelled at, which was to understand the politics of the union, to sense what the membership wanted, and who were the key players in forming the attitudes of workers on the shop floor. The Canadian Region was larger and more complex than it had been in Tommy's day, but the importance of staying close to the rank and file was still crucial for people in leadership.

FOR THE NEXT YEAR I sweated buckets. I was really struggling. I didn't share it with very many people, but the work load was a killer. I tossed and turned at night, worried about the decisions I had to make the next day, going through the bargaining session of the day before, aware that the paper work was piling up. My hours were crazy, but they always had been. At membership meetings on weekends someone was sure to criticize what I had done or complain about what I hadn't done.

I wondered if I'd ever get over the hurdle and feel confident again. One source of relief for me during that difficult first year was my regular Friday-night steam bath. Frank Moroz, a personal friend as well as a colleague, and Carl Anderson and a few others used to meet Friday nights in Hamilton at the Barton street steam baths and I joined them every time I could.

Frank Moroz mentioned one time that he was getting a growth on his neck. He joked that he might be getting an extra testicle, which he figured would stand him in good stead for his old age. It turned out to be cancer. They figured he had about nine months to live. He was forty-nine years old. I watched him in the steam baths go down from 190 pounds to about 140. He refused to miss a day of work even when he was taking chemotherapy.

He laughed about his hair falling out, and when it came back in curly, he laughed about that. A couple of times I went home from the steam baths and cried. We had a staff meeting in Bracebridge and he was there, looking terrible. He gave us all shit for not taking our annual medicals. He hadn't done that and he wanted us to see what a mistake it was to skip the medicals.

"You owe it to yourselves and to your families," he told us.

There wasn't a dry eye in the place. We figured he was saying goodbye.

Still, he didn't give up. I played golf with him at the Richview golf course near Oakville on his fiftieth birthday. It had begun to look as though he was turning a corner, putting on weight. On the third hole, he was taking a practice swing when he paused and looked up at the sky. "Thought I wouldn't be here for my fiftieth, you sonovabitch," he said in a friendly way. "Well I'm here, and I'm staying." He did, too. He beat it. Today he's living a full life in retirement.

Carolynne and I were getting along pretty much as we always had, superficially all right but not very connected. With the boys now approaching their teens and active in sports, I got involved in coaching, particularly minor-league hockey. I wasn't home much, it's true, but we had friends over for barbecues, took family vacations together, enjoyed the skating rink that I built in the back yard, that sort of thing.

They never seemed to resent how much I was away, but now that they're grown they tell me they did. To tell the truth, I never thought about it much. There wasn't time in my life. Living in Burlington had been convenient when I was an organizer based in Malton, but it was a hell of a drive, fifty miles a day, after Dennis moved the union offices to the east end of Toronto. It added two hours onto every working day.

One of the duties Dennis turned over to me was to answer all his long-neglected mail. It was common knowledge that Dennis was getting complaints about unanswered mail.

"Answer it as if you're me," he instructed me. "Handle all the goddamned mail yourself. If you have a problem with anything, talk to me about it, but otherwise use your own judgment."

McDermott had two secretaries, Claire Preney and Anne Brooks. His marriage had broken up and he and Claire planned to marry after he got his divorce. When George Specht and I moved into the office beside his, he assigned Claire to be my secretary. That was a lucky break because Claire, an attractive, bright woman, was very efficient and had a good idea how Dennis wanted his mail answered. Between us, we did all McDermott's mail and rarely needed to consult him.

That meant I had to know what was happening in every aspect of UAW activities, including McDermott's keen interest in the community. I started to get a sense of the people in other labour organizations with whom Dennis was in contact and with a variety of people in the community, such as heads of social agencies, civil libertarians, mayors, NDP politicians, church leaders, peace activists and, an emerging group, feminists.

CHAPTER NINE

McDermott in Charge

D ENNIS MC DERMOTT MADE some far-sighted decisions, not well understood at the time, which helped to make the Canadian Region more independent than American regions in the international UAW. Previous directors like George Burt had griped privately about Detroit's dominance of Canadian affairs, but they did little to change it. Dennis complained less but quietly went about laying the groundwork for Canadian autonomy.

Today's independent Canadian Auto Workers Union really began with Dennis. The first step was achieved with the constitutional change that made the Canadian Region director automatically a vice-president of the UAW, giving Canada a unique voice in the inner circle of the union and the prestige that goes with it. McDermott's next move changed the labour movement in Canada. He was the key figure in the decision to strike a new code of conduct in the Canadian Labour Congress, part of which said that Canadian unions that were part of international unions should elect their own directors, rather than have them selected by the U.S. head office.

The CLC, it must be noted, has no teeth to enforce the policy. Some of the more than forty international unions in the Congress insist on having their directors chosen at conventions in the States where the Canadians are vastly outnumbered. The 58,000 Canadian members of the International Association of Machinists, for instance, form only 10 per cent of the IAM delegates at the convention that picks their director.

Dennis was busy making changes within the Canadian Region that were long overdue. He took exception to the fact that the UAW newspaper *Solidarity* was written and printed in Detroit, with only a page or so devoted to Canadian news. He insisted that the Canadian membership should receive newspapers written and published in Canada. Though it put some noses out of joint in Detroit, he got an all-Canadian *Solidarity*.

He also persuaded Detroit that we should have our own research component, as American data wasn't always relevant in Canada. Next he maintained that Canadian unions should have independent affiliation with international bodies instead of being lumped in with the American parent.

That last was the result of the first meeting Dennis attended of the International Metalworkers Federation, an organization with which the UAW is affiliated and which represents all the metalworkers unions in the western industrial world. On the first morning, he strolled into the convention room and found there rows of tables, each one marked with a small flag and nameplates to identify the country of each group of delegates. Dennis was seated with the American UAW and his nameplate was behind the American flag.

"I don't see the Canadian flag," he said to a conference organizer. "Where the hell is the Canadian flag? I'm not from the United States."

The response was, "Where do you get your goddamned paycheque?"

That infuriated Dennis. He promptly arranged for affiliation fees for the American membership of the UAW and the Canadian membership to be paid separately. Even though the Europeans continued to think of the UAW as an entity, the red and white Maple Leaf marked where the Canadian UAW delegate sat, not the Stars and Stripes.

Dennis was influenced by the debate on Canadian nationalism that was stirring many people in the seventies. A fiercely nationalistic group, the Waffle, had formed in the New Democratic Party. The Committee for an Independent Canada, headed by Peter Newman, Walter Gordon, Jack McClelland, Abe Rotstein, Pierre Berton, Mel Hurtig, and others, talked of Canadian ownership of natural resources and industry. Dennis was smooth and moved cautiously in a middle position. We had to make changes, he said, but not a revolution.

Still some people found him too aggressive. In the Canadian Region, and outside the labour movement, he had critics who saw him as vain and pushy. Canadians often take an uncharitable view of the activities of other Canadians who occupy the spotlight. We seem to have a constitutional aversion to people who get ahead of the pack.

I supported Dennis all the way in his efforts to get some autonomy for the Canadian Region. Dennis was having a lot of influence on me on that issue as well as contributing to my views on union philosophy and international affairs. We found, to our mutual surprise maybe, that we were a good team.

He had decided that he could trust me and that I would carry out his instructions to the letter even when I didn't agree with him.

We used to have strenuous arguments, but neither of us held a grudge afterwards. As he promised, he did consult with me before he made a significant decision, but he made up his mind on his own. One of his best skills was delegating. He assigned responsibility to people he trusted and then left them alone to do the work.

I appreciated that. He didn't send me into a bargaining session with a set of orders. Because he had confidence in me, I gained confidence in myself. His attitude was, "You're making the call. If you blow it, I'll give you shit, but it's up to you to go out there and use your judgement. If you want help, you can consult with me, but I won't be bugging you."

That's the way I work today. I don't want it said about me that every decision winds up being made in the corner office.

I worked hard and for long hours, which I enjoy, but Dennis could sleep until noon, no problem. It was better that he did because he was a menace in the morning. I tried to avoid him at breakfast if we were travelling together because he'd raise hell if his coffee wasn't delivered the minute he sat down. You had to treat Dennis with kid gloves in the morning.

On the other hand, I get up ready to go. I'm up and running around seven, listening to the news on a Walkman, driving to work or to an airport before eight and using the long time in slow traffic to sort out my day, plan a speech, review a position, make phone calls. I had a cellular phone installed in my car a few years ago and it has been a great asset. Mornings are maybe my best time of the day, so between the two of us there was a good trade-off.

Dennis had a big picture in mind and I was stretching myself, learning from him. I watched him at dinners with delegates from Japan or the Soviet Union or Israel, moving around comfortably with absolute assurance. He knew what was going on in those countries and was an excellent representative for Canadian labour. I could see I still had a lot to learn.

The first major collective-bargaining year after I became Dennis's assistant was 1973. Dennis made the assignments, giving General Motors to George Specht and Ford to me. The Chrysler contract was bargained in Detroit because, at that time, Chrysler Canada workers wanted to be in an international agreement. Dennis went over from time to time to see how the Chrysler talks were progressing, but otherwise the Canadian Region was represented at the international level by our staff person from Windsor.

The big issue in 1973 was voluntary overtime. The practice had been that employers could schedule large amounts of compulsory overtime, often with very short notice. The membership wanted the contracts to say that they couldn't be compelled to work more than forty hours a week. That clause had been in our contracts in the agricultural-implements industry and elsewhere for years, but we'd never got it in the auto industry. This was the year to go for it.

Some locals already had made significant gains in that direction. After a long, tough campaign, Local 444, the Chrysler local in Windsor, had just won acceptance from the company of no involuntary overtime after forty-eight hours. They did it by filing a blizzard of grievances against the company and keeping up the pressure. Finally Chrysler agreed to the change, but on an informal basis; it wasn't in the contract. The Chrysler workers were anxious to see it in the new agreement.

The Ford plant in St. Thomas had a good local. The workers were mostly young, tough, and smart. When the company compelled them to work nights or Saturdays without prior consultation, they were furious. One Saturday the company, insensitive as hell, told them they had to work, knowing that they had a hockey tournament scheduled. There was a shop-floor rebellion. The workers said they wouldn't work, they were playing hockey. If the company disciplined them, they'd shut down the plant.

That confrontation led to meetings with the company at which there was agreement on a selective voluntary overtime system and no weekend overtime work. That agreement in St. Thomas put heat on the union leadership to get the same thing in the new contracts.

Voluntary overtime was a hot issue in the States as well. People were wearing Voluntary Overtime buttons in all the plants.

Solidarity House decided that year to make Chrysler the target company. That meant discussions on the voluntary overtime issue were taking place in Detroit without a strong Canadian presence.

We heard that Chrysler and the UAW had an agreement. It happened so abruptly that even Dennis, as he later told me, had no knowledge of it. Although he was in Detroit, he hadn't been involved in the final decision, which we in Canada found unacceptable. The UAW had agreed that overtime was to be voluntary only after an employee had worked fifty-six hours. Until then, the company could demand that employees stay on the lines at any time. Further, workers were entitled to refuse to work only every third Saturday.

Dennis was furious that the Americans had left Canadians hanging out to dry. In the Windsor Chrysler plant and in the St. Thomas Ford plant, workers would be losing gains they had made for themselves after a hard fight.

The U.S. Ford agreement followed the pattern of the Chrysler agreement. We could see the steam rising over St. Thomas as Dennis led us into the King Edward Hotel in Toronto, where negotiations with Ford Canada were held. We split into small groups. Contracts are so complex that bargaining is divided into sessions, each one directed to a particular issue such as health and safety or pensions. Ford asked for a main-table session on voluntary .overtime, which involved the total bargaining team. It was here that Dennis showed what a strong leader he was.

I was sitting next to Dennis as Ken Holsworth, Ford's vice-president in charge of industrial relations, walked us through a twelve-page document on voluntary overtime that was a replica of the one signed in Detroit. We maintained a polite silence as he read the clauses, which he knew were full of everything we didn't want.

Holsworth was considered a master at bargaining, a man who was always courteous and smooth but determined and skilled. He finished with a friendly grin and reminded us that the international UAW had signed that same agreement with U.S. Ford. He could anticipate no problems with us, he said.

Dennis had scribbled some notes while Holsworth was reading the clauses. With only an occasional look at the notes, he took the clauses apart, piece by piece. His tone was scornful, his language profane. At the conclusion, he declared, "Before I put my name to any garbage like that, my director's card will be on the table and I will no longer be the leader of this union in Canada. You can take that paper and stick it where the sun doesn't shine."

Dennis demanded voluntary overtime after forty hours and he wouldn't budge, though tempers exploded on both sides of the table. Ford argued that we weren't playing the game by the unwritten rules, that we had an obligation to accept whatever was decided in Detroit. Dennis shouted that this was Canada, not the United States, and the Canadian Region didn't have to swallow whatever bilge Detroit pumped out.

Ford yielded at three in the morning, December 4, 1973, only hours before the strike deadline. We compromised on voluntary overtime after forty-eight hours, which was not what we wanted but still a helluva lot better than after fifty-six hours.

We knew we would face a blast from our St. Thomas local if we didn't work out something to allow for the special situation there. We finally got them an unprecedented clause that there would be no compulsory weekend shifts, period.

Getting voluntary overtime was a significant victory for the Canadian Region. For the first time, we had a contract that differed markedly from the one signed in Detroit. The Big Three heard the message that we wouldn't rubberstamp American agreements as we had in the past. We were an independent organization that had to be considered separately – and we were tough.

THE YEARS BETWEEN contract negotiations with the Big Three always seem comparatively quiet to an outsider, but the UAW deals with a lot more than the auto manufacturers.

In 1974, we had the famous strike against Pratt & Whitney in Quebec. Pratt & Whitney was a multinational employer based in Connecticut, who gave us a lot of trouble when we tried to organize. When finally we got Local 510 certified in the plant, management refused to move on even such basic collective-bargaining issues as union security and the checkoff of union dues. The result was two thousand workers out on strike.

Because the issue was fundamental – the right to have a union – labour and political forces in Quebec rallied to help. Unhappily, the already bad situation was complicated by internal problems in the handling of strike funds. There were accusations that workers drawing strike pay were not appearing on the picket lines. Worse, rumour had it that strike funds were being misappropriated. I have no idea, to this day, how much of that was true, but there certainly was a suggestion that a few people were taking advantage of the situation.

Emil Mazey, national secretary-treasurer of the UAW, was in poor health at the time. Just before going into hospital for an operation, he decided to send a devastating letter to the strikers, intimating strongly that the UAW was about to cut off strike funds for the Pratt & Whitney local.

I happened to be acting director of the Canadian Region at the time as Dennis was in the Soviet Union leading a study tour. I hit the roof when I saw Mazey's letter blasting the strike leadership. The way to deal with misappropriation of funds is to sit down and deal with it internally. You don't devastate a strike.

I tried to reach McDermott in the Soviet Union by phone, but it was two days before he got the message and called back. In the meantime I had to act. The leaders of the Quebec strike had come to Toronto for help, shaking with anger. The strikers were in a state of panic that they would lose their strike pay. If that happened, the strike would be destroyed. I called Leonard Woodcock, the UAW president.

"We've got a helluva mess here," I said, without much preamble. "Dennis is out of the country, so I need to talk to you. We can't have this. I don't know what Mazey was thinking about, but this is nuts."

I knew I was putting myself in a tough spot by being critical of Mazey, who was the number-two man in the UAW. Moreover, Mazey was in hospital so it looked like I was attacking a man when he was down. I wasn't surprised that Woodcock was frosty on the phone, but he agreed to see me in Solidarity House.

I took two people with me because I knew confronting Woodcock was not going to be pleasant. He was a cold, calculating man who would not make my task one bit easy. He greeted the three of us in an icy manner, crossed from his desk to a small table nearby, and sat down without saying a word. I assumed we were to sit in the empty chairs opposite him. As we did so, one of his assistants joined us silently, staring coldly at us.

The approach I had been hoping for was that he would say something reasonable like, "We've got a problem here. How do you see us solving it?"

That wasn't Woodcock's style. "This is your goddamned meeting," he said in a nasty tone. "You asked for it. Get on with it."

I was disconcerted but plunged in with all the composure I could muster to describe what Mazey had written and its appalling effect on the Pratt & Whitney strikers.

Woodcock interrupted angrily. "You've got no godamned right criticizing Mazey," he snapped. "He's secretary-treasurer of this union. Who do you think you are? Those people are stealing money. They've got no goddamned right to steal the membership's money."

I wasn't there to defend that, if it was happening. My point was that we deal with that issue separately but that we shouldn't, for Christ's sake, destroy a strike that was holding on by the skin of its teeth.

"You've got to understand the sensitivities in Quebec," I argued.

We were at it for hours. At one point I could feel the sweat running down my back. My associates said almost nothing, leaving me to do all the talking and take the heat. My objective in meeting Woodcock was to get him to make a commitment to the Pratt & Whitney workers, in writing, that the UAW wouldn't terminate their strike benefits. I stuck to that. When we parted Woodcock had agreed to reconsider. Woodcock never did write a reassuring letter, but there was no more talk about cutting off strike pay.

In fairness to Woodcock, all he could see was a young guy from Canada coming to Detroit to tell him the secretary-treasurer of the UAW had screwed up. It wasn't something that was likely to put him in a friendly mood.

I awaited McDermott's return with some uneasiness. The minute he arrived in the office, I told him what had happened, step by step. He listened, showing no expression, nodded curtly when I finished and made no comment. A Canadian Region council meeting was coming up in Port Elgin and Dennis went home to prepare his report. The next day he told me, "I'm going to take Mazey to task. He had no goddamned right to write that letter."

Dennis not only backed me, but he was taking on the fight himself. You've got to know the importance the UAW attaches to loyalty in order to appreciate the guts it took for Dennis to take that stand. Emil Mazey had been a pioneer in the UAW. He represented the Reuther years, and that meant something almost sacred in UAW history. Mazey was a legendary figure from the time when the union was pioneering collective bargaining rights. It was Mazey who kept the union clean financially, a singular accomplishment in the larcenous early days of the labour movement. As well, Mazey was the only UAW leader who supported Dennis's position against the Vietnam war. Even Walter Reuther had been reluctant to be critical of American involvement in that war.

Dennis first talked to the staff, explaining why he felt that Mazey had been out of line. Most agreed with him but were apprehensive, too. Some thought Dennis should settle the matter quietly in Detroit in a closed meeting and not criticize Mazey in front of local union leadership.

Dennis disagreed. "The membership has to know about this," he insisted. "They have to know what's at stake here."

He went to the Canadian Council meeting at Port Elgin ready to condemn Mazey. When he learned what was going to happen, even Charlie Brooks, president of the Canadian Region Council and a former left-winger, was alarmed.

"Christ, Dennis," he protested. "Isn't there another way to do this?"

Dennis snapped, "No, there isn't."

The comments on Mazey's letter were the last item on his report. When he finished reading it, he said he wanted a vote of the council censoring Mazey.

I thought to myself, we're into it now.

A few people protested, uneasy about an open challenge of Mazey, but McDermott had laid out the arguments very clearly and there was much less fuss than I had expected. I was to remember how careful and effective he was that day. Ten years later, when I was facing the Canadian Council to explain why I thought the Canadian Region should become a fully autonomous union, I followed McDermott's lead in making that recommendation the last part of the report, and I made sure that I had all the points in as logical an order and as sharply defined as he had done the day he criticized Mazey.

McDermott took the resolution censoring Mazey to the next meeting of the International Executive Board in Solidarity House. Woodcock saw him coming. Woodcock and the others were shocked that Dennis wanted to deal with the difference openly, rather than in the club-like atmosphere of a caucus or private meeting. They decided to handle it by keeping it off the agenda. Dennis was satisfied, however, that Woodcock and Mazey got the message.

McDermott's stock in the Canadian Region soared. Mazey's letter had raised hackles in the locals, where a threat to cut off strike funds looked very much like strike-breaking. They were proud of Dennis for challenging Mazey, for making his fight out in the open, and for getting away with it.

Quebec workers were astonished that Dennis championed them so vigorously. They were accustomed to unions that were run by Americans with little consideration for Canadian differences, and certainly none for French-Canadian sensibilities. Dennis became a hero overnight in Quebec. Later he endorsed the right of our staff and local unions to support the PQ and Quebec's right to determine its own future in the referendum on separation. His credentials in that province are solid.

The Pratt & Whitney strike went on and on for months, exhausting everyone involved. As the strikers and their families fell into debt, Local 510 did fund-raising to help them. They sold thousands of leather straps from which hung a cross made out of horse-shoe nails, which became the symbol of the 510 strike.

The strike headquarters was in the basement of a church. Many priests were sympathetic and gave sermons about supporting the strike. The artistic community rallied and put on benefits which attracted huge audiences. I went to some of those union meetings and I'd never seen anything like it. The strikers made them open session, even inviting the media to attend.

"We've got nothing to hide," they explained.

Then Pratt & Whitney management started to hire scabs. Desperate strikers put down their placards and slipped back into the plant. By the time that bitter, violent strike was over, Pratt & Whitney had something like 1,600 scabs working inside the plant. Many times there was violence on the picket lines as Quebec police waded in with clubs, beating the strikers bloody. Along with others, I went to Quebec City to meet with the premier, Robert

Bourassa, to beg him to put some pressure on the company to bargain in good faith, but to no avail.

Our staff man in Quebec in charge of the 510 strike was Bob Dean. The strike had worn him down so completely that he could hardly make a speech about it without breaking down. One weekend during a staff seminar in Port Elgin, we were just sitting around talking in Dennis's room there, when someone called. The man was so excited he was hard to understand. He said some strikers had taken an empty Brinks' truck. Using the armoured vehicle as a kind of battering ram, they had crashed through the plant gates and were holed up inside the plant. They were still inside with a CBC reporter who had agreed to the desperate stunt, but riot police had been called to get them out. Dean feared for the lives of people inside.

Dennis and I were aghast. Their illegal act could put the strike leadership in a bad light. The company could play the aggrieved party and make bargaining even more difficult. At the same time, our trade unionist sympathies were with the workers.

"I wish they hadn't done it," I said, "but they've got a lot of guts."

Dennis nodded somberly. "I just hope they come out without their heads getting bashed."

Doctors and nurses rushed to the scene, prepared to treat the casualties. The sight of the ambulances and stretcher bearers cooled everyone's passions. It dawned on both sides that people were about to get seriously hurt and somehow the confrontation got sorted out without much damage. It marked the turning point. A chastened company began to bargain and we got enough in the contract to salvage something out of the long debacle. But a number of workers were fired, and stayed fired despite the union's protests, and we did not get the checkoff of union dues.

That strike fuelled the growing resentment in Quebec of foreign domination of industry. Local 510's terrible ordeal became part of the political base from which the Parti Québécois was built. Almost every night, news programs had shown film of the strikers and the way they were being treated. The strike at Pratt & Whitney entered the turbulent history of the union movement in Quebec. It was the direct reason for the new labour legislation brought in by the Parti Québécois under René Lévesque to prohibit scabs and to make the checkoff of dues compulsory. Bob Dean, our staff man on that strike, was subsequently elected to the Quebec legislature, and became a proud cabinet minister in the PQ government.

THE PRATT & WHITNEY STRIKE was winding down, and McDermott

turned his attention to the lack of a research department in the Canadian Region. The person lost during the 1970 cutbacks caused by the GM strike had not been replaced.

"We've got to get someone good on this," Dennis said. "We need to develop a good analysis of what's happening in the industry."

We were beginning to see the first signs of a recession in the auto industry. Jobs were being lost in all the Big Three as customers turned to cheap, small, well-constructed import cars. The gasoline shortage had sent a wave of panic through North America. Almost overnight, buyers switched from gas-guzzlers to the small compact cars made in West Germany and Japan. Those cars had been sitting on dealers lots for years, attracting few buyers outside of a handful of conservation-minded people, whose passion for the tiny cars was considered to be mildly eccentric. Suddenly, they were on the roads everywhere and dealers who depended on sales of the huge, powerful Detroit-designed cars were hurting. We talked about the change we were seeing, but none of us had a handle on what was happening or what to do about it.

We advertised for an economist-researcher in newspapers and labour publications. Dennis gave me the task of screening the applicants. One stuck out because it was from a Ph. D. student in Wisconsin. He said he was a Canadian, raised in Manitoba, and he was interested in the position. Dennis said to give him a call.

I arranged with the man to come to Toronto for an interview and I met him at the airport. I stood outside the doors, watching people coming from customs. No one who passed by looked the way I imagined an economist working on a doctorate would look, and I was beginning to worry. Finally all the passengers had departed except for one man, wearing jeans, work boots, and a windbreaker.

"Hi," I said tentatively.

"Yes," he replied with a grin, "I'm Sam Gindin."

In the car Gindin peppered me with questions about the Canadian Region. I had planned to use the time to learn about him, but I couldn't find an opening. I got one bit, that he had studied at the University of Manitoba under a left-wing professor of some renown, Cy Gonick. I introduced Gindin to Dennis and we showed him around. One staff person took an immediate dislike to Gindin. He didn't like the Cy Gonick connection, he told me later, because Gindin was likely to be full of socialist ideas. I didn't think that was such a bad recommendation. I was beginning to be impressed with Sam. Dennis questioned him about what he knew of the labour movement and Gindin turned out to be knowledgeable.

I drove him back to the airport, warming to him by the minute.

When I returned to the office, Dennis asked me what I thought.

"The guy's got an MA in economics," I exclaimed. "For Christsake, I dropped out of school when I was fifteen. How do you expect me to be able to judge a guy like that?"

He waited for an answer.

"To tell you the truth, my gut feeling is that I like him," I went on. "He asked more questions of me than I asked of him. He's bright. And besides, we've got nothing to lose. He wants to work for the union so I think we ought to try him."

"Fine," said Dennis. "We'll give him a chance."

We had a Canadian Council meeting coming up in Windsor in two or three weeks. I suggested we have Sam Gindin attend to get a feel for the organization. I told him he had the job and he was pleased but concerned that starting so soon meant it would interfere with his Ph. D.

"Don't worry," I assured him. "We'll give you a sabbatical when this crisis is over."

Sam never found the time to write his doctoral thesis, but he has turned out to be without a doubt the best labour economist in Canada. People ask me who is my right arm. I tell them I don't know, but Sam is my left arm. He's a world authority on the auto industry. He's a genius at writing an economic analysis so that anyone can understand what is at stake. When I'm in a bargaining session, he'll give me figures on profits and costs that help me debate management's arguments. I can trust his data; it won't blow up in my face, he's always right. It was Sam who helped me with the arguments to make against free trade, and Sam who laid out the facts about the costs structure underlying the issue of wage concessions.

He's an innovative, committed, bright man. Sam could make four times as much money in the corporate sector as we're paying him, but he has a great love for workers. He gets quite left-wing sometimes and I have to pull him back a little, but he's got a good social conscience and a grasp of international issues. It's Sam who keeps reminding me that I should be going to Nicaragua, or making statements about South Africa.

Not long ago I made him my assistant. He's a key part of the team that keeps the CAW going. He puts in an enormous number of hours on our behalf. Maybe someday, when he retires, he'll write that doctorate.

Soon after Sam Gindin came on staff, George Specht reached retirement age and Dennis had to appoint another administrative assistant. He talked to me about it and the name of Frank Fairchild naturally came up. Frank was a little older than I was, but not much. He came out of the local in Thunder Bay and had joined the staff a short time before I did. Frank was a warm, bright individual whose time was spent mainly in the service department of our union, first in Ottawa and then in St. Catharines. He also taught members about union history and philosophy. He was moved to Toronto as the service person for McDonnell-Douglas and de Havilland aircraft companies, tough locals where he had gained enormous respect.

There had always been a bit of friendly rivalry between Frank and me. Frank's supporters resented that Dennis and I had become quite close, and that Dennis seemed to consult me more than he did anyone else. Others wanted to be in the inner circle, too. I don't suppose I made it easy for them by giving away any ground. Frank, however, had a different relationship with Dennis than I did. They had a warm personal relationship and visited one another's homes.

Frank had a spotty medical history. He had a heart attack during one of his regular compulsory checkups at the UAW clinic in Detroit. Afterwards, he took off some weight, quit smoking, and appeared to be in good shape. The matter of his health didn't occur to anyone when Dennis named Frank his other assistant.

With Frank there, my work load was considerably relieved. He moved in quickly and aggressively to take responsibility. I have to admit I had a sense of losing a bit of territory, but I had been carrying a heavy burden and needed the help. Still, it took a bit of adjustment for me when Dennis began to consult both of us instead of me alone. Frank made no bones about his determination to get involved in everything that was happening.

Frank was put in charge of the General Motors department, the largest responsibility of all the departments in the union. In 1976, Ford was selected as the target company so he was idled while those bargaining talks were going on. On Monday, October 18, we were meeting with Ford at the King Edward Hotel. Around seven in the morning, my phone rang and it was Dennis. I knew at once from his tone that something serious must have happened.

"I've got some bad news," he said.

"What now?"

"Our buddy Frank Fairchild died of a heart attack last night."

Frank had been involved in a very complex arbitration on behalf of some union leaders fired at McDonnell-Douglas, an incident known as "the Douglas five." He could have delegated that to someone else, but he took an interest in it himself. On Sunday when he went to the office to check his mail he found he had won one of the cases. He telephoned Dennis in some glee with the good news. A few hours later he died in his sleep.

I got up and took a shower, and cried like a baby. I felt some kind of doom was stalking labour people. We were dropping like flies.

By the time I dried myself I was thinking what we would do to fill the hole. Dennis had part of the answer.

"When you finish the Ford bargaining," he said, "you'll come with me to GM. You'll take Frank's place there."

The GM negotiations opened in the Royal York Hotel a few days after Frank's death. I met first with the GM bargaining team and saw at once that they weren't going to make things easy. They were a tough, clannish crew who weren't giving me an inch. One of the guys, Phil Bennett, a burly, gruff type, took a few strips off me, but I gave it back as good as I got.

Bennett came up to me after the meeting.

"I like you," he said levelly. "You've got balls."

At ten in the morning, Friday, negotiations with Ford fell apart and our workers went out on strike. That afternoon we had our first meeting with General Motors' committee. One of the union GM staff from Detroit started by reading a list of layoffs in the United States that GM had just announced. We listened in horror. The recession we had been dreading was suddenly upon us.

Dennis and I had both felt confident we would get what we wanted in the Ford strike. That optimism vanished. Now that cutbacks had started, Ford would be tough.

The meetings adjourned for the weekend, leaving us a badly shaken group. Dennis and I met in our temporary office in the King Edward Hotel.

"We've got to find a way to settle this Ford strike," he said. "We've got to get a solution right away."

We told the Ford bargaining committee how the recession would affect our positions. We scrambled to find a compromise that the membership would accept, recognizing they had to make the best of a bad situation. The strike was settled and the Ford line was running again in a week.

CHAPTER TEN

Moving On, Moving Up

F RANK FAIRCHILD'S DEATH shook us all. Many people on staff had
hoped that Frank would be the next leader of the Canadian
Region when Dennis McDermott left. Others favoured me, but it would have
been close.

No one moves through the ranks to reach a position of prominence solely
on the basis of his or her personal ability and talent. People in such jobs as I
now have don't get there entirely on their own. A certain amount of hard
work and skill is necessary, but luck and timing count for a lot. Somewhere
along the way, the rising leader becomes the beneficiary of someone else's bad
luck. If Frank Fairchild hadn't had that heart attack, he was just as likely to
have become Dennis's successor as I was.

Dennis had to find someone to replace Frank as his other assistant director. Gordon Parker seemed the best of all the likely contenders. Gordie was a
good, solid choice. He had been around a long time, a sort of diamond-in-the-
rough type who could be cantankerous and difficult. Gordie wasn't innovative and he tended to fly off the handle when his authority was challenged,
but he was a plugger who worked hard and was totally devoted to the union.

Gord was in his fifties, which Dennis saw as an advantage. That meant the
position would be vacant in a few years and our younger staff people, now too
green to be considered, might be ready. You have to look ahead when you fill
positions; you have to think about how the organization can grow.

Gordie was difficult to work with. I wasn't his favourite kind of trade-
union man. He was suspicious of me and maybe envious. He wanted to be at
least my equal, if not my better, and he resented that my relationship with
Dennis was closer than his. His manner with me, as with almost everyone,
was abrupt, critical, and testy. You couldn't get close to Gordie.

Gordie was assigned General Motors, which he managed creditably, but much of the work that Frank Fairchild had insisted on doing fell back on my shoulders.

Some time in 1977 we began to hear rumours that Dennis McDermott was a leading candidate for presidency of the Canadian Labour Congress. Joe Morris was retiring and Dennis had perhaps the highest profile of any union leader in the country. None of us knew, at first, how Dennis felt about it. I didn't raise it with him, but one day as I was leaving his office, Dennis brought up the subject himself.

"I guess you've heard the scuttlebutt about me going to the CLC," he said. "What do you think about it?"

"Dennis, you should stay here," I replied promptly. "You've started to make important changes in the UAW in Canada and I think you should see them through. Just so you know where I'm at, I never expected to be the administrative assistant. If you go, obviously I want to be considered for your job, but I want you to know that I'm happy where I am."

I was sincere about that. I knew I was the obvious choice to succeed Dennis but I had doubts that I was ready. It is one thing to do some of the director's work while someone else is in the director's office and takes the responsibility for it, and quite another to be in that office alone.

Dennis consulted a number of people. He polled most of the members of the executive of the CLC and found that he was their favourite candidate. If he wanted the job, it was his. He wouldn't have to do much politicking. He decided in the end he couldn't resist the challenge and the prestige. He told me he was leaving the UAW to go to the CLC.

I think he had mixed feelings. The UAW has a mystique in the labour movement. It's world famous as a progressive, clean, democratic union, and Dennis was the Canadian leader at an exciting time.

The Canadian Labour Congress, on the other hand, could be a minefield. Because the CLC is a collection of more than eighty unions representing more than two million workers, the leader can't move the organization along at a pace that is faster than the affiliates will allow. Some of the affiliates are very progressive, but some don't think unions should be involved in anything but collective bargaining. A few, to put it frankly, are less than admirable in their internal operation.

Dennis was concerned that he wouldn't have the patience to tolerate the frustrations he knew lay ahead, but he also thought he had almost an obligation to try. If anyone could bring that huge organization along, stir it to use the power it possesses, get it more involved in improving the quality of life for all Canadians, it was McDermott. He saw the job as a chance to make the CLC more active on social and political issues and move it closer to the NDP.

Dennis began preparations to leave. He seemed to take it for granted that I would be the new director and we talked about who should be my assistants.

"Are you going to stay with Gordie Parker?" he asked.

"I don't think I'm going to do that," I said. "I don't know all the director's tasks, but I do know the administrative assistant's tasks. I know it takes hard-working, younger people. I don't see Gordie fitting in."

He nodded. He wasn't surprised.

The staff speculated about a possible challenger to run against me. Gordon Wilson, a seasoned trade union man, well-liked by all, was seen as the most likely. He had been a close associate of Frank Fairchild's and had many of Frank's assets. Gord's background was solid. He came out of our Local 27 in London and for a while was on the CLC staff. Dennis brought him back into the UAW to do servicing work in Chatham and then made him education director. Gord had proved himself to be capable, industrious, and popular. Gordie Parker also was encouraged to try for the job.

I took little part in the manoeuvring that had begun. I knew others were working on my behalf. People told me that Dennis was making calls, telling people why I was the right man. I didn't make a lot of calls myself or go out of my way to talk to people about it. I was fairly assured that I had no real opposition to worry about on the staff and I knew I had good support in the locals.

I'm not saying that I hadn't made any mistakes. I'd made a lot of them. But I had a good working relationship with most people on the staff and in local leadership; despite my fast rise I had few enemies.

Gord Wilson had an advantage over me in that he spent a good deal of time socially with some of the newer staff. For instance, I wasn't close with Sam Gindin outside the office but Gord and he would go to each other's houses for dinner. Gord thought he could count on Sam for his support.

I discovered otherwise. One morning when Sam and I were flying to Ottawa, the subject of the new director came up. I told Sam he had to make a decision about which man he would support.

"There's no question about it," he said. "You're the director."

A few days later, Gordie Parker had a heart attack. At the same time, discussion of Gord Wilson's candidacy seemed to evaporate. That left me alone in the running.

Early in 1978, just before he was to depart for the CLC, Dennis called a staff meeting and announced he wanted us to sort out the leadership question so the staff wouldn't be divided. A couple of people pushed for a postponement of the decision. They said it was too soon for people to know who was available for the job.

I listened to the discussion without concern. I'd learned the lesson that Tommy McLean pounded into me, that you don't go into a meeting unprepared. In the room of about fifty-five people, I knew who was for me, who was against, and who were the doubtfuls. I had a solid majority. You can't be a leader and not know what people who work with you are thinking. In fairness to Gord Wilson, it should be said that I'd had a better opportunity to be more active than he had in the union at different levels and I'd developed a good rapport with many more people than he had.

Eventually someone got up and, sounding genuinely perplexed, said, "I don't know what this debate is about. Bob White is the only one for the job."

Someone else said, "I don't know what you guys are hearing, but in the local I'm servicing the guys are saying that it better not be anyone else but White."

At the end of a good discussion, it was agreed that I was the staff's choice for the position of director of the Canadian Region.

Dennis' resignation came between international conventions so we were obliged to hold a special, emergency one-day convention in Toronto, bringing in 300 delegates from every local in the Canadian Region for the single purpose of electing a new director. Emil Mazey and Doug Fraser came from Detroit to supervise. Fraser was the new president of the UAW, having succeeded Leonard Woodcock when Woodcock retired.

In the UAW, any delegate can nominate another for the position of director, and any delegate can nominate himself or herself and run against the designated candidate. If there is more than one candidate, there must be a roll-call vote.

I was nominated by Jack Dunn from my local in Woodstock. There was a pause, and then Gus McCarthy from Local 707 in Oakville, got up. He said he wanted to nominate someone who had been active in the trade union movement all his life, a talented person who had never been a bureaucrat – a lot of emphasis on that – and never taken a full-time staff job; a paragon. In short, Gus McCarthy.

He wouldn't back down and withdraw, though his friends urged that he should. We had no choice but to hold a roll-call vote.

Helen Kramzyk, my secretary from the days of the organizing team, had arranged a happy surprise. Without telling me, she invited my parents and sister Rachel from Woodstock to attend the meeting and witness my triumph.

My son Todd and his girl friend Tracey were also there. My dad was alarmed by Gus McCarthy's challenge. He was so worried about me that he was hanging on every vote anxiously as the locals responded.

After several locals had voted without one vote for Gus, he got to his feet.

"Mr. Chairman," he said, "I'd like to withdraw and make it unanimous."

There were cheers, an emotional speech of thanks from me, a few words about working together in what looked like a period of hard times for the North American automotive industry, more cheers, and it was over.

I'D DONE SOME THINKING about who to appoint as my assistant. Bob Nickerson was our staff man in London, a very strong man out of Local 1256 in Oakville who had good rapport with workers. He had been in bargaining sessions with me and I knew him to be able. I'd already spoken to him about it, and he had accepted with delight.

My other pick was another young man, Basil Hargrove, known as Buzz, who had been on staff only about three years. He came out of Local 444 in Windsor and was assigned to service American Motors and a lot of other plants in the Brampton area. I'd kept an eye on him. Listening to him during staff meetings, I had been impressed. He made good sense, had a sharp feel for the issues, and he wasn't afraid of work. I wanted him for my second administrative assistant but I still hadn't spoken to him about it.

As the convention was breaking up I asked Hargrove to meet me for breakfast the next morning. When I asked him to be the other administrative assistant, he was surprised. He hadn't expected it because he hadn't been on the staff very long. I told him being a bit new was no handicap. Rather, I saw it as an asset because I felt it was important that the Canadian Region have a fresh perspective.

"My problem is Gord Parker," I admitted to Hargrove. "He's lying in hospital recovering from his heart attack and obviously I've got to tell him right away. I can't let the news that I've picked two other guys get back to him third-hand."

The next morning I drove to the hospital in Scarborough where Gord was recuperating, agonizing all the way, wishing I could be doing anything else but this. I kept saying to myself, "What a bastard you are, White."

I could rationalize it because I knew it would kill Gordie to work as my assistant. The edge of conflict between us and the pace I would set would be too much for a man with a heart problem. Still, I didn't think Gordie would see it from that angle. Nevertheless, I had to face him.

He greeted me without enthusiasm and offered congratulations on my election. We chatted while I summoned up nerve. Finally I raised the topic that was on both our minds.

"I don't want you to get upset, Gordie," I began, "but I'm going to tell you a few things. I've made my decision about my administrative assistants. I want you to know you're not going to be one of them, for a couple of reasons. One of them is that it is too demanding for you."

His expression registered pure fury. I hastened on. "Look where you are today," I said, looking around the hospital room. "It makes no goddamned sense for you to take on the kind of workload that's ahead. The second reason is that I want to put together an entirely new team."

He was almost apopletic. I hoped there was a nurse not too far away. "You're getting more money than the regular staff but I've worked it out with Fraser," I went on. "We'll red-circle your rate so you don't have to take a cut. I'm not trying to push you out of the union. When you get better we'll sit down and talk about what you want to do, but right now I have to get on with things."

I was finished. I added lamely, feeling awful, "I don't feel very good about doing this to you when you're in here with a heart attack."

Parker exploded. "You goddamned sonovabitch," he yelled. "If I had known this would happen I would have run against you as director."

"I know you're upset and I don't blame you," I said, "but it's not a question of running against me or not running against me. It's a matter of who can get the job done. I think when you reflect on this in a year or so, you'll agree it was a wise decision for both of us."

When he recovered, Gordie came back on staff, surly but resigned.

By that time we were in a new building, the one we still occupy, a square, two-storey, glass-sheathed building on the crest of a breezy hill in the northeast part of Metro Toronto. I made sure every office had proper walls – no more of McDermott's open plan for me – and I moved into a large corner office on the second floor with my two assistants next to me. I assigned Bob Nickerson, whom everyone calls Nick, all of Toronto and everything east of it, including Quebec, together with responsibility for General Motors, the Independent Parts Council, aerospace locals, organizing, retired workers and the Canadian office staff. Buzz got everything west of Toronto, plus heading up Ford, American Motors, Chrysler, Rockwell, the Technical Office and Professional department, the agricultural-implement plants, and citizenship. I gave Gordie Parker Massey-Ferguson and some other bargaining chores, making him a sort of overseer for the Toronto area, and he did fine. His personality didn't change, he was still a bit of a grump, but it worked out all right. Unhappily, only a few years after he retired, he got cancer and died very quickly.

The selection of Nickerson and Hargrove turned out to be one of the best decisions of my life. They have been my confidants, my supporters, my advisers. They carry enormous workloads in their various responsibilities and never complain. Buzz and Nick have different personalities, each with his own strengths and weaknesses, each with his own point of view, sometimes quite different from the other. I have consulted them on almost every major decision, whether it is collective-bargaining strategy, staff appointments, or leaving the international union. Though the discussion can get heated and can last for days, we've always reached a consensus.

I was going through a rocky time personally. In 1976, Carolynne and I separated, leaving Todd, then fifteen, and Shawn, thirteen, feeling very bitter. When parents separate it's initially a terrible blow for the children. They are great survivors, however. If parents behave as mature people and resist the temptation to use the children as pawns or engage in long legal fights over custody or material possessions, the kids can live reasonably normal lives and sometimes are stronger for the experience.

I went through that dismal routine of seeing my sons only intermittently. I would take them out and try to find the old mood of camaraderie. The boys, however, were distant. Todd was sometimes openly hostile. It was hard work for us all. Carolynne didn't demean me with the boys, but the three of them shared a sense of grief that formed a bond. I was the outsider, the villain, a role I couldn't escape.

Carolynne and I didn't fight about money or possessions. Our lawyers quickly arrived at an appropriate amount, and that was all there was to it. I took my clothes and a radio and left everything else to her and the boys. When I walked out, the boys were crying and Todd was cursing me. That's something you never forget.

One of the first people I told about the breakup was my parents. I drove to Woodstock and waited until we were almost finished dinner before I said, "I've got something to tell you."

My mother said calmly, "You and Carolynne are separating."

I stared at her. "How did you guess?" I asked.

"We don't know how it lasted this long," my father observed. "We've often wondered how you two could stay together, you're so different."

They've never been critical of Carolynne, then or since, and she still visits them. Their quiet support and understanding of my point of view helped me greatly at the time.

Though the marriage wasn't working for either of us, Carolynne and I probably could have gone along in our own strange, cool way. It happened, however, that there was someone else in my life. I met Marilyne Kuhn in 1976 at a CLC convention in Quebec. She was a flight attendant and a delegate of the Canadian Air Line Flight Attendants' Association, a bright, pretty woman, thirty years old and newly divorced, and enthusiastic about the labour movement.

She was among a group of delegates from her union who met in my hotel room to decide on a candidate for the CLC executive. The discussion turned to the subject of women in the work place. With a straight face, looking to provoke a reaction from her, I said, "I think women belong in the home, in the kitchen, at the sink."

Marilyne came out of her seat in indignation. "I just got rid of a man who thought that way," she told me furiously. When people started to laugh, she realized I'd been kidding.

Before she left, I asked her for dinner. She said she would call and let me know. When she did, she suggested we make it a foursome. She brought one of her union's delegates and Cliff Pilkey also joined us. I invited her for dinner the next night and she insisted again on a foursome.

Marilyne was chairperson of her bargaining committee and following the merger with Pacific Western Airlines became a member of the PWA bargaining committee, chair of the Toronto union, and subsequently national vice-president of CALFAA, the Canadian Airline Flight Attendants' Association. She soon found out that because of petty jealousies in her own organization, being married to Bob White was not an advantage.

Marilyne and I were drawn to one another but the courtship wasn't easy because she was living in Winnipeg. I have never been much for chasing around, as the expression goes. The situation with Marilyne, however, drew me strongly. I am a romantic person and I had reached a point where I wanted to be in love.

After I left Carolynne, I lived in a basement apartment for a while. Marilyne and I then bought a three-bedroom town house in Etobicoke and she moved in with me while we waited for the divorce. Her mother wasn't too pleased about that arrangement but most people accepted it. I had to attend an International Metalworkers Federation meeting in Helsinki, Finland, and while I was gone Marilyne scouted around and found a minister who would make a house call. In October 1978, not long after I took over from Dennis as director, we were married in the livingroom of that house with my sons, my parents, and Helen Kramzyk in attendance. Todd was my best man and we all went out to dinner afterward to celebrate. The next morning I had to be in Port Elgin for a meeting of the Chrysler Council so we didn't take time for a honeymoon until the following January, when we went to Hawaii.

My sons suffered greatly in the breakdown of my marriage to Carolynne. Todd and his mother fought so much that later on, when Marilyne and I were living together, he came to stay with us. That was hard on Marilyne because he took some of his anger out on her. With my help, he got a job in Toronto but he goofed it. I went to bat for him a couple of times, finding him other jobs, and he'd be all right for a while and then he'd mess up again. He was at an age, seventeen, when he was trying to find himself and it wasn't easy. I felt a lot of guilt, knowing that one of the reasons he was having such a hard time was my decision to leave his mother.

Eventually I made another tough decision and told him that he had to leave.

He moved into a hovel in downtown Toronto, scaring me to death. Despite my alarm at what might happen to him, I also knew in my heart he would survive. Todd always was street-smart and he was certainly his own man; I couldn't see him letting himself get pushed around. I told him that if he ever was in trouble, if he ever needed me for anything, he had only to call.

I saw him from time to time because I took him food and stuff I thought he could use. One day he called to say a teenaged girl in his rooming house was in trouble. Some guys were pumping drugs into her and she had been picked up by the Toronto police youth division. She was in the Jarvis Street detention centre for juveniles. He asked me to help get her out and drive her to her father's home in Weston. I said sure.

I was shocked by how young and ravaged the girl looked. She was maybe fifteen. Driving to Weston I heard Todd in the back seat lecturing her like a parent, warning her to stay away from those guys. Look where it had landed her. "You're crazy putting all that shit into yourself," he scolded her.

I felt good listening to him. I'd been wondering how far he was going with drugs but obviously he hadn't lost himself in that culture at all. It served Todd in good stead that he had never been one to run with the herd – dress like everyone else, do what everyone else was doing. Not long ago we went to a wedding in Woodstock and Todd turned up in a white tuxedo jacket with an earring in his ear. That defiance of the mainstream kept him out of trouble on the street. He was smart enough not to get caught in the drug mess.

It wasn't too much longer after that that he said, "I'm ready to go to work."

"Okay," I said, "I'll give you one more shot."

I asked a guy I knew at de Havilland if there was an opening for an inexperienced young man and there was. I warned my friend, "I have to be fair about this. Todd's screwed up twice. If he does it again I'll kill him." The man wasn't concerned. "We'll give him a try," he said. "Maybe this time it'll be all right."

It was. Todd worked there for a long time and did fine until he was laid off, which was not his fault. We get along all right these days though he and Shawn will still take a shot at me that hurts. I try to reason it out. If I can keep my cool around a bargaining table when the crap is really flying, why can't I take the occasional dig from my own kids? They saw their dad leaving, so they're entitled to be hurt and angry. All I can do it try to establish some kind of relationship so we can reach one another, still be a family.

Todd never minds arguing with me openly, but Shawn usually prefers to be friendly, at least on the surface. He stayed longer with his mother, but when he was ready to leave and go to work, he asked me to help him. I was able to find him a job at one of the auto companies and it has turned out fine. He doesn't particularly like the work – I don't know how anyone can like that kind of work – but he's a good young man and he meets his responsibilities stolidly.

Dennis was sympathetic with my distress while I was separating from Carolynne because he'd been through a marriage breakup himself. But as he was preparing to leave, we both had other matters on our minds because we were in the middle of one of the most significant strikes of the decade in, of all places, the tiny Fleck Manufacturing plant in the small community of Centralia, forty miles north of London, Ontario.

IN THE BEGINNING Fleck looked like a routine, first-contract bargaining situation. It was a small auto-parts plant with 140 employees, mostly women. Conditions in that place were simply terrible. It was infested with rats and mice. The safety precautions were negligible, the machinery was dangerous and there were only four toilets. Women who started work there were paid $2.85 an hour; after ten years they could earn $3.24 an hour, and that was almost without benefits. To make a bad situation worse, a good many of the women were being sexually harassed by men in senior levels of management.

They approached us for help. We sent in an organizer, Lorna Moses, who quickly signed up enough workers to allow a new UAW local, 1620, to be certified at Fleck by the Ontario Labour Relations Board. We set a strike deadline date for March 6, 1978, and approached management in the routine way to negotiate a contract. We asked for improvements in the plant, some benefits in the wage packet and an increase of seventy-five cents an hour.

We were turned down flat. Further, to our astonishment, management was adamantly opposed to a compulsory checkoff of union dues. They announced they would not collect dues from employees who didn't join the union.

Fleck was challenging a fundamental principle in union contracts called the Rand formula, on which labour stability has depended for thirty years. Without the Rand formula, the company has what we call a one-contract union. We get a contract out of the first collective bargaining but the company immediately starts to favour the non-union employees and intimidate the workers who are paying dues. Management makes the point that those who didn't join the union are enjoying the same benefits as union members without it costing them anything. In no time, particularly if the workers are inexperienced in trade unionism, people start turning in their cards. That's an old management trick to destroy a union.

The Rand formula is something the UAW won for the labour movement during the famous Ford blockade of the forties, when the workers in Windsor abandoned their cars in the streets and tied up traffic for miles. A Supreme Court judge, Mr. Justice Ivan C. Rand, was asked to look into the root causes of the disturbance. In 1945 he made a recommendation, known ever since as the Rand formula, that when a union is certified and has a bargaining agreement, the employer must collect union dues from all employees, whether they belong to the union or not.

The reasoning is that since all workers benefit equally from the agreement that the union has secured, all workers should pay into the union. That isn't the most important aspect of compulsory checkoff, however. As Rand understood very well, the real point is that the checkoff protects the union's very existence. When some people in the plant pay dues and some do not, and yet all are working under the same conditions, why would anyone pay dues? If workers can opt out of the check-off, resignations would run like a cancer through the plant and decertification would follow rapidly.

Fleck was counting on that happening. There was no question in my mind that if those Fleck women went back to work without the Rand formula and a decent collective agreement, very soon we wouldn't have enough members to keep our certification.

Al Seymour, our staff representative, began to feel uneasy about what was happening at Fleck. He warned me that something odd was going on, and that we might have something nasty on our hands if there was a strike. He figured management was preparing to hire scabs.

On the Friday before the Monday strike deadline, the company representatives walked out of the bargaining session. Fleck called a meeting of employees in the plant and the Fleck vice-president, flanked by two uniformed officers of the Ontario Provincial Police, addressed the workers. He warned the employees that they would lose their jobs if they went on strike. Then the police took over and lectured the women about violence on the picket lines. They were advised not to carry baseball bats, knives, or chains and were told that they could be arrested if they tried to stop anyone passing through their picket lines to enter the plant.

That devastated the women, some of whom were only teenagers and none of whom knew much about their legal right to picket peacefully. The company was able to persuade a good many of them to come to work despite the strike.

We thought it odd that police would be in a plant telling employees that a strike was a bad idea, but events were moving too quickly for us to react. The strike began Monday morning and scabs arrived in great numbers by a company-hired bus. Before noon we had a call from a staff man there, Bert Rovers.

"There's a real Donnybrook going on here," he gasped.

He told us the police in full riot gear were "throwing women into the snowbanks like cordwood" to clear room for the buses to enter the plant. No one had ever seen so many police for one small strike, especially one involving mostly women. Trying to protect one of the strikers, Al Seymour and another UAW member from Northern Telecom, Rene Montague, got into a scuffle with the police and were arrested. Al was tossed in the back of a police cruiser and taken to the Stratford jail, where he was held without bail. That set the tone for the rest of the strike.

Eventually the two were told by the Justice of the Peace in Exeter County that they could be released if they signed a statement agreeing to stay out of the township in which the Fleck plant was located. Seymour refused to do so. He said the strike was his responsibility and, besides, there was another plant in the township that was also part of his assignment.

We told him to sign and got our lawyers busy on an appeal of the bail conditions. The judge who later lifted the conditions had some stern things to say about that Justice of the Peace.

We couldn't understand where the company got the clout to have so many police there until we looked into the company's background. We learned that the Fleck plant had a significant political connection. It was founded and 50 per cent owned by the family of James Fleck, deputy minister of industry in Ontario and a close personal friend of Premier William Davis. Moreover, the premises were owned by the Ontario Development Corporation, a branch of Fleck's ministry. Dennis McDermott was outraged.

"We've lit a match on a fuse," he said, "and found that the string leads to dynamite in the premier's office."

The women on the Fleck picket line took another beating at the hands of the police the next day, and the day after that. We don't often make a calculated decision to get tough on a picket line, but this time we did. We had a good local union in the Ford Talbotville plant in St. Thomas, not far from Centralia. The members were young burly guys who rather enjoyed a good fight. We called them and some others in Local 27 in London and Budd Local 1451 in Kitchener. We said we couldn't allow the Fleck strikers to be terrorized and asked for a show of strength and solidarity to hearten the frightened women.

At our request, several hundred took a day off work, sacrificing pay. Some had to get up at three in the morning to be on the picket line for the first shift. They got to the plant in time to meet the buses carrying scabs. You can be damned sure the police didn't try to throw any of them in the snowbanks. Some arrests were made, but we got our message across clearly that we weren't going to stand for police abuse of workers in a legal strike.

We threw everything we had into supporting that strike, politically, financially, organizationally. In that kind of labour negotiation, when the usual systems have broken down completely, you have to grab whatever you can. You can forget about dialogue, you're really in a war. Around the Canadian Region headquarters, the Fleck strike took on the mood of a holy crusade.

It was our good fortune that the strike caught public attention, with feelings strongly favouring the strikers. It had some unusual features that people found appealing. These weren't automotive workers on the picket lines, men with relatively good incomes. Instead there were plucky women making little more than minimum wages and taking a bruising from the police for trying to get a fair income. When television showed police shoving the Fleck women around, the police raided television stations in London and Toronto, confiscating the film.

Centralia was in the provincial riding of Huron-Middlesex, represented in the Ontario legislature by a Liberal, Jack Riddell. Riddell lined up solidly with the company. He told the media that the Fleck workers didn't want the UAW and signed union cards only because they were threatened by our organizer. I asked our lawyers to prepare a libel and slander action against him.

The Ontario government was horrified and took the view that Riddell's remarks were privileged, though he had made them outside the legislature. I was hauled before the Procedural Affairs Committee. The UAW lawyer who went with me was not allowed to ask questions while I was subjected to almost three hours of hostile examination. I was told that the union faced a possible fine and I could be jailed, which I didn't for a moment believe. Despite the committee's lawyer giving the advice that they were in error, the members voted to find me and the UAW guilty of violating a member's privilege. The legislature later tossed out the charge.

James Fleck tried his best to keep out of the limelight, but hot questions began to be asked in the Ontario legislature about his possible conflict of interest.

Dennis McDermott waded in, insisting that there be an investigation of the police. The government's reaction was to ask the Ontario Provincial Police to study the matter. The NDP house leader, Elie Martel, scoffed, "That's like putting Dracula in charge of the blood bank."

We approached the Ford Motor Company in Detroit, Fleck's major customer, to ask them to buy their products some place else. We said we couldn't continue to have a good relationship with Ford when one of their suppliers was trying to destroy our local there. Ford rejected our request, so we put Fleck strikers on a picket line in front of Ford Talbotville and shut down the plant.

Ford got a Supreme Court injunction banning Fleck pickets and UAW officers from picketing any Ford location in Ontario. We appealed the injunction without success.

During the Fleck strike, and other first-contract strikes I mention later, the women's movement played a key role. Feminists turned out to support the strikers and promoted their cause widely through the movement's network. Unions have an important ally in the women's movement and should understand better their potential to organize support during difficult strikes such as Fleck.

The strikers grew spunky. Some of them toured the province, speaking to the media and addressing gatherings about the strike, winning friends wherever they went. The Toronto Workshop theatre produced a play about the strike and, on June 19, staged a benefit before a packed house. I spoke briefly and Madeleine Parent, a legendary figure from the textile workers' union, also made a speech. That raised $2,000 for the strikers. Donations came in from all over the country, the largest of which was $10,000 from the Ontario Public Service Employees Union.

Fleck was unmoved. Despite everything we could do, we found it impossible to talk with the company.

We next tried a desperate tactic. We applied for permission to prosecute the company, Grant Turner, a Fleck vice-president, three members of the Ontario Provincial Police, and MPP Jack Riddell. We charged that they had violated seven sections of the Ontario Labour Relations Act, among which were failure to bargain in good faith, intimidation, failure to comply with a certification order, and so on.

In April 1978, with the Fleck strike still unsettled, Dennis left the UAW and was elected president of the Canadian Labour Congress at a convention in Quebec City. As was customary in the CLC, as the UAW's Canadian director, I was elected vice-president.

In his presidental address following his election, Dennis made an impassioned plea for the entire labour movement in Canada to throw its weight behind the women on the Fleck picket line. He said the implications of what might seem a small, tempestuous but unimportant strike in Centralia extended beyond the UAW. What was involved at Fleck was a direct assault on trade unionism itself.

In a flourish that was vintage McDermott, he announced he was going to Centralia himself to face the police.

"I'm an old street fighter from way back," he said with a cocky grin. "Let me see them throw McDermott in a snowbank."

Al Seymour went with McDermott. Driving to London on highway 401, they were struck by the number of black and white provincial police cars all around then. They checked into the Holiday Inn in London and were amazed to find the hotel bristling with provincial police, some in riot gear. The media, which accompanied Dennis on this pilgrimage in great numbers, estimated that there were 500 police in Centralia.

Of course the company didn't send buses through the lines the day McDermott was at the Fleck plant. They didn't want any incidents and the police, aware of cameras everywhere, behaved with perfect propriety.

As the new director of the Canadian Region, I had to find a solution to the Fleck strike. Despite all the media attention, the workers' families were suffering and the strikers were growing discouraged. Luckily, the political heat finally got too much. The Ontario Ministry of Labour appointed a mediator, Fred Joyce, to bring the parties together.

Joyce was an experienced labour-management negotiator. He usually represented the management side in negotiations, but he was a reasoned, fair man. He instigated one-on-one meetings between me and the president of Fleck, Fred Berlett. I refused to yield on the issue of compulsory checkoff, and so did the company. Fred Joyce found a middle road. He suggested that I agree that everyone in the plant could vote on the contract ratification, the scabs as well as well as the strikers. If I did, he thought Berlett would accept compulsory checkoff.

The rule was that only dues-paying union members voted at ratification meetings. We would run a big risk if we allowed everyone to vote. If some of our members didn't like the contract and voted with the scabs, we would lose the ratification. I consulted with Buzz and Nick and we came to the conclusion that we had to take the chance.

"We have a majority of the workers," I pointed out. "If every one of our members votes for the agreement, we'll win."

The agreement was not great, and I knew some strikers would be disappointed and tempted to vote against it. We got a forty-cents-an-hour increase over the two years of the contract and some improvements in health benefits, but not as much as the women deserved, especially after holding out for 163 days. I called a meeting in Centralia and told the strikers why they should vote for the agreement whether they liked it or not. Every vote mattered because the scabs would vote solidly against the agreement.

The strikers joined hands and walked to the polling station in the Huron Recreation Centre singing "Solidarity Forever." The thirty-nine non-strikers, driven to the Centre in a dusty company-hired bus on which was scrawled "Strikers are pigs," voted first. The seventy-three strikers voted an hour later. To a person, the Fleck UAW women voted in favor of the agreement and we won the ratification. The vote was seventy-three to thirty-seven, with two spoiled ballots.

I wanted the Fleck strike to be the last time in Ontario that workers had to walk to picket lines in order to get union security. On August 17, 1978, I wrote Ontario Premier William Davis a sharp letter about his government which, by its inactivity, supported an employer practicing nineteenth-century labour relations.

"Never again in Ontario should workers have to do what Fleck workers did – strike for a Rand Formula checkoff," I told him. "Never again in Ontario should massive use of police be used to support an employer trying to break a strike and deny workers their right to have a union. It is time for action by your government on this issue. The compulsory dues checkoff should be automatic by legislation, once a union is certified by the Ontario Labour Relations Board."

Our union and others – notably the United Steelworkers at Radio Shack in 1979 – were later also involved in strikes on union security, but eventually we got laws to assure that when a union is certified there will be compulsory checkoff. The tradeoff in the legislation was the same as the compromise we accepted in the Fleck strike. By law all workers, union or not, participate in a secret vote on ratification.

As I said in my September report to the Canadian Council a few weeks later, the Fleck strike will go into the history books of the labour movement. The women at Fleck were not striking for a good contract but for their basic right to have a union. They were a gallant group of workers who never wavered. Although scabs were going through their lines every day, not one of the Fleck women returned to work during the strike.

CHAPTER ELEVEN

The Men from Detroit

I BECAME THE UAW's Canadian director at a fateful time, just as the North American automotive industry plunged into recession. In 1977, employment in the Canadian auto industry was at an all-time high, but early in 1978, in an effort to cut losses, the industry tried to rationalize and restructure its huge operation. People were laid off by the thousands and plants were closed. The Big Three started shopping around for government subsidies, bargaining with the promise of jobs in stricken communities for the sweetest deals they could get.

The first sign of cutbacks came at a strike at the Columbus McKinnon Company in St. Catharines, which began in October 1977. The company was the first in the industry to demand that we accept cutbacks in our contracts. The company insisted on a 25 per cent cut in future cost of living and some other concessions. We refused.

The plant was completely closed all that winter. Spring came, and then summer, but the company wouldn't budge and neither did we. Suddenly, in August 1978, the company announced it would never reopen the plant. The operation would be transferred to its plants in the United States.

I protested hotly to the Ontario government. The minister of labour, Dr. Bette Stephenson, arranged a meeting with me and the U.S. president of Columbus McKinnon. I tried to persuade him to rescind the decision, but he blandly stated that his hands were tied. The Canadian president insisted on it, he explained. This was nonsense, of course. I was certain that the company intended all along to close that plant. It just wanted to blame the UAW for it.

Plant closings were becoming common in the States and were starting in Canada. We were never to suffer as severely as American workers did for a number of reasons. As the industry has acknowledged many times, quality is higher in the Canadian automotive plants than the American. Also, the return on investment in plants in this country is one and a half times greater than the return in the United States. Simon Reisman headed a federal review of the Canadian automotive industry at that time, which confirmed Canada's marked profitability margin.

In 1978, however, General Motors, Ford, and Chrysler were in trouble. Facing huge losses for the first time in their corporate lives, they appealed to governments to help them, and they were successful. Governments all over the world were willing to play the game of corporate give-away with taxpayers' money in the hope of getting new plants or of saving existing ones. The beneficiaries, of course, were the shareholders.

We were skeptical about the need for government handouts to the automotive industry, but our main concern was for the workers who were losing their jobs outright or being laid off for indefinite periods. The union's supplementary unemployment benefits fund, called SUB, had been designed for short-term layoffs created by model change or sales decline, but not for the kind of long-term layoffs we were seeing.

I thought if the Canadian governments, federal and provincial, could give Ford $68 million to locate a $500 million plant in Windsor, it could certainly afford to establish a fund to compensate workers affected by corporate decisions to relocate. I wrote the federal minister of industry, trade and commerce, Jack Horner, proposing a Transitional Assistance Benefit, calling his attention to a Chrysler shutdown in Windsor and American Motors layoffs in Brampton. He dismissed the suggestion.

Because Dennis McDermott had been good at delegating responsibility, the transition from administrative assistant to director wasn't as difficult as I had feared. I just had a few more things to juggle, a few more meetings to attend, some homework to do on foreign affairs, a lot more speeches and interviews to give, a whole lot of decisions to make, and that was about it.

I was interviewed by a reporter for the UAW's *Solidarity* soon after moving into the director's chair. I observed that the team that built the UAW in the forties was almost completely gone and a new team was moving into place.

"The new people," I observed, "haven't been in there for twenty years. They don't feel cynical about trying new solutions to problems."

We certainly had new problems now the automotive industry was in recession. There was talk about colossal investment in new plants and updating production lines with robotics. What wasn't clear was how much of that new investment Canada was going to get. While the Canadian Region's membership had bounded ahead in the years 1965 to 1970 when I was organizing, that increase came about because the whole auto industry was expanding. To keep growing we'd have to organize office workers, a huge untapped group, and we'd have to move into the new electronics industries.

I talked about Canada being distinct in the UAW. "It's a constant struggle to remind people in the United States that we are not a region," I said. "We're not a region, we are a country, separate and distinct."

As for our goals in the immediate future, 1978 and 1979, I listed our commitment to retirees and getting a shorter work week. We got shorter hours in 1976 in the form of a paid personal holiday plan, which allowed a person to work a four-day week once a month. That was a big step because to keep the machines running, management had to hire. The question I was considering was whether to expand that program or go for a shorter work day on Friday.

I complained about the absence of women in the top union jobs. I made it clear that I wanted to see more women on the Canadian Council and on the staff. Also on my agenda that year was the defeat of Pierre Trudeau's Liberals in two forthcoming federal by-elections. I was still sizzling that Trudeau, who had been elected on a platform of no wage controls, had turned around after the election and on Thanksgiving Day 1975 had slapped on wage controls.

It was obvious that the only control during the period of so-called wage and price control had been on workers' wages. We had figures to show that wage controls had cost the average worker in Canada $2,200 over the three-year control period, or about $20 billion for the entire work force, and that we were about to lose another $1,100 per worker in 1979, or $10 billion overall. Meanwhile corporate profits were up. In the first quarter of 1979 they rose by 58.3 per cent over the first quarter of 1978.

That was a lot to work on. I developed my capacity to cope with many activities simultaneously when I was heading the organizing team. On any given day we had every possible stage of organizing going on all over the province, from door-knocking to signing up members to negotiating a first agreement with management. I had to learn to keep it all in my head at once.

What makes it possible for me to deal with seven or eight urgent matters in one day is that I can drop information out of my head just as quickly as I can absorb it. If I think a problem is over, closed, I clean the slate. I make a decision, see it carried out, and then I forget it.

Usually I sleep well, even when we're in the thick of negotiating, but if I have six or seven matters jumping around in my head that are unresolved, I can have a hell of a time, waking up at four in the morning and unable to get back to sleep. Most times I enjoy pressure and even thrive on it, but occasionally it gets to me. I can't tolerate being rattled and disconnected, so when that happens I concentrate on getting some of the mess resolved. I think about it while jogging and figure a way to handle this, and what to do about that. I can then go to work with my mind made up, get busy and by the end of the day I have enough problems resolved that my mind is at peace again. Jogging usually cools me out when the pressure gets too much.

As a man who knew lean times as a child, I suppose I should enjoy my present standard of living more but I'm pretty casual with my own money. Marilyne says I spend my paycheque, her paycheque, and someone's we don't even know yet.

I like nice things – a soft leather windbreaker, good wool sweaters, a new car, a meal in a fine restaurant – but if I didn't have money for them tomorrow, I could get along fine. I don't have a fancy house, or a cottage, a boat, or a condominium in Florida. I have no desire to accumulate wealth. I figure that I'll always get by all right, no need to worry now about my old age.

IN APRIL 1979, I'd been director of the Canadian Region for about a year when I had a curious conversation with the UAW president Doug Fraser. We were in Anaheim, California, at an international aerospace conference to discuss strategy in the forthcoming round of bargaining talks in that industry.

"Before the meeting breaks up," Doug said to me, "I want to have a conversation with you about something."

I met him in his suite and he took me out on the balcony overlooking the pool and slid the door shut behind us. He started to talk about the future of the union. As everyone in the UAW was aware, the Reuther era was coming to a close. In four years, five of the greats, president Doug Fraser, secretary-treasurer Emil Mazey, and vice-presidents Pat Greathouse, Irv Bluestone, and Ken Bannon would reach the compulsory retirement age of sixty-five.

He began to speculate about the new leadership the union would need. He thought Ray Majerus would be good as the next secretary-treasurer. I agreed with that, wondering where this conversation was going. His greatest concern, he said, still circling around, was for the office of the president. He didn't see many people around him who could handle the job. Then he paused and looked hard at me.

"You've got the potential," he said. "You could handle it. You're in the Reuther mould. You're a social democrat and you've got a good social conscience."

I was stunned.

"Have you thought about it as a possibility?" he asked me.

I said, truthfully, that I hadn't. "I've only been director for a year," I pointed out. "It hasn't occurred to me to think about being president. But right off the bat I can say that I have no doubt about my ability to handle the administrative and collective-bargaining role in the international union, if I wanted to do that. My concern is how a Canadian could be transplanted into the American political milieu, especially since the UAW president is expected to play an important part in political affairs in the States."

Reuther had been trusted adviser to Democrat presidents and Leonard Woodcock, his successor, had been the same. After his retirement from the UAW, he was appointed the first U.S. ambassador to China.

A Canadian could be at a distinct disadvantage in understanding the shifts and trends below the surface in the States and in having credibility if or when the UAW wanted to criticize Washington. I know that a Canadian, Lynn Williams, is head of the international Steelworkers, but Lynn spent a long time as an international secretary, deeply immersed in the union's business in the States, before that happened.

Doug brushed my reservations aside. He said I had four years to groom myself. I could start to travel around the States, get a feel for things, make friends in the regions, get to know politicians. It wouldn't be too difficult for me to grasp how state government worked and how to relate to the Congress and Senate.

I wasn't sure. "For the first term, at least, I'd be easy to dismiss as persona non grata because I'm not an American," I told him. "I think that's the reality."

Doug wouldn't accept that either. He insisted I could be ready in four years if I started right away to become more involved in the U.S. UAW. My assistants could take over more responsibility for the Canadian Region and that would free me to spend much of my time in the States.

He didn't say clearly that he would back me if I wanted to try for the job. In politics you avoid making a blanket statement you might have to deny later, but we both knew what he was saying: I was his choice as the next president of the UAW. He insisted I was right for the job, that I was acceptable to a lot of people, and that I should start right away thinking about it.

The concerns I expressed were real, but I didn't mention a more important reason for my reluctance – I didn't want to leave Canada. I love this country. It was a lucky day for me when my parents decided to come here. There are opportunities here that are available nowhere else in the world. I believed then, as I do now, that I could have more effect on developments here than I could in the United States.

I assured Doug that I would give the presidency of the UAW a lot of thought before I made my decision, but I had pretty well made up my mind on the spot. Though I was sure I didn't want the job, I wanted to keep the option open. I decided to tell no one about that conversation, not my family, not my friends, not my closest associates.

It's interesting how the political process works in a powerful organization like the UAW. Right after that talk with Doug in California I started to get invitations to address meetings all over the United States. Schools and conferences suddenly wanted to hear from the Canadian director of the UAW. I knew Fraser was pulling strings. The process of getting me exposure in the key regions of the UAW had begun. Some of the invitations I accepted, and some I didn't. I found it was interesting to watch how the system worked.

That summer, the UAW's public relations department called me to say that *Fortune* magazine wanted to arrange an interview with me. When I met with the writer in the London Chop House, a famous Detroit restaurant, he wanted me to talk about the politics of the UAW and about the coming change in leadership. I was astonished. I thought, God, things are starting to happen and I haven't really sorted my mind out yet.

When the article appeared, it was about the two prominent contenders for the UAW presidency, Bob White of Canada and Don Ephlin, a vice-president close to Fraser. The article wasn't complimentary about either of us and suggested that the UAW's greatness was behind it.

In the wake of the *Fortune* article, people in Solidarity House were openly resentful and envious of me and Ephlin. At the next meeting of the International Executive Board, someone commented furiously that it "looks as though we've got a goddamned leadership race on here already."

Doug was very smooth at handling that kind of outburst.

"I didn't give them the story," he said easily. "I haven't annointed anyone as my candidate."

"There's nothing to worry about," I joked. "I don't know what happens here, but in Canada *Fortune* is not a big seller. I think there were only two copies in the whole country and my mother bought both of them and sent them to Ireland!" Someone else pointed out that *Fortune* doesn't have a vote in the UAW and we all laughed. But no one forgot. Afterwards, I started to get very special, very friendly treatment around Solidarity House.

DESPITE THE RECESSION, we were making progress in Canada in introducing paid educational leave (PEL) into our contracts, though management fought hard against it. The idea came from the Scandinavian countries, where employers pay into a fund that the unions use to educate their members about union history, collective bargaining, and about social and political issues in their communities. We were asking for one cent an hour, paid by the employer into a PEL fund, and we would choose workers from that plant to put through what is now a four-week seminar. By 1987, over two thousand members had taken the course.

The PEL program has been a huge success. Some of the people we've trained have emerged with great leadership qualities and all of them have gained an interest in what's going on in this country that has led to their involvement in the social and political life of their communities. Some have run for municipal government, some have headed local bargaining teams, some have become volunteers in non-profit organizations helping battered women or disabled people.

Gord Wilson, our education director, had pushed for this program and it had been developed by Dan Benedict, who has a long and illustrious career in the labour movement. He worked for the UAW in Solidarity House when Walter Reuther was there, then he went to Geneva as assistant general secretary of the International Metalworkers Federation. Then he taught at McMaster University in Hamilton because he wanted to work in Canada. He spent some time working with the Latin American labour movement as well. Dan speaks eight languages fluently and is a warm, understanding, reasonable individual. He was sixty-one when we hired him to head our PEL education program, a North American first.

Management complained that we were asking them to pay to train a bunch of socialists to cause trouble, but they grudgingly yielded to our insistence. The first place we got PEL was at Rockwell in Milton and Chatham, one of the smaller operations of Rockwell, where Gord Parker negotiated the breakthrough.

In September 1978, thirty-one union members embarked on the first PEL program at our Port Elgin facility. By the end of the year we had PEL in 117 of our contracts covering 33,500 workers, and we were looking to get it in our Big Three contracts during the 1979 round of bargaining talks.

We didn't yet have the Ontario legislation to protect union security, so we were fighting yet again on the issue of the compulsory checkoff. We were on strike at Blue Cross, a hospital-insurance company operated and controlled by the Ontario Hospital Association. Ironically, most of our workers in the automotive plants were covered by Blue Cross for such extras as semi-private rooms. Our members were giving Blue Cross, literally, hundreds of millions of dollars worth of business while Blue Cross was fighting a union among its own employees.

Our locals complained about this situation but none more loudly than those in Windsor, where Green Shield, a rival hospital insurance company, was fully unionized by us. Our members wanted us to switch companies, but the corporations insisted on choosing the health insurance carrier themselves.

We tried to organize Blue Cross office workers in the head office in Don Mills, directly across from the Ontario Federation of Labour building. Management fought us tooth and nail but finally, early in 1979, our organizing team led by Clare Meneghini succeeded. We were certified by the Ontario Labour Relations Board, but when we attempted to get our first contract, we ran into a stone wall in the person of the president, Alan Hay, a retired British officer in his seventies. He looked the way a character actor would portray a stiff-necked tyrant, even to the monocle. He maintained that he would never grant us the compulsory checkoff.

We went on strike. Like the strike at Fleck, it was a women's strike and again the police were very rough with the picketers. The company hired security guards to open holes in the line to bring in scabs.

In the middle of the Blue Cross strike we opened the 1979 round of bargaining talks with the Big Three. This was the biggest test of my leadership I had faced since becoming Canadian director. As before, Ford and General Motors would bargain separately with Canada, but the Chrysler workers in Windsor still wanted to be under one international agreement to be negotiated in Detroit.

I didn't like the Chrysler arrangement. It meant that Canadians could never defeat a ratification vote because all the votes were counted together and we were greatly outnumbered by the Americans in Chrysler. We had three Canadians on the international UAW Chrysler bargaining team that year but they kept a low profile. Doug Fraser, himself a veteran of a Chrysler assembly line, led those negotiations, and the Canadians at Chrysler loved and trusted him.

We were worried about what was happening in Detroit, but Buzz Hargrove, Bob Nickerson, and I had our hands full in Toronto with GM and Ford. Hargrove was with me as I headed the Ford negotiations and Nick was at my side when I talked to GM in Toronto's Royal York Hotel.

One day I led the whole GM bargaining team up to the Blue Cross picket lines to bolster the women strikers. The company president later referred to us as "the goons from Oshawa and St. Catharines." I swore that when we came out of negotiations with the Big Three, Blue Cross wouldn't be our carrier.

The bargaining with GM in Canada always had an insulting edge to it. When talks reached the final phase, a team would come from Solidarity House and top management would come from GM in Detroit and they would take over. The rest of us, GM's Canadian management and the Canadian Region team, moved down to the end of the table, clearly no longer in charge.

Accordingly, as we were getting close to the strike deadline, Irv Bluestone turned up from Detroit with his team of UAW negotiators. I had nothing against him personally. He was of the Reuther era and a fine man, one of the intellects of the UAW and a long-time head of the international union's GM department. General Motors sent its "first team," headed by George Morris, vice-president in charge of industrial relations.

I knew that would happen. I'd watched the same thing occur in 1973 and 1976, but I didn't resent it any the less. The big guns from Detroit sat down opposite one another, worked out the final details of our contracts, picked up their briefcases, and went back to Detroit – leaving us to live with whatever they had decided.

The UAW talked about paid education leave in the States but no one had ever tried to negotiate it. I was insisting on it for the Canadian GM contract, and to my relief, Bluestone was supportive when he saw that we were serious.

George Morris of GM was a short man, a bright, tough sonovabitch. He strode into the room, sat down opposite Bluestone, and demanded curtly, "Well Irv, what are the issues?"

Bluestone and Morris were old adversaries, who liked and respected one another. Unperturbed by Morris' manner, Bluestone calmly went through the list while Morris listened without comment and his assistants made notes. A day later, Morris came into a subcommittee meeting where Irv and I were bargaining on the economics. Morris pulled an envelope out of his pocket and unfolded it, consulting some notes on it.

"All right," he announced, "let's get at it. Number one, no fucking way. Number two, okay you got it. Number three, no goddamned way. Number four, all right we'll do it. Number five, we'll do part of it. Number six, you got it. Now the fucking negotiations are over."

Education leave was number one.

"We want paid education leave," I said coolly, "and we're going to sit here until we get it."

"No fucking way," Morris retorted. "We're not going to pay into a fund for the goddamned trade unionist guys to have a good time. This looks like another Jimmy Hoffa slush fund to me."

I argued back. He asked what we planned to teach. We had a copy of the program ready, which he scanned and threw down contemptuously.

"You're going to make goddamned revolutionaries out of people. We're not interested in turning people into revolutionaries. We want goddamned workers who'll be productive."

I explained that we weren't teaching only trade union history, we were training workers to be better citizens. "I think GM should share our interest in making people more aware of current affairs," I said.

I knew that our membership couldn't care less about paid education leave. I could picture a picket being asked what the strike was about and having to answer, "We want a penny an hour for paid education leave." The membership would have killed us for holding out on this issue, and Morris knew that. As with much of what happens in collective bargaining, the issue really was the credibility of the leadership of the union.

"I know this isn't a membership issue," I told Morris frankly. "You know goddamned well it isn't. It's a leadership issue. But it's a commitment to our members in Canada and we're going to fucking well get it here. We'll keep arguing here until we do."

We had set up a temporary UAW office on another floor of the Royal York Hotel. I sat there, watching the clock and sweating because the strike deadline was close. Finally George Morris called me.

"All right," he said. "We're going to give you one more goddamned chance. I'll tell you what we're going to do for your paid education leave. We'll give you $250,000 a quarter for the next five years. I'd like to see you strike your goddamned membership after we tell them that that's what we got on the table for you."

I was doing the arithmetic rapidly. It wasn't a penny an hour.

He anticipated my protest. "It's not a goddamned penny an hour and you're not going to get a penny an hour," he went on. "If you don't want it, just say so and I'll take it back."

I didn't like giving up the penny-an-hour principle, but it was a lot of money to get out of GM. It meant we had our foot in the door for paid education leave.

"I want it and we'll take it," I said.

We still had other issues to resolve. One was the firing of five workers in an earlier confrontation on the plant floor in the Ste. Thérèse GM plant. With a day left before the strike deadline, Irv Bluestone was desperately trying to get those five people their jobs back. Morris was being very difficult. If he took those workers back, the Canadian GM management would be left with egg on its face.

We argued until three in the morning with neither side yielding. Four hours later, my phone rang and I answered groggily. Irv Bluestone was on the line.

"Get your pants on," he said. "We've got to go up to George Morris's suite right away. Quebec has created a helluva problem for us. They've jumped the gun. The guys at Ste. Thérèse are out on strike!"

Morris was waiting in his suite on the seventeenth floor. Coffee and Danish were laid out and the room was full of GM staff people I'd never seen before, the backup he kept out of sight while he did his number with notes on an envelope. Morris introduced us to a Quebec lawyer and pointed to a stack of law books on a table.

"We've consulted our lawyer," he told us, "and what those goddamned guys are doing in Quebec is illegal. They've got no goddamned right to do it. They can't break up the master agreement. We're going to take them to court."

"George, you can't do that," I said. "That's not the law in Quebec."

"There's no goddamned law," he roared. "We've got our lawyers here. This guy" – pointing to the Quebec lawyer – "says it is. Tell 'em."

The lawyer gave a long explanation of Quebec labour law. I listened impatiently.

"With great respect, my friend," I said, "you don't know what the hell you're talking about. I'm not a lawyer and I'm not from Quebec but I know the law better than you do. I know the guys are on a legal strike. We may not like it, but don't tell me that they're on an illegal strike and don't tell me you can put them back to work by threatening to take them before the labour board."

"What makes you so goddamn sure," Morris said furiously.

"We can argue about the mess we're in, but I'm telling you that the guys are on a legal strike. Tell you what I'll do. We've got a young lawyer in Quebec, Gaston Nadeau. I haven't talked to him yet. Let's get him on the phone and see what he says."

"Put him on the conference phone," Morris said.

I called Nadeau at his home and woke him up. I carefully explained what was happening.

"You know what has happened in Ste. Thérèse," I said. "The corporation is taking the position the strike is in violation of Quebec law and it can take us before the labour board and order the strikers back to work. Tell me, are they in violation or not?"

He asked some questions and quickly came up with an opinion. The strike was legal, he said, and he cited the statutes in the Quebec labour code that applied.

"That guy sounds like he knows what he's talking about," Morris admitted, glaring at GM's lawyer. He sighed and turned to me. "We've got to solve this problem, I guess."

We got down to work. Irv Bluestone got those five guys at Ste. Thérèse their jobs back.

CHAPTER TWELVE

Solidarity versus Sovereignty

W E WERE AN UNTIDY lot as we dealt with those last pieces of the contract in George Morris' suite, only hours before GM strikers would hit the bricks. Unshaven and hastily dressed in sweatshirts and jeans, all of us were red-eyed from lack of sleep and edgy from too much coffee, too much stress, and too many meals gulped at erratic hours. We all knew that ON STRIKE placards were stacked by the plant gates. We'd reached the point where we had to say what we meant and mean what we said.

You can't write a text book on how to bargain at the eleventh hour. It's a gut instinct, it comes from sheer nerve, from the integrity that the participants have been able to generate, and from the respect that either has developed, or hasn't.

The feeling between Morris and the UAW in these negotiations couldn't be described as camaraderie, but there was mutual appreciation of each other's skills. I can give an illustration of what kind of a man Morris was. Not long after the GM agreement, I was invited to be on a television show in Windsor hosted by Warner Troyer. The format was a bearpit, with the guest fielding questions from Troyer, people in the audience, and people who called in.

Immediately after the show, the floor director told me there was an urgent message that I call George Morris in Detroit.

Mystified, I found a pay phone and called Morris at his home. He said gruffly, "I was watching you, kid, on that television show. I thought you were great. I just wanted you to know."

Not that Morris was friendly when we told him in 1979 that we wanted GM to drop Blue Cross as the carrier for workers' health benefits. Morris said there was no way he would let us tell him where that contract would go.

"Look," I said to him, "Blue Cross isn't giving us a nickel in the pay cheque. We aren't talking about breaking some company. We're talking about a bastard who is getting all our business but who won't recognize our union."

Morris shook his head.

I asked, "Meet with Hay. See what you think."

Morris refused, but later that day he quietly made arrangements to do it.

The next day he was shaking his head. He told me, "We've met him. We can't figure him out either."

General Motors made a deal that they pull some business from Blue Cross and split it between Green Shield, the company we favoured, an emerging Canadian-owned company in Windsor, and Etna, a big American insurance company.

The Ontario minister of labour, Dr. Robert Elgie, made a last-minute attempt to resolve the dispute at Blue Cross. He set up a one-on-one meeting between me and Alan Hay in a little restaurant in a shopping plaza.

Hay strutted in, swinging his cane like an officer leading his troops against colonial riffraff. He sat down stiffly and launched into a tirade against me and the union.

"I'll not stand for your audacity, bringing goons from General Motors to our picket lines," Hay said, refusing to look in my direction. "You've browbeaten our employees into accepting your union. This is still a democracy, sir. We're not going to force people to pay union dues. *Never* so long as I am president of Blue Cross." For more than an hour I tried to reason with him, but it was hopeless.

We ended up losing the strike and were decertified because we couldn't settle with Alan Hay on the fundamental issue of union security. Despite the pressure on them inside the company, 123 brave workers inside the office voted for the UAW, but were outnumbered. Alan Hay then offered his company union better terms than he had been willing to give us. He refused to hire back fifty-nine strikers. Clare Meneghini of our staff succeeded in finding other jobs for them.

We were defeated at Blue Cross at the same time as negotiations with the Big Three moved into the next phase. As soon as the GM agreement was ratified by the membership, Buzz Hargrove and I packed our bags in the Royal York Hotel and unpacked them ten minutes later in the Westbury Hotel, where the Ford bargaining team was waiting. Bob Nickerson left for Detroit to sit in at the Chrysler talks in Detroit, which were just concluding.

Doug Fraser called me early one morning. Chrysler had just invited him to come on its board of directors. The company thought it would be helpful to have his perspective during its present period of financial crisis, he explained. What did I think?

"I think it would be an interesting experiment," I replied.

I wasn't opposed to Doug being on the Chrysler board, but I couldn't see any great advantage to his being there. Doug promised that he would remove himself from the discussion if there was a conflict of interest. I didn't comment on that, but I wondered what the point was of being there if you didn't speak up about the union's position in a discussion of a labour issue.

Rumours about the Chrysler negotiations in Detroit were alarming. Chrysler was insisting that if the new contract couldn't be delayed six months, until March 1980, the company would be destroyed. We had 130,000 workers in those Chrysler plants and thousands more in parts plants that supplied Chrysler. Fraser agreed to the delay, though it would cost Chrysler workers in the Chrysler plants $203 million off their incomes. For the first time in its history, the UAW negotiated a contract with one of the Big Three that meant deferrals in pay increases.

The company's financial problems were real, but to a considerable extent they were Chrysler's own fault. Management had made some bad decisions, one of which was to cut back on small-car production just before buyers switched away from the big gas-guzzlers. In Windsor, for instance, a plant had recently retooled at great expense to build six-cylinder and v-8 engines. When big cars stopped selling in 1979, the work force in the engine plant had to be cut from 2,200 to 450. The Canadian operation wasn't as vulnerable as the one in the United States, as it was smaller, but we were worried about a complete shut-down at the Windsor plant where those large engines were made.

Chrysler needed to get its design staff back together and retool for lighter, smaller cars. The company estimated that it needed $8 *billion* to become competitive again or it might fold. Chrysler said it could raise more than $6 billion privately but it was asking Washington for the rest. The cuts in the new UAW contract were to be used as evidence that Chrysler and Chrysler workers were serious about making a come-back.

We Canadians could do nothing about what was happening to our members at the Chrysler bargaining table in Detroit as they had chosen to come under the international agreement. We had another headache to address, which was to work through the non-economic issues which lay outside the Chrysler international agreement. In the States, the Chrysler locals took a ratification vote on the international agreement and then spent months sorting out the other problems, but in Canada we could have just one ratification vote. We had to conclude negotiations in time to have the local agreements in the package when the membership voted on ratification of the international agreement.

We faced this enormous pressure on negotiations every bargaining year, but we always got through it without anything memorable happening. In 1979, however, something occurred which was to prove fateful for me personally and for the future of the UAW.

Buzz Hargrove, I, and the bargaining team successfully concluded negotiations with Ford in Toronto, and I hurried to Windsor. With the Chrysler international agreement on the brink of being settled, we could lose no time at the bargaining sessions between our Local 444 in Windsor and the Canadian Chrysler corporation. Soon after my arrival in Windsor, the international agreement was signed in Detroit, leaving Nick free to come across the river to help me with what were some thorny issues.

It was the first time a Canadian director had headed Chrysler bargaining since the days when George Burt was leader of the Canadian Region. McDermott hadn't thought those local negotiations worthy of his attention. Chrysler sent Tom Miner, head of labour relations, from Detroit to sit down opposite me. Like Morris of General Motors, he was a tough, bright man.

The Chrysler meetings took place in the company's executive offices near the plant gates. Chrysler provided us with a small office so we could have some privacy and access to phones. We were all exhausted. I was feeling the strain of four months of pressure and I was unhappy with the international agreement Fraser had negotiated with Chrysler. I suspected that the membership of 444 wouldn't like it any more than I did. I was right. They were furious about the concessions. The local bargaining committee warned us that workers were saying the UAW had sold them out.

A strike deadline had been set in order to put some force into the lagging negotiations. As it approached, we were still in a deadlock. Management, encouraged by the mood of conciliation in the international agreement, wouldn't give an inch. We were going to have to strike.

At the appointed time, Nick and I stood in our temporary office to watch the men burst from the plant on the dead run, headed towards the gates. When a strike starts, there's always a group of workers whose pent-up emotions simply explode. I saw that they had effigies dangling by their necks from poles. Some were labelled "Hang Doug Fraser," some "Hang Iacocca," and a few, "Hang Bob White."

They were mad as hell at everyone, but at Doug Fraser especially. From their point of view, Doug had joined the Chrysler board and immediately they'd been asked to take wage deferrals.

They milled angrily around the building, shouting at us. I heard glass breaking. Tom Miner and Bill Fisher, Chrysler's head of labour relations in Canada, came running down the hall. A striker had just thrown a brick into the room where they were meeting.

"This is insane," I told them apologetically. "This isn't how our union behaves. This is one crazy person who's wound up about the strike."

Some of the 444 bargaining team, including Kenny Gerard and Larry Bauer, went out into the boiling mob. It took courage to do that but they were counting on the fact that the guys knew and respected them. They bawled instructions to the angry workers to line up and prepare to march in a demonstration. The guys marched around the plant until they cooled down. I decided we wouldn't meet in Windsor again. The next round of Chrysler talks, I promised Buzz and Nick, would be in a hotel in Toronto, not only because of this, but because that's where all of the major auto industry negotiations take place.

With the workers out on strike against a shaky Chrysler, both sides were anxious to conclude the talks. Negotiations picked up. Around four on a Saturday morning, we had an agreement. We fixed on Sunday afternoon for the ratification vote. We were too wound up to sleep and ravenous with hunger so Frank LaSorda, president of Local 444, took us to his house. His wife good-naturedly got out of bed and made us scrambled eggs and bacon and sausages, which we washed down with gin and tonics. The pressure got to me and I got absolutely smashed, something I rarely do. Someone had to help me back to the Richelieu Hotel, where I fell into a bottomless sleep.

When I wakened Saturday afternoon, I turned on the television and watched a news show from Detroit. G. William Miller, the U.S. secretary of the treasury, was saying that Washington had been approached by Chrysler for loan guarantees of $1.5 billion. There was no way Lee Iacocca would get government money, Miller said, unless the Chrysler president tore up the contract with the UAW and negotiated a new one with more cuts.

That night Bob Nickerson and I had dinner together.

"We won't get this agreement ratified tomorrow if our members think it's a charade," I said. "If the U.S. government is going to take the agreement away from them, there's no reason for them to vote for it. They don't like the contract anyway."

Nick nodded.

"So we must take the position that no U.S. government is going to change the terms of a collective agreement in Canada."

"We've got an international agreement," Nick reminded me. "Maybe one view is that we're bound by that."

I shook my head. "I don't know what they're going to do about this in the U.S., but I'm going to tell the membership tomorrow that we won't stand for any interference from Washington in a Canadian matter."

The ratification vote was scheduled to happen in a hockey arena. I hate meetings in arenas. It means that I'm down on the ice surface along with the bargaining committee, freezing, and the crowd is around us like Romans watching Christians being fed to the lions. Something about the association with hockey encourages the crowd to be unruly. One time when Dennis McDermott brought Leonard Woodcock to a ratification meeting in that Windsor arena, the crowd booed heartily the minute the men stepped out on the ice. Woodcock was appalled.

"What the hell's going on?" he asked Dennis. "Is there something wrong with the settlement?"

"Nothing's wrong," Dennis said, shouting over the noise. "They just like to boo their president. Over here they don't go to that obedience school you run for your locals in the States."

Local 444 is renowned in the UAW for its efficiency. The guys had a podium set up on the ice at the end of the arena and I noted gratefully that the seats at our back were roped off and vacant so no one could hit us from behind. They had put shop stewards in front of the podium, facing the crowd, to catch eggs or whatever else the audience threw at us. I heard an egg drop behind me but I didn't look around.

Kenny Gerard, Local 444's bargaining committee chairman, introduced me and mentioned that I was the first Canadian director to participate in local negotiations since George Burt. That got me a good hand. I thanked them, made a joke about the security arrangements, and then talked seriously to the membership about the international agreement and about the good relationship between the Canadian Region and Solidarity House.

Then I got to it. "I'm sure that many of you saw the statement by a U.S. government official on television last night that the terms of the recent UAW-Chrysler agreement you're being asked to ratify today have to be changed in the States. I want to make it absolutely clear to all of you today that if this agreement is ratified by you, this agreement will stay and in full force in Canada."

Cheers.

"No government, least of all the U.S. government, is going to change the terms of an agreement in Canada."

More cheers.

I went on, "An international agreement is an agreement to represent workers in both countries. No American government official is going to change what happens here."

Cheers, whistles, and workers on their feet applauding.

I knew what a road I had put my foot on. If Doug Fraser didn't support my stand, it would tear the union apart. I hadn't warned Doug what I was going to do. Still, I felt I had no other choice.

The agreement was ratified by 444 and by the Chrysler locals in Ajax and Etobicoke. The next morning Nick and I flew to California to join Buzz. The International Executive Board was meeting there the next morning.

I found Fraser and the others upset over Miller's statement, which obviously they hadn't expected. The executive would have to decide how to respond to Miller. I described to several of my colleagues on the International Executive Board what I had said in Windsor and repeated that no one should expect Canada to be bound by something the American government decided. To my surprise no one paid much attention. They were so concerned about Chrysler's state of near-bankrupcy they couldn't think about much else. I could see that the UAW was inclined to accept the new cuts to save Chrysler. They didn't see the situation that was developing – the Canadian director publicly taking a different position from that of the international union.

I wanted Doug to hear my arguments so he would have the ammunition he would need to explain the Canadian position to the rest of the UAW. I went into considerable detail, explaining that in the States workers had some recourse if they had to accept something they didn't like from their government. They could go to the ballot boxes and vote the bastards out of office. Canadians couldn't do that. They didn't vote in American elections. There was no way they should submit to something the American government wanted.

I emphasized Canadian sovereignty, of course, but there were some sound economic arguments to make as well. The Canadian automotive industry is different from that in the States. Canadian workers have a medicare system for which the company pays little, while in the States companies pay large premiums for workers' doctor bills. Our labour legislation is markedly different. Canadian workers don't have the right to strike during the life of an agreement, but Americans do.

Fraser didn't appear to be paying attention.

"Look guys," I said, "when this crisis is over, our members will be looking at pay cheques that are the lowest in the Big Three. Who do you think they're going to blame for that? Chrysler? Hell no. Jimmy Carter? No way. They're going to be mad at us."

THE RECOMMENDATION for a bailout of Chrysler went before the U.S. Senate banking committee. I went with Fraser and other UAW executives to show our support for Chrysler. We had to listen as several Senators took up Miller's line that the Chrysler workers had to take more cuts or else they wouldn't vote for the guarantees.

I thought their talk about "equality of sacrifices" was a lot of American hype. It wasn't the workers' fault that Chrysler was having problems and I didn't hear much about management being asked to make sacrifices. In my view the reason the UAW was being asked to take cuts was that the government needed something to throw to the wolves of public opinion. Spending taxpayers' money to bail out a big corporation like Chrysler wasn't a popular move.

The banking committee discussed a three-year wage freeze across all Chrysler plants. I immediately called a press conference to say clearly that the Canadian Chrysler workers would not accept a freeze. Chrysler had already made approaches to the Canadian government for loan guarantees. If those guarantees were tied to wage concessions, I said we would deal with that in Canada, but we would not be bound by what Washington wanted.

The U.S. Congress then passed a bill requiring Chrysler unionized workers to take an additional $259 million in concessions, on top of the $203 million that Chrysler saved because of the delay clause in the contract. The total loss for Chrysler workers was $462 million.

I was disgusted, but I did not criticize the deal in public. I maintained that Americans should not dictate to us what we should do about Chrysler and I had to refrain from telling them what Washington should do.

Over the Christmas holidays Fraser started to take my comments more seriously. He scheduled a meeting on January 2, 1980, of the Chrysler international bargaining committee and I asked his permission to explain how the Canadians felt. He invited me to meet with him in his office ahead of the meeting to resolve our differences so we could present a united front. I didn't see how that could happen, but I could only try. I went to his office with Bob Nickerson and we found Doug had invited Marc Stepp, head of the UAW's Chrysler department, to join us.

The confrontation that had been brewing for weeks was about to come into the open. There was no way this dispute could be contained within the walls of Solidarity House. Over the holiday Buzz, Nick, Sam Gindin, and I talked for hours about the split with Doug and the American UAW, but none of us could see an honourable alternative.

I went through it all again. I was amazed that it was necessary. I couldn't understand why Fraser wasn't helping me. I was sure that his membership would understand that Canada couldn't be dragged around by Washington. Instead what I got was that we selfish Canadians weren't willing to share the load of Chrysler's misfortunes.

"Look Doug," I said in exasperation. "If the positions were reversed, what would you do? What if Ottawa decided to ask American workers to take pay cuts because Ottawa wanted to guarantee Chrysler loans. You'd tell Ottawa to go to hell, and you'd be right."

But Doug just kept on insisting that we were bound by the international agreement and had no right to opt out. We had to accept the same cuts as American workers.

"There's no way that can happen, Doug," I told him. It would be the end of the international agreement if it happens. Our members won't stand for it. Goddamn it, it's so fundamental I don't understand why you can't see it."

He looked at me levelly.

"You know what this means Bob," he said.

He didn't have to spell it out. He was talking about withdrawing his support of me for the presidency of the UAW.

"Yes I do," I told him quietly.

There was a heavy silence. Then he said, "I never thought the international agreement would last forever anyway."

"I don't think it has to go," I said. "If an international agreement is really international, and not an American agreement with a Canadian piece to it, then it has to reflect the political differences in both countries."

"No," he insisted. "This is the end of the international agreement."

After a gut-wrenching, fruitless hour, Fraser and I gave up. We were both depressed and hurting. Doug was one of my closest friends in the UAW. We shared the same views on social and political issues and we'd fought side by side to get support for them inside and outside the union. We walked in silence to the UAW's executive committee room where the Chrysler international bargaining committee was waiting.

Once more I laid out the Canadian position as eloquently as I could. Doug Fraser and Marc Stepp offered not a word of support as the bargaining committee tore into me. They accused the Canadians of "walking away" from Chrysler's troubles.

"We're not walking away from anybody," I insisted. "If the Canadian government wants us to make wage concessions, we'll deal with that. But we won't let the American government take money out of the pockets of Canadian workers."

One man said, "Well, fuck you Canadians. If you're not going to make the sacrifice with us, then we're going to demand that all the jobs come over here. Chrysler Canada's gone."

"Goddammit Bob," a UAW staff man exploded, "if the American Congress had meant to exempt Canadians, it would have said so. It didn't, so the legislation includes Canada."

I couldn't believe what I was hearing. I felt sweat trickling down my back. Doug said nothing except to repeat his prediction that the international agreement was dead.

Finally, I told them that if the UAW reopened the Chrysler contract to make the cuts, the Canadians would have nothing to do with it. We had an agreement and nothing Washington said could change it. I asked Fraser to notify Chrysler of our decision that the agreement would remain intact in Canada. But, as I was leaving, I happened to overhear Fraser in an aside to Joe Zappa, chairman of the Chrysler bargaining committe.

"Well this will make it easier to ratify in the U.S.," he was saying. "We'll just say the Canadians walked away from us and we'll do this alone, as Americans. And we'll kick them out of the international agreement."

I was shocked. It put a whole new complexion on my relationship with Doug Fraser.

FRASER WASN'T THROUGH FIGHTING. He asked me to arrange a meeting for him the next day with the Chrysler Local 444 leadership in Windsor and the leadership of Local 1090 from Ajax and 1459 from Etobicoke. Those guys loved Doug and he knew it. He'd worked on the line at Chrysler himself and liked to sit around, talking shop with them. I knew that he figured he could do an end run around me and get these local union guys to repudiate my position.

The night before the meeting, Nick and I were back in the Richelieu Hotel in Windsor. Fraser called me about midnight.

"Christ, Bob," he said, "there's got to be some goddamned way to sort this out. How about this? You Canadians make the same concessions as we're making but we'll put your money in a fund. If the Canadian government doesn't ask concessions for loan guarantees, then you'll get the money back."

"Like hell," I replied. "That's like giving our government a blank cheque. It would be nuts not to put concessions into the loan-guarantee agreement if we'd already accepted them."

Doug was silent. I felt terrible. "Doug, I'm sorry," I said, "but there is no compromise."

I didn't sleep. Around four I called Nickerson's room. "We gotta have a meeting," I said.

"Come on down," he said.

I pulled on some pants and went down to his room. He was sitting in his underwear. "Is there any way out of this?" I asked. "Let's go over the whole thing one more time. We've got to try to find an answer or else there's going to be a Donnybrook that will tear our union apart."

We went over the ground again, inch by inch, until dawn broke. We couldn't see how we could do anything but what we were doing. No compromise was possible.

The next morning we went to the Local 200-444 union hall. We found Kenny Gerard there, one of the Chrysler bargaining team in 444 and a huge man, over six foot, heavy set and tough as nails. Gerard was a union stalwart. He was recognized in 444 as a natural leader, a man of strength and credibility. His face was ashen.

"You look troubled, my friend," I said to him.

He nodded. "Doug Fraser is a good friend of mine. It's hard to do this to this guy."

I said, "Kenny, you don't feel any worse than I do. I love him too. Do you have any other answers?"

He had tears in his eyes. He shook his head, "No."

"Then we have to make a choice. I've wracked my brains to find some other solution and I haven't come up with one. We're being boxed in here and we have to stand up. If we don't it's goodbye. Your membership will run over you at some point down the road. This isn't just important for our union, it's important for Canada."

"I know we have to do it," he said. "I'm just troubled by it."

"If it's any consolation, I feel exactly the same," I told him. "But we have to do it."

Doug Fraser arrived with Marc Stepp and Joe Zappa. He was trailed by newspaper, radio, and television reporters from Detroit. Fraser was a master at using the media. I knew I wouldn't have any friends among the reporters because the mood at that time was strongly pro-Chrysler and Canadians were being portrayed as deserters. The Canadian media weren't much evident. For some reason, the implications of what was happening were lost on them.

The media went downstairs to wait the outcome of the meeting while we gathered behind closed doors. Doug sat among the 444 guys, comfortable and easy, talking at first about the old days.

He got around eventually to describing the present difficulty Chrysler was in, and how the UAW had to do its bit to save the company. He laid out the option he'd offered me, which I again rejected, and then he talked about solidarity.

I did something that wasn't easy. I asked Doug and the others with him to wait in the office while I talked to the Canadian members alone. Fraser didn't like that, but he went.

When the door shut behind him I said, "Look, nobody likes what we're doing here. If there are any faint-hearts who don't want to do this, you'd better tell me now. Once we make a decision here this morning, you don't turn back. I've tried to find another answer but there isn't one. This is the crunch."

In the uneasy silence which followed, a Chrysler worker, John Gatens, made a motion to support my position. It was seconded and the question was called. They were unanimously in favour.

I called Doug upstairs and he returned, looking quickly into faces to see if he could read what had happened.

I was crisp. "I just want to tell you, Doug, that we've voted unanimously that we're not going to participate in these concessions."

He was devastated. It was clear that he had expected that his popularity with the guys would win the day. Their rejection was as painful for them as it was for him. He recovered and said brusquely, "Okay, that's the end of the international agreement. Now, what the hell will we tell the media?"

"The truth," I suggested. "Tell them what happened."

The Detroit media looked on us with loathing. It was very unpopular that winter to do anything that might be seen as damaging Chrysler's chances of recovery.

"It's the end of the international agreement," Doug told them somberly.

Maybe because the Canadian media wasn't there, our newspapers, radio, and television people took the same view as the Americans did – that we were being disloyal. I was amazed. These were the same editorial writers who constantly criticized Canadians unionists for taking their instructions from head offices in the States. Now they were criticizing us for acting independently.

Doug went back to the States and immediately exchanged letters with Chrysler that threw us out of the international agreement. Canadian Chrysler locals had joined the international agreement by twice taking a vote of all members, but now they were being thrown out by a means that was less than democratic.

Doug wrote me a letter setting out the conditions he was imposing. We were forbidden forever from rejoining the international agreement, or suggesting that we might rejoin the international agreement, or submitting any amendments asking to discuss rejoining. The tone and terms were so appalling that I never did show the Canadian Council that letter. I didn't want to inflame the situation.

Letters went to all the UAW's Chrysler locals in the States, along with comments that portrayed us as greedy Canadians kicking our brothers when they were down. As Fraser knew it would, it angered the membership and stiffened them to ratify the wage cuts.

We were still bound by the international agreement until the next round of talks, so Frank LaSorda and two other Canadian representatives were at the meeting of the international bargaining committee when it was decided how the additional $259 million in cuts would be made. Frank told me later that Tom Miner, the Chrysler vice-president in charge of industrial relations, also attended. Frank said Miner seemed pretty pleased at the way things were going and had unflattering things to say about me.

"I can't wait to meet that sonovabitch Bob White at the bargaining table in 1982," he announced.

The UAW had been through splits before, but not like this one. In the past, membership often had fallen out with the leadership, but this time the division was in the union leadership itself. I gathered that I was being pictured as a new director who was puffed up with his own importance and didn't understand the meaning of solidarity. I was baffled that unionists who talked about internationalism couldn't see that internationalism won't survive without respect for one another's territory.

As it turned out, Canada wasn't nearly as hard hit by the auto recession as the United States. Sales of domestic cars actually *increased* in Canada in 1979, while they had declined by 11 per cent in the States. Layoffs in the States were massive – 71,000 at General Motors, 37,000 at Ford, 40,000 at

Chrysler, and an estimated 50,000 more in the parts industry. In Canada we had 1,000 on indefinite layoff at GM, 3,000 at Ford, 3,000 at Chrysler, 500 at American Motors, and 8,000 in the parts industry.

Import cars, led by Japanese models, had risen from 18 per cent of the American market in 1978 to 22 per cent in 1979. It looked as if they would have a bigger share of the market in 1980. Detroit had no economy cars to offer as competition – only gas guzzlers that promised higher profits. Fraser asked the American government for protection against the imports and he even went to Japan to see manufacturers there about setting up plants in the States. He was seeking the same safeguard over content that Canada has in the Auto Pact.

The UAW had its international convention in the spring of 1980 in Anaheim, California, where the Canadians were as popular as skunks. The recession was in full swing and 300,000 UAW automotive workers were on indefinite layoffs in the two countries.

Fraser was entering his last term as president. Everyone on the floor of the convention became quite emotional as Pat Greathouse, Emil Mazey, and some others of the legendary Reuther team retired. New faces appeared on the executive. Ray Majerus was made secretary-treasurer and Owen Bieber got the top assignment as head of the UAW's General Motors section.

Meanwhile Chrysler was seeking loan guarantees from the Canadian government in Ottawa. Herb Gray, minister of industry, was from Windsor and had an unusual degree of sympathy for labour for a cabinet member. He was in constant contact with me. Our position was that we weren't opposed to loan guarantees for Chrysler, but we wanted them tied to commitments from Chrysler to keep Canadian plants open and to protect product lines and jobs.

Chrysler was getting anxious. Some of the loan guarantees in the States were contingent on their getting a loan guarantee in Canada. This gave the government here some leverage.

In May 1980, I was at the CLC convention in Winnipeg when Herb Gray phoned to say he wanted me to meet with him and Chrysler people right away in Ottawa. I told him it was impossible for me to leave the convention. Obligingly, his chief negotiator flew to Winnipeg. Chrysler sent Gerry Greenwald, the number-two man in Chrysler, after Iacocca, and Don Lander, president of Canadian Chrysler.

At the meeting late that night, Gray's negotiator pushed Chrysler to make a commitment to protect Canadian jobs. He was anxious to get such a guarantee because the Trudeau cabinet wasn't too keen on bailing out Chrysler. We were afraid that Chrysler was going to stop production of cars in Canada altogether, so we wanted a further guarantee that they would continue to make cars in Canada. Our task was the same as the government's, to make sure Canadian jobs were protected and that Canadian taxpayers got value for their money.

I overheard a Chrysler man grumbling, "It sure is different in Canada. In the States the union and Chrysler are lined up against the government. Over here the government lines up with goddamned union."

I thought, "Right. That's just the way it ought to be."

Eventually Ottawa guaranteed Chrysler a loan of $200 million, in exchange for a Chrysler guarantee to continue building cars in Canada, including a new wagon for the Windsor truck plant and a new front-wheel-drive car for the Windsor plant. There was no mention of cut-backs in wages, in sharp contrast to the agreement made in Washington. Not only did we not give up one cent, we got Chrysler to commit itself to maintaining a certain percentage of jobs and plants in operation. Chrysler already had all the wage cuts it needed in the States – half its work force was laid off.

Lee Iacocca, Chrysler's flamboyant president, asked for a meeting early in December 1980 with Fraser. Chrysler was going back to the U.S. Loan Guarantee Board for another $400 million. Iacocca wanted to show Washington that he was tough about cutting costs and making Chrysler profitable again. He demanded that Doug reopen the Chrysler agreements and accept more wage cuts. He said, "If the workers at Chrysler don't take a $4 an hour wage cut, the lights will go out."

I sent Buzz Hargrove to represent me at the talks that followed. As I expected, Fraser and the committee agreed to a wage freeze at the level due to be reached on January 1, 1981, a freeze on pensions, a reduction of paid personal holidays, and immediate elimination of the cost-of-living allowance, which alone meant an immediate loss to workers of $1.15 an hour. There was no mention in the agreement that Chrysler would ever have to make restitution to their workers.

Fraser admitted that it was "the worst economic settlement our union has ever been involved in." Buzz described it to the Chrysler membership in Windsor as "a piece of shit." Iacocca called it "a super deal." The total value of the concessions made by Chrysler workers now reached an estimated $662 million.

No one disputed Iacocca's figures. The media was giving him an easy ride and never questioned his doomsday proclamations. Maybe he wasn't exaggerating the situation, but I often wondered.

The cuts had to be ratified. Buzz, Nick, I, and the local leadership wrestled with the problem of what recommendation to make to the membership. We knew the shop-floor leadership was furious. They wouldn't stand for it if we told them to advise the membership to accept cuts. On the other hand, we didn't want to worsen our relationship with Solidarity House by suggesting the locals fight the agreement.

Finally we decided to do something we have never done before or since. We made no recommendation at all. We told the Chrysler locals that we knew it was a shitty deal and we told them what Iacocca had said. But we left it up to them to decide what to do. The agreement was accepted in Canada by a narrow 51 per cent majority.

CHAPTER THIRTEEN

No Concessions

E VEN BEFORE THE agreements for concessions at Chrysler were signed, companies were bombarding us to reopen their agreements and negotiate cuts in pay. We had five such requests in one week alone. Now the powerful UAW had given up the COLA, which it had pioneered in the labour movement, had given up paid personal holidays, and had taken a wage freeze, the path was greased for everyone else.

Doug Fraser announced that the Chrysler agreement was unique. Concessions would not apply to Ford, General Motors, or anyone else. Iacocca disagreed. He said that this marked the end of the COLA everywhere. The UAW sent him a sharp letter suggesting that he stick to Chrysler's problems and not try to be spokesman for the entire auto industry. But the damage was done already. Employers everywhere saw the Chrysler concessions as a break in labour's front. All over North America, they started pressuring their workers to accept cutbacks by threatening to close their plants. Over the Christmas holidays I read a staff report on a plant in Belleville, where the bargaining committee had agreed to a dollar-an-hour cut in pay in return for a company promise that more people would be hired. Another report described how a plant in Quebec lost 138 jobs because the work was transferred to the Belleville plant. Unwittingly, UAW workers in Belleville had undercut UAW workers in Quebec.

I called Buzz and Nick for a long consultation. "We've got to stop the haemorrhage," I told them. "We can't accept any more concessions. This could run through every agreement we've got and spread to every union in the country. Chrysler has to be not only the first time the UAW agreed to such massive concessions, but the last."

I told John Deverell, labour writer for the *Toronto Star*, "We can't let our members get into a bidding war for jobs and tear each other's throat out to see who can work cheapest. That's not what unions are for."

I made a "no-concessions" recommendation at the Canadian Council meeting a few weeks later. I said that if we gave out major concessions, it wouldn't stop until workers in every union in the country were stripped of the gains that had taken fifty years to achieve. We had to declare that we were through making concessions.

The debate was a long one. Too many in the room were looking down the barrel of a gun at the choice between a wage cut or a job. The papers were full of the news that Canada's unemployment rate was rising to levels of the great Depression in the thirties.

"If you're a worker sitting around the dinner table with your family and you're told that you have to take a dollar-an-hour pay cut or lose your job," I said, "you'll take the cut. But losing a dollar an hour off your wages won't guarantee your job. The whole economy is going through a bad time. This is monetarism at its best. These bastards are using high interest rates and high unemployment to restructure the economy. People are making fortunes out of these high interest rates. The 'inefficiencies' they talk about are workers and their families. The idea that taking a wage cut will protect jobs is absolute nonsense."

I'm told that one of the contributing factors to the Great Depression was that workers agreed to one wage slash after another, undercutting one another in a frantic effort to keep their jobs. That took money out of the economy and deepened the Depression.

The vote to support a no-concessions policy was unanimous. It wasn't just Bob White's policy any more, it had been ratified by the plant-floor leadership of the entire Canadian Region. That locked us into the position. If the plant-floor leadership had been opposed to the policy, they would have wasted me.

We started a "no-concessions fund" into which every local paid. If workers were forced out on strike for refusing to give up wages or benefits, we had money to top up their strike pay for a while.

I had warned the Council that there would be sacrifices, and there were. In some cases plants closed because, they said, we wouldn't give up wages. But many of those plants were going to close anyway. Places like CCM wanted to take $4 or $5 an hour from the workers and they closed the plant when we refused. But the CCM plant was obsolete. For years, the owners had bled it of every cent they could take and had invested almost nothing.

I had word from Chrysler that the company wanted to back out of the loan-guarantee commitments it had made to Ottawa. Chrysler had two assembly plants in Windsor, one, an older plant building a large van, and the other, a newer plant that was building Cordobas. Chrysler had promised that the newer plant would get a new, super-secret T115 van wagon, and the older one would get one of Chrysler's new front-wheel-drive cars. Now, Chrysler had changed its mind. It didn't want to put a car in Windsor at all.

One of our main concerns was that the new mini-van would compete directly with the larger van, and we would eventually lose jobs in the larger van plant. We were informed that the T115 would be a big seller, a better deal for Canadian jobs than the Cordoba, but I was skeptical. Federal Industry Minister Herb Gray checked with me and I said we would insist that Chrysler stick to the deal. We wanted one of the new front-wheel drive cars in Canada. Gray told Chrysler that the company would have to secure the Canadian UAW's agreement before he would accept a change in the loan conditions.

Then Solidarity House got into the discussion. Marc Stepp invited me to talk to Chrysler U.S. about the Canadian operating plan. I prickled at this. I thought that any discussion about Chrysler's plans for Canada should take place in Canada.

The new president of Chrysler Canada, Maurice Closs, called. He was prepared to meet me at the Chrysler parts depot in Mississauga and show us the T115. I brought in Kenny Gerard and some other guys from the Chrysler locals 444, 1090, and 1498. Closs came with some top executives from Detroit, and with Chrysler's design team. The meeting began with an hour-long lecture, complete with charts showing the surveys and projected sales of what was described to us as a brilliant engineering achievement. We were thinking, *it's not a car.*

Then we were led to closed-off area surrounded by security guards, where a row of vehicles was shrouded in sheets. With a dramatic flourish, one of the Chrysler guys pulled off the covers and revealed a New Yorker and an unfinished model of the T115. They were good-looking vehicles, we had to admit, but we didn't want to let on how much we liked the van. Our guys walked around the T115 wearing expressions of disdain. "It looks like a goddamned Volkswagen," they said. "It isn't a car. It looks like a goddamned van."

The New Yorker, however, *was* a car, a big one. Big cars were still selling because people who could afford them weren't bothered by high interest, as low-income people were. We didn't appreciate that at the time, so the big, gas-guzzling New Yorker worried us.

Closs took us back inside and asked how we felt. We told him, "When Ottawa asks us if we agree to this, we'll tell Gray that there's no way," I told Closs.

"Do you know what you're doing?" Closs said furiously. "You're going to put the Chrysler corporation under."

"I'm not going to put the Chrysler corporation under – Iacocca is," I replied. "Tell him to put a car in Canada. We're not going to have the Canadian section of Chrysler without a car."

"I don't believe this," Closs said disgustedly.

He walked out and was gone about twenty minutes. When he came back, he was calmer.

"What kind of a car are you talking about?" he asked.

"A fuel-efficient, front-wheel drive," I told him. "One of the new K cars. We want some job security."

Closs said he would think it over, so I knew there was some flexibility in the plan. Never before in the history of car-making in Canada had the Canadian UAW been consulted about product lines, and we were pleased to be part of a historic moment.

Chrysler later announced that it had changed its plan. It would be putting a car in Canada. But, eventually, it went back to its original intention. Despite the wild talk that Chrysler Canada would go under on February 3 without Canadian loan guarantees, they never drew of penny of that money – they didn't need it. We built the New Yorker for a few years and then Chrysler invested $750 million and put the mini-van, the T115, into Canada. A solid seller, it has been providing jobs six days a week ever since.

General Motors and Ford had been pressuring Fraser to reopen their agreements, too, ever since the Chrysler deal had been signed. They wanted the same concessions. In June 1981, Fraser called the UAW International Executive Board together to talk it over. We met at Sawmill Creek in Ohio, a pleasant resort area.

I was still the outcast from Canada, but, on the surface, people at the meeting behaved cordially toward me. Doug was again his old friendly self. I think he felt the Canadians were back on track. Along with a few others, I argued strongly against concessions, and the board agreed not to reopen the Ford and GM contracts. General Motors officials flew to Ohio to convince Doug to relent, but he stood firm.

At that meeting, we also discussed postponing the next international convention a year, from 1983 to 1984, so that Doug could stay on as president past the mandatory retirement age of sixty-five. Younger men on the executive, particularly Ray Majerus, were pushing for the extension to gain extra time for themselves before they declared their candidacy for the position.

They didn't put it that way, of course. All they said was that we shouldn't change leadership in the middle of a crisis.

To his credit, Doug opposed the idea. He didn't want the UAW to fall into the situation that occurred in the AFL-CIO where the leaders stayed on until their eighties. The idea died.

THROUGHOUT 1980 car-assembly plants in Canada were putting workers out on indefinite leave, but none were closed. It was the auto-parts plants that were hardest hit by the recession. Every few days there was news of another parts plant closing somewhere in Ontario or Quebec. Without warning, workers were notified that they were out. The owners locked the doors and moved away, making little effort to pay a decent severance or settle fairly on pensions or health premiums. Many of these plants were in small cities, which were left bloodied by the shutdowns. Merchants felt the pinch almost as soon as the workers.

We went into a Canadian Council meeting in Port Elgin just as the Bendix plant in Windsor announced one morning that it was closing for good that night. Owned by a multinational company, it had been building brake shoes for years. The employees worked with asbestos, unaware of the risk that they could get lung cancer. When the man from the Bendix local got up to speak at the Council meeting, he had tears in his eyes.

"We can't let this happen," he said. "It isn't right that employers can just walk away like this."

Worker after worker got up to talk about other plant closings, and I resolved that we fight back. We needed a tactic. There was no point putting pickets in front of a deserted plant. I remembered the days when the Reuthers occupied plants so that scabs couldn't get in and workers wouldn't be exposed to the company-instigated violence against picket lines. The only weapon we had against plant closures was to occupy the plants so the company couldn't get its equipment out.

I spoke off the cuff, for about ten minutes. "If it takes occupation of plants to stop this," I announced, "then we'll occupy them." At the end, the delegates leapt to their feet cheering.

The members' enthusiasm had a momentum of its own. Some went back to Windsor, rounded up the leadership of the Bendix local and the next morning tried to climb the fence around the shuttered plant. Of course they were caught right away and there was a tremendous holler.

"That's exactly the wrong thing to do," I told my staff. "We've got to think this through before we act and make ourselves vulnerable."

Another closing was scheduled for October, the small 240-employee Houdaille plant in Oshawa, which had been making auto parts for over thirty-five years. It was a good, locally owned operation which hadn't taken a strike in thirty years. A multinational company, KKR, had recently purchased it and had obtained money from the federal government for new equipment. Soon afterwards, KKR announced it was closing the plant and moving the equipment to South Carolina, one of the right-to-work, anti-union states.

The company was reneging on pensions, a serious matter because most of its workers were older people. The person lowest on the seniority list had been working eighteen years and thirty-eight workers, younger than fifty-five, had more than thirty years' service. The company proposed to give them credits up to the age of fifty-five but told them they would have to wait until they were sixty-five to get the full pension.

When we met with them, KKR management proposed one week's wages for every eight years of service as severance pay and refused to make any payment toward health costs. We learned that the same company had awarded its president on his retirement a lump sum payment of $1,062,432, plus deferred compensation, supplementary retirement benefits, full medical coverage, stock options, and so on.

Employees and union leadership, headed by Bill Rudyk, the local chairman, talked it over in the plant cafeteria, trying to think of a strategy to fight back. They eventually decided to mount a peaceful occupation.

Keeping the organization tight and everything in good control, they walked into the plant and blockaded the gates. We didn't want to lay ourselves open to charges of malicious damage, so the workers cleaned the plant until it was spotless. They even mowed the lawn and trimmed the hedges around the building.

A UAW banner was hung outside of the building, DAY 1 – TILL HELL FREEZES OVER, and someone changed the figure each morning. Cots were set up and shifts arranged, though a few workers decided they would stay inside until it was over. Relatives brought food, and workers scrupulously tidied up after they ate.

Laura Sky, a gifted film-maker, made a documentary about the Houdaille shutdown, which became quite a beacon of hope in that unsettled time. After the first week the occupation became a major news story. People were touched by the plight of these older people, many of them war veterans, who were far from the stereotype of labour radicals. It was obvious that they were not likely to find employment again in their lifetimes.

At the end of the first week, I paid a visit. One of the workers said to me,

"We may not succeed, but maybe what we're doing will help other workers."

I called Doug Fraser in Detroit. "This is a *very* special situation," I told him. "I know what we're doing is an illegal action and the UAW can't pay strike pay during an illegal strike, but this time we've got to do it. I'm going down to Oshawa and I want to be able to tell those workers that they'll be getting strike pay."

He said something about law suits. Everyone was worried that if the UAW was seen to advocate the sit-in, the company would mount a punitive suit.

"We can't worry about law suits right now," I argued. "Here's a group of workers who have taken on the fight against plant closings. This isn't a strike anyway. The company closed the plant, not us. We've got to support these workers."

To his great credit, Fraser said, "Okay. We'll take the chance."

I think that was the first and maybe only time the UAW ever has paid for what was clearly an illegal action. I felt great. We were doing something to stop a trend that was sweeping the industry. Maybe we'd win, maybe we'd lose, but goddamn it, we were trying.

I went to Oshawa and spoke at a rally, announcing to cheers that the UAW would provide strike pay. I was worried about police intervention.

"In case anyone is thinking about trying to break up this sit-in," I shouted, "I want to make it clear that we have 14,000 UAW members in the General Motors plants in this city, and we'll empty those plants if need be. If someone tries to force these Houdaille workers out of here, those 14,000 workers will come over in waves."

Driving home in the car that evening, my assistant said in a friendly voice, "Bob, you want to know something?"

"What?" I said, feeling mellow.

"All the GM guys in Oshawa are on vacation. Right now those plants are empty."

I broke up. "Maybe the government doesn't know that," I grinned.

One of the GM workers told me at the next Council meeting that he heard the news while he was camping in New Brunswick.

"I had the goddamned radio on," he said, "and I heard how Bob White was going to empty the GM plants. Man, I couldn't wait to get back to work so I could leave."

We learned that Ford, General Motors, Chrysler, and American Motors had dies and other equipment in the plant that they wanted to remove. We told them we wouldn't allow that. To show the kind of support the workers had, we staged a demonstration attended by 600 people, including the wives, children, and grandchildren of the men occupying Houdaille. The media took great pictures.

In August the company yielded. It agreed to pay thirty-year workers their full pensions, to pay severance pay, to give terminated employees a lump-sum payment toward their health premiums and to give older workers with less than thirty years' service a full pension when they reached sixty.

We not only won that battle, we won the war, too. We were part of a dramatic Ontario Federation of Labour demonstration in front of the Ontario legislature. Workers from the thirty plants that had closed carried coffins and placed them in a row on the steps of Queen's Park. There were moving speeches about the hardships the workers and their families were suffering. We kept up the pressure by appearing before parliamentary committees with documentation of the abuses workers were experiencing when their plants closed. Finally the Ontario government passed legislation making it obligatory for workers to get severance pay on the basis of one week for every year of service when a plant shut down. I was disappointed that the legislation didn't require corporations to justify plant closings, but still it was valuable legislation and we welcomed it.

THAT SUMMER I called a meeting of the presidents of all UAW locals and told them what had been going on at the highest level of the union, including the friction between the Canadian and American leadership. I was so nervous about bringing all that stuff into the open that I video-taped it and took the tape home with me. I wanted proof of exactly what I said and how I said it, in case there was any problem afterwards. I was taking a chance but these people were the shop-floor leadership in Canada, and I wanted them to know about the issues and conflicts that were developing.

In September 1981, the regular meeting of the International Executive Board started as usual with department reports from each person – Mark Stepp for Chrysler, Owen Bieber for GM, and then Don Ephlin for Ford. Ephlin talked about the trouble Ford was having and concluded by suggesting that we have a look at the possibility of opening up the Ford agreement.

Doug Fraser and others on the board promptly reminded him of our decision in Sawmill Creek not to do that. The next man reported without mentioning concessions, and the next, but then it was the turn of Ray Majerus, the international secretary-treasurer, who also was in charge of American Motors. He announced enthusiastically that American Motors had proposed an innovative scheme to take the COLA away and replace it with what was called a wheel tax – for every car sold, a sum would be put in a pool to be later divided among the workers through a complicated formula.

I listened in horror as the American Motors proposal was discussed seriously. Here we were talking about concessions, right after saying we wouldn't.

My Irish temper rose. "This is a violation of our policy," I protested. "I've just told our membership in Canada that we're together as a union on the issue of no concessions, and here we are talking about concessions for American Motors. This is nuts."

Doug exploded and I yelled back. Finally Doug sat back and spread his hands in resignation. "The hell with it then," he said. "We won't do the goddamned thing."

"Fine," I said. "That's exactly what we agreed to in Sawmill Creek, and I'm happy we're going to stick to that position. If we open that concession door one more crack, we're dead."

Later I was told by workers in other unions across the country that they had been feeling apprehensive. If the UAW cracked, they would have to give in, too.

Doug Fraser seemed unusually upset during that fight at the board meeting. A friend in Solidarity House confided in me that Doug had expected Owen Bieber and Ephlin to support the opening of the American Motors agreements and was dismayed that they hadn't. Doug's game plan was to open the door at American Motors for discussions at Ford and GM, both of which were pushing him hard to reopen the agreements.

A short time later I read the respected *Labor Letter* written by John Hurling, an old labour writer. In it he quoted a speech by Steve Schlossberg, general counsel for the UAW and a man very close to Doug Fraser. Schlossberg had said that if workers expected to keep their jobs, they would have to start paying more attention to quality and absenteeism – and give up some wages and benefits.

I was outraged. I shot off a letter to Doug Fraser demanding to know what right a UAW lawyer had to make such statements. What authority did a high-paid union bureaucrat have to say that workers had to give up wages to save their jobs? Somehow the issue blew over, but I was left with a very uneasy feeling that something was softening at the top of the UAW.

In Canada, plant closings and threats of closings continued. White Farm Equipment in Brantford, which employed about nine hundred people, had laid off its entire workforce for nine months. The company maintained it was going bankrupt in Canada and wouldn't reopen unless we agreed to substantial wage cuts.

The company had been bought by the TIC Corporation in Texas, which got its UAW local in the States to agree to concessions amounting to three dollars an hour in exchange for a cute promise. If the Canadian workers in Brantford got a better contract out of TIC than the Americans had accepted, TIC would have to match that settlement in its American plants. The agreement, which came to be known as the "me-too letter," was signed by Steve Yokich, UAW vice-president in charge of White Farm Equipment, and was designed to make sure that Canadians didn't get a better contract than he had negotiated with White in the States.

Gargoulis was the TIC head in the States. He asked us to open up the agreements with his company and negotiate concessions. Buzz Hargrove notified him we weren't going to cut the collective agreement, even if the plant was headed for receivership. "Your problems have nothing to do with workers' wages," Buzz said. "Even if we gave you five bucks an hour, it wouldn't solve the problems. We're not going to do it."

Because of the difference in the value of the dollars, Canadian workers had a distinct cost advantage over American workers. In other words, there was no rational reason why Canadians should take deep cuts.

Gargoulis was a real bullshitter. "I'd like to pull the blind on the UAW in the United States," he said ingratiatingly, "but I have this 'me-too letter' and I have to get this contract signed so it doesn't embarrass Yokich."

Buzz told him that was his problem.

I called a meeting of the White Farm bargaining committee in my office to explain why we were being so tough. The workers shuffled in looking very depressed. The long lay-off was crushing them and they were beginning to believe they would never get their jobs back. I told them if we gave concessions at White Farm, we couldn't refuse them anywhere else.

The youngest man in the room was scowling.

"You've got something on your mind, haven't you?" I asked.

"Well Bob," he said slowly, "it's okay for you to take this position. You've got a job. But I've got three kids and I ain't working. I understand your policy, but if I haven't got a job that policy don't mean anything to me."

"I care about you and your kids," I told him, "but if you give this guy a few bucks an hour it won't change anything. He's here to rip everyone off."

The same thing had just happened with Massey-Ferguson in the United States, a Canadian-owned company. They got three dollars an hour off the workers and then they closed every plant in the States anyway.

We refused concessions in White Farm and the plant survived. As I had insisted all along, the crisis had nothing to do with wages. The company was just using hard times to break our agreements. The real problem was the high-interest rates that made it difficult for farmers to buy new equipment, particularly as an over-abundance of wheat had driven down their incomes. This created an over-capacity in the agricultural-implements industry, and this plant, among others, was closed three years later.

TIC found a way to get out of the "me-too letter" promising to match Canadian wages and benefits. They gave a Canadian company, Lenamar in Guelph, 51 per cent ownership of White Farm so TIC could say it didn't have controlling interest in the plant any more. Lenamar went on to make a cool million that year, so TIC hastily bought its shares back.

Not all the confrontations turned out so well. We lost many jobs during that no-concessions fight. Budd in Kitchener, a huge auto-parts plant, said it had been underbid by another plant, A.O. Smith, whose shop union had taken a dollar-an-hour wage cut. The company insisted it couldn't be competitive unless we took the same cut. We refused and a lot of jobs at Budd were lost.

I took some heat for that, but I argued that if we took the dollar cut, wages at A.O. Smith would go down fifty cents, and then we'd be asked to match that, and so on. When you start down that road, there's no end to it.

IN NOVEMBER 1981, there was a conference in Detroit of General Motors workers from around the world, sponsored by the International Metalworkers Federation. It was the first time the conference had been held in North America in a long time, so I invited the entire Canadian GM bargaining team to go with me.

At the meeting, Doug Fraser made an unequivocal speech in which he said that if GM and Ford thought the UAW would open its agreements before they expired in 1982, they'd better bring a deck of cards with them to the bargaining table and learn how to play solitaire because the UAW would not be there. Owen Bieber, head of the GM section, made an equally clear statement that we would not be asking our GM workers to take concessions. Our guys were delighted. They went back to their local unions to tell the workers that the GM agreements were locked in until September 1982.

Our next International UAW Executive Board meeting was on December 7, 1981. A few days before the meeting I read in the papers that we would be discussing opening the agreements with Ford and General Motors. Shit, I thought. We just went through this at Sawmill Creek and we had it out again in September. *What the hell is going on?*

I knew Doug Fraser must have leaked the story to test the waters. That meant there had been internal discussions at Solidarity House about reopening the agreements.

The officers meet in advance of the board, and I went into that meeting in a fine state of controlled rage.

"I've been reading the papers," I said. "Are we going to have another discussion about opening up the goddamned collective agreements? I thought that was behind us."

"This situation has changed," Doug said. "Some people on the board want to have another discussion."

The main person on the board who wanted another discussion, I knew, was Doug Fraser.

The debate opened right away at the board meeting that afternoon and lasted more than six hours. Fraser had an ingenious twist on the argument. He said we weren't talking about concessions. We were merely deciding whether we should open up our agreements.

"The workers are scared," Doug said. "They want to see us doing something to save the industry."

I said that we were obliged to give the workers leadership in both good times and bad times. If we had left it up to the workers to decide what we should do, we wouldn't have pensions, we wouldn't have SUB, we wouldn't have health care. Young guys, especially, don't care about those benefits and would rather we went only for higher wages.

"We should be explaining our position to the membership," I said. "We should show why it makes sense to fight concessions and get their support. We're caught right now in a massive restructuring. The Japanese have forced the American car industry to make changes in order to compete. But we can't compete with the Japanese by cutting our wages to seven dollars an hour, and it wouldn't make any difference if we did that. Concessions aren't the answer.

"The UAW has been a trail-blazing leader in the labour movement both in the United States and Canada. If the UAW starts opening up our collective bargaining agreements to give back wages and benefits, we will be making a hole in the dike that will flood every union in North America. We have a responsibility not only to our own members but to all the labour unions in both countries.

"Look," I implored, "workers don't need a union to walk them backwards. They can do that on their own."

Bob Nickerson told me afterwards it was the finest speech I'd ever given in my life. When I finished, one person after another got up to say, "I agree with many of the points Brother White has made, BUT. . ."

Doug was sitting back looking very comfortable. He knew he had the votes to open up those agreements. I passed him a note.

"With all these people agreeing with me, I want a secret ballot vote. I think I can win."

He laughed. He knew that I knew that I didn't have a chance.

I was thinking ahead. I needed a way to continue to fight concessions in Canada no matter what the Americans did. I found it when I heard Doug explaining that we weren't opening up the agreements, we were merely giving permission for the councils – the GM council, the Ford council, and so on – to make that decision.

If they were saying that the Ford council in the U.S. had the right to make a decision and the GM council in the U.S. had a right to make a different decision, then they couldn't turn around and tell me that the Ford council and the GM council in Canada didn't have a right to make their own decisions, too.

"Let me understand this," I asked the board. "You're not advocating that we open the agreements?"

"No, no, no," they shook their heads. "We're going to let the councils decide. That's the democratic way to handle this."

"Okay," I said.

The vote was called. I said I wanted my vote recorded, which isn't usually done. The vote was twenty-five to one – me.

Doug announced we'd have a major press conference the next morning. I asked for time. "I'll have to deal with the Canadian media on this," I said. "The direction we're going is fundamentally different from the one I thought we had when I came here yesterday." I was flying to Ottawa the next morning for a meeting of the CLC, so it was agreed that the announcement in Detroit would come around eleven, giving me time to get to Ottawa and prepare myself to respond to the Canadian media.

Nick and I went down to the bar in our hotel and drank about three gin and tonics and two bottles of wine. I had a sinking feeling in my stomach that Canada was headed into one helluva fight with Solidarity House.

"We're in it now," I said gloomily. Nick agreed.

One thing was sure, the idea that the councils would make their decisions independently was nonsense designed to get the leadership off the hook. I knew the councils were going to be lobbied to vote the way Doug wanted them to vote, which was to open up the agreements. The UAW executive had just opened up the whole auto industry. If assembly workers in the States went ahead and gave up wages and benefits, the parts industry would follow. We were facing a staggering fight to keep those concessions out of Canada.

Our Ford council in Windsor had met the day before. I called the chairman of the council, Ray Wakeman.

"I have to see you at six o'clock tomorrow morning at the Windsor airport," I said, without explanation.

He didn't hesitate. "I'll be there."

Next, I called Phil Bennett, chairman of the GM council in Oshawa, which was meeting in Toronto the next day.

"I'm on an early flight from Windsor. I want to see you guys as soon as I can after my plane gets to Toronto."

"We'll be waiting," he promised.

The next morning I met Wakeman at the airport and told him what had happened.

"Don't worry about us brother," he assured me. "We just voted yesterday that we're not going to give in on concessions. We're on side."

At seven I flew to Toronto, and by nine I was in front of the GM council at the Carlton Hotel. The guys were furious when I told them the UAW had decided to allow the councils to open up the agreement if they wanted. They raved about being betrayed by Fraser and Bieber.

"Look," I told them, "let's not do something we'll regret. This is much deeper than how Fraser or Bieber behaved. This has to do with the future of our union in Canada. We made the decision not to open up those agreements, and I'm telling you that the leadership in Canada is going to keep the faith."

Some talked of pulling out of the UAW. I said, "This doesn't mean the end of the international union. We'll have a discussion at some point when we're calmer and more objective, but right now what matters is that we stick to our policy and refuse to open up the agreements."

Two men were there from Owen Bieber's staff. I knew they would take all this straight back to Doug.

I caught a plane to Ottawa at noon and arrived at the CLC executive meeting just as the afternoon session was about to begin. I requested an opportunity to speak. I was heavy-hearted and very emotional. This would be the first time I had ever criticized my union openly before colleagues outside the UAW, but I wanted the CLC to throw its weight behind a no-concession stand right across the union movement in Canada.

"This is so fundamental, we have no choice but to go a different direction than the States is," I said. "These concessions are a cancer in the labour movement. We have to fight them even if it means a break within the international unions. I hope that won't happen in the UAW. I hope we can keep it together. But right now we have parted ways."

Louis Laberge, CLC vice-president, immediately supported me. He said my statements were important to the entire labour movement in Canada. Someone else said the same and then the executive started to applaud. That was a heart-warming moment for me.

The media swarmed around and I made moderately worded statements about Canada intending to go a different route. I was anxious not to inflame the situation. Wilf List of the *Globe and Mail*, a thoughtful analyst whom I respect, disappointed me by writing a critical article on how the Canadians weren't showing the proper mood of cooperation with Detroit in a time of crisis.

TWO MOMENTOUS THINGS had happened in my personal life. Within a few days of each other, our daughter Robyn was born and my friend and mentor Tommy McLean died of cancer in the remote corner of northern Michigan where he had retired.

His wife had died soon after he retired. He had been devastated and had moved to a place he built in the northern lake country of Michigan. A daughter, who lived near him, had been sworn not to tell anyone he had cancer, so his death came as a shock to us all.

Marilyne's pregnancy wasn't planned, and I have to admit that, at first, I didn't welcome being a father again. I knew there was no way I could find the time that a child needs and deserves.

Marilyne wanted me to attend prenatal classes with her, but I never had the time. I went into the delivery room with her at the doctor's invitation and he assumed that I was prepared to help. He told me what to do and I did it.

Later he congratulated me, commenting that I certainly must have paid attention in the prenatal classes.

Marilyne laughed. "He didn't go to even one," she told the doctor. "He learned that cool from years of collective bargaining under pressure."

The period after Robyn's birth was quite stressful because we had to adjust to living with a stranger in the house, a woman who took care of

Robyn so that Marilyne could continue to work. As in most situations, time passes and problems find solutions. Robyn has grown to be a beautiful child, bright, intelligent, and independent. I love her very much.

The day after Robyn's birth I was on a plane to Michigan for Tommy's funeral, reflecting on how one life had started at the same time as another ended. McLean and I hadn't seen much of one another for a few years because his cottage was so inaccessible, but I knew he was pleased with his star pupil. I felt the loss of him as acutely as if he had been my father. In a sense, he had been a father me.

When I came back, I arrived back in the thick of the no-concessions argument. The GM and Ford councils in the States were preparing to vote on whether they would start talking with the companies about opening up the agreements. The Ford council in Canada took the position that it was none of its business what Ford workers did in the States, but the GM council had a different view. They decided to go to the States and try to persuade the GM council to vote against concessions.

I disapproved. I told them we couldn't have it two ways. We couldn't tell the Americans to stay out of our business in Canada and then go down there and tell them what to do in the United States.

"This is against our policy of autonomy. This screws it up," I told them.

"Bullshit," they replied. "We know these guys. They don't want concessions any more than we do, and we're going to go down there and prop them up."

They prepared a bushel of leaflets using some of the excellent material Sam Gindin put together on why workers shouldn't give concessions. They wore sweatshirts printed with NO CONCESSIONS and stormed past the UAW staff people in Washington who tried to bar them from the meeting.

I was in Hawaii. For the first time in my life since joining the UAW, I felt too exhausted to carry on. I should have hung around for the GM and Ford council votes but instead I took a vacation.

I watched the results on television. Though both the Ford and the GM councils in the States voted to take the first steps toward concessions, there was no question the guys from Oshawa had had an impact on the GM council. The GM vote for opening the agreements was nowhere near as large as the Ford vote.

I was sickened. The Canadian Region was now in Solidarity House's direct line of fire.

CHAPTER FOURTEEN

Up Against the Big Three

O UR GM BARGAINING TEAM who went to Washington said that I had a lot of support with UAW people there who hated Solidarity House for accepting concessions. They praised me as the one person on the international executive who had the nerve to vote against all the others to protect wages. Fraser didn't name me, but he said a few times that certain parties were behaving like Custer at Little Bighorn.

Most feeling in the States, however, was against us. One of our guys had remarked at the GM council meeting that there wasn't a Canadian flag. The response he got was, "If they bring in a Canadian flag, someone will stick it up a Canadian ass."

When GM opened talks with the UAW bargaining committees, they found that opposition to opening the agreements was stiffer than they had expected. The committees sent the matter back to the GM council for review, and our Canadian team went down again in force. UAW staff pushed them into a roped-off area, but they were still able to get the message through that wage freezes and cutbacks weren't the answer to the recession. The council once again voted to continue the discussion on the agreements, but the margin this time was so narrow, only a shade over 50 per cent, that GM realized it would have a huge battle on its hands. The company backed off and gave up trying to get those contracts renegotiated.

On the other hand, the Ford council strongly approved reopening the contracts and the Ford bargaining committee made substantial concessions. To be fair, the situation at U.S. Ford *was* serious. Ford workers had suffered much more downtime than GM workers had, and many Ford plants had closed.

The UAW agreements with the Big Three were due to expire in September 1982. Before the expiry date, the UAW always holds a collective-bargaining convention, which draws 2,500 delegates to talk about the future of the union and decide what the priorities will be in the coming negotiations.

I urged the International Executive Board to use the 1982 convention to mount a fight-back campaign against concessions. With that as our mandate, the companies might not push so hard for concessions in 1982-1985.

Fraser wouldn't buy that. Worse, it looked as though there wouldn't be a collective-bargaining convention in 1982. The new Ford agreement wouldn't expire until 1984 and the Ford concessions, if ratified, would extend the contract to the same date. That left only GM in the 1982 bargaining.

I was at the skilled trades conference, one of the conventions always scheduled in a bargaining year, just as the Ford talks concluded. The contract was full of deep concessions. Canadians at the conference were given a rough time. We were blamed for scuttling the GM talks and, by extension, for jeopardizing jobs at GM.

The conference always opens with a speech by the UAW president. Customarily, his introduction is greeted with a standing ovation. I was on the platform with the other members of the executive, so I had a good view of the Canadians seated at two or three tables in the second row. When Fraser was introduced, they didn't stand.

In Canada we're not much for automatic standing ovations anyway, but this was a deliberate snub and everyone knew it. One of the vice-presidents, Odessa Komer, leaned over to me.

"What's the matter with the Canadians?" she asked. "They're not standing."

"No," I told her. "They're mad. They're mad at Doug and they're mad at the UAW over here. And it's a funny thing about Canadians, when they're mad they don't give you a goddamned standing ovation."

Komer stared at me.

"You ought to quit worrying about what the Canadians are doing," I told her, "and start worrying about where we're going as a union. I'm not going to ask our guys to kiss ass. These guys are mad and I'm mad, and we show our feelings. That's the way we built the union and that's the way it's going to stay at this convention."

In his speech, Doug made no attempt to explain why Canada was opposed to concessions, which he described as "innovative bargaining" and "new ideas." He might have said that Canada was a different country, that it had different labour costs because the U.S. dollar was worth more than the Canadian dollar, because the Canadian inflation rate was different, and because Canada had medicare. He could have at least said that although many members didn't agree with the Canadian position, the Canadians still had the right to act autonomously.

Not a word of that. Instead he spoke of people "storming the barricades," people who "couldn't look to the future," who "didn't understand change." We heard about Custer again. "Custer stood his ground," he declared, "and look where it got him."

After his speech I went up to him.

I said mildly, "Doug, couldn't you at least point out that the Canadians have the right to do this?"

Doug's expression was drawn and full of pain. With the auto industry in a major recession, it was a difficult time to be head of the UAW. It was his misfortune to be the first president in the union's history to participate in bargaining in which the union gave back gains. He was exhausted and haggard from the strain.

"Don't you know what this is doing to us, Bob?" he asked. "Your relationship and mine? It's tearing us apart."

"I know that Doug, but I can't help it. Goddamn it, we're not going down this road."

"Don't you know what this is doing to me personally?"

"Doug, I fundamentally disagree with you on this issue."

"I'm furious about that shit Sam Gindin is putting out," Fraser said, switching the subject. "It's full of bullshit and propaganda and lies."

"What are you talking about!" I said, bristling.

Our conversation was witnessed by the entire convention, but both of us had forgotten the audience. We couldn't be heard, but the delegates could plainly see us waving our arms and red-faced.

"There are forty-five gross errors in it," Doug said.

"There are not," I retorted. "That's a goddamned good piece of economic analysis and policy argument for our union. It's no more propaganda than the stuff you guys used to prepare for Walter Reuther when he wanted to make the union's case for advancement. We all use it. We all fix our positions, and Gindin's arguments are just as rational as those were. The information we're putting out is to counter the slanted propaganda coming from the goddamned corporations."

Doug reached into his briefcase and pulled out Gindin's *No Concessions: A Canadian UAW Council Policy*. "Look right here," he said furiously. "He talks about company profits. GM isn't making any goddamned profits."

"They will when it's over," I snapped. "But what will the workers get out of this? They aren't going to get any goddamned money when this is over."

Doug was breathing hard. He said, "Did it ever occur to you, Bob, that you might be wrong and the other twenty-five people might be right?"

"Quite frankly it did, Doug," I answered coldly, "but not for very long."

Later, Wilf List of the *Globe and Mail* interviewed Doug, who rejected everything we said and even our right to say it. If he had made even a small comment about the labour-costs difference, the inflation differences, the mortgage-rate differences, the differences in the value of the dollar, my position would have been a lot easier. I read the article with despair. I felt I had been betrayed.

About two weeks later, we went on to the production workers' conference. I hoped Doug would soften his opening speech somewhat this time, but he didn't. I heard again about Custer's Last Stand. The only reference to autonomy came at the end, when he said "Each council's going to make its own decision on this – the GM council, the Ford council, the agricultural implements council, and the Canadian council."

The stage was being set to open up the GM agreements early. General Motors was starting to play hard ball, and the company knew how to do it. They had just announced a series of plant closings to take effect in 1983 and 1984.

Despite that, a young GM worker from California got up at the convention and made an impassioned appeal against concessions. I thought, the roots for fighting back are here. If the UAW leadership would only explain that wage concessions wouldn't solve the problems the industry was having, that plant closings would go on happening anyway until the industry shook itself out, I was sure it would get the same support in the States that we had found in Canada.

I happened to see the young Californian the next morning in the hotel coffee shop. I picked up my cup of coffee and went over.

"I just want to introduce myself," I said. "I thought your speech yesterday was right on the money."

"Yes," he said, "but last night we got news that our fucking plant's closing down, twenty-five hundred jobs."

U.S. Ford workers ratified the concessions contract by a significant majority and locked themselves into the punishing cuts until September 1984. The International Executive Board then cancelled the 1982 collective-bargaining conference, as I had anticipated, and in April went straight to collective bargaining with General Motors. A badly shaken UAW gave GM a two-year contract with the same punishing concessions that Ford had been given. The agreement saved GM $2.5 billion in the States.

These contracts introduced something called profit-sharing, which was supposed to make up for the losses in wages. In Canada we opposed profit-sharing, predicting – correctly – that in the long run it would be to no advantage to the workers. (In 1986 Ford workers in the States finally collected about $2,200 out of profit sharing, while at General Motors, which made $2.5 billion, workers got nothing.)

A GM official threatened that jobs would start to be scarce in Canada if the UAW in Canada didn't agree to concessions. GM's new president in Canada, Don Hackworth, spoke in Montreal in January about GM's "serious cash flow problems." He observed that GM had plants on every continent and could build cars "wherever we must in order to ensure that our vehicles are cost competitive."

The ratification vote in the American GM plants was a blow for Doug Fraser. The contract was approved only by a narrow 52 per cent. The UAW leadership didn't have the backing for concessions that it thought it had.

Suddenly Canada didn't look as isolated as we had. We needed that psychological boost. For the first time in union history, the Canadian UAW was going into collective bargaining with Ford and GM at different times than the Americans.

General Motors made a colossal error. The day after the concession contract was ratified in the States, the company called a meeting of the board of directors to talk about bonuses for its executives. Fraser raised such hell that the company backed off.

The talk everywhere was about "equality of sacrifice." The phrase "equality of sacrifice" even appeared in a UAW pamphlet, which I thought was inexcusable. The corporation executives never did sacrifice. Very few of the top executives changed their life style one bit during the recession in the American auto industry. Bonuses may have been smaller, but there were certainly no salary cuts and the perks, like executive dining-rooms and chauffeur-driven limousines, didn't stop. Lee Iacocca gave up his jet. Big deal. Workers were losing their cars, their homes, their marriages.

Early in 1982, the Ford Canada vice-president of industrial affairs asked to meet with me. The company knew what our position on concessions was, but the letter I received said that as a result of what had happened with the Ford agreement in the United States he wanted to sit down with our bargaining team to discuss issues such as competitiveness and jobs.

We knew Ford's plan was to open the door for concession negotiations, so some of our Ford team thought I should refuse to meet. I disagreed. We had said we would give no concessions but we never said we wouldn't meet. When we met, Ford said the company had lost $214 million in 1981 in Canada and now, in 1982, was losing a million dollars a day. The stockholders had just missed a dividend payment, things were so bad. If there wasn't some relief in the contracts right away, jobs would be lost in Canada.

The Ford spokesman wasn't specific, but there was pointed reference to the contract U.S. Ford workers had accepted, "a model of union-management cooperation."

I listened without interruption, as I always insist we do. Then we asked for a recess to consider our reply.

Our position was a tricky one. We knew that the major cause of the million-dollars-a-day loss was the fact that Ford Canada was not manufacturing enough parts in Canada and was having to pay high exchange rates to buy them from the States. Gindin did some calculations and discovered that if we gave Ford Canada the same cuts in wages and benefits that American Ford workers had given, Ford would still lose $900,000 a day in Canada. The solution to the company's financial problem, as we saw it, was to build more parts in Canada.

I didn't want to make a flat rejection of the company's request. The million-dollars-a-day loss was real, and tough for us to handle. I didn't want Ford to push us into premature negotiations, but I also didn't want to look intransigent. I said we'd meet with the company in June, right after our collective bargaining convention.

In the meantime, I suggested, we could set up three joint company-UAW study groups, one on labour costs, one on productivity, and the last on sourcing.

"We're willing to open up negotiations early," I told Ford, "but let's take the time before our collective bargaining convention in April to hold study talks. Then we'll be ready to start negotiations with clear understanding on both sides of what's happening at Ford and how we can be helpful."

The local leadership in the Ford plants was pleased with our counter-offer. They had been encountering uneasiness on the shop floors about our no-concession policy. Some workers feared that I was being too tough and Ford would break.

I waited to hear from Ford. Typical of big corporations, it couldn't respond quickly. Ford was represented by Stanley J. Surma, vice-president in charge of industrial relations, a man for whom I have a lot of respect. I sent a letter to Ford stressing that one of the issues to be discussed had to be labour costs. We knew that when Canadian labour costs were compared to those in U.S. Ford, our position was unassailable. The corporations were paying out about

$7 an hour less to Canadians than to American workers because of the exchange rate and such other differences as medicare.

Three weeks passed and then Ford rejected our offer. The company would agree to study sessions on productivity and sourcing, but not on labour costs. I chuckled. Here was Ford, crying crisis, refusing our offer to discuss labour costs. With that stupid decision, they had boxed themselves in. The unreasonable party now was Ford itself.

At press conferences, I made the point that if Ford was afraid to talk about labour costs, it was clear proof of our contention that Canadians weren't overpaid. The media was still unsympathetic to our position, but our position was being heard.

GM CANADA was quiet that spring. There was no approach to ask us to open the agreements before September. I think the narrow ratification of cuts in the States gave the company some concern, knowing that the Canadians were even more set against concessions than the Americans. Also, GM wasn't taking the heavy losses that Ford was.

Rodney Andrew, GM's director of industrial relations, put out a feeler. Andrew was new to the job in Canada. A former big-league pitcher, he's a tall man, then in his early fifties, gregarious and easy going, but *very* smart. He said casually to me, "Look, do you want us officially to ask you to open up the agreements?"

"If you want me officially to refuse, go ahead," I told him. We like one another.

"Well, if that's your position there's no point in going through the exercise," he shrugged.

"That's our position," I assured him.

The situation with American Motors was slightly different. The agreement negotiated in the States called concessions an "employee investment program" and offered a pay-back promise for the cuts the workers took. When the gimmickry was stripped away, it was nothing more than a plan to take $150 million from the workers in return for little.

In Canada, American Motors in Brampton was pushing to reopen the agreement and accept the "investment" cutbacks. If we didn't, we were told that Brampton would shut down. We refused and something odd happened. Far from shutting down, Brampton hired a second shift and put production on an over-time basis. The leadership of Local 1285 called a meeting of workers and recommended that they vote to reject the company's proposal,

Shortly after White arrived in Canada, aged fourteen, he bought a bike with his dollar-a-day earnings as a farm hand.

The happiest man in the world. In Atlantic City during the 1957 UAW convention. Left to right, George Burton, Frank Kenney, White, Clarence Chattington (*G. Dobkin Studios*)

ABOVE From the high of Atlantic City to the hard task of recommending an unsatisfactory settlement to Wellwood strikers. White with Roy Brown in 1957. BELOW LEFT Back in Atlantic City in 1959 at the union's biennial convention with Frank Moroz, looking every bit the union man (*Central Studios*). BELOW RIGHT In 1964, White's job was to keep de Havilland workers in the UAW. He pulled out all the stops, including bringing UAW president Walter Reuther to speak at a mass rally at the Crang Plaza in Malton (*Fednews*). OPPOSITE, TOP After the success of the de Havilland campaign, White was chosen to head up a new Canadian organizing team. Left to right, Les Rudrum, Bruce Lee, White, and Carl Anderson. MIDDLE The organizing team worked under UAW vice-president Pat Greathouse (left). Tommy McLean (right), assistant to the Canadian director, was White's friend and mentor. BOTTOM In 1968, shortly before McDermott's election as the new Canadian director, outgoing director George Burt (right) met with (left to right) Herb Kelly, Tommy McLean, and Dennis McDermott (*Photo by Jack Mitchell*).

ABOVE, LEFT One of the most bitter strikes of the decade was the 1978 Fleck strike. Left to right, Fran Piercy, White, Al Seymour, and Mary Lou Richards at the ratification meeting. ABOVE, RIGHT On day six of the 1980 sit-in at Houdaille in Oshawa, White threatened to empty the GM plants in support of the laid-off Houdaille workers. BELOW General Motors was the target company in the 1982 round of negotiations. Left to right, Rod Andrew of GM, Bob Nickerson, Pat Clancy, Phil Bennett, White, and Sam Gindin. Wendy Cuthbertson is in the back row. OPPOSITE, TOP After negotiations with Chrysler broke down in 1982, White addressed a mass meeting of Local 444 at the Windsor race track, unaware of a bomb threat to his life. MIDDLE White and UAW president Doug Fraser twenty-four hours before the settlement of the five-week strike against Chrysler in 1982 (Globe and Mail, *Toronto*). BOTTOM In 1983, Owen Bieber was elected sixth president of the UAW by acclaim at the 1983 convention in Dallas.

TOP In July 1983, the Canadian
government capitulated to U.S.
requests to test the cruise missile
over northern Alberta. White
addressed a protest rally of 20,000 in
Toronto, criticizing Trudeau's
decision. ABOVE White with Chrysler
heavyweights Tom Miner, Lee
Iacocca, and Moe Closs at the 1984
Auto Show (*Vern Harvey*). LEFT
Dennis McDermott on the podium
with White during the UAW-Canada
founding convention in September
1985 (© *Photo Features Ltd.*).

LEFT Victor Reuther delivering his spellbinding speech during the founding convention (© *Photo Features Ltd.*).
BELOW In its first negotiations as an independent union, the UAW Canada settled with Chrysler before an agreement was reached in the U.S. Left to right, Jim O'Neil, Bob Nickerson, Kenny Gerard, White, Buzz Hargrove, and Sam Gindin.
BOTTOM The cheque at last! Nineteen months after the Canadian Region split, the UAW finally signed over $43,500,000.63 to the independent Canadian union in October 1986. Buzz Hargrove (left) and Bob Nickerson (right).

ABOVE Marching against free trade with Bob Nickerson at the Labour Day parade, September 1986 (*Tim McKenna*). BELOW Delegates from the Newfoundland fishermen's union receive a standing ovation at the 1987 CAW collective bargaining convention. Left to right, Bob Nickerson, Helen Kramzyk, Kevin Condon, Father Des McGrath, Richard Cashin, Frank McNally, and White (© *Photo Features Ltd.*).

which they did by a margin of over a thousand to one. A few weeks later, the second shift was laid off.

The Canadian agreements with General Motors and Ford expired on September 15, 1982, and the Chrysler one on October 15. The industry was full of speculation about what the Canadian UAW would do. The no-concessions policy was under heavy fire from the corporations and from the media, which asked the question, "Why doesn't Bob White act responsibly in this crisis, like Doug Fraser has?"

In 1982, there was no collective-bargaining convention in the States to set the pattern. We went ahead with plans to hold our own conference. For the first time in the union's history, the Canadian UAW was acting on its own in major bargaining. I decided we should prepare by locking in our membership's support for the no-concession policy one more time.

The conference was held in Toronto on May 8 at the Sheraton Centre, with 400 delegates representing 130,000 workers. We were surrounded by media, much of it from the United States because of their keen interest in the open split that was developing in the UAW. Though pushed to make incendiary statements criticizing Solidarity House, I took a mild tone. What happened in the United States was one thing, I said, but the UAW was a strong organization and we had the autonomy in Canada to do whatever was best here.

The UAW collective bargaining conventions are watched intently by the auto manufacturers. In Canada we don't allow them to attend our bargaining conventions, but they can learn from the media what has happened and also we mail them a copy of the collective bargaining program when the convention is over.

"We all understand that with the conditions that exist now in the auto industry, this won't be a year of substantial progress in collective bargaining," I told the delegates. "But it's not going to be a year in which the corporations have a licence to attack our wages and benefits."

The corporation could read between the lines. We were determined to fight concessions, but we were aware we couldn't make a lot of progress. It was not business as usual.

I had invited people I thought might strengthen our resolve and also show the corporations we weren't alone in our fight against concessions. Dennis McDermott came as president of the Canadian Labour Congress and, without any guidance from me, gave the speech I hoped he would. He tied the CLC to the Canadian UAW position. Bob Rae was also there, the New Democratic Party's rising star in the federal legislature. He called concessions, "the most destructive idea of our time." The convention then voted to stand behind our policy against wage or benefit concessions.

An editorial in the *Montreal Gazette* on May 14 was typical of the media reaction across the country. The Canadian UAW's position was described as "remarkably short-sighted." It said that "Canada's 300 auto companies and other UAW shops, to say nothing of the workers, don't need this . . . the effect could be devastating . . . tough talk will set a regrettable example for other unions."

The CLC met in Winnipeg on May 25, 1982, right on the heels of the UAW bargaining convention. Dennis analysed the recession exactly as I did and the CLC leadership wrote a well-thought-out paper against concessions and in support of bargaining in the public sector. That national policy meeting of 2,500 delegates, representing two million workers, voted overwhelmingly to reject employer demands for wage concessions. McDermott said the CLC would support that policy "to the bitter end."

Dennis' speech was so tough that there was speculation after the convention that the CLC planned to lead the country into a general strike.

"This will be a test of our collective ability to pull together," Dennis warned. He used my phrase when he added, "Who needs a union to walk backward?"

Dennis had agreed to recognize me as the first speaker at the floor microphones in the afternoon session. As I was introduced, an enormous ovation began that lasted for several minutes. It wasn't really for me, though it felt wonderful to hear it after all the condemnation I'd taken. It was for the UAW's fight against concessions and for the endurance we'd shown in such strikes as Fleck, Blue Cross, and CCM. The unions across Canada were saying, "Okay, White. We're with you on this."

I was too choked up to give a good speech, but I talked about the labour movement sticking together. The UAW could handle the fight ahead, we were strong, but small unions across the country needed to know the CLC was behind them in their fight against wage cuts. The UAW was the only big union in Canada going into major bargaining that year. What we did, I knew, could not help but set the pattern.

That night we had a meeting of all the heads of unions: Don Nicholson of the Railway and Transport Workers, Dave Patterson and Gerry Docquier of the United Steelworkers, Pierre Samson of Public Service Alliance of Canada, Grace Hartman of the Canadian Union of Public Employees, and Jack Munro of the International Woodworkers. Dennis wanted them all to line up and swear there would be "no retreat." Not everyone was happy about the no-concessions policy, but Dennis was looking forward to the battle. At one point he said, "This policy is locked in blood, and any sonovabitch who doesn't agree with it should be thrown out of the trade union movement." I thought he could have handled it a little more diplomatically than that.

The media tore into the CLC. One cartoon showed Dennis with sticks of dynamite in every pocket and in his ears, fuses lit. Politicians said the labour movement lacked proper consideration for the struggling companies. Corporate executives earning top salaries were giving speeches about how workers should take pay cuts. At the same time, the entire labour movement in the United States was taking cuts whenever and wherever asked. The AFL-CIO had no cohesive policy on concessions. The Canadian labour movement had no support anywhere and Canadian union leaders realized they had to be in touch with their members as never before.

In the Canadian UAW we almost completely reorganized our communications network to bring the local union leadership closer to the rank and file. We had to be certain that our membership understood why we were going against the wind, so we had to put out good material. Our communications department, headed by Wendy Cuthbertson, put out a booklet titled *Working People Under Attack*. Sam Gindin was kept busy sending his economic analysis papers to other unions. We held education sessions in every local. Committee people were urged to get out on the shop floor and talk to workers. The staff was ordered to stay close to the members and I went around the locals, meeting with the workers to answer questions and talk about our reasons for opposing concessions.

We knew that people were saying "White is nuts," and "He can't win. When is he going to give in?"

There was still no one in Solidarity House, from Doug Fraser down, who was willing to tell the UAW membership in the States why the Canadians were behaving differently. They didn't have the political nerve to do that or enough confidence to admit that we were right. I think they kept hoping we would mess up and justify their position.

We went to government to explain our position, meeting with leaders of all the parties at all levels. Prime Minister Pierre Trudeau was getting ready to issue his restraints policy and didn't want to see us, but Bill Snare from the Prime Minister's Office sat down with us.

Snare said, "You obviously want Canadian content legislation to protect the Canadian industry against imports."

I nodded.

"I think it would be immensely important for you in that regard," he said smoothly, "if you would endorse the prime minister's restraint program."

I considered carefully. "Sometimes I'm not too bright," I said. "You'd better run that by me again. Are you saying to me that if I endorse the restraint program, we'd have a better chance of getting content legislation in the Canadian car industry?"

He backed off. "I'm not saying it's that black and white . . ."

"I'm telling you," I said curtly, "the answer is no. The answer to the prime minister's restraint program will be given by the whole labour movement, not by the UAW alone. We have no intention of endorsing the restraint legislation as a trade-off for getting content."

My meetings with the Ontario government were more fruitful. Premier Bill Davis and his cabinet understood but didn't agree with the arguments against concessions. However, with the exception of one cabinet minister, Gordon Walker, they never spoke against our position.

The Ontario New Democratic Party held a leadership convention that summer. I'd had some influence in persuading Bob Rae to leave his seat in the federal legislature and run for the provincial party leadership. The UAW people in Oshawa were for Mike Breagh from Oshawa, but when I got to the convention, I found that almost all the other delegates in the UAW favoured Bob Rae. Rae is an intelligent, articulate, capable man, who has the ability to grasp and explain complex issues. I was happy when the NDP convention elected him as the new Ontario leader.

The UAW's fight in 1982 had enormous impact. When the CLC staged a demonstration in Ottawa against high interest rates, the UAW contingent was one of the largest ones there. We had busloads of people in front of the parliament buildings, and we made plenty of noise.

Despite the heavy plant closings and layoffs, we were not in any financial trouble. Interest rates were running around 21 per cent, and our huge strike fund was turning over five or six million dollars a month in interest.

Nonetheless, because workers had taken concessions, Doug Fraser decided it wouldn't look right unless staff took pay cuts, too. Solidarity House circulated waivers we were supposed to sign, authorizing Detroit to cut our wages. It put me in a difficult spot. I didn't see how we could have a no-concessions policy in Canada and then turn around and ask our own employees to make concessions.

In May 1982, I wrote Doug my decision:

"I am sure you clearly understand, Doug, that if our union was in financial difficulty, I would have no hesitation in deferring wage increases, in working for half pay, or drawing no salary at all. . . . The current situation, however, and the resulting decision of the International Executive Board is not based on any financial difficulties our union currently faces. . . . We have adopted a different position on concessions in Canada, and therefore, I do not intend to participate in the most recent IEB decision and will not be returning the waiver form. In addition I am also holding the waiver forms for my assistants and other members of our staff."

I proposed to the staff that we give up $100 a month on a voluntary basis – more than the UAW staff in the States was giving – and put it in the fund to help workers on strike against no-concession contracts. To a person, the staff voted to do that.

NOW I HAD TO TURN my attention to the negotiations that lay ahead. I decided bargaining should open with GM, then Ford the next day, and move to Chrysler on the third day. After that, the talks would run concurrently until we picked our target company.

On the morning of July 14, 1982 we began with General Motors in the Royal York Hotel. I went to meet with Ford in the Westbury the next morning, and then drove to Windsor on July 16 for the preliminary rounds with Chrysler.

Each day in my opening statements I laid out the case against concessions very clearly. We knew there were real problems in the industry and we were seeking a settlement that was fair to all parties. After each session, I held a press conference to explain our position again.

I met with GM's Rod Andrew privately just before we opened the bargaining sessions, each of us probing to see where the hot spots were. I was impressed with him. Our chemistry was right and we each felt good about the other's integrity. That doesn't mean we didn't argue.

John Deverell of the *Toronto Star* once asked Andrew what he thought of me and Rod replied, "He has a very clear philosophy of where he wants to see Canada and Canadian labour go. . . . He knows where to draw the line between rhetoric and what is possible at the moment." I thought that was a generous comment, coming from an adversary.

Very little happens in the first few weeks of bargaining. We sparred with the companies in desultory work sessions, looking for soft spots. We still had no authorization to strike from Solidarity House. We began to feel uneasy. If we didn't get it soon, the corporations would think we were easy picking.

"Why don't you ask Doug about the strike authorization?" I was asked.

"Like hell," I replied. "I don't ask a question I don't want to hear the answer to."

I was running on nerve. My plan was to go ahead as if we had strike authorization, take the strike votes, and only then meet with Fraser about authorization.

We decided to make GM the target company for a number of reasons. The company hadn't ask us to open up our agreements early, which suggested that they recognized we were serious about not taking concessions. Also, GM as a huge multinational has a lot of flexibility in any one country and could accept differences in Canada. Besides, GM was in much better financial shape than Ford, so we had our best chance of holding the line against concessions there, after which Ford might fall in line. The reverse was not necessarily true. A deciding factor was the militancy of our GM guys.

I don't usually attend strike-vote meetings, but I accepted the invitation from the GM local in Oshawa to be there on August 22. It was a somber meeting. I told the workers what we were facing and expressed the concern I knew they felt for the danger we were in. None of us wanted a strike against an industry in deep trouble. However, the bargaining team couldn't be effective unless it had the confidence of the membership. The vote was over 90 per cent in favour of striking if they had to.

On August 23, the day after the Oshawa strike vote and about three weeks before the contract expired, I went apprehensively to Detroit to meet with Fraser. The rumour around Solidarity House was that many of the UAW international executive opposed giving Canada strike authorization for fear we would get a better contract than the Americans got.

Doug and I had an affable discussion about the way the bargaining in Canada was going. I didn't tell him everything, but I was fairly open. He pressed me for details about the money, but I evaded him. "We're still playing around," I said. "You've got to give us some room to work these things out."

Then I told him I thought we would make General Motors the target company in Canada.

"This is a big issue, and we might as well go to where the power is," I explained. "Go where we have the power in the plants and where the corporation has the power in the industry."

He agreed, so there was nothing more to say except to ask for strike authorization. To my relief, he agreed readily. He had a concern, he added, about the PPH, paid personal holidays. The UAW has had PPH in our contracts since 1976. It gives workers nine extra days off a year. The first concession

Fraser gave up were all the PPHs, the easiest cut of all to make because it didn't take money out of the workers' pockets.

"You can have strike authorization," Fraser said, "but not if you want to strike over the PPH. We can't handle that over here."

Rod Andrew already had warned me on the same score. "We're not going to agree to keep the paid personal holidays," he told me sternly. "I want to tell you, my friend, that if you strike us over that, you're in for a long goddamned strike. We'll take you right through Christmas."

The PPHs were always cited as one of the big labour-cost disadvantages that the Big Three faced when competing with Japanese imports. Andrew wanted to get the PPHs out of Canada, now they were gone in the States. If we were tough on this issue, we'd be gone.

I had scheduled a meeting Thursday, three days after seeing Fraser, with all four bargaining committees, GM, Ford, Chrysler, and American Motors, where I planned to announce the selection of General Motors as the target. Doug would have to canvass the other UAW officers by telephone before that date in order for us to have formal authorization. He'd agreed not to go into details with them about our agreement, just explain that I had accepted certain terms, in light of which he was recommending that they approve the strike.

I had a card up my sleeve. I knew there were three PPH days in October, November, and December, which were outside the agreement. When I was younger I might have blurted out to Doug that we had some negotiating room there, but I had learned to keep some things quiet. I discussed them with Nick and Buzz, and we agreed to try to keep those extra three days.

I waited impatiently for Fraser to call. Tuesday passed without word. All day Wednesday went by with no word. Buzz Hargrove asked me, "What if he doesn't call?"

I said, "I'm going anyway. I'll give GM the deadline."

"You *are* nuts," Hargrove grinned.

I knew that Fraser had to give us the right to strike. To deny it would have been the end of the international union. We had followed the rules exactly and they had no grounds on which to refuse us. Fraser just wanted to make me sweat and I did. The phone rang just before midnight Wednesday. We had the strike authorization, he said.

Just before the meeting the next morning, I called the chairmen of the bargaining committees up to my room in the Skyline Hotel. There was Ray Wakeman, head of the Ford team, Phil Bennett of GM, and Kenny Gerard of Chrysler. They all understood Chrysler wasn't a contender as the target.

Because workers there were at a disadvantage and the fight was to get back lost ground, it couldn't set the pattern. The choice was between GM and Ford, and Wakeman and Bennett were each keen to lead the negotiations.

I looked around the room at the three guys heading our bargaining and felt good. They were all bright men, strong and intelligent. I turned to Phil.

"Are you ready to go to work, Bennett?"

He got up with tears in his eyes and paced rapidly up and down to get control of himself. "Goddamn it," he said in a choked voice.

As a courtesy I called Owen Bieber, head of GM for the UAW. There was no warmth between us. He accepted the news without wishing us well.

The next step, before facing the media waiting for me, was to notify Stan Surma of Ford and Rod Andrew of GM.

"I've got some good news for you," I told Andrew. "You're going to be the target. Are you ready to go to work?"

He replied, "Let's get at it. We'll meet your committee this afternoon."

Then I called Surma.

"I've got some good news for you. You can take a rest for a few weeks while we sort our shit out with GM."

He paused. "I've got mixed feelings," he said. "I don't like being first, but sometimes it's nice to have a say in your own destiny."

It was the first time Canadians had ever made the announcement of the target. I pushed my way through a lot of media on the way to the room where the leadership of the Ford, General Motors, Chrysler, and American Motors locals were waiting for the news. We were making history and everyone knew it.

CHAPTER FIFTEEN

Target, General Motors

I N THE ROOM WHERE our bargaining committees had gathered, the atmosphere was extremely tense. I could see money changing hands as last-minute bets on the target were placed. I rather cruelly prolonged the suspense. I opened by saying that I'd been to Detroit that week and things were fine with Doug Fraser. Then I complimented the local leadership for getting the strike votes in the face of the fear that was running through all the plants. I complimented the workers on their courage in voting to strike if they had to.

I looked around, taking my time and savouring it, and then said, offhandedly, "I just hope the GM guys are ready to go to work."

The place broke into deafening cheers and applause. Men shook hands with the grinning GM bargaining team and clapped them on the back.

When it was quiet I said, "Of course most of that applause came from the Ford guys," and they laughed.

The evident solidarity and comradeship in the group filled me up with pride. A Ford worker got up and said, "I wish it had been us, but we want to tell you guys at GM, if you have to hit the bricks, then we'll go to our membership right away and raise money for you. We won't screw around, we'll raise our dues to help." The Chrysler guys said the same.

When I announced to the media that General Motors was the target, they all asked *why?* My reply was simply that GM was the largest company and it was making money in Canada.

"What we've done here today is not select a strike target in the hope of having a strike, but select a strike target in the hope of getting a settlement."

We had three weeks to get an agreement. If we didn't have one by one minute past midnight in the morning of September 15, 34,000 workers would strike General Motors.

That afternoon we began the first bare-knuckle bargaining session with GM, knowing we'd be at it seven days a week until the deadline, if that's what it took. Our first decision was to establish an artifical deadline, September 14. That gave us a cushion of twenty-four hours to call off the strike before the workers went out, so they wouldn't lose a day or two of pay.

The twenty-five General Motors negotiators sat on one side of a long table and the twenty-five-member Canadian UAW bargaining team on the other. Andrew and I sat opposite one another. Expressionless, he read the General Motors proposal, a replica of the concession contract signed in the States. We said it was an insult. He next tabled a slightly better version, which we also turned down flat. Then we got serious.

Andrew handled himself well during this round. I found him an interesting man with a fresh approach to GM and a good deal of flexibility on some issues. On others, and I could read him very well, he was not flexible at all. My hunch was that he had more elbow room than he was revealing. I didn't know how much, but I suspected that GM in Canada wasn't going to hold out for the same deep concessions it had extracted from the UAW in the States.

After a few days, I was certain that Andrew was getting interference from Detroit. I couldn't figure out why Andrew wasn't being consistent. At times he seemed to agree that GM in Canada wasn't in the same boat as GM in the States and then, the next day, he'd harden and insist that we were. I realized I needed to talk to him in private, and soon.

I met with Phil Bennett, the burly, bearded head of the GM bargaining committee, and members of his team to tell them what I wanted to do. When negotiations are in a logjam, it sometimes helps if I can meet privately with my counterpart, I explained. I needed that privacy in order to say, "Look, we're stuck. We're not bound by anything we say to one another here, so let's talk to see if we can get through this block."

I explained to Bennett and the others, "Obviously this is the most critical bargaining the Canadian UAW has ever been in and I intend to use every means, including private meetings, to work it out. Without question, you guys will make the final decision, but I hope everyone in this room understands that I have to have the freedom to hold one-on-one meetings with Andrew when that seems advisable."

There was no argument; everyone accepted it.

So there would be no misunderstanding, I always informed Phil Bennett fully of every meeting I had with Andrew. Bennett almost lived in the temporary UAW offices we had established in a row of hotel bedrooms. I spent hours talking to him, to the staff, and to the other GM guys about the PPHs, about plant closing benefits, about pensions, and the other major issues on the table.

The inconsistencies continued. One day I had a session until late in the evening about a certain increase of thirty-five cents in March 1985. The next morning I again met with Andrew alone and he referred casually to "the increase of twenty-eight cents."

"Wait a minute, what are you talking about?" I asked. "Last night we said thirty-five cents."

Andrew looked at me levelly. "It can't be thirty-five cents," he said.

I didn't think GM was balking at seven cents. That left only one possibility.

"What are you telling me?" I asked quietly. "Are you saying that there's interference from my own union in the United States?"

He didn't reply, but I knew I was right. I had been suspecting it for some time.

I hadn't been telling Fraser much about what was going on, so he and Owen Bieber had been calling General Motors. GM had no reason not to tell the president of the UAW what the GM Canadian bargaining team was doing, so Fraser and Bieber were getting a full report of our negotiations. I believed that because thirty-five cents would create problems with the GM locals in the States, Fraser had knocked the increase down. I appreciated that Fraser didn't want Canada to get too good a contract with General Motors, but I was so furious at the sabotage that when I left Andrew I was shaking.

Marilyne had come to the Royal York to visit me, bringing our daughter Robyn, then a baby of about one. They were waiting for me in the union's temporary office. On an impulse I plucked Robyn out of her stroller and went back to Andrew's suite. I rapped hard on his door, not concerned who might be with him. He opened it, amazed to see me standing there with the baby. Over his shoulder I recognized some top GM brass, astounded expressions on their faces.

I indicated Robyn. "I just want to tell you that when we're in trouble, I bring in the heavyweights to help me in bargaining."

Andrew was amused. He took an immediate interest in Robyn and became so fond of her that he used to send cards on her birthday.

I was still sizzling about Solidarity House. To protect their asses with their members in the States, the UAW leadership was doing its best to defeat a good settlement in Canada. We were also taking a beating in the media in both countries, which portrayed the Canadian UAW as stupid, arrogant, and irresponsible. A strike at General Motors was almost certain, people said, because White was pig-headed. One respected research group in New York predicted a three-month strike in Canada. I felt beleaguered from all sides.

The new GM president in Canada, Don Hackworth, made a speech at the Automotive Day luncheon at the Canadian National Exhibition. Protocol required that he make no reference to the contract negotiations, and he observed it. However, reporters crowded around him when he left the platform, asking questions about the bargaining. Hackworth used the scrum to made some dumb remarks to the effect that if the Canadian UAW didn't follow the pattern in the States and make major concessions, General Motors would start to pull out of Canada. He said that GM could cut production in Canada by 40 per cent and still meet the conditions of the Auto Pact.

Public sympathy swung against the company. Peter Trueman, a thoughtful commentator on Global television, made a statement that was almost vicious, the most critical of an employer that I'd ever heard from the media. He declared that companies elsewhere in the world had been nationalized for less, and he lectured GM for behaving like a child who picks up his marbles and goes home when the game starts to go against him.

The tone in editorials was "Does GM think we're a banana republic?" Whatever ambivalence there had been in the plants about no concessions vanished. Outraged workers demanded to know who the hell Hackworth thought he was. Premier Bill Davis of Ontario declared that a GM pullout was "unthinkable."

I didn't take Hackworth's threat seriously. GM was paying wages in Canada, in real terms, that were seven dollars an hour cheaper than wages in the States. I was busy thinking how we could get the most out of Hackworth's blunder. I didn't want Hackworth's statement to become the focal point of the bargaining.

I discussed it with staff and the bargaining team, and we agreed that I should put a lid on it. My comments to the media were mild. I said Hackworth was uninformed and I thought he should cool his rhetoric. His remarks about GM being in trouble in Canada were "at variance with the facts."

I called Andrew. "I'm going to tear your ass off at the bargaining table," I warned him. He was expecting no less.

The full bargaining teams met later that evening and I opened with a blistering attack on Hackworth. Andrew had no defence. The other guys on our side then had their say, after which I slapped my hands on the table and said, "Okay, that's behind us. Let's get back to bargaining."

That night I happened to encounter Hackworth as I was getting off the elevator in the hotel.

"Howya doing?" I asked.

"I've had better days," he responded.

"Good," I grinned.

As USUAL, we had divided up responsibilty for various parts of the contract. My part included most of the economics – wages, the cost of living allowance, and the paid personal holidays. I had been hoping for a three-year agreement, but Andrew insisted on a two-year term. Nick was my assistant on health care and pensions, Buzz on SUB, and all members of the bargaining committee played key roles.

The first time we formally addressed the issue of the PPHs, Andrew was emphatic that GM wanted them out of the agreement.

I gave him a level look. "That's very nice," I nodded. "That's fine that you've given me the message and I hear you, but I'm not impressed one goddamned bit. I've got a message for you, my friend. Maybe if we don't get the PPHs, we'll have a strike. Giving up the PPHs spells concession, and we're not taking any concessions."

Many people have the idea that these sessions are all-night bargaining by men in shirtsleeves, but that's rare. Most of time we work long hours but knock off in the evenings to play cards, go to hockey games, read, or whatever. Those marathon sessions usually only happen when we're facing a strike deadline the next day. We look at our watches and say, "We've got twenty-four hours to settle this. Why don't we try to get it done by ten tonight?"

The system being what it is, we usually go through midnight or beyond. Sometimes you have to bump your nose on the deadline before the pieces of the agreement really start to come together.

I don't get my jollies out of all-night bargaining. In many cases it doesn't make sense and I try to avoid it, but once the momentum starts you can't say, "Look, it's ten o'clock and we're all tired. Let's get some sleep and come back at it at six tomorrow morning. We'll be able to clean it up in a couple of hours." It doesn't work that way. There's always something that comes out of the blue at the last moment that takes much more time to discuss and find a consensus on. When you're rolling, you have to keep going.

In my first heavy bargaining session, the one with Ford in 1973, I didn't know how to take care of myself. Now I try to eat properly and get some exercise. I schedule a run almost every day and I try to get enough sleep.

I get through an all-night session by taking two or three showers during it. When I put on a fresh shirt, it almost feels like I'm getting up after a night's sleep. Exhaustion catches up with me later.

Much bargaining is done in small committee work. The guys take turns stepping back from the table to catch an hour or two of sleep across some chairs or stretched out fully dressed on a bed, alert for the phone to ring to summon them back.

There is no booze. That would complicate things. I've been in some bargaining when the guys got into the sauce and the pace has really slowed down. Something that would normally take an hour to get passed takes five hours instead. I throw up my hands and say, "Look, let's pack it in and go to bed."

You learn from experience. In the beginning I thought that if you argued long enough, you'd get the job done. Now I know that if you keep banging your head against a stone wall all you get is a headache. Sometimes you've got to step back and give it up. It's not the end of the world. You'll get it, but not that night, maybe not in that agreement.

Over the years, people who meet across the bargaining table get to know one another pretty well. For example, the Ford team and Ford management have built up a good rapport and some respect for each other. They still argue about issues, but the tone of the arguments is different. I've heard one of our guys say to another who has been bearing down on a management person, "Hey, back off. That guy is having a helluva problem at home."

Sometimes the people across the table are unpleasant, but that doesn't happen much with the big corporations. They are represented by people with whom you can have a basis of camaraderie. You don't go out to dinner with them, but you can joke with them, which I think is useful to reduce tension. On the other hand, anyone walking in on a hot bargaining session would think there was a war going on. Both sides can give and take with the best. I've been in some heavy sessions with a lot of emotion flowing, each side cursing the other blue. We try to avoid the word "liar" because that word is an attack on integrity. I've used it a few times, but always with the knowledge that it means the relationship is over.

A lot of people seem to think that I'm a moderate at the bargaining table, a reasonable and calm man, but our bargaining committees know that when we have a point to make, I do it forcefully. Civil exchange becomes very difficult if the company is using scabs or threatening to close a plant. Mostly, though, I think it's important to keep the dialogue going and I make every possible effort to do that.

During these sessions with GM, the mood in the plants, stirred by some skillful propaganda by the company, was that PPHs were something workers could give up. Our members were braced to lose, so the paid personal holidays seemed the most dispensible of all their fringe benefits. The message to me was that they didn't want a strike if it was over the PPHs. Our GM bargaining team understood the mood of the members but I agreed with Sam Gindin, who believed that giving up the PPHs was a major step backward.

My position wasn't good, however. Andrew was willing to leave the COLA intact, do something about income security, give something to retirees, and even provide one wage increase. That meant we had a much better contract than GM workers got in the States. Our members wouldn't be pleased to strike because the PPHs were missing from the package. Andrew knew the situation. I never doubted that he also knew I didn't have Fraser's authorization to strike over the PPHs.

Nevertheless, I pressed to save them and got a compromise. The PPHs would be kept for 1982, which gave the workers October, November, and December that year, but would come out in 1983. I hated it and made no secret of my distress. We had promised no concessions, but we were making one. Still, I knew it was the best we could get. General Motors certainly wasn't going to let us keep the holidays, at least not without a long strike.

With the strike deadline a week away, we were all showing the strain. I admitted to the media that the negotiations were the most stressful collective bargaining sessions I'd ever been in.

Somewhere around three in the morning on September 13, Andrew read us the final draft of their proposal. Just before, Bennett and I had talked to Andrew privately. He had assured us this was their absolute final position, nothing more would be on the table, and we believed him. Andrew read out the clauses one by one, raising his voice to be heard the length of the long table where some fifty exhausted people slumped.

Only a few reporters were still hanging around at that hour. I saw four, John Deverell from the *Toronto Star*, Sheila McGovern from the *Windsor Star*, Mike Phillips from the *Tribune*, the Communist Party paper, and Mike Babad from the *Oshawa Times*. Unknown to us all, they had located a way to get behind the hotel freight elevator next to the room in which we were meeting. By putting their ears against the wall, they heard every word of the proposal that Andrew read.

The UAW caucus withdrew to consider. We listened, haggard with fatigue, while Sam Gindin went over an analysis of the economic issues, writing the figures on a blackboard. We finally agreed by a vote, formally moved and seconded, that we would accept GM's proposal. The non-economics hadn't yet been completed, but we figured they would fall into place quite easily. Bennett and the other committee members hadn't wanted to lose any of the PPHs. However, they thought it a victory that they wouldn't be lost until 1983.

GM agreed that we would keep the details secret until the membership was notified. I called Doug Fraser to tell him we had a settlement and he congratulated me. He, of course, knew exactly what was in it and he couldn't have been happy. With the Canadian UAW's success in getting a good contract out of GM without a strike, Fraser knew he would by criticized by his U.S. membership. Maybe things were tougher in the States, but the UAW, in my opinion, hadn't given the proper leadership against the direction the corporations wanted to take them.

Fraser met this criticism in a letter sent to all UAW locals in the States, in which he explained for the first time the wage differential in Canada. The implication was that given our big cost advantage, we really should have done better in our agreements.

I thought the explanation of the differences between conditions in Canada and the United States had come a little late. If Solidarity House had done that from day one, we would not have had the split in the international membership.

I called McDermott with news of the GM settlement, hauling him out of a CLC executive meeting. His comment was, "Bloody marvellous." I then notified Premier Bill Davis, who was warmly courteous.

Around ten the next morning, we called a press conference to announce the settlement. I said it was a good one but I was noncommittal about the details. I simply called it "the best collective agreement possible short of a strike."

John Deverell asked innocently, "Is this a concession agreement?"

"No, it's not," I said, "but I'll let the workers decide that."

"Did you give up the PPH days?" he went on.

"I'll deal with that when we announce the details," I told him.

He asked some other pointed questions, but I continued to stonewall. It wasn't until I read his story on the front page of the *Toronto Star* that afternoon that I realized he had been playing with me. He knew the answers to his questions as well as I did.

When the GM workers got news of the settlement, only twelve hours from the strike deadline, they celebrated. The guys told me later that the GM plants, especially the big one in Oshawa, erupted like New Year's Eve. Workers cheered, blew horns, and threw their arms around one another. No one ever remembered seeing such jubilation and enormous relief. The workers' families were absolutely ecstatic to learn that there wouldn't be a strike. Few had expected that we would avoid it. They knew GM would be asking for concessions and it was certain that we were committed to no-concessions. Everyone was convinced we'd never get a settlement without a strike.

We were all pleased with ourselves. Given the mood of the times, it was a major achievement to have a contract with gains in it. Canadian workers, braced for cuts, got increases instead. For the first time in labour history, GM workers in Canada were paid more than GM workers in the United States. We had managed to keep the COLA. Also, we had fulfilled our commitment to our retirees and we got major plant-closing benefits that meant lump sum payments starting at $10,500 for twenty-five-year employees. We had also got improvements in the SUB, and improvements in health care benefits.

I went to the Local 222 ratification vote in an arena in Oshawa packed with 8,000 members. There were some questions about the lost PPHs but they accepted my explanation that GM simply wouldn't budge. Eighty-nine per cent of production workers and 85 per cent of skilled trade workers voted for the agreement, the highest ratification vote that we had registered in years.

The reaction everywhere was heartwarming. For the first time in UAW history, Canadians had bargained with General Motors entirely on our own, and we had acquitted ourselves so creditably that even GM had some complimentary things to say.

The public profile of the Canadian UAW was changed by the 1982 General Motors contracts. The media hailed us as heroes. The *Toronto Star* had a congratulatory editorial under the heading WELL DONE, BOB WHITE. My staff and I, unaccustomed as we were to such praise, immediately worried that it was meant sarcastically. But the tone of most comments was admiring. The media seemed to be saying, "Those auto workers aren't stupid after all, they're not trying to drive industry out."

Dennis McDermott called his wife, "Let's buy a bottle of champagne and celebrate. Today General Motors recognized that Canada is a foreign country."

ON THE SAME DAY as the press conference announcing the GM agreement, Buzz, Nick, Sam, and I, with others of our support staff, moved into the Westbury Hotel. That afternoon we met with our Ford bargaining team, which had been sitting around for three weeks waiting for us to get the GM contract concluded.

Jim Donegan, chairman of the Ford passenger car plant workers, listened as I outlined the details of the GM settlement. He's a great speechifier and when I was finished he really let me have it. He said that I'd made a lot of noise about no concessions, I'd made a commitment to no concessions, but when it came crunch time I'd waved a white flag. "It was the biggest retreat since Dunkirk," he said disgustedly.

I hadn't been to bed in two days, so I was in no shape to take that crack about the white flag. The hair stood up on the back of my neck. Enraged, I tore into Donegan.

Ray Wakeman, head of the Ford bargaining team, touched me on the shoulder and said softly, "Hey brother, slow down." I shook him off. "I just ain't gonna take this," I snapped.

I traced all the stages of the GM talks, punctuating each step with, "Is that a white flag?" I couldn't get over Donegan attacking me that way.

When the meeting ended, I went up to Jimmy with my hand out.

"I just want you to know," I said, "that there was nothing personal in what I said."

"I think if you'd been through what I have, you'd have responded the same way," I added. "I hope you'll look at the settlement differently when we get through with Ford."

I took the subway back to the Royal York where my clothes still were and I almost was physically sick. I discovered I could scarcely stand. I think that run of adrenalin when I blew up at Donegan just finished me.

My eye caught my own face on the cover of Maclean's magazine on a newsstand, with the line, LABOR'S BIG RETREAT. I was shocked. I thought, as most people did, that it referred to the GM contract. The story inside, however, was complimentary to me and the Canadian UAW. The heading wasn't about me, but referred to the general trend across the labour movement because of the recession.

The Ford team had to pull itself together to face the company. We told Stan Surma, head of Ford's industrial relations, that we wanted only twelve days of bargaining before the strike deadline. I called Solidarity House and advised Don Ephlin, the UAW vice-president in charge of Ford, that we had a deadline for one minute past midnight on September 28. That took us to the only week before November when all Ford assembly plants would be working. Ford was down all over the place. While we bargained, St. Thomas had worked only a few weeks of the preceeding months. If we had a strike, we'd be taking workers off unemployment insurance and SUB to put them on strike pay.

Ford was prepared to take a strike. For months the company had been stockpiling engines and glass. Ford had so much glass in warehouses that after the settlement, Niagara Glass was almost totally shut down for three months.

Ford's proposal to us was full of drastic cuts and take-aways. As well, the company wanted to change seniority provisions, job postings, layoff provisions, and other non-economic matters. I explained to our bargaining team that I would have private meetings with Stan Surma as necessary to get things going. When Surma and I were alone, I made it plain that we would tolerate no concessions beyond the PPHS – none at all. He knew I meant it but declared that Ford wouldn't meet those terms. Then we went back into the general session.

Day after day, Ford insisted it wouldn't accept the GM agreement as the pattern and we maintained without wavering that nothing less was acceptable. The talks were deadlocked.

Along with the 14,000 hourly workers in our Ford locals, we were also representing some 500 salaried office workers in Windsor and another hundred or so in Bramalea, who had formed white-collar locals. Usually, when the work force is mixed between salaried and hourly wage earners, we clear away the heavier part of the bargaining first and then address the office workers' contract. This time, however, Ford wanted deep concessions from its office staff. We didn't have the bargaining power with the 600 office workers that we did with the 14,000 plant workers and Ford wanted to take advantage of that.

I consulted with Ray Wakeman and his bargaining team and they agreed that we had to protect the office workers. I told Ford that we wanted the economic settlements for the plant and office workers to be done together. If they were going to mess around with the office workers, they would face a strike in the plant as well.

I wasn't sure that the plant workers really would have gone out for the office staff, but we certainly convinced Ford that they would. Otherwise Ford would have left the salaried employees out to dry. Close to strike deadline, we pushed our point home by suspending talks on all plant issues for two days, refusing to discuss anything but the office workers' agreement.

Right up until the final day Ford talked about shutdowns and waited for our nerves to crack, but we stood up to the pressure. That wasn't easy. We knew if we struck Ford, the company would leave us out a long time. Wakeman worked his head off. Office workers represented only a small fraction of the membership, but he fought like hell for them.

With only hours to go before the strike deadline, the company finally gave up its major demands on the office workers, and we had a mad scramble to put the rest of the pieces together. Eventually we got an agreement, which differed in some parts from the GM agreement, but basically matched the economic package.

Just before midnight, we went over the final offer clause by clause with our full bargaining committee and the Ford Council. For the first time in its history, that group accepted the tentative settlement without a long debate. Jim Donegan was more than satisfied with the agreement, which he had criticized so strenuously two weeks earlier.

The ratification vote at Ford got an overwhelming response – 90 per cent of the production workers, 73 per cent of skilled trades, and 95 per cent of office workers voted in favour of the agreement.

WHILE THE FORD NEGOTIATIONS were running, I gave what attention I could to Chrysler and the next round of collective bargaining coming up. The prospect of going to Windsor did not appeal to me at all. For one thing, there were the memories of the near-riot outside the Chrysler office, but what bothered me more was being so close to Detroit and Solidarity House's interference.

I called Bill Fisher, the Chrysler labour relations director in Canada.

"I think it's bad for us to conduct our negotiations in Windsor," I told him, reminding him about the near riot at the plant gates. "We might as well be holding our bargaining in the middle of a Local 444 membership meeting."

He chuckled at that and agreed it wasn't the best place to meet. He sent people down to look at the facilities in the Westbury that Ford was using, and agreed to the move.

Our Chrysler bargaining people in Windsor weren't pleased when I told them about the move. It would mean leaving their families for maybe weeks. I pointed out the advantages, one of which was increased media attention. Some of the Chrysler guys had been in the Westbury during the conclusion of the Ford talks and they had been impressed at the masses of media packing the corridors. Nothing remotely like that ever happened in Windsor except on the rare occasions when the Detroit media took an interest, so that aspect appealed to them. In Toronto, they would have a chance to talk to the media about their issues instead of always being asked about Solidarity House. So they agreed to move.

On the day we settled with GM, I had received a phone call from Tom Miner, Chrysler's vice-president in charge of industrial relations in Detroit.

He was the man who had gloated in 1980 that he couldn't wait to meet me across the bargaining table in 1982, he was going to make me eat concessions.

"Howya doing brother?" he asked. It amuses him to call me brother, which is how male UAW members refer to each another formally at meetings.

After the pleasantries, he said, "I just want to tell you, brother, that the GM settlement is too rich for our blood. If you have any idea about coming to us for the same kind of stuff, you can forget it."

"As a matter of fact Tom," I responded, "I'm glad you called because I was about to call you. You're right. The GM settlement doesn't apply to Chrysler. We want a lot more from you. It's time you started paying workers back for the concessions they've already taken."

"I guess we both know what our fight will be about then," he said heavily.

Chrysler came to Toronto full of fight. Doug Fraser had just finished negotiations with Chrysler in the States and a one-year contract was about to go to the locals for the ratification vote. It was a shocker, full of bad news for workers who had been expecting to get back some of the three dollars an hour they had given up for two years. Instead, the tenatative agreement provided only twenty-five cents an hour up front and some profit-sharing.

Chrysler was asking the same from us. It didn't make sense. Chrysler had turned the corner and was pulling out of the slump. We spent a day talking over every aspect thoroughly, using Sam Gindin's analysis of Chrysler's improving financial position. The company had started to pay back the banks and some of its parts suppliers, but it was unwilling to be fair with its workers, who had made serious sacrifices when Chrysler was in trouble.

Our Chrysler guys were absolutely determined to get back some of that lost pay. I took a more cautious approach. I agreed with them and admired their spirit, but I wasn't sure we could get as much as they wanted.

"We'll try to get as much as we can," I said, "and I agree that you have a right to get that money back, but I'm just not sure we can do it."

I talked to Doug Fraser about a strike deadline. He said he was facing a potentially adverse ratification vote in the Chrysler plants, and he'd like us to wait before getting in position to strike in Canada. If his members turned down the contract, he didn't want to go right back at Chrysler. He planned another ballot to ask the workers if they wanted him to reopen negotiations on November 1 or postpone them until some time in the New Year. I understood his reasoning. The workers almost certainly would opt for the delay, since asking them if they want to look at a strike before Christmas is like asking them to vote to shoot their mothers.

I said it would be difficult to postpone our strike deadline while he sorted that out, but to help him we would do it.

Chrysler workers in the States rejected the agreement by about 70 per cent. For the first time in UAW history, the membership repudiated an agreement with one of the Big Three. Doug was prepared for the defeat, but it stung. He was not only the president of the union, he also headed its Chrysler department.

The vote only complicated matters for us. We'd been hoping that Chrysler and the American UAW would get a settlement so we could see what we were dealing with, but now everything was up in the air. Once again, we would be setting the pattern.

CHAPTER SIXTEEN

A Buck Fifteen Up Front

W E MOVED NEGOTIATIONS with Chrysler to the Westbury Hotel on October 5, 1982. Chrysler expected us to set a short deadline as we had with Ford, but that was out of the question. Not only had we promised Fraser a delay, but there were literally hundreds of amendments to make to the old Chrysler agreement. This was our first independent negotiation, after years of being covered by the international agreement, and the paperwork alone was mind-boggling.

We fixed a strike deadline of November 5. That meant the chilling possibility of a Christmas strike, with loss of paid holiday time. The Chrysler bargaining team wasn't pleased with the date. Five weeks to the deadline looked like a stall. The guys were troubled, but they understood the situation and went along with it.

Their concern was valid, they knew their membership. When the strike date was announced, all hell broke loose in the plants. The workers, who had expected a strike deadline of October 15, simply exploded. They thought I was no better than Fraser.

Some guys in Windsor walked out. When the stewards got them back, a smartass foreman came along and said the workers would be disciplined. With that, the plant was gone, a wildcat strike. Some four or five hundred workers angrily milled around one of the Chrysler assembly plants, drinking, setting bonfires, and tipping over a truck to vent their frustrations. The police were afraid to interfere for fear of touching off a riot. People living in nearby houses didn't dare go out.

Almost same thing happened at the Chrysler trim plant in Ajax. People stopped working, put on their coats and walked out. That surprised me because there were no militant agitators in Ajax as there were in Windsor.

"What the hell is going on?" I asked Gerard. "I know the workers are fed up, but this is crazy."

We had to get the workers back. I sent Buzz Hargrove and Jimmy O'Neil, our staff man for Chrysler, to talk to the Ajax workers.

"No problem," Buzz said as he left. "They just feel like raising some hell. They're probably cooled down already."

He called about two hours later. "Holy Christ," he said. "This is almost a riot. I've never been at a membership meeting like this in my life. They're about ready to lynch me. There're people running on the stage screaming about the union taking away their wages in the concession agreements. I tried to tell them that we didn't recommend that agreement, but they're blaming us anyway. The whole place is yelling *Sell Out!*"

He stayed and talked to the night shift until they calmed down and agreed to go back in. Then he drove to the Westbury, a worried man, to talk it over with me.

"This is bad, worse than we thought," he said. "Some of those workers have lost their homes because of the concessions. They're bloody mad – at us. They don't trust us. They think we're trying to manipulate them like what's happening in the States."

We designated the Local 444 chairman and two full-time local union officials to talk to the guys in Windsor. They went in with a loudspeaker, but the mob just ran them off the grounds. It scared the hell out of them. Buzz Hargrove, who is from Local 444, and Kenny Gerard hurried down on a plane. Around eleven that night, they bravely waded into the angry crowd. It was a wild, dangerous scene. They saw guys with switchblades cutting the cables of TV cameras.

Kenny and Buzz kept talking and talking. Buzz later admitted he'd felt his life in danger that night. They called a meeting of the whole steward body for the next morning and, after a lot of hard work, they got the guys back in the plant. Chrysler, meanwhile, announced it wouldn't negotiate until we got the wildcat strikes under control.

"Isn't that great," I snapped. "You guys are sitting in your comfortable goddamned offices and your stupid foreman precipitates a dispute. Our guys have to take all the shit from workers who are mad as hell because of the lousy concessions your company pushed on them two years ago."

It was desperately important that we get those workers back inside. It was a test of our control of the membership. If we didn't succeed, we'd lose our credibility with Chrysler, and bargaining would be in chaos.

Someone from the Windsor Chamber of Commerce had the audacity to send me a telegram condemning the Canadian UAW for taking a different policy from the American one. It suggested we were stupid not to postpone the negotiations, as Fraser had done, and that we weren't showing any decent concern for the future of Chrysler.

I retorted with a blistering telegram to say that I expected them to show more interest in workers getting some money back so they could spend it in the Windsor area, and that I didn't appreciate their advice on collective bargaining. They had been silent when Windsor workers at Chrysler were forced into concessions, so the least they could do now was give workers their support.

We printed both telegrams in a leaflet, which we distributed in the Chrysler plants. The mood changed overnight. Workers saw that we were speaking up for them and started to feel better about their leaders.

We were getting more media attention than we had ever had before. The Canadian UAW appeared to be on a victorious roll after GM and Ford; now it faced Chrysler, where concessions in the auto industry had started. Fraser was saying that the industry would improve in the New Year. "We can do better in January than we did in September," he promised. Yet, here were the crazy Canadians with a November strike deadline. Everyone wanted to know what was happening at the Westbury.

Not much. We were insisting on a major up-front increase and further increases in the second and third years that would give us wage parity with GM and Ford at the end of three years. Chrysler acted hurt and incredulous that we could be so unreasonable.

I told them that I knew Chrysler was paying back the banks and its suppliers, it was about time they started to pay back their workers. We had an edge on Chrysler workers in the States. The company's labour-cost per hour in the States worked out to about twenty dollars, while in Canada it was around twelve. We also knew that the New Yorker, which was built in Windsor, was Chrysler's best-selling car.

In September, Maurice Closs, president of Canadian Chrysler, had announced that Chrysler-U.S. made a profit of $256.8 million in the first six months of 1982, a dramatic turnaround from the $268.6 million loss in the same period in 1981.

"The workers made the greatest sacrifice to help Chrysler when it was in trouble," I said. "Now that it's coming back, some of Chrysler's investment now has to be in human relations."

On the night of October 23, a Saturday, Buzz called me at home. "I have some bad news," he said. "Kenny Gerard just had a heart attack."

We both immediately remembered how Kenny had waded into that near-riot at Chrysler only two weeks earlier. I was devastated. I was scared I was going to lose a good friend and scared because Kenny was the head of the Chrysler bargaining team, and I depended on him to lead the negotiations in the committee. John Gatens, the vice-chairman, was a capable person, but Kenny was one of the best negotiators anywhere. The next day, Kenny had a second heart attack, a massive one that nearly killed him.

With heavy hearts, we resumed negotiations on Monday, October 25, where we were faced with something new to deal with – the presence of a CBC television crew. A veteran reporter, Fraser Kelly, host of a news documentary show called "Fraser's Edge," had asked permission to follow me around through the Chrysler negotiations. I'd thought it might help the public to understand that the Canadian UAW was not a monster out to destroy poor Chrysler. I had discussed it with the bargaining team. Some worried about having to watch their language, but on the whole it seemed a good idea and they agreed.

The crew was now in place. The reporter was Susan Ormiston, who later became one of the CBC national news on-camera reporters, and there were a researcher and technicians. Television crews aren't exactly inconspicuous, but we rapidly discovered that when we really got down to work it was easy to forget that they were there.

We had been negotiating with Chrysler for three weeks but very little was happening. The final weekend before the Friday strike deadline was upon us. I called a Sunday-morning meeting of the Chrysler plant and office leadership from all the locals. We were headed for a real Donnybrook, and I needed to know what the mood was.

I listened for almost four hours as some 120 leaders talked about how angry the membership was. Caught between concessions, inflation, layoffs, and high interest rates, people had lost their cars and their homes. I heard stories of marriage breakups, suicides, heavy drinking. In 1980, Chrysler workers had given up wage increases, their PPHS, their COLA, part of their pensions, and other benefits. The plant leadership was unanimous in its opinion that Chrysler had to start making up for those losses.

"That means we'll have to take a strike," I warned.

"That's fine with us," they said. "We're ready."

On Sunday night about 300 leaders from across the Canadian UAW were to meet in Black Lake, Michigan, for a week of education sessions. Our Chrysler bargaining team couldn't make it, of course, but everyone else was there, and I was scheduled to give the opening speech. Doug Fraser gave me permission to charter a plane so Buzz, Nick, and I could get to Black Lake and back the same night.

I had an uneasy feeling. "There's something funny going on in the Chrysler negotiations," I said to Buzz and Nick as we prepared to go. "Chrysler's misreading us. They don't think we're serious. There's no proposals, there's no movement on non-economic issues. They're just sitting there. They don't think I'm in control here. They think Fraser's calling the shots and there's not going to be a strike. We've got to get our message across."

I called Bill Fisher, the head of labour relations for Chrysler. "I'd like an off-the-record meeting," I said.

"Who will you have with you?" he asked.

"Buzz, Nick, and Jimmy O'Neil."

"Okay, I'll have Bob Weiske and Bill Lobeck." They were his closest assistants.

Fisher was staying in the Westbury in a corner room directly above mine. I went there.

"Let's put away the pencils and papers," I told him. "This is off the record. There's something going on in these negotiations that I don't understand. I know you're not the decision-makers, but you'd better get to whoever the hell is the decision-maker. You're going to have a strike on Friday if we don't get money up front, and a lot of other things on the bargaining table."

They weren't impressed. "Fraser isn't going to stop the strike," I went on. "We're in charge of these negotiations, and a strike is going to happen whether Iacocca wants to stop it, or Tom Miner wants to stop it, or Bill Fisher wants to stop it. Someone better get the goddamned message through to Detroit that we're not screwing around here."

I told Fisher, looking at him levelly, that someone was misreading us. "Someone thinks we're going to cave. I've just met with our local leadership and I can tell you that we're not going to cave. They thought that in GM, they thought it in Ford, and they were wrong. They're wrong as hell here."

With that we left. "Let's see where that one goes," I said to Buzz and Nick. "If they feed that message to Detroit, we'll start getting some calls."

At the education meeting, I told our leadership about the negotiations we'd just been through with GM and Ford and what was happening at Chrysler. A strike at Chrysler looked very likely, and if it happened, we'd be asking all of them to raise money to help the strikers.

The mood was very good. We seemed to have gained confidence in ourselves from the GM and Ford contracts and some other victories we'd achieved that year in the auto-parts industries. No one was happy about the strike, but they were all behind the principle that Chrysler workers had suffered enough. If it took a strike to get something back for them, then a strike it had to be.

Buzz, Nick, and I went back to the airport to return to Toronto, but Toronto was fogged in. When I called home, Marilyne said that Doug Fraser was trying to reach me.

"If he calls again, tell him I'm tied up in fog," I said. I didn't want to talk to Fraser. I knew that Chrysler had delivered my message straight to him, and I didn't want to hear what he had to say. When I eventually got to my room in the Westbury in Toronto well after midnight, the message light on the phone was blinking. Fraser, I figured. I put a pillow over it and went to sleep.

The phone started to ring first thing in the morning, but I ignored it. I showered and went to my office in the hotel. "If Doug Fraser calls," I said to the staff, "tell him I'm tied up in a committee caucus."

I met the committee and told them, "We're getting down to the wire guys. We're going to have to hold hands. Something's going to happen soon. Either we're on strike or something's gonna break."

Around eleven, I went back to the office and put in a call to Fraser.

"Christ, I've been trying to reach you since last night!" he started.

"Really?" I said. "That's too bad. I was tied up with fog and meetings. What's on your mind?"

"It's probably too late now, but I wanted you to come to Detroit to meet with me and Marc Stepp and Lee Iacocca about the Chrysler negotiations."

I didn't want to meet with Iacocca in Detroit, and certainly not along with Fraser and Stepp. That would be three against one, as far as I was concerned.

"Yeah, you're right. It is too late," I told Fraser. "If Iacocca wants to meet with me, why don't you tell him to get his ass to Toronto?"

Fraser said, "They've got a smartass named Greenwald. I think they're going to send him."

Gerry Greenwald is Iacocca's right-hand man, the second most powerful person in Chrysler. He runs the day-to-day operation of Chrysler, not Iacocca. Greenwald is young, bright, well-dressed, very smooth. Only the day before, Greenwald had made a speech at Windsor University, in which he said Chrysler wasn't strong enough yet to start restoring the concessions.

"Tell him to come up," I said to Fraser, "and tell him to bring some money with him."

Our guys were excited. The mountain was coming to Mohammed. This was the first piece of good news we'd had since Chrysler negotiations had opened.

"This isn't a bullshit meeting," I warned them. "Greenwald is coming to find out if we're serious. We don't need a lot of rhetoric here. We need an honest expression of how people feel. After he speaks, I'll lead off the discussion, and then we'll get down to the issues. We've got to get our message through to him."

On the afternoon of Wednesday, November 3, 1982, only two days from the strike deadline, we met with Greenwald. He looked cool, calm, and collected, with a three-ring binder under his arm. Behind him were Moe Closs, Bill Fisher, and Tom Miner, followed by their entire bargaining team.

After the usual pleasantries, Greenwald started into his pitch, a long, long presentation about Chrysler's financial situation. He had figures on the whole range of economic issues – inflation, mortgage rates, interest rates, unemployment – and he lectured us with our own statistics as if we'd been on some goddamned island for the last five years.

What he was after, it transpired, was a postponement of the strike deadline until after January. If we went on strike in Canada on November 5, he said, 6,000 workers would be laid off immediately in the States. He warned us it would be a long strike and Chrysler would lose $100 million in the final quarter in Canada. American workers in Chrysler wouldn't get the increase they were hoping for in the collective bargaining that would begin in January.

The postponement was impossible for us. For one thing, the membership would never stand for it. For another, I knew Chrysler was stockpiling in order to take a long strike. I wasn't going to give them another two or three months to get set.

I waited patiently, not interrupting, until he was finished. Closs, Fisher, and Miner had nothing to add. It was our turn. I was furious.

"Who the hell do you think you are?" I said to Greenwald. "A goddamned economics professor? Coming here to lecture us about inflation, unemployment, plant closings? Christ, we live it every day of our goddamned lives."

The Chrysler workers had made sacrifices, I said, "a lot more than you guys ever made – this 'equality of sacrifice' is bullshit. You've sacrificed nothing. There are workers in Windsor who've been laid off for months. They've loaded their families into cars and driven to Alberta looking for jobs. And you're telling us we're not going to get more money? The hell with that. If we don't get more money, you're not going to get any goddamned cars. It's that clear and it's that simple."

After about fifteen minutes I stopped. "I think the committee may have something to say," I said.

Every member of the committee had something to say, the men and the women. They told Chrysler about the hardships, the family stresses, the alcoholism, the suicides. Up and down the room, office workers, skilled tradesmen, and production workers told devastating stories. The language was atrocious because they were really spilling their guts. Even the ones who rarely said much gave Chrysler hell.

Sweat was dripping off Greenwald's chin, plopping on his three-ring binder. Much later, after we knew one another better, he admitted to me that it was one of the toughest meetings of his life.

He said, "Well, I guess we understand what your position is."

The session lasted two and a half hours. Outside, the media mobbed him. He stuck to the company line. If Chrysler had a strike in Canada, he said, "At worse it would be so crippling that we'd never come out of it." The current wages, he claimed, were "all that we can afford."

Later that day, Fisher called for an early evening meeting to put a final offer to us. I hoped it meant a breakthrough, but he warned me carefully and slowly, "My instructions are that the proposal we will make to you tonight will be the identical proposal that was made in the United States."

"You guys are nuts," I said. "That proposal was rejected overwhelmingly by the membership in the States. Your strategy is stupid."

We met across the bargaining table and listened while he presented the same offer that had been turned down by Chrysler workers in the States.

"I'm not even going to get angry about this," I told Fisher. "This is an insult to your intelligence and to mine, and to all the members of both bargaining teams in this room. Whoever told you to do this is a dumb sonovabitch."

The bargaining committee was enraged. Seeing them red-faced and cursing, I feared that the Chrysler plants also would explode. We put out the word to keep the lid on. We needed to show ourselves in total control, and I was sure we could. A week or so earlier, we had started getting telegrams from Chrysler workers, telling us we were doing a good job. The trickle had now become a flood. One telegram was signed by more than 700 workers.

Late that night, Bill Fisher called again. "Can you come up to my room?" he asked. "Tom Miner wants to talk to you on the phone."

Miner said, "Howya doing brother?"

"We're not doing worth a damn," I told him. "We're not going any place. We've got a strike."

"Will you meet Iacocca if he goes to Toronto?" he asked.

"Sure," I answered.

Miner was matter-of-fact. "He'll be in Toronto tomorrow afternoon then. Someone will let you know what the arrangements are as soon as we get it fixed up."

"Fine," I said, using the same impersonal tone.

I tore back to the office, ecstatic, and got Helen Kramzyk to round up the staff and the bargaining committee. We were working all hours, living in the hotel, nobody going home, so it wasn't difficult to pull everyone together in a few minutes.

"Guess who's coming to town?" I asked them, grinning from ear to ear.

"Doug Fraser?" someone guessed.

"No, Iacocca."

They cheered. "Lee Iacocca," someone yelled, *"Come on down!"*

"I don't know what this means," I told them, "but at least he's coming to Toronto. We've got his attention."

I COULDN'T SLEEP that night. When I gave up trying, showered and dressed, it was early Thursday morning. We were a day away from the strike. I had promised not to make a media announcement that Iacocca was coming to Toronto but I was burning to have the story get out. It was unfair as hell to keep this out of the news, the biggest thing that had happened at a Canadian labour negotiation in years. I had to figure how to do that.

A radio station in Ajax had scheduled a phone interview with me that morning around eleven o'clock.

"Do you think you can get this settled without a strike, Mr. White?" the reporter asked.

"I can't answer that," I replied. "I really won't know until after I get through my meeting with Mr. Iacocca this afternoon."

"What!" the reporter said.

When I finished the interview, I warned Wendy Cuthbertson, our media-relations person. "I think those phones are going to start ringing."

I still didn't know where I was going to meet Iacocca.

By a coincidence that was almost bizarre, the federal government had just decided to establish a task force to examine the shaken auto industry in Canada. The industry had been studied to death but always by analysts without first-hand knowledge. The government this time wanted the industry itself to make recommendations. Edward Lumley, the minister of industry, trade, and commerce, had called a meeting late that same morning of the

Canadian heads of the auto corporations and auto parts industry and the head of the Canadian UAW – me.

Moe Closs was at that meeting, representing Chrysler, as was Ken Harrington, president of Ford Canada, Don Hackworth, president of GM Canada, some senior federal government officials, Patrick Lavelle, executive director of the Automotive Parts Manufacturers' Association of Canada, and James Dykes, president of the Motor Vehicle Manufacturers Association. Lumley announced that he wanted recommendations on what must be done to make sure that Canada's auto industry survived. We would be called the Federal Task Force on the Canadian Motor Vehicle and Automotive Parts Industries.

Lumley knew that if he named a president of one of the major auto companies as chairman, the report might be seen as self-serving. So, he suggested I be a co-chair with Pat Lavelle, a former civil servant.

We sat in our good suits, nodding at one another, relaxed and smiling as though we were in another world from the grim bargaining at the Westbury. Closs and I behaved impeccably. We made no reference to the Chrysler strike one day away. The group struck an agenda and agreed to work quickly, reporting in only nine months, on such issues as productivity, new technology, the Auto Pact, and the vexious question of Japanese imports.

At the end of the meeting, Moe Closs approached me with a man I didn't know. Moe Closs introduced him and said, "He'll take you to meet Lee."

The man drove me to the Harbour Castle Hotel on Toronto's waterfront. He opened a door and said, "Mr. Iacocca? This is Mr. White."

Lee Iacocca came toward me, a big cigar in his mouth, hand outstretched. "Bob," he said. "Howya doing?"

Iacocca started pacing around the suite, talking rapid-fire, cutting up Pierre Trudeau, Margaret Thatcher, Ronald Reagan, and "all the dumb sonovabitches who don't know how to run a country."

"Look at the interest rates!" he cried. "How can people buy fucking cars with interest rates so high?"

I watched the performance from a small sofa near the window. Knowing he smoked cigars, I had prepared myself with a cigar of my own. When he got through stomping around, he sat on a sofa opposite me. I leisurely lit my cigar.

"We've got a goddamn problem here with the leadership and the membership, eh?" Iacocca said, looking at me quizzically.

"Pardon?" I asked to give him a chance to rephrase.

"I said, we've got a goddamned problem here with the leadership and the membership."

I sat forward. "Lee, let me tell you something. We've never met before. Let me tell you how I operate. We have no problem here with leadership and membership in Canada. *You* have a problem with *me*. I'm with the leadership and membership and they're absolutely right on this. They want a good piece of money and if they don't get it, you're going to have a strike starting tomorrow."

"Jesus Christ!" he yelled. "That's not fair. I'm in the U.S. bargaining and I get a goddamned agreement that's rejected by the U.S. workers. Fraser says if I give the goddamned Canadians a penny more than I give the Americans, the U.S. plants'll go down, and here you're telling me I have to put in a lot of up-front money or the goddamned Canadian plants'll go down. I'm only the chairman of the board. I can't do anything about it."

"I can't help that, Lee," I said quietly. "The guys have made concessions. . ."

He waved a hand impatiently. "I don't want to hear the sad speeches about the mortgages and the loss of homes. Greenwald told me all that yesterday."

"You may not want to hear about it, but that's the reality," I told him. "There's no point in you and me fooling ourselves. You've got to put money up front."

He looked me over. "What are you talking?"

"A buck fifteen up front," I said, rapping the table. "A buck fifteen up front, and then we'll take a look at a three-year agreement to start putting back the cost of living and . . ."

"We're not going to talk about goddamned parity," he said. "Jesus Christ, you're fighting with Fraser. You're either one union or you're two unions. Goddamn it, I'm caught in the middle . . ."

"I'm not fighting with Fraser," I said.

"Yes you are," he retorted.

"No I'm not."

"You're talking about a Canadian Metalworkers Federation."

That was true. I'd been floating the idea of a loose umbrella organization made up of auto workers, steelworkers, machinists, moulders, rubber workers, and maybe some others to improve co-operation and information sharing.

"Lee," I said, "it wouldn't matter today if we were called the Canadian Association of Sweethearts. It's going to cost you a buck fifteen up front. The workers are entitled to it and we've got to find a way to do it."

"We can't find a way to goddamn do it today," he snapped.

"There's no other way out of this," I told him.

Then he launched into a speech about the state of the industry. I said nothing. He stopped and sat back. "I guess there's gonna be a strike," he said quietly.

I said, "Yes, I guess there is."

The meeting lasted more than an hour. I couldn't get in the door of the Westbury lobby for the media inside, waiting for me. I told them that I couldn't talk until I reported to our committee, but I would hold a press conference immediately after that.

"Can you tell us where the hell he's staying?" someone yelled.

"I promised I wouldn't do that," I replied. "Some hotel close to the water, I don't know where."

Dozens broke away to get down to the Harbour Castle. The *Toronto Star* posted photographers at both airports, and one happened to catch Iacocca sitting in the front seat of a limousine, water streaming down the windshield, on his way back to the Toronto Island airport. It was a great picture and the *Star* ran it on the front page.

With Iacocca in town, industry analysts had to revise their view that the Canadian UAW didn't have any bargaining power with Chrysler. We knew all along that we had bargaining power. Chrysler was recovering, wages were lower in Canada, and the New Yorker car we were building in Windsor was the best in the Chrysler line.

Still I was worried as I faced the committee. "There's no question that we're going to have to strike," I told them. "Even if Iacocca gives us what we want tonight, we'll have a strike tomorrow. There's a helluva lot more work to be done on the agreement."

At the press conference that followed, I described my interview with Lee Iacocca as "frank and dramatic." I said, "He wanted to meet me and see how serious I was. Now he knows we're very serious."

Moe Closs was asked what he thought. He answered that Chrysler was "determined to keep our labour costs under control. Only by doing so can we save this company – and your jobs. We will take a strike if we must, even though we are aware it could put us out of business."

"Robert White has a gun in his hand," John Deverell wrote in the *Toronto Star* that day, "and it's pointed right at Lee Iacocca's head. The chief of Canada's UAW union has the fate of the Chrysler Corporation in his hands – or so it seems. If 9,000 Canadian production workers strike Chrysler Canada Limited tomorrow, they'll cause a fast-moving chain of disruption in many of

Chrysler's North American operations. If the strike lasts long it may create a crisis of buyer confidence that could send Chrysler into the final tailspin it has been struggling since 1979 to avoid. After all his harrowing performances for bankers, shareholders and the U.S. Chrysler Guarantee Board, Iacocca, Chrysler's chairman, must find it bizarre to see all the chips at risk at a union bargaining table in Toronto."

The strike deadline on Friday, November 5, was ten in the morning. At a quarter to ten we had a perfunctory meeting with Chrysler, where we sat looking at our watches. Bill Fisher is a droll man, a towering person who used to play basketball. After ten minutes of gloomy silence, he looked up and down the two rows of dejected faces and said, "You know what this reminds me of? A New Year's Eve party in a funeral parlour."

Ten o'clock came and the Chrysler plants emptied very carefully, 9,600 workers walking out with complete discipline. There wasn't the slightest sign of the unruliness that had occurred only a few weeks earlier. Chrysler was incredulous. Management told me later that the last car off the Windsor assembly line was perfect, not a scratch on it.

Right after the press conference where I announced the strike had begun, a man I'd never seen before started to ask questions. Though he seemed to be a reporter, I doubted it from the dumb things he said. Once or twice he bumped into me hard, pretending it was an accident. I ignored the incident but one of the guys on our bargaining committee, a former motorcycle gang guy, took it very seriously.

"Get some security for White," he advised Buzz. "I don't like the looks of that guy."

I'm not paranoid, but I took his concern seriously. He wasn't one to panic, he knew his way around the street scene. Others were alarmed, too. We'd been getting calls from the States from small companies, the owners screaming at our secretaries that if the sonsofbitches Canadians pushed Chrysler into bankrupcy they'd be ruined, and they'd be coming after us. Other angry calls came from Chrysler parts workers in the States, who were facing immediate layoff when the Canadians walked out. A doctor called from Hamilton, raging that his life savings were in Chrysler shares and threatening to sue me if their value went down. Another time, as I was walking through the airport in Toronto, I heard someone say in a loud, angry voice, "There goes that bastard who's trying to break Chrysler."

I put a call in to Tim Armstrong, the deputy minister of labour, who contacted someone in the office of Premier Davis. In an hour, the Ontario Provincial Police were in our office. They told Buzz and Nick they'd assign someone to watch me for a while. Buzz and Nick explained we didn't want anyone around who had been involved in helping strike-breakers. The OPP said that was understood. They'd find someone we could work with, and they did. He was Ken McLeod, a former National Hockey League referee and OPP officer who was doing some security around the legislature.

He worked out well, a discreet and sensitive man, who became my side-kick right through the Chrysler strike. But he wasn't available that first day. Instead, another man arrived as I was talking to the media later that night, a big guy who pulled a notepad and pen out of his pocket and stood in the crowd scribbling notes, trying to blend in. One of the guys on our bargaining committee came up to me. "Who's the fucking cop down there with a note pad?" he asked. You can't fool workers.

McLeod turned up to escort me home. Marilyne and Robyn were away and the place was empty and felt eerie. McLeod went around, checking the windows, watching the street.

Doug Fraser always had a bodyguard. All the UAW presidents did because of the assassination attempts on Walter Reuther, but it didn't feel right that I should need one in Canada. McLeod slept in a spare room and the next morning checked my car before letting me get in.

I was feeling miserable. I'd figured Chrysler wrong. I thought they should have known from the GM and Ford negotiations that we meant what we said. What we asked was realistic. Why didn't Iacocca grab it?

We had to meet the membership right away. I decided to include the media in those membership meetings. We had nothing to hide, and I was beginning to see that we were getting public support by showing our side of the argument.

We started at Ajax that weekend. "Iacocca is paying back the banks. He's paying back the suppliers. It's about goddamned time he started to pay back the workers," I told the cheering members.

We went to Windsor next. Bob Nickerson had rented the Windsor harness race track. It turned out to be an excellent facility. We put up a temporary stand in front of the glassed-in grandstand so the members sat in comfort.

Our 7,000 members in Windsor were in a happy mood. They'd been waiting to get back at Chrysler ever since Iacocca took away their money. Kenny Gerard, still in hospital, had taped an hour-long message, which the local leadership wanted to play at the meeting. We had a row about it. I said we couldn't ask the membership to sit for an hour and listen to Kenny's voice coming from heaven. Finally it was agreed to cut the tape to five minutes.

Harness horse drivers were training on the track behind the platform.

Every half-minute, one or two sulkies would pass by drawn by a high-stepping horse kicking dirt. We ran Kenny Gerard's tape at the beginning of the meeting. Kenny's voice was strange, floating bodiless from the loudspeakers. It seemed to last forever. I love Gerard, but I couldn't wait for it to end.

"Let me explain what's going on behind me here," I opened my speech, pointing at the sulkies going by. "Those are Chrysler supervisors. They're a bunch of horses asses running around in circles and they don't know what the hell they're doing."

Then I got serious about the strike. I said we couldn't know how it would end, but we would keep the faith. "I can't promise you parity, I can't promise you the moon either. But we'll do our best."

At the press conference later in a dark room under the grandstand, a seasoned, sardonic American labour reporter asked me, "Bob what makes you think the tail can wag the dog?"

I said, "I don't know if a tail can wag a dog," I answered, "but my mother told me a long time ago if you grab that dog's tail long enough and squeeze it hard enough, at least you'll get his head turned around to see who you are. I think we'll get Iacocca's head turned around."

To my surprise, the 444 guys started to hustle me out of the building by an entirely different route than we came in.

"What the hell is going on?"

McLeod replied, "Just when you got up to speak, we got a tip that there was a bomb in one of the television cameras."

There was no bomb. But someone was trying to disrupt the meeting.

I visited the picket lines in Windsor. The strikers assured me that if they had to take a long strike, they could.

As often happens at the beginning of a strike when both sides are miles apart, negotiations in the Westbury were recessed to give both sides a chance to reflect. Our local leadership started to plan Christmas parties for the children of Chrysler strikers. We had to move quickly to get money together to supplement the strike pay. If the strikers couldn't manage on the wages they were getting in the plants, they sure as hell couldn't keep their heads above water long on strike pay.

Ford and GM workers went around their locals asking the membership to double their dues voluntarily to help Chrysler workers. Local 200, in the big Ford plants in Windsor, voted 99.9 per cent in favour of pledging about $40,000 a month – $10 a person – to help the Chrysler strikers. I talked to Dennis McDermott of the CLC and Cliff Pilkey of the OFL, warning them we might need financial support from their organizations.

Tom Miner, Chrysler's head of industrial relations, then made the alarming announcement that Chrysler didn't intend to make another economic proposal until some time in 1983. The company had no intention of allowing the pattern of its agreement to be set in Canada, he said, so Canadian workers would have to wait on the picket lines until Chrysler and the American UAW settled their contract.

An editorial in the *Globe and Mail* described the Canadian UAW as lemmings. The *Toronto Sun* showed me with a gas tank registering empty, and another cartoon showed me going over a cliff in a Chrysler car. I had them framed. They were great cartoons.

Doug Fraser stepped down from the Chrysler board of directors, saying his participation during a strike was "inappropriate."

IN MID-NOVEMBER, I went to a caucus of the UAW international executive in Solidarity House to select the candidate to succeed Doug Fraser as president. Owen Bieber, who came out of the auto-parts industry and was head of the General Motors department, and Ray Majerus, the UAW secretary-treasurer, were the two contenders. I supported Majerus and I thought Fraser did too, but it turned out that he was behind Bieber. Don Ephlin also put himself forward as a candidate but he only got one vote, so he dropped out quickly.

While Majerus and Bieber were committed to trade unionism, I didn't think that either of them – or anyone else on that board – had a vision of where to lead the UAW in the future. Doug hadn't encouraged any younger people to take over leadership, people who would have been willing to take on the corporations and lead the UAW in a different direction.

Majerus and Bieber were tied on the first ballot. On the second, Bieber got four more votes than Majerus. Though I was disappointed, in retrospect I believe Bieber was the better choice, a solid, balanced trade unionist who is committed to the social ideals of the UAW.

That night in Detroit, I went to a meeting of the steering committee for the upcoming international convention. I was not popular. I was asked, "How come the Canadians didn't postpone negotiations when we did? How come they're out, hurting jobs over here?"

That day Doug was quoted in the press as saying that the Canadian strike was "dangerous." He added, "I happen to think we'll have the good sense to settle that strike in Canada before there is any permanent damage."

Gerry Greenwald replied in the same story that Chrysler wouldn't budge. "If the pie was small before, it's going to be almost non-existent by January."

Doug Fraser took me aside. He was worried about reports that shutdowns were imminent in sixteen Chrysler plants – eight in Michigan, five in Ohio, two in Indiana, and one in Alabama. He asked how I felt about the Canadian and the American Chrysler bargaining teams sitting down together. If we picked a common settlement date and agreed that one side would not settle until the other did, we might use our combined clout to get Chrysler to the bargaining table before Christmas.

I'm prepared to explore anything, as long as we're in control, but our guys were nervous when I told them about it. They thought Fraser was trying to lump us in with the American Chrysler workers, just when we'd voted to get out of an international agreement.

"Let's meet with them," I urged. "We can't lose anything by listening to what they have to say."

We arranged to meet on November 17, and Doug suggested that we announce the meeting at a press conference the day before. I objected on the grounds that the Canadian media couldn't get to Detroit.

"They only have to come from Windsor," he said.

"No, there's more than Windsor interested in this," I told him. "People from Toronto are interested, too. They've been following the Chrysler story for two months and you've got to give them a chance at it."

We arranged that I would tell the Canadian media in advance to give them time to attend if they wished. When I notified the Toronto reporters, they pounced on me with questions about the significance of the Detroit meeting. Were we going back into the international agreement? No, I said, we were just looking into possibilities.

The two bargaining committees met on November 17 at Solidarity House. Kenny Gerard insisted on being there, though he had just been discharged from hospital and was heavily sedated and the colour of a sheet. Once I caught him popping a nitroglycerine pill for the heart pain he was experiencing. I wondered if he could live through this.

Dave Mitchell, a bit of a pompous ass who worked for the public-relations department in Solidarity House, was seated next to Wendy Cutherbertson, our communications person. He made some snide comment about the Canadian Chrysler workers being lemmings. The mood around rest of the table was similar. A few American guys shot off their mouths about Canadians putting their jobs in jeopardy and how we were hurting Chrysler. In the end we agreed that Fraser would tell Iacocca that both U.S. and Canadian committees were ready to resume bargaining and that the Canadians would to go back into bargaining in Toronto on Monday.

The next day, Tom Miner was asked for his views on the UAW request to reopen negotiation. He replied that he was willing to talk but "there won't be any new offer."

The Chrysler U.S. workers reopened their negotiations a week later than we did. We reopened negotiations on November 22, and later that same day, I slipped away to attend the Ontario Federation of Labour convention. I wanted to get the OFL to endorse a fight-back policy not only in the private sector but also in the public sector. The discussion had already started when I arrived. Bob Nickerson was at one of the floor microphones and yielded his place to me. When I started to speak, everyone stood and applauded. It choked me up.

Chrysler threatened to move work from the stalled Canadian production lines to the States. "We'd be stupid if we didn't," Tom Miner said. Marc Stepp of the UAW behaved well. "That sounds like confrontation," he said. "We will meet confrontation with confrontation. Our members will refuse to accept the work."

Somewhere toward the end of November, Iacocca made a statement that if we didn't have a settlement by December 13, he would take the strike into the New Year. We knew all along that there would come a point in December when it would be cheaper for the corporation to wait out the year rather than pay wages over the Christmas shutdown.

CHAPTER SEVENTEEN

Winning One and Losing Many

J UST WHEN IT SEEMED the strike was stuck, we heard some great news. Despite the bitterness in the American UAW over the Canadian strike, some Detroit Chrysler workers came across the river and walked the picket lines in Windsor. "We support you guys," they said. "Whatever you get will help us."

Doug Fraser called me on December 6. "Chrysler wants to know what the hell the bottom line is," he said. "They're all through screwing around. What will it take to make a settlement?"

Obviously, Fraser had been negotiating without consulting us, but I wasn't offended. If that's what it took to get this thing settled, I didn't care. I told Doug I'd have to consult and called a session with Buzz, Nick, Sam, and Kenny Gerard. Kenny was back in negotiations, which were scheduled so he could lie down for a couple of hours every afternoon. There were some inherent dangers in giving Chrysler our final figures, but the way things were, we weren't going anywhere anyway.

"Look, we might as well," I said. "I gave it to Iacocca anyway, a buck fifteen up front. There's no water in the pail, that's it."

With a raise of fifty cents an hour in the second year of the contract, a dollar in third year, and restoration of the COLA and some payment for retirees, we'd get back to parity with GM and Ford. We took it that night to the bargaining committee. They were apprehensive, fearing that Chrysler would bargain it down. I said that wouldn't happen. The bottom line was the bottom. After a long, worried discussion, we gave the formula to Bill Fisher and he conveyed it to Tom Miner in Detroit.

"What's your deadline to get Chrysler's response?" Doug Fraser asked me. "Iacocca says you've got to have it settled by the thirteenth."

We'd talked about that. My guess was that Chrysler was playing with us.

We needed time to prepare material and hold ratification meetings, so our deadline was December 9. I told Doug it was midnight Tuesday, December 7, one day away.

I heard nothing from Chrysler or from Fraser all day Tuesday. We sat around, trying to keep from looking as discouraged as we felt. If we lost it now, the negotiations would go flat for a month and the Chrysler workers would be walking the picket lines on Christmas day.

I was preparing to go downstairs for a press conference when Doug Fraser called.

"I've got bad news for you. They can't meet you. I guess we'll just have to let it go until after Christmas. They're not interested in getting a settlement on those terms. And Marc Stepp tells me his talks here with Chrysler aren't going any place either."

We talked a bit, both feeling lousy. He wondered how I felt about asking for less up front. I assured him that was impossible.

"Have you got any ideas?" he asked.

"No," I replied heavily. "If Chrysler isn't willing to meet that buck fifteen up front, there's no point in continuing."

I told Fraser I had the media waiting for a briefing.

He said casually, "Why don't you give me a call when you get finished?"

My neck prickled. Maybe there was something going on that I didn't know about yet.

It was ten at night and I still had to face the media waiting downstairs in the Westbury. My statements were as bleak as I looked. We had almost 10,000 people on strike, shivering in the winter winds, and now it looked as if they were going to be out for another five, six weeks minimum. I said we had given Chrysler the bottom line twenty-four hours ago, but they weren't buying.

About midnight, I called Fraser back.

"I was talking to Tom Miner," Fraser told me. "He's thinking of coming up to Toronto."

"Tell him to come up," I said, "if he's got some goddamned money."

Fraser said, "He didn't say that he has any money."

"Then tell him to stay the hell home," I told Doug.

"What he was saying is that maybe we both should come up," Fraser said, testing the water.

"Sure, come on up."

"You don't mind if I come?"

"No, not at all. Come on up. Doesn't matter to me."

Fraser said, "Let me call you back."

I sat looking at the phone, trying not to let myself get hopeful. Finally it rang.

"We'll be there tomorrow morning," Fraser said.

Despite the lateness of the hour, I pulled the committee together to consider this latest development. I told our communications people to let the media know that Miner and Fraser were coming to Toronto.

The next morning the Westbury lobby was packed with reporters and camera crews, all watching the doors. I stood back in the crowd. The first to arrive was Tom Miner. He's a robust, white-haired man, who has talent as a put-on artist.

"I think if we can find a key to the Canadian situation," he said to the reporters, "things in the United States will fall into place. We have to get a settlement in the next day or so."

When asked about his hopes for a settlement, he answered genially that he'd brought his toothbrush.

That's interesting, I thought.

Doug Fraser was next, trailed by a number of reporters from the Detroit media. He was quite taken aback by the battery of lights and microphones that confronted him. I joined him and we ploughed our way to the elevators, tossing off statements carefully balanced between optimism and caution. "If we try this and fail," I said, "then we've tried everything."

We went to my office upstairs. Doug had one guy with him, Howard Young, the director of the UAW social security department. I had Kenny, Sam, Buzz, and Nick for what I knew would be a hard meeting. I was certain Doug was there to convince us to lower the bottom line. Miner's presence indicated there would be some money, but not what we wanted.

The discussion was frank. How much more up-front money would Chrysler pay in the States? How much more in Canada? Should we be trying for the same amount? Doug kept saying that we couldn't possibly get a buck fifteen out of Chrysler Canada because it was more money than we got out of Ford and GM. That reasoning made no sense to me. We needed Chrysler to pay back concessions that Ford and GM had never had. He stuck to his point. A buck fifteen was too much.

"If that's the case," I said flatly, "there's no point in going to the bargaining table. We might as well decide right now to postpone negotiations until the New Year."

Howard Young doesn't usually say much, but he interjected, "How come you Canadians expect to get more than the Americans?"

"Because we've got a good strike on, that's why," I told him.

I said we weren't going to fight with our committee, which had been promised that we wouldn't waver from the bottom line, and we weren't going to outrage our membership, which was fed up with sacrificing wages to help Chrysler. If the international union tried to force a settlement on us from Detroit, it would split the UAW. In any case, the workers would reject any contract that wasn't fair.

After a brutally tough session that lasted almost three hours, Kenny Gerard, Fraser, and I went to see Miner. We told him that we hadn't changed our position. Miner wasn't ruffled. He's a great poker player. "Well, we're wasting our time then," he said.

We left him to go to the diningroom for lunch. I love the big round table in the middle of the Westbury diningroom. I have a great affection for it because that's where the turning point in the Chrysler strike happened.

We were talking about the strike, musing really. Doug loved the toughness of our Canadian bargainers. He saw where they lived, all on one floor of the Westbury, sleeping two to a room to save money, little hot plates for their coffee, clothes all over the place. He admired how solid they were and how hard they worked. It reminded him of his youth; it was good for his soul after all the years of concessions and internal politics and bullshit. In a few months he would be leaving the UAW but, for the moment, he was back in the trenches and he was loving every minute of it.

Somewhere in the course of our almost aimless discussion, it finally dawned on Doug that we weren't kidding about the bottom-line. He stopped leaning on us.

"I'll go up and talk to Miner," he said suddenly.

I wasn't too pleased. These were our negotiations, not his.

"That's fine," I said.

Doug went to work. From time to time he'd call me in the office, or come down to say how things were going. I had to wait it out. I felt that I was being torn apart.

Late that evening, Doug and I were in the office when Miner phoned down. He wanted to see Doug right away because Iacocca was calling. As we nervously waited for his return, Howard Young and I walked up and down the corridor to ease the tension. We met Doug as he came off the elevator.

"I've just had a yelling match with Iacocca," he said. "Lee says you've got your buck fifteen an hour up front. You don't deserve it he says, but you got it. And seventy-five cents for the Americans."

That was fifty cents an hour more than Chrysler had offered U.S. Chrysler workers only six weeks ago. The Canadian strike had helped the Americans.

"It's a one-year agreement," Fraser went on. "It expires in October next year."

"That makes no goddamned sense," I said. "Christ! We'll be back negotiating in another ten months. I can't stand it and it's not fair to the membership to ask them to go through this again in less than a year."

Doug tried to soothe me. "You'll be in a good position in another ten months," he said. "The industry will have turned around a bit more. Anyway, Iacocca won't gamble long term. You should have heard him. He called it blackmail. He said the goddamned Americans aren't entitled to seventy-five cents either but he had no choice, he had to get the goddamned plants open."

I was sure that Fraser wasn't exaggerating. That's how Iacocca talks. And I knew the rumour was that Chrysler was losing $4 million a day because of the strike.

"He's mad at you," Fraser warned me. "You'll probably have to pay a price for this."

"I expect that," I said nodding. "Let's go try this on Kenny Gerard."

I knew Gerard wouldn't mind the one-year agreement, so long as we were in a good position for the next negotiation. When I told him the terms, he said, "That's good enough."

We had a press conference around eleven that night. Nothing was tied down and we had a lot of non-economic issues to resolve before we had an agreement, so Doug and I didn't reveal that we were close on the main issue. We reported only that we had talked to Iacocca and there was a little light at the end of the tunnel.

Peggy Berkowitz, a reporter from the *Wall Street Journal* asked, "What are you going to do now Bob, go to bed?" I had been trying to keep the tone easy but I was tired. My judgement slipped.

"That's the best offer I've had all day, Peggy," I said. The press corps broke up, but Peggy was devastated and I thought, oh shit.

Despite the late hour, Doug called Tom Miner, and Miner invited us to come up. When we met in his room I could see that Miner didn't like the idea either of going into another collective bargaining session in ten months.

"This is crazy," he agreed, "but Lee makes these decisions and that's it."

"We should get at least two years," I insisted.

We tried to piece something together to make a two-year agreement. He wouldn't buy the escalation we wanted in the second year. I argued that in ten months we'd be asking for that and more, such as restoring the Canadian

COLA. Suddenly it struck us both that we were already into 1983 negotiations. We gave up.

The next morning, we met with the bargaining committee and made the presentation. There were some sharp questions, but essentially the committee felt the same way about it that Kenny did, that we'd be in a good position to go after Chrysler in the next round. The vote was unanimously in favour.

Before we broke up, I paid tribute to Doug Fraser. I was feeling emotional and it wasn't easy to speak, but I struggled through some remarks about the difficult times we'd had in the last eighteen months. I said I thought it was fitting that Fraser's great career in collective bargaining should finish in Toronto, where we were defending a position that was fundamental to trade unionism. I thanked him for his help in getting the settlement and paid him the credit he was due. Without question, it was Doug Fraser who had ultimately convinced Iacocca that we wouldn't back down.

Doug thanked me, his voice also breaking. He said we Canadians had come through the strike with our integrity intact and he was proud of us. He had a long history with Chrysler, he reminded us, and what had happened in Canada meant a lot to him. Then we opened a few beers to celebrate and, spontaneously, someone started us on "Solidarity Forever." Then we sang a "For He's a Jolly Good Fellow" to Fraser.

Doug had to get back to Detroit to tell Marc Stepp and the U.S. Chrysler bargaining team about the seventy-five cents an hour. I heard later that he flew back to Solidarity House on cloud nine, talking everyone's ear off about the solidarity in our Chrysler team and how we represented trade unionism at its best.

We called a press conference to announce that we had a tentative settlement on economic issues only. If we could work out the non-economics by the weekend, I explained, we could get a ratification vote and return to work before Iacocca's December 13 deadline.

After I'd answered all the questions, I spoke again. "Last night at a critical time in bargaining I was cracking some jokes around here," I said. "Peggy Berkowitz asked me a question and I said something which is considered a sexist remark. I want to apologize for it."

The next few days of bargaining were full of rancour. Having yielded big on the economic issue, Fisher and his guys tightened up on the non-economics. He started to get cute, telling us that we shouldn't be concerned over these matters. We had our money settlement, and we ought to be satisfied.

"Bullshit we've got a settlement," I told him. "My friend, don't test us again. We'll take the strike past the weekend."

I really was playing Russian roulette. The steam had gone out of the strike and we all knew it. We finally had an agreement in time to schedule the ratification votes for Sunday, December 12.

There were three Chrysler members' meetings to make in that one day, Ajax and Etobicoke in the Toronto area, and Windsor. I asked Fraser's permission to charter a jet for the trip to Windsor. When we took off from the Toronto airport in that six-passenger Lear jet, I said to Buzz, Nick, Wendy, Sam, and O'Neil, "Isn't this wonderful. Iacocca flew in in a little private plane and said we'd get nothing, and we're flying out in a Lear jet with a buck fifteen for our workers. That says something good about our union."

I felt great, absolutely great. The Chrysler strike was a monument to union solidarity. The media went to our picket lines almost every day, probing to see if the workers were getting fed up with the leadership, and they didn't get one complaint, not one. Workers said, over and over, "We trust White. We trust Gerard. We trust the Canadian leadership." When the tentative settlement was announced, the media went back to the strikers. They were in the same mood. "If Bob White says it's okay, it's okay with me," they said. "White won't sell us out."

We went into those ratification meetings almost dizzy with relief from the long tension. At Ajax and Etobicoke, the workers were thrilled with the upfront money and happy to be back to work before Christmas.

Then we flew to Windsor to a tumultuous welcome from some 7,000 Chrysler workers in the Windsor raceway grandstand. Some were so anxious to vote YES that they didn't want to wait to hear us read the terms. We had to close the ballot boxes to keep them from voting prematurely.

More than 90 per cent of the membership of the six Chrysler plants voted in favour of the settlement. It was a historic occasion for the UAW in Canada. We'd done a number of things. We'd forced Chrysler, who a few weeks before claimed to have no money, to pay workers better wages. We'd forced Chrysler, who a few weeks before said it would not settle in Canada first, to settle in Canada first. We'd also forced Chrysler to settle with workers in the United States a full month before negotiations had originally been scheduled to reopen there.

"I want to cry or get drunk," I confessed to a reporter afterward. "I'm not sure which. That was a tremendous show of solidarity. When ten thousand workers feel good about a settlement, that's good for the future of the corporation too."

Iacocca wasn't in nearly as fine a mood. He was reported as feeling "a bit wounded." He guessed Chrysler's losses over the five-week strike at $60 million. The new contracts, including the one in the States, which was ratified by 43,000 workers, would cost the corporation another $80 million, he said. A few months later the actual figures were released. Chrysler reported a loss of $96.1 million in the final quarter of 1982. Since sales were rising sharply in that same period, the company believed that it would have shown a profit but for the Canadians.

"It was unnecessary," Iacocca commented of the strike, "but it's behind us, thank God. It came at a time when we could least afford it."

Doug Fraser was delighted and magnanimous. "It took a strike either in Canada or the United States before January so we could get this," he said.

Our office in Toronto was inundated with telegrams and letters of congratulations. Our stock was very high all over the country. The odds had been so much against us that when we won it seemed like David beating Goliath all over again. To our astonishment, we had mail praising us from all over the States. The result was a higher profile all over the continent for the Canadian UAW, which could only strengthen us in future bargaining. It was, in fact, an enormous lift for the entire Canadian union movement.

A few days later, I was in Saskatoon waiting for a plane when a man approached me. "I'm not a trade unionist," he said, "but I think what you did in the Chrysler strike was bloody good for Canada."

I flew to Miami the morning after the ratification vote in Windsor in time for the meeting that day of the UAW International Executive Board. I was so exhausted I was shaking. I looked at my food and couldn't eat. I told Doug that I wouldn't hang around long, I needed sleep. He wanted me to give a report on the Chrysler strike, and I said it would be brief.

Doug opened with some warm comments about the Canadians and the great spirit of solidarity they had shown. As he spoke, beaming towards where I sat with Bob Nickerson, a wave of astonishment went through the executive. They weren't prepared to hear the Canadians praised, especially by Fraser. Then it was my turn to report.

I thanked Doug for his participation and said we'd achieved the settlement because our membership was strong and united. As a result of our collective bargaining power and Doug's assistance, the strike had turned out well. We were happy.

Marc Stepp, who had done almost nothing in the Chrysler negotiations – Doug had done it all – then gave a long, glowing report on his accomplishments in the Chrysler negotiations. He spoke for about twenty minutes without once acknowledging that the settlement really was reached in Canada and that the Canadian settlement had helped American workers. I listened to him without betraying what I was feeling, remembering that no one in Solidarity House, except Doug Fraser, had ever contacted me, let alone offered help, support, or congratulations.

Later I was complimented for what one man called "a class act." He meant he was glad I hadn't gloated, and he was a little disgusted with Stepp.

I touched Dave Mitchell on the shoulder as we were leaving the room. He was the man who had made the remark to Wendy Cuthbertson about the Canadian lemmings.

"Can I speak to you a moment?" I asked.

He said, "I want to offer my congratulations."

"Fuck you," I told him. "When we were at a very critical stage in the bargaining you referred to our Canadian workers as lemmings. They're paying your goddamned wages and I never want to hear that from you again. You're a paid bureaucrat, you're not even a member of this union. You've got no right to call any worker a lemming."

"I didn't," he said.

"You're a liar, you did," I told him. "So I don't need your congratulations, thank you very much."

I WENT STRAIGHT from the brief respite in Miami to face another crisis at home. American Motors had given all its employees notice of layoff just before Christmas, then cancelled the layoffs when it discovered it had to build another car in Canada to keep within the requirements of the Auto Pact. A few weeks later, the comedy and tragedy of errors wasn't over. American Motors said it would take off a shift in the summer.

It was a dizzy situation. American Motors were threatening to close their Brampton plant if we refused to reopen the agreement. Because the Brampton contract expired a year later than the GM contract, AMC workers in Canada briefly were the highest paid in the industry, working for a company that hadn't made a profit in three years.

We had little bargaining power because AMC is a small operation: approximately 1,400 workers, of whom 500 were laid off. Finally, less than two hours before strike deadline, we reached a settlement that was basically the same as those at Ford and GM. Much later, the company announced it would build a $764-million, state-of-the-art car assembly plant in Brampton, recall the workers it had laid off, and add another 1,800 to the payroll.

At the same time, we had strikes all over the place against other companies that were insisting on wage freezes in their contracts. We had to renew contributions to our No Concession Fund, which we had stopped when the fund reached $60,000, when we thought we had enough. Seven hundred members were out on strike against International Harvester in Chatham, for instance, because we wouldn't accept a wage freeze there.

International Harvester Canada was wholly owned by International Harvester Chicago, which reported a loss of $1.64 billion in 1982. As I pointed out, "We could work for nothing and still not wipe out the company's loss."

In January 1983, General Motors called back 1,500 laid-off workers in its Oshawa plant and 110 in Windsor. The second shift in a transmission plant, which had been laid off since April 1982, was put back. Car sales were rising, but the industry was still not out of trouble. Ford had overbuilt its Escort, the company's answer to the small Japanese cars. The glut in Escorts forced its Edison, New Jersey, workers to take concessions. Workers in a Ford steel mill in Dearborn, Michigan, took a 15 per cent wage cut, when Ford convinced them that the mill otherwise would be shut.

Since August 1981, 400,000 jobs had been lost in Canada, 40 per cent more than were lost during the Great Depression. The Canadian Gross National Product was down 7 per cent in a year, and the glut in oil had set the stage for an oil-price war that was to bankrupt Mexico.

The high-tech companies, de Havilland, Pratt & Whitney, and Canadair, all experienced major layoffs, and the Canadian agricultural implement industry was among the hardest hit in the country. The president of one company came to me to ask for concessions, not necessarily for those working, because there were few still in the plants, but for those on layoff. He said they had a year and a half's worth of production still unsold and they owed the banks millions.

The Japanese auto industry was the chief beneficiary of the poor economy in North America, as customers switched to their smaller and cheaper cars. Japan deliberately sold its cars cheaply to undercut North America, causing much of the suffering in the auto industry. Early in 1983, I talked to Prime Minister Trudeau about our concern that Japan had pushed its percentage share of the Canadian market to intolerable levels. While the Big Three were retooling in their Canadian plants at the cost of hundreds of millions of dollars, the Japanese created very few Canadian jobs and invested almost nothing in Canada.

"Quite frankly," I protested to Gerald Regan, the new federal minister for international trade, in a telex dated February 7, 1983, "the Japanese have outmanoeuvred us in every phase of discussions about restraints – either pitting us against the United States, or moving from calendar year to fiscal year, or ignoring our situation on trucks [where Japan had 20 per cent of the market] and doing little or nothing to improve Canadian content by parts purchasing."

Regan then went to Japan and announced a six-month limitation on imports from Japan that was a disaster. In the first half of 1983 Japan would be allowed to export to Canada 79,000 vehicles, more than in the whole of 1982, when it already had 25 per cent of the market. I had been urging a two- or three-year restriction on Japanese imports into Canada and Canadian content regulations such as those we placed on American cars under the terms of the Auto Pact. I also warned that the problem with Japanese trucks was getting out of hand.

Regean didn't consult with me, as his predecessor Ed Lumley usually did, but went ahead with the appalling six-month agreement which didn't even mention trucks.

Fuming, I called a press conference and delivered some scathing criticism, saying that Japan had Canada's permission to "flood the market again." Regan was very hurt. He had been passing his position off as having been endorsed by me, a blatant effort to protect his political ass. Meanwhile, the States was being tougher on Japan than we were. Japan, seeing the writing on the wall, already was moving into the States with assembly plants, parts plants, and a joint venture with GM in California.

In Canada, the Japanese Automobile Dealers' Association spent a lot of money on a campaign to advance the idea of unlimited imports, which it described as good for consumers. The suggestion was that we were trying to prevent Canadians from buying cheap cars. That wasn't the case at all. My quarrel wasn't with Japan or Japanese cars, it was with Ottawa for not insisting on Japanese investment here. A healthy, competitive auto industry in Canada means jobs, not just for auto workers but for hundreds of thousands of other Canadians.

THE GOVERNMENT'S TASK FORCE on the automotive industry was taking much more of my time than I had expected. We talked to experts all over the country and in the States. Sam Gindin, who was named to the task force at my suggestion, really proved his worth. In less than nine months of intense work, he came up with statistics and analyses that helped us to put together the best report on the industry that has ever been done. None of us were paid, but we had a budget of $125,000 that allowed us to hire an outside consulting group to write the sharp, readable report. Lumley didn't want another long academic report that would gather dust. He asked us to study labour costs, structure, productivity, labour relations, quality and what to do about the off-shore producers.

While there were the expected collisions between the views of corporations, parts manufacturers, and the UAW, our common concern to help the industry kept us civil. We weren't in collective bargaining, we were trying to save the industry, so we were forced to accommodate our different viewpoints. No one wanted to weaken the effect we could have on the government policy by splitting our recommendations into minority reports.

Hackworth turned to me during a discussion of General Motors when I was being mildly critical of the corporation. He said in exasperation, "White, will you quit whipping the lead horse! We're at least making investments in Canada." Indeed General Motors was investing heavily in Canada. The *Financial Post* in October 1983 estimated that GM was pouring $4 billion into this country to modernize and robotize its plants.

That line about whipping the lead horse got around. When the task force was finished, a GM cartoonist drew a picture of us on a chuckwagon, with me whipping Hackworth and GM, the lead horse.

This investigation of the automotive industry by insiders turned out to be an interesting and worthwhile endeavour. We gave the government our 188-page report in May 1983 – the most exhaustive, in-depth study of the auto industry ever done in Canada. We discovered, for instance, that the Canadian auto industry accounts for 8 per cent of all manufacturing in Canada, that it represents 20 per cent of all merchandise exports, and that it accounts for 100,000 jobs directly and another 150,000 indirectly.

The recommendation that drew the most attention was the proposal to limit off-shore producers. We wanted Japan and other auto-exporting nations to conform to the Canadian content rules that govern the United States under the Canada-U.S. Auto Trade Agreement. One is the requirement for an assembly-to-sales ratio. For every vehicle a manufacturer sells in Canada, the manufacturer must produce a vehicle in Canada. That's how Canada got the huge auto-assembly plants in Ste. Thérèse and St. Thomas and kept the assembly plants in Windsor and Oshawa. Also, we asked a 60 per cent Canadian content regulation for cars assembled in Canada, a rule applying to American cars that had created a lot of jobs in the auto-parts industry. Our bottom line was that we wanted Japanese assembly plants and part plants in Canada. To illustrate how careless Canada was about off-shore imports, in 1982 Japan shipped $1.2 billion worth of automobiles and trucks to Canada and purchased only $10 million worth of Canadian-made parts. The deficit is much higher today.

Gerry Regan said the government would adopt our proposal only as "a last resort." Others described auto quotas as "a licence to remain inefficient." That was the picture much of the public had about the auto industry in Canada – delapidated, obsolete industry that should be allowed to die. The government had reports declaring that the auto industry in Canada was hopelessly out of date. Our study showed the opposite was true. Canadian-built cars, the corporation presidents themselves said, were of better quality than American-built cars. We found that absenteeism is less in Canada and productivity higher. Labour relations in Canada admittedly were tougher for the corporations to deal with than in the States, but there was a history of good faith.

Further, the auto industry in Canada is as high tech as anything in the country. We have more computers and robotics in our plants than most people realize. General Motors is currently spending over $300 million to train Oshawa workers in the new technology.

Ed Lumley, Regan's predecessor and the man who had appointed the task force in the first place, had been a real asset for the government when he had the portfolio of minister of industry. He could deal with the bureaucracy like a hot knife cutting through butter and was a hard-working person I came to like and respect very much. Unlike Regan, Lumley was sympathetic to our position that there should be quotas, although he didn't pursue all of the task-force recommendations. He appreciated that we were not saying that Canadian consumers shouldn't have the choice of buying foreign cars. Our point was that foreign-owned auto makers, who wanted to sell significant amounts of vehicles in the Canadian market, should be required to produce a certain amount of vehicles in this country, just as we required the Americans to do under the Auto Pact.

The position was completely misunderstood. The *Toronto Star* complained in an editorial that quotas on Japanese cars would hit Canadians in the pocketbook. Though we had figures to show that a 60-per-cent-Canadian-content rule on imports would create 21,000 new jobs in Canada, no one was listening. In the States, where the UAW succeeded in having local-content rules introduced in Congress, expectations were that if it passed, it would create 580,000 jobs.

The government eventually did adopt a few of our recommendations on limitations of imports. But they never did address the principle recommendation, which was to stop giving auto manufacturers in Japan and South Korea an advantage that our Auto Pact denied U.S. manufacturers.

We campaigned hard to get the public aware of the issue. The industry sent out speakers and petitions and our UAW members went into the streets and shopping malls to get people to sign postcards saying they were concerned that Canadian-content rules weren't being applied outside North America.

In February 1984, I headed a delegation that took 110,000 cards to Prime Minister Trudeau and dumped them in front of him. The next day, he announced he was resigning. When I heard about his resignation, I joked to friends, "I told Trudeau, either give us the auto policy or get out."

All our predictions of doom have come true. To get around the off-shore competition, GM, Ford and Chrysler are entering into co-production deals all over the world, taking jobs out of North America, while the investments by foreign auto makers in Canada remain token. The industry in this country is living under three sets of rules: the Japanese operate with some restraints plus some investments, the South Koreans, who sell 100,000 cars a year here, have no restraints and a token investment, and the Americans have to meet the strict terms of the Auto Pact.

We've had two meetings with Prime Minister Brian Mulroney, but we can't get his government's attention. Nobody in Ottawa is looking at the future. Even when the president of GM Canada said we had to have similar rules for off-shore producers or we would lose thousands of jobs in this country, the prime minister was unmoved.

I was part of a joint CAW-corporation delegation to Ottawa recently, during which I said to the prime minister, "The people in this room are together on this. We represent the union, the Big Three, and the auto parts industry. We know what we're talking about, and we're all saying the same thing." That was significant, but Mulroney didn't seem to appreciate it. Canada has something unique in that partnership. In the States only the UAW has lobbied for content rules. The Big Three haven't supported the union, though I think Lee Iacocca takes the same view; the auto manufacturers and the auto parts people there are divided. In contrast, the Big Three, the parts industry, and the union in Canada are all on the same side on this issue.

I was disgusted to find Ottawa bureaucrats skeptical because the Big Three in Canada were taking a different position from the Big Three in the United States. After years of hollering about Canadian independence from American influence, when it happened they couldn't believe it. They thought there was some kind of manipulation going on.

The irony is that Japan and South Korea themselves don't have the kind of open door we provide them in Canada. Japanese content rules are very strict, and you can't sell a car in South Korea that doesn't have 90 per cent South Korean content.

In 1983 we had, for the first time, a demonstration of how good the Auto Pact could be for Canada. After the inception of the Auto Pact, each year the States had benefited and Canada had suffered a trade deficit, but suddenly that turned around. For the first time since 1972, Canada had a surplus in automotive trade with the States amounting to $4.6 billion, a substantial boost for the troubled economy.

THE UAW INTERNATIONAL CONVENTION was held in Dallas in May. Doug Fraser, the last of the UAW vice-presidents who had served with Walter Reuther, retired as president. Owen Bieber was elected by acclamation as the sixth president of the UAW. Don Ephlin took over from Bieber as head of the union's General Motors department, Marc Stepp retained Chrysler, and Steve Yokich was given responsibility for Ford.

Bieber was fifty-three, a relatively young man, who could be expected to lead the UAW until he retired in twelve years. An immense man, six-foot-five and bulky, Owen was described in the press as methodical, aloof, and a hard-worker. But he was unknown, so business analysts leaped into print with speculations that the UAW might turn away from Fraser's conciliatory stance and return the union to Reuther's confrontation style.

Bieber gave impetus to these conjectures when he said in his presidential address that the UAW "has given all it is going to give and it is now management's turn to do some giving." He was interrupted twice by standing ovations.

"The most disastrous thing that could happen in this industry," Tom Miner observed the next day in the *Wall Street Journal*, "is to return to normal relationships. It concerns me very much that we might. And Bieber is where the buck stops."

David Dyer, a Harvard University professor sympathetic to labour, said, "The UAW's problems cry out for a guy who can lead them to a different future and who can manage the change to that future elegantly. Nothing in Bieber's past indicates that he is going to be able to do that."

At a press conference during the convention, Bieber was asked about relations with the Canadian UAW. He said that one of his priorities was to bridge the gap. Doug Fraser interjected that he was sure Solidarity House was interested in "repairing the rift."

Bieber was assuming the leadership at a very difficult time. Bargaining with Chrysler was due to begin in a few months, and his Chrysler membership was clamouring for parity with GM and Ford. Then he would face the 1984 bargaining with GM and Ford, whose workers were enraged about the cutbacks they had taken. Convention delegates were sporting buttons reading RESTORE AND MORE IN '84.

The *Wall Street Journal* that month painted a bleak picture of the state of the U.S. labour movement. In the past year, the AFL-CIO had lost about 1.2 million members in the States because of plant closings and layoffs. The UAW had cut its staff of 900 by more than 10 per cent. To avoid losing programs, the UAW decided to divert some money from its strike fund. When the strike fund reached $550 million, only 15 per cent of individual union dues would go to the strike fund instead of the usual 30 per cent. UAW locals would get back two-thirds of the remaining 15 per cent to relieve their financial difficulties and the balance of 5 per cent would go to help Solidarity House meet its overhead.

Meanwhile, Chrysler was trying to decide whether to invite Owen Bieber to join its board of directors. Iacocca and Doug Fraser had had such a good relationship that when Doug stepped down as UAW president, Iacocca urged him to remain on the Chrysler board. Doug didn't think that was appropriate and declined. We all waited, but Iacocca didn't offer the vacant directorship to Bieber.

The Big Three finally were showing signs of recovery, but there wasn't much cause for rejoicing among workers. The profits were secured through flexible automation, imported parts, and leaner production, all of which meant fewer jobs: 200,000 were on indefinite layoffs in the auto industry.

During this period, I was making some structural changes in the Canadian Region to accommodate our Quebec members. We had some 7,000 members certified in the assembly and parts plants in the Eastern Townships and thousands of others in the aerospace industry.

Quebec delegates, naturally, were entitled to participate in the Canadian Council. That looked fine on paper, but in practice it didn't work worth a damn. Few Quebec locals bothered to elect delegates. They objected to the travel expenses to Ontario, the fact that most of the discussion was in English, and that the agenda was dominated by what was happening in Ontario and Detroit.

Soon after I became director in 1978, I named Claude Ducharme from Quebec as my assistant. That worked a little better but still Quebec didn't have a forum in which to discuss their particular issues, of which there were many, and a way to mobilize themselves to confront René Lévesque's PQ government, which was trying to balance its budget by union-bashing such government employees as teachers.

One suggestion coming out of Quebec was that the province should be a region within the UAW, separate from the Canadian Region, with its own director and its own office. I objected on the grounds that there were so few members in Quebec, comparatively speaking, that they couldn't be self-supporting or politically effective.

In 1982, I recommended to the Canadian Council that we establish a Quebec UAW Council to deal with local social, political, and economic issues, and this was accepted. The founding meeting of the Quebec UAW Council was in Montreal on March 26. Buzz and Nick went with me for what proved an exciting weekend. John DeFalco, chair of the GM plant at Ste. Thérèse, was named president by acclamation, and I was pleased to see two women, Denise Bellalite and Carol Froment, elected to the executive.

To make sure we didn't pull in different directions, we established interlocking representations. The Quebec president attends all Canadian Council meetings with voice, not vote, and all Council executive meetings. Similarly, a representative from the Canadian UAW Council executive attends the biannual Quebec Council meetings.

CHAPTER EIGHTEEN

Collision with
General Motors

I N JULY 1983, seven months into our one-year contract, Chrysler tried to reopen negotiations. Iacocca explained virtuously that the company was recovering and he wanted Chrysler workers to share in the success. My hunch was that Iacocca wanted to extend the existing agreement into 1984 before we found out just how well Chrysler was doing.

Chrysler was asking for early bargaining in the States as well. Bieber had the same suspicion I did. He notified Chrysler he would be asking for a dollar an hour up-front raise for American workers.

I met with Kenny Gerard and his Chrysler bargaining team. If we could get a good one-year agreement to take us to 1984, we'd have the Big Three negotiations back in sync again. But, when we met with Chrysler, we learned they wanted a two-year agreement expiring in September 1985. They were prepared to offer a dollar an hour up front, but nothing more to close the parity gap with wages at Ford and GM. Chrysler was asking the same in the States. In each proposal they'd inserted a clause stating that the offer had to be accepted in both Canada and the United States to be effective. Chrysler knew Canada was no longer part of the international agreement, but they still wanted to impose a common settlement.

The UAW in Detroit turned it down before it even came to us. In rejecting it unanimously, we warned Bill Fisher that we would not be bound by any agreement Chrysler might reach in the States. Iacocca had misread the UAW again. He appeared genuinely surprised that Bieber didn't jump at the offer. Instead Bieber was talking to the media about how much money Chrysler executives and stockholders were making. The bailout had been such a success that the U.S. government had a potential profit of $230 million on its stock warrants. Chrysler earnings in the second quarter of 1983 were $310.3 million, the largest quarterly profit in its history, and the company was repaying the remaining $800 million on its federally guaranteed loans. Predictions of the 1983 profits were between $800 and $900 million.

In late August we were approached by Chrysler again to get back to the bargaining table ahead of schedule. Chrysler was alarmed by the new militancy in the American Chrysler locals. If contract talks waited until January 1984, the corporation feared there would be a long strike. Chrysler Canada was particularly vulnerable to a January strike because it had just invested $750 million in the Windsor assembly plant and its hot new T115 van wagon was ready to roll in November or December.

We weren't anxious to negotiate in January either. A mid-winter strike is tough on everyone. So we opened collective bargaining with Chrysler in Canada on Labour Day weekend. We had a settlement by the following Tuesday. That same day, the U.S. bargaining team met with Chrysler and got a settlement in a few hours.

This time, the only real issue was the wage rate. Chrysler agreed to a dollar an hour retroactive to August 1983 and additional increases at intervals until the contract expired in October 1985. We got back the Canadian COLA, to start running in March 1984, made the pensions equal to those at Ford and GM and made substantial improvements in the SUB plan. It worked out to about five dollars an hour more for Chrysler workers in Canada from 1982 levels.

Chrysler workers now had parity with the existing GM and Ford agreements, but the contract made no provisions for any increase we might get in 1984 bargaining with Ford and GM. We pushed, but we couldn't get Chrysler's commitment to maintain parity in the final year of the agreement.

Still it was, as I said, "a tremendous victory" to get back the COLA that Iacocca had said was dead in the auto industry and to return Chrysler workers to parity with GM and Ford. "The membership will be tremendously relieved we got parity without a winter strike," I told the press.

We went straight from the Chrysler settlement into last-minute bargaining with Massey-Ferguson in Toronto and Brantford. Massey-Ferguson was deep in financial trouble, with losses of $11.3 million in the preceding quarter and 60 per cent of its workers on layoff. The strike deadline was already just a day away.

The Massey-Ferguson workers, who hadn't been laid off, were expecting no more than five weeks work before a total winter shutdown. That put Massey in an excellent position to keep us out on strike all winter. Figuring they were in the driver's seat, they offered a three-year wage freeze, no COLA for two years, reduced vacations, and so on.

In the public perception, the union was irresponsible not to give concessions to Massey-Ferguson. In an effort to meet that criticism and avert the strike, we made a modest proposal of a one-year extension on the current contract, keeping the COLA, and making some SUB changes to help the laid-off workers. And at Massey-Ferguson in Toronto, anyone with less than thirty years seniority was on layoff. I maintained to our critics that wage concessions would make no difference because the company's problems lay in the marketplace. "If we make concessions, Massey-Ferguson won't make one more combine or recall one more worker from layoff."

A strike was inevitable, and we went into it reluctantly. Though our situation looked hopeless, because the company held all the cards, I decided the bargaining team should stay in the hotel and keep trying. We had ten years of good relations with Massey going for us, which they knew would be shattered if they kept us out all winter.

It helped that I had a long-standing good relationship with Massey's labour relations director, Bob Rzonca. Both of us were determined that those negotiations would not collapse. The discussions were dicey, however, because Massey had nothing to lose by taking a long strike. I described our situation as "walking through an alligator pond in our bedroom slippers."

Because Rzonca and I were experienced and trusted each other, we were able to work quickly without getting sidetracked by misunderstandings. We bargained around the clock and got a basic agreement around ten in the morning on the second day of the strike. The settlement was a two-year agreement with full continuation of the COLA. Massey, however, agreed to put $1 million in the SUB fund for laid-off workers.

It wasn't a model agreement, but the Massey-Ferguson workers were so relieved to get an agreement at all that they ratified it by a vote of 90 per cent.

LATE ON A FRIDAY AFTERNOON in July 1983, the Canadian government revealed that it had given the U.S. government permission to test the Cruise missile in Canada. Despite the government's effort to bury it, the announcement roused the peace movement in Canada. I joined in the opposition to Cruise tests and took part in demonstrations and marches that followed the announcement. Later, I reported to the Canadian UAW Council on the dangers of Canada's participation in the nuclear arms escalation and won the endorsement of many locals.

At a protest rally of 20,000 people in Toronto, I criticized Prime Minister Pierre Trudeau's position on the Cruise testing. Along with church and disarmament groups, UAW locals signed petitions to Ottawa asking the government to reverse its decision.

All of these activities raised my profile across the country. I could no longer go anywhere in Canada without being recognized. Some people got the impression that I spent little time on union business, but our members knew otherwise. If a union leader is seen romping around on other issues and isn't at the bargaining table at a critical time, that says that the leader hasn't sorted out his other priorities. If you work hard, you aren't open to criticism. I try to keep my perspective. I know I have influence on national issues only because I'm president of the Canadian Auto Workers and have the support of my members. I make sure, first and foremost, that I don't jeopardize that.

A public profile opens doors and opportunities. I've been invited, for instance, to speak to such groups as the Canadian Clubs in Toronto and Vancouver, organizations that rarely open their doors to a trade unionist. Because they want to take a look at me, I get the opportunity to speak to business and political leaders about union concerns such as free trade or Canadian content regulations in the auto industry.

I made a calculated decision long ago to be accessible to the public and to the media because the labour movement has a lot to say about social and political issues.

I studied Doug Fraser, who was good with the media. He created an enormous profile for the UAW in the United States by making himself available, fair weather or foul. He enjoyed a good press conference, as I do today, and the give and take that goes with that questioning.

Whether we like it or not, the public forms its opinions on the basis of what it hears on radio, or reads in the papers, or sees on television. If a labour leader opts out of the media, the leader allows that platform to be taken over by someone else.

I'm very aware, when we're in a strike, that workers and their families turn on the television news to see if there's hope of a settlement. There's no way we can reach our members as quickly to tell them how the talks are progressing.

Almost every day I get at least one request from the media and I rarely turn anyone down. I can't say the same about the requests for speeches that come into our offices. I receive an average of ten a week so I can accept very few. I try to take it in stride when the *New York Times* runs a quarter-page story about me or *Maclean's* magazine puts my picture on the cover, and I think I've kept my feet on the ground.

I see stories about me that I don't like, sure, but once I give an interview, it's behind me. Only once have I ever protested to a reporter about a story that was unfair. I have some complaints about the media. One of my peeves is that some still refer to labour leaders as "union bosses" when, in most cases, we are elected.

When the media come down hard on the labour movement or on our union, I tell my staff that we must respect their right to do so. They are not the voice of the CAW. If they were, they would be on our payroll.

Over the years I've met hundreds of journalists. In the 1982 Chrysler strike I met Susan Ormiston, co-host of "Fraser's Edge," which filmed the documentary while we were bargaining with Chrysler in the Westbury Hotel in Toronto.

The program was shown shortly after the strike began, but I continued a friendship with Susan Ormiston. I've learned a lot about journalism and, in turn, she's learned a great deal more about the labour movement. Frankly, without her I don't think this book would be possible. It was she who suggested early in 1983 that I put on tape the events leading from 1979 to the 1982 Chrysler strike so there would be a historical record of those three years. That tape was very valuable to me in working on this book. During the writing of this book, she kept stressing to me that this was a once-in-a-lifetime opportunity and that, in spite of my schedule, I should set aside the time to do it right.

Late in 1983, we had a request from the National Film Board for our cooperation in a documentary on collective bargaining.

"We thought about doing it in 1982 and didn't get around to it," John Spotton of the NFB explained. "We could have kicked ourselves, because we missed getting the Chrysler strike."

"You really missed the labour story of the decade," I agreed. "That's too bad."

He explained that the documentary would be an educational film. The public was curious about collective bargaining and what went on in those sessions, he said, but no film had ever been shot of an actual session. He was asking my permission to follow bargaining from beginning to end.

"It's all right with me," I said, remembering that the crew for "Fraser's Edge" hadn't bothered us at all. "Which corporation do you want?"

"We thought it would be interesting to do Chrysler," Spotton said.

"I don't think Chrysler would agree," I told him. "Of all the Big Three, Chrysler is the least receptive to any innovation like that."

The NFB went to Detroit to talk to Chrysler anyway and got a short "no" from Tom Miner. I suggested they try General Motors. "Hackworth is president here and he's a reasonable man," I said. "Rod Andrew is a good person to deal with."

I called Andrew myself. "I think it would be interesting to do this," I told him. "It'll cause some hiccups in the bargaining process, but so what? Why don't we try it?"

General Motors ended up agreeing to allow filming of the 1984 bargaining. We met with the NFB crew in our board room to go over the ground rules. Among those at that meeting were John Spotton, the executive producer, Bob Collison, who wrote, co-directed, and co-produced the film, Sturla Gunnarsson, director and producer, and John Kramer, senior producer. We had Wendy Cuthbertson, our communications director, Sam Gindin, Bob Nickerson, Buzz Hargrove, and a few others from the union.

The NFB people asked what they could expect.

"I can't tell you," I said. "There's no map. I can say that we'll open July 23 and things will be fairly quiet the first few weeks. But after that it's unchartered. The bargaining process will get into high gear when we set a deadline and choose the target company."

I explained that there was a lot going on within the UAW that would interest them. Solidarity House and Toronto didn't always see negotiations the same way. I commented idly, grinning, "You never know. You could be filming the breakup of the international union." Everyone chuckled.

The NFB crew started travelling around with me. I got so accustomed to the routine that it became automatic for me to put on a body-pack battery and clip a microphone on my tie when I dressed each morning. The crew went with us on March 8, 1984 to the UAW international bargaining convention in Detroit. I explained to the delegates what the crew was doing and their presence was accepted without much comment. Later, the NFB was all over the place at the Canadian bargaining conference, while we developed our proposals to present to Ford and GM.

The talk of both conventions was a leaked internal General Motors memorandum, titled *Actions to Influence the Outcome of Bargaining*, which disclosed GM bargaining strategies. What we had to prepare for, it seemed, was the abolition of wage increases and the substitution of what was called profit-sharing, or lump-sum payments. Bieber told the media that profit-sharing wasn't enough for his workers. I repeated that Canadians wanted wage increases, not profit-sharing or lump-sum payments.

"If the company wants to share the profits after the wages are paid, fine," I said.

When I first talked about the NFB documentary to Phil Bennett, chairman of our GM bargaining committee, he was nervous. He worried it would inhibit the process. So, at a candid session with the GM bargaining committee, we went over all the objections carefully.

"Initially you may think that you have to act differently and you'll be feeling self-conscious," I told them. "I can assure you that concern doesn't last. You'll be surprised how soon you'll forget they're in the room."

The Film Board people warned me that they wouldn't be happy if they were only allowed to film meetings where nothing much happened. The word they kept stressing was *access*. "We'll have to have access to everything that's going on," they said, "especially when the fur starts to fly."

"Don't worry about that," I told them. "Once I agree to do something, that's it. You'll have your access."

In June General Motors sought to unsettle us by complaining that its labour costs, $35,000 a year on the average, were at a record high. We pointed out that Roger B. Smith, the new GM chairman earned $1,058,000 that year in salary and bonuses and F. James McDonald, GM president, got $1,330,000 annually.

When we opened bargaining with General Motors, the Film Board recorded us moving our desks and files into the Royal York Hotel to set up the temporary offices. With GM's permission, the crew was in the room when both bargaining teams made their initial presentations. The crew came into our committee caucuses, they were in my office when I was on the phone or talking to Helen, they filmed Sam Gindin giving the bargaining team a strategy analysis using the blackboard, they followed us down halls and stood over us with cameras while we ate. They had a lot of access.

During the early part of August, the crew grew bored. "Nothing much is happening," they complained. I reminded them of my warning that collective bargaining always is slow in the first stages. It would pick up, I promised, when things started to progress with GM and Ford bargaining in the States.

The unhappy crew went to Oshawa and talked to GM workers, filming them on the production line and catching some sharp confrontations with plant foremen.

We took strike votes at Ford and GM. In both, the mood of the workers was strong, 97 per cent at Ford and 95 per cent at General Motors voted to strike if necessary.

We were encouraged by signs of recovery in Canada's automotive industry. The press spoke of "skyrocketing sales." Ford-Canada's profits in 1983 were $153 million and GM-Canada's profits were $676 million. The *Wall Street*

Journal estimated that the Big Three's profits in 1984 would be around $6.3 billion, more than thirteen times their combined 1982 profits. The following year, 1985, profits were expected to be even higher, with earnings soaring nearly 50 per cent to about $9.2 billion.

The Big Three were planning to expand operations in Canada. GM announced it would spend $1 billion in Oshawa in the next two years, mostly in high-technology like robots that could weld and spray paint, automated press systems to stamp out roofs, doors, and trunk lids, and robot-guided "smart carts" to take raw material to the machines and make deliveries to the shipping department. It was rumoured that GM might spend as much as $3 billion in Canada over the next few years. Already there was a $255-million modernization underway in the St. Catharines engine-assembly plant.

When GM advertised job openings that summer in Oshawa, the line-up of applicants stretched around a city block. Chrysler was talking of reopening its engine plant in Windsor. The Honda Motor Company of Japan revealed that it would build a $100 million automotive plant in Alliston, the potato capital of Ontario. I was unimpressed and commented that, "All told, Japanese automakers owe Canada about twenty thousand jobs." Indeed, a number of people weren't impressed. Honda had built a plant in Marysville, Ohio, that would turn out 200,000 Accords a year. The Alliston plant was expected to produce only 19,000 cars a year.

Our GM and Ford contracts were due to expire September 14, 1984. With three weeks to go, I went to Detroit for a meeting of the UAW's International Executive Board (IEB) to select the target company in the United States. Bieber reported that he wasn't quite ready to decide between Ford and GM. He recommended that we keep both companies on the burner a little longer and continue probing. The proposals from American GM and Ford were much alike and followed the line of the leaked GM bargaining manual. Neither contained across-the-board wage increases. Instead there was a scaled increase and lump-sum payment of $600 in the first year, a lump-sum payment of $300 in the third year, and nothing in the second year. The corporations were smart to dream up lump-sum payments. It's hard for workers not to think the lump sum is wonderful when they get it. It takes a while for them to realize they are the poorer for it. The Big Three's strategy was to blame high labour costs in North America for the success of the Japanese competition. They insisted the industry could be saved only by shrinking workers' incomes.

I was appalled. In Bieber's inaugural address he had vowed that the UAW was finished with concession agreements, yet the corporations were trying to keep the door shut on the UAW tradition of an annual 3-per-cent raise on top of the cost-of-living allowance.

I was dead against lump-sum contracts. Under lump-sum payments, a worker gets nice bundle in the pay envelope once, but at the end of the year it's gone and the worker's wages are the same as they were at the beginning of the year. The next year, the wage is the same, with maybe another bonus, and in the final year he's still making the same hourly wage as he did three years earlier.

To my dismay, the UAW executive board's discussion of the Ford and GM proposals didn't touch on the absence of wage increases, only the lack of lump-sum payments in the second year of the contracts. That aspect of the proposal hadn't troubled me. It was clearly a bargaining ploy, and I was certain the corporations would come through during negotiations. What alarmed me was that Bieber and the others were seriously considering these agreements.

"I don't like the direction these negotiations are going," I said with some heat. "I think we should reject these proposals on the basis of their direction. It is irrelevant that the amount of the lump-sum payment isn't enough."

A few people nodded, but no one really supported me. I was amazed. Owen Bieber should have been just as worried as I was. He should have argued that we had to insist on a return to the guaranteed annual hourly wage increases. I waited for him to say, "We'll tell the corporations that there's no goddamned way we'll accept lump-sum payments. They have to put some money in the pay cheques each week." Only a month before he had written an article in the *Wall Street Journal* titled, "Why a Higher Auto Wage Isn't Too Much to Ask." But there was not a word, not a hint, that he was opposed to the lack of regular wage increases.

I was thinking ahead. It was clear to me that if the UAW in the States went for lump-sum payments, the corporations would push lump-sum payments in Canada. I had to make sure I had room to manoeuvre.

"I have no problem with whatever you do regarding the selection of a target in the States," I said casually, "so long as I have flexibility to select either GM or Ford in Canada when you guys get through." That went over without a comment.

A few days after the meeting, the International Executive Board decided the UAW in the States would target General Motors. Because Bieber didn't want a full-scale strike of General Motors, which pundits were saying would hurt the Democratic presidential candidate, he proposed to take out only a few plants if it went to a strike. If bargaining still didn't go well, he'd shut down a few more, and so on.

On September 15, a strike was called in thirteen GM plants in nine American states. As the walkouts spread, the strike was said to be costing GM between $100 million and $150 million a week and lost production of 45,600 vehicles. Nine days later, it was over.

Somone phoned me from Detroit to tell me the details of the settlement. The *Wall Street Journal* said the new UAW-GM contract was "good news for the economy ... not inflationary ... won't drive up car prices." The substance of it was that the union had accepted the General Motors plan to shrink its labour costs in exchange for what the union saw as job protection.

It was hailed as a landmark pact, "a new cooperative relationship," but not by me. Bieber had accepted bonuses instead of contractual wage increases. The contract also provided that GM would establish a $1 billion fund to retrain, relocate, and readjust laid-off workers. Bieber was said to be elated, and was reported as saying the UAW, with 100,000 members laid off in the States, would be "suckers" to forget about job security and insist instead on the money package. He called the contract "historic" and he won immediate praise in the *Wall Street Journal* for "resisting the temptation to take a hard line in his first big bargaining test and opting for moderation."

The U.S. agreement, however, didn't fit Canada at all. Here, our workers were fully employed and the Big Three were hiring.

Here we go, I thought.

At a press conference in Toronto following the U.S. tentative settlement, I was careful not to criticize it. I confined myself to the statement that it was "totally unacceptable in Canada in its form and in its substance," and that it could not be considered in any way the basis of a settlement.

I told GM's Rod Andrew very clearly how I felt. "I don't want any misunderstanding with you, my friend," I said. "This isn't rhetoric. There is no way the lump-sum payments are going to fly in Canada. We aren't going down this road without a fight. You'd better be ready for a helluva confrontation."

Following UAW bargaining procedure, Bieber called an IEB meeting for September 25 to discuss the tentative settlement, which would be followed immediately by a vote in the GM council. The board meeting was in St. Louis, but the plane I was taking had mechanical trouble and I arrived late. I missed the full discussion, but I said flatly the GM settlement in the States was not acceptable in Canada.

That night in the bar Bob Nickerson almost came to blows with a staff guy from Solidarity House who was attacking me for "pissing all over the settlement before the ink was dry."

The next day the GM council met. Bieber encountered little opposition to his settlement from the elected representations of GM workers in the States. By a show of hands, the 300 delegates voted overwhelmingly to support the agreement. I listened to the discussion but took no part. I was there only to get Owen Bieber to agree on a strike deadline in Canada. Under the UAW structure, strike deadlines must be authorized by the president. The consent of the IEB is required but this is a mere formality. The UAW president calls the shots.

Nick, Buzz, Sam, and I had talked a dozen times about whether Ford should be the target this time in Canada or if we should go with GM again. I had decided to go after GM. Bieber had gone to GM in the States to set the pattern for Ford, and I believed we should do the same in Canada. I knew Ford Canada would fight to rubberstamp the Ford agreement in the States, but I hoped Hackworth and Andrew of GM-Canada would be more flexible.

I confided my decision to Bieber, who told Steve Yokich, the UAW vice-president in charge of Ford. Yokich asked Bieber to hold off the GM strike deadline in Canada until he finished the Ford bargaining.

"Hell, we can't do that," I said. "We've got two bargaining teams going in Toronto and we want to get at this."

Owen and I talked privately. I gave him a date I wanted for the GM strike deadline but I put a little water in the pail. If he extended the deadline a few days to get his pound of flesh, we'd have it just where I wanted it.

He called me the next day from Kentucky to say I had strike authorization and set a date, twelve noon October 17, that was two days later than the one I'd requested.

"It's just going to cause all kinds of hell over here because it's taken so long," I said. "It's going to make it tight. But I'll do it. I'll do it on the seventeenth. Okay."

When I put down the phone, I grinned at Bob Nickerson. October 17 was the date we wanted in the first place.

We would start negotiating on Monday, I told Nick gleefully. "We're going to finally get our hands on the steering wheel. One foot on the gas and get the money in the tank." This comment got around and was eventually used as lyrics to "Roadblock," the theme song of the NFB's film *Final Offer*.

I called Andrew at GM and Art Hanlon at Ford to tell them that the target was GM. I said to both, "I want you to know that the settlement in Detroit doesn't fit here."

At the bargaining session with Andrew I was blunt, "It's completely opposite to where we intend to go in Canada. If we start to see an indication that that's the direction GM of Canada wants to go, then I can tell you we are headed for a confrontation."

"We've made money," Andrew acknowledged. "There's no question about it. And I can understand your apprehension about what you saw come across the table in the United States. But there's also no question in my mind that we're so stable that we can return to what we've done in the past. We're not as viable as everyone thinks we are."

We were warning each other, sparring. We each knew where the other stood.

No ONE WAS SURPRISED when we announced we had targeted GM. I had been maintaining publicly that both options were in balance, but people figured GM was a foregone conclusion after Bieber went to GM in the States. As reporters questioned me about what our goals were in the bargaining, I noticed a man I assumed to be from General Motors quietly taping everything that was said.

When Rod Andrew held his press conference we had someone there quietly taping. Later, we listened intently to the tape on which Andrew explained that GM understood that Canada's position differed from the States. He said he was willing to bargain a made-in-Canada agreement. He also stressed, however, that the auto industry was competitive and Canadian workers had to be prepared to accept competitive conditions. Meaning: something close to the GM agreement in the States.

That didn't worry us. We knew we had a seven- or eight-dollar-an-hour wage advantage over the States. We already were as competitive as hell.

A few days later, Lee Iacocca announced the appointment of Owen Bieber to the Chrysler board of directors. Iacocca explained, "His specific experience as a labour leader will be valuable as we close ranks to meet the Japanese competition."

I found it interesting that although there was little opposition at the GM council in St. Louis to the lump-sum agreement, the U.S. GM settlement was only ratified by 57 per cent. Leadership in many of the locals urged their members to reject the agreement and ten locals did, though Bieber warned that a "no" vote would put them on the picket lines. Owen Bieber didn't have the backing for lump-sum payments that he thought he had.

After Rod Andrew's remarks about understanding how Canada was different from the United States, I wasn't prepared for the proposal he tabled. It was a complete duplicate of the agreement in the United States. The only difference was that in some parts, it was a worse offer.

Only eleven days from strike deadline, we knew we were in serious trouble. The National Film Board crew was delighted at the way things were going. In order to give them some sense of what was happening, I had taken them into my confidence to some extent. The producers were fully aware that two stories were developing, the collision with GM and a confrontation within our own union. I don't think I excluded the NFB from more than two meetings or two telephone conversations. They knew exactly what was shaping up. We all got accustomed to stepping over a cameraman prone on the floor, shooting up at Buzz, Nick, Sam, and I as we huddled for a quick conference, or walking around a script assistant to get out the door, or making room for their cameras and lights at the committee caucus's meetings.

The crew got into a couple of private meetings between me and Rod Andrew until Don Hackworth was transferred out of Canada. Jack Smith, the president who replaced him, was aghast to see cameras inside the bargaining room. He withdrew access by the Film Board to all meetings involving General Motors, so that left the crews with no one to film but us.

My bargaining committee was firm about what it wanted from GM. John Clout, chairman of the St. Catharines plant, assured me that the membership was willing to take a long strike rather than cave in. "They're going to have to give them a raise," he said. "We're going to have to go for more bucks."

Once again, much of the media and public opinion seemed to be against us. We were taken to task for jeopardizing the recovery of the Canadian economy, which depended on a healthy auto industry. "Nobody in his right mind wants a strike at GM," moaned Robert Baguley, a Royal Bank of Canada economist. "The Canadian dollar may never see seventy-seven cents U.S. again."

A CBC news commentator said, "For the Canadian economy, some experts say an auto strike is like pulling a lynch pin from the economic recovery." He was fair enough to add, "General Motors has never been more profitable. Labour costs here are cheaper than on American assembly lines. So the workers argue the company can afford to give them some breaks and a uniquely Canadian deal."

General Motors made a second proposal only twenty-four hours before the strike deadline of October 17. It was almost a replica of the first one. It still included lump-sum payments and take-aways in many of the benefit areas, with no wage increases.

Our bargaining guys were furious. "I would never, never, stand up and recommend that bag of shit to my membership in Local 222," one guy said.

"It has nothing to do with the reality of what we proposed," said another disgustedly. "It's a waste."

Someone else commented, "It just seems to me that they don't want to settle the son of a bitch."

We turned it down unanimously, but I was worried. We had 35,000 workers facing a strike only hours away.

As far as I could see, GM was counting on Bieber to put pressure on us to take their offer. I knew Solidarity House was nervous about the possibility of a GM strike in Canada. It embarrassed them that we were rejecting a pattern settlement that GM workers had accepted in the States.

About that time, Bieber called. He expressed annoyance that I wasn't keeping him apprised of day-to-day developments. In truth, I told him, there were no day-to-day developments to report. We knew where we were going, so didn't need his help, and it didn't occur to me to tell him what we were doing. What was really on his mind was his desire for a quick settlement, which meant, take the company's terms.

I was curt. "Well I'm not going to get an agreement that I know won't be ratified by my membership," I told him. "I'm not going to tear the union apart over here, my friend. I know where I'm going. I'm a responsible bargainer and I'm going to try to get this thing done by Wednesday. If I can't, I'm going to stay till I do it. But I think I know my way around here."

Owen protested that I should consider the well-being of the total union. He said we would hurt the entire auto industry in the States if we took a strike in Canada, and warned that about three days into our strike, we would start to hurt even U.S. Ford.

"Yes, I understand that," I said. "The last thing I want to do is put this thing in the ditch and start affecting the income of U.S. workers, I can assure you of that."

When I hung up, Bob Nickerson speculated that Bieber might withdraw the authorization and cut off our strike benefits. Privately, I thought there was a good chance that might happen, but I said, "I won't lose one second sleep over that because I know, come Wednesday noon, we are on the march."

On Tuesday, when GM made its second proposal, Beiber telephoned again. His voice was tight with anger.

"I see you got another proposal," he said. "Did you reject it?"

"Yeah," I replied.

"I read just it in the newspaper," he said furiously. "I am the goddamned

263

president of this union. You'd think you could pick up the fucking telephone and tell me."

"I was going to call you later today, Owen," I said, and that was true, "but there really was no reason to call. The proposal is unacceptable and I've told them that."

"What's unacceptable?" he asked.

"We're not going down the road of lump-sum payments," I explained wearily. "You've known that from Day One."

"We can't keep doing this," he went on.

"Doing what?"

"You're causing all kinds of political problems over here," Bieber said. "We've either got one union or we haven't."

"We have one union, but we've got two countries," I told him. "We're going in two different directions. If that means we take a strike at GM, then we take a strike."

I was getting sore myself. "I'll tell you," I went on, "that's a fundamental issue. We're going to have to come to grips with this because I can't keep doing this every two or three years. I'm just not doing to do it, arguing with my own goddamned people about putting together a settlement."

We had a further hot exchange and then he snapped, "You're not going to get AIFs over there."

That's the 3-per-cent Annual Improvement Factor – in plain words, the wage increase.

"We're going to get some increases," I responded stubbornly.

"You can't be on strike for AIFs in Canada when we didn't get them in the United States," Bieber said. "If you strike on the AIFs, I'll call the board."

He didn't have to spell out what he meant. He was threatening to call the IEB to revoke the strike authorization.

I sighed. "Owen, unless we get a change in the proposal, we're going on strike tomorrow. And the strike will be about more than wages."

The guys in the GM bargaining committee knew that something was going on between me and Bieber. I didn't say much, except to joke that I was keeping my eye on Detroit, but they could see I was under a lot of strain and they knew some of it was coming from Solidarity House.

Owen called again in a threatening mood. He said he had called a special meeting of the IEB to discuss developments with Ford in the States. I thought I might only make matters worse by getting involved in a personal confrontation, so I sent Claude Ducharme, the Quebec director, to represent me in

Detroit. He returned the same day to say I didn't have a friend in Solidarity House. The executive might revoke the strike authorization the next morning.

We were in a committee caucus in the hotel at eight o'clock Tuesday night, sixteen hours before the October 17 noon deadline, when the phone rang. It was Helen Kramzyk. She had a call from Rod Andrew, she said. The night shift at GM's Oshawa truck plant, 3,000 workers, had just jumped the gun. They were out on a wildcat strike, and their picket lines were already humming. Word was spreading quickly – self-appointed leaders in Ste. Thérèse were also taking the workers out early.

A wildcat strike is death to bargaining because it removes our leverage. The corporation has nothing more to lose by standing pat. The final sixteen hours on which we had been counting were wiped out.

Phil Bennett got on the phone at once to his committee man in the Oshawa plant. I had a flash of panic. Bieber could use the illegal wildcat strike as an excuse to deny strike funds.

"You're playing exactly the games some people want us to play," I told the bargaining committee. "I don't have to draw any more drawings on the blackboard than that."

I tried to keep calm. "I hope those guys are as militant at Christmas as they are tonight. This hurts us. I'm not going to lecture anybody. There's nothing you can do now."

Nickerson said to Bennett, "You'd better get the word in there that they don't have the right to do that and the day shift is supposed to go in tomorrow." Phil, already with a phone in his ear, nodded.

Bennett was getting feedback. The workers thought they were helping us.

I said, "Let's try and not tear each other apart here. It's a difficult situation. The leadership ought to try and get at least an announcement out that the plant should operate tomorrow until twelve o'clock. And the responsibility belongs back there in the local union."

I called Rod Andrew.

"I guess you know our goddamn plants are down," he said.

"Yes I do," I replied. "I feel bad about that, but it's behind us. I've raised hell about it but let's move on."

I had to tell the bargaining committee that Bieber might stop the strike funds.

"There's been no decision taken," I told them. "The board was advised this afternoon that depending on the issues, they may have to make a decision tomorrow about whether or not to authorize a strike in Canada. I just want to make it absolutely clear that these plants are going down tomorrow at twelve noon."

The next morning, the Oshawa truck plant was still shut tight. A group of members lit some tires and blocked the gates, stopping people who wanted to pick up their paycheques. It was a very bad scene.

Bieber called to ask what I thought I was doing.

"I'm trying to get a fucking agreement, my friend," I told him. "We're going to have a strike. I don't know where we'll end up, but we're going to have a strike."

Bieber was upset. He said something about not striking on the issue of the AIF.

"What are you telling me?" I asked quietly.

He repeated it.

"That's not the only issue in this strike," I protested. "There's a number of other issues and we won't be settling them before twelve o'clock today."

"Just so you know," he said, "we're not going to continue a strike on the AIF."

"I hear what you're saying," I told him. "You'll have to make a decision if that becomes a last issue, I guess."

When I hung up I sighed, "God, he's an unhappy president." The only consolation for me was that Bieber hadn't cancelled the strike authorization. We were running.

I went into a room teeming with media to make the announcement about the strike.

"At twelve o'clock today we will be commencing the first Canadian strike against General Motors in fourteen years," I said. "We got another offer from General Motors yesterday that was almost identical to the offer we received ten days ago. I talked to Mr. Bieber this morning and acquainted him with the situation here. We have to find a solution to this problem in Canada. We intend to do that."

Someone asked a wicked question, "What did Bieber say to you?"

I joked, "Good morning and how did you sleep?"

CHAPTER NINETEEN

Across the Table from
Two Adversaries

W E WEREN'T PREPARED, and neither was General Motors, for the immediate consequences of the Canadian strike on the United States. General Motors had stockpiled in anticipation of the strike, but supplies were inadequate and, in some cases, entirely lacking. Within days an assembly plant in Detroit was shut down. By the end of the first week of our strike, some 40,000 American workers were laid off.

The *New York Times* published a Wall Street estimate that the strike in Canada cost GM $30 million in lost profits in the first week. It was expected that their losses in the second week would mount to $60 million. If all nine GM assembly plants depending on Canadian supplies had to close, as was likely to happen with a long strike, their loss would be about $100 million a week.

In spite of the hardship the strike was causing to American workers, we got telegrams of support from GM locals in the States wishing us well and saying they wished the UAW had done the same thing for them. Owen Bieber, when asked about the strain on the UAW's $500 million strike fund, responded that he hoped the strike in Canada would be settled quickly.

General Motors took a different view. We were advised that the GM chairman, Roger Smith, had told Rod Andrew to tell me that General Motors was not prepared to yield on the issue of wage increases.

I took that message to the bargaining committee. "Roger Smith has said there is no way they're going to put anything but lump sums in the second and third year, and that if this means the 1970 strike all over again, then that's the way it's going to be. It's going to mean a lot of jobs and it's going to mean a lot to investment in this country. There's no question this is tough stuff. My guess is when Roger Smith says that today, he probably means it."

The influential *Globe and Mail* chastized me severely. An editorial on the day of the strike observed, "Looking stoutly backward, Mr. White leads his membership into the picket lines demanding the same fixed percentage increase for all workers over the contract's three years. . . . A strike for the old rigidities that helped bring the auto industry to its knees only three years ago seems wrongheaded. . . . If this strike for the past continues much into the future, many people will suffer. Is the 'traditional pattern' for the few worth so much?"

The *Toronto Star* agreed with the *Globe*. Its editorial writers declared, "The only way that the attitude of Bob White and the UAW toward GM would make sense would be if they believed they're travelling on the Titanic and might as well go first class. . . . It's hard to see what they hope to accomplish by this strike. . . . The strike shouldn't have happened. It should be settled quickly."

Rod Andrew and I were meeting several times every day, in a frantic effort to find a formula. It was obvious to me that the problem was in Detroit. Rod didn't have the authority to move from lump-sum payments and give us some money. I didn't hear from Owen Bieber for a couple of days. When he finally called, we had a long talk.

"I am the president of this union," he reminded me frostily. "You can't settle this without me. I'm willing to give you some assistance."

"That's fine with me," I assured him. "All I want is to get this goddamn thing done."

"What does it take to get a settlement there?" he inquired.

We'd been working on little else. Sam Gindin had written the figures on a blackboard and every day we went over and over them with him, Buzz, Nick, Phil Bennett, and Pat Clancy. We looked at the U.S. pattern to see how we could use it as a framework in the first year but still get the 3-per-cent increase, and we explored what we would need in the second year, and what we would need for retirees, in pensions, and legal services, and so on. But our focus was still to discard the lump-sum payments and get increases instead. That's what the strike was about. That was the bottom line.

I laid it out for Bieber exactly as I had for Andrew. "We have to get *exactly* this," I explained to Bieber. "In the U.S. contract you got a two and a quarter per cent scaled increase in the first year, plus lump-sum payments in the second and third years. We're arguing here for a two and a quarter scaled increase in the first year plus a special increase of twenty-five cents an hour to bring us to three percent. And we want a twenty-five-cent-an-hour increase in the second year and twenty-five cents in the third." We also wanted to keep the COLA intact and we would be asking for improvements in pensions and in other areas.

"I'll give you what it takes to settle this," I told Bieber, "but there's no screwing around with this. We want that twenty-five cents."

"What are we going to call the goddamn thing?" Bieber asked. "You can't call it AIF."

"I don't care what we call it," I retorted. "We can call it CFI."

"What's that?"

"Canadian Fucking Increase. I'm telling you we're not settling this until we get the money."

We weren't interested in the General Motors' billion-dollar job bank. That might be useful in the States, but in Canada responsibility for social programs to help out-of-work people lies with the government. We could implement short-term assistance in our agreements, such as the SUB (supplementary unemployment benefits) or some minimum plant-closing benefits, but we didn't think the wellbeing of laid-off workers should depend on what happens every three years at a bargaining table.

I didn't agree with the American UAW's premise that job security could be bargained successfully. The auto industry is dependent solely on the consumer. No collective agreement, however wise, can protect workers against the vagaries of the marketplace. If a worker is in a good plant where they build one popular model after another, he can expect to work maybe a lifetime with few layoffs. But if the worker is making Edsels, he's likely to be on the street in a hurry. No matter how high the plant productivity or how low his wages, his job will be gone. A union can't do much about that, but we can negotiate long-term income security.

Some members of our UAW bargaining team had grown discouraged with the long stalemate. They thought that we should break off negotiations and come back fresh in a week or so. We had been living in the Royal York for two months and the strain of bargaining and the monotony of hotel meals and living out of suitcases was getting to us. I argued that we had too much at stake, we shouldn't quit quite yet. We had a responsibility to stay in the hotel and keep trying.

The crew from the NFB had become part of the background – like furniture, only friendlier. We were so accustomed to having them around that we didn't notice them any more. Whatever curbs on language we had imposed on ourselves in the beginning were forgotten and our behaviour had become normal and unselfconscious.

I think the NFB shot, in all, about sixty-two hours of film in the making of what became the award-winning documentary *Final Offer*. It wasn't until Buzz Hargrove and I saw a rough cut that I realized how blue the air had become at times when we were under pressure.

Buzz said, "Bob, I was going to tell you during bargaining that your language was the worse I've ever heard in all the years I've known you. I decided you had enough to think about, so I shut up. Your language is bad at times, but never as bad as it was those days when you were under so much pressure."

"Wait until my mother sees this," I groaned.

I decided in the end not to ask the NFB to edit. A documentary is a documentary; it isn't fair to turn it into fiction by trying to make it prettier than the reality. From the beginning of the project, my only stipulation was that if the equipment picked up the voice of anyone I was talking to on the telephone, the Film Board would have to get that person's permission to use it.

The GM bargaining team discussed breaking off negotiations but I was still reluctant. We were in a ballbuster. We were on strike against the biggest corporation in the world over an issue that was directly contrary to the position that our parent union had taken in the States. I didn't want us to leave the hotel until we were absolutely certain that the stalemate couldn't be broken.

The media were fascinated with developments in the GM strike. "What is involved is nothing less than a fundamental change in the basis for negotiating income improvement," observed Wilfred List in the *Globe and Mail*. "A lump-sum increase is really a euphemism for profit-sharing, with the money up-front. It looks attractive but it does not carry over into the next contract. . . . Never has the UAW in Canada steered so independent a course as it is doing today, undoubtedly to the chagrin of the leadership south of the border."

I continued to meet privately with Rod Andrew, but there was no change in GM's position. He seemed to have no bargaining room at all. To make matters worse, there were rumours flying around the hotel that Bieber was thinking of ending the strike by cutting off strike funds to Canadians.

"I don't want you to lose a moment's sleep over that, my friend," I told Andrew. "If Bieber cuts off our strike funds, I've got a cheque for ten million dollars in my hip pocket from the Canadian Labour Congress and there's more where that came from. We can keep this strike running without Bieber."

I related this later to the bargaining team.

"That's great," someone commented, "but do you *really* have a cheque for ten million from the CLC?"

"I don't have a cheque for ten cents," I replied with a grin, "but Andrew doesn't know that, and neither does Bieber. If we need to, we'll find a way to raise some money."

Six days into the strike, estimates of GM's losses had risen to $200 million a week. Still there was no change in the corporation's position. I noted at a press conference, "The only light at the end of the tunnel is on the front end of the freight train. We're trying to stay to the side of the track."

I was puzzled at GM's rigidity. "This is nuts," I said to Buzz and Nick as we paced the halls. "We've got thirty-six thousand workers out in Canada and forty thousand workers laid off in the States, and Bieber and Roger Smith are holed up talking to one another some place, and no one's telling us what's going on. What's happening here?"

The committee was also frustrated and angry. John Clout, an explosive man anyway, shouted, "I'm the chairman for eight thousand goddamned people and I want to know what the hell's going on. All I'm getting from you, Bob, is that you're having some conversations with Bieber. That ain't good enough." He was right.

We all felt like we were on ice with the motor running, our foot on the gas, spinning our wheels, and getting nowhere.

My strong hunch was that GM was getting a message from Bieber that the corporation didn't have to worry about yielding on wage increases. The Canadian bottom line could be negotiated away if General Motors simply put a little more in the lump-sum payments. No other explanation of the stalemate made sense. It just wasn't possible that GM would continue to keep us out unless the corporation had good reason to believe that we were soft. The money we were asking wasn't that much and the labour costs in Canada gave GM an enormous advantage in this country. We had a pretty good idea of what was going on inside Solidarity House.

I had another telephone conversation with Bieber a day or so after giving him our bottom line. "They're not buying your bottom line," he told me, sounding regretful. "Here's what the corporation is prepared to do. They won't go for the wage increases you want, but they'll improve the lump-sum payments. That's the best you can get."

I didn't yell and scream. I was thinking through my next move.

"So that's where they're at?" I said to Bieber in a calm voice.

"Yeah."

"Well, that's rather disappointing."

On Wednesday, October 24, seven days into the strike, we met as a committee to schedule mass-membership meetings at all GM locations for the weekend beginning Friday, October 26.

Then I called Rod Andrew. "I think someone is misunderstanding this," I said. "Someone thinks we aren't serious about wanting the wage increases. We have to hold a session with both our full bargaining teams."

Andrew came with only four or five people.

I led off by declaring that in another twenty-four hours we would be leaving the hotel, breaking off negotiations. "We're planning membership meetings this weekend. We's going to the membership to lock in our position," I told the GM bargainers.

"I don't believe this," I went on. "Look at Roger Smith's income and his executive bonuses. Contrast that with the way you treat your workers. First you make them take concessions, and now you want to take away the increases to which they're entitled. Someone wants us to take lump-sum payments, but I can tell you that we're not taking them."

I banged my fist on the table. "Someone, again, thinks that this strike is going to be taken away from us. That's not going to happen either. I want to tell you, my friend, that when we go out to the membership this weekend, and I wrap myself in the Canadian flag and talk about Roger Smith's executive bonuses and stock options, we won't have to meet with them again for another six or eight weeks. They'll be so charged up they'll be ready to strike until hell freezes over. Better get that message to Detroit."

Next the committee members took him on, just as tough.

Rod came back. He talked about making the industry competitive, about the precarious state the industry was in, about payrolls in the Japanese auto industry being 60 per cent lower than payrolls in North America. He went over the danger we were in, repeating the warnings he had given me in our one-on-one sessions, that we could lose the GM plant at Ste. Thérèse, we could lose the London diesel plant. The guys were furious at being threatened like that. They exploded and the meeting became as irate as the one we had with Greenwald during the Chrysler strike.

The weight on my shoulders was enormous. I was leading an organization which had 36,000 workers on strike. The wellbeing of those workers and their families depended on us. One wrong move could mean the closing of some plants and a strike that could last for two months, with all the sacrifices and pressures that go with a protracted strike.

Every morning, when I turned on the news, I heard of more GM workers laid off in the United States. I didn't feel good about that. We had the power to hurt ourselves.

If Andrew had been hoping in that session to find a weak link in our bargaining committee, he was seriously disappointed. Everyone was solidly behind the principle of a wage increase. We knew we would have no problem with the membership once we told them what was going on. The strikers would support us and their enthusiasm would carry us a long way. Eventually, though, we would have to go back to the bargaining table to find a solution. I was hoping we could take a shortcut. By showing Andrew how strongly we felt, maybe he could convince Roger Smith that Bieber was giving him wrong information.

As soon as Andrew and his GM people left the committee room, our guys broke into applause. I grinned at them, very moved. "That was a very important meeting," I said. "I think we just gotta hang tight for a few hours and see what happens. And we may have to play a little hardball later today. I'm proud of this committee. Let's just keep going. Let's not panic. I love it."

I called Bieber.

"I just want you to know, my friend, that we've had a very tough session with Andrew," I said, making no effort to keep the fury out of my voice. "I've told them that if they haven't changed their position in twenty-four hours, we're getting the hell out of here. We're all through fucking around, Owen. We're going out this weekend to lock this goddamned thing in with the membership, and then we'll sit and see if GM wants to do some serious bargaining."

Bieber didn't think I was being reasonable.

I blew up. "The membership will sit," I told him angrily. "We'll pay a hell of a price for that, but we're not going down that road for nickels and dimes. As of ten o'clock tomorrow morning, I will have Andrew at that bargaining table and tell him these negotiations are finished. I may get grey hair, but I'll get grey hair fighting the goddamned corporation before I'll get grey hair going to ratification meetings to have the membership cut me up. I ain't going to work that way."

I talked it over with the bargaining team. "You guys know this isn't Joe's Garage we're negotiating with. This is a tough company we've got. And they are mean. They're going to grind, make no mistake about that."

Things started to break almost immediately. Phone calls between the hotel and Detroit picked up suddenly. A different Bieber talked to me a few hours later.

"I'm going to see Roger Smith again," he informed me.

I didn't object. I didn't like it, but as long as he was giving Roger Smith a straight message, I didn't protest. After all, Roger Smith was the decision-maker. Rod Andrew didn't have the money.

"It won't be easy," Bieber warned me.

"Look at it this way, Owen," I said genially. "If the candidate I wanted for president of the union had been elected, you wouldn't have this problem."

Bieber didn't think that was too goddamn funny.

I told the committee, "I would just like to say that I'm more hopeful tonight than I've ever been that we can break this log-jam." John Clout was annoyed. He didn't like me being vague. "The clock's fucking ticking," he snapped. "I know where my membership is on the wage issue, but I'm not sure if the union's there anymore."

I said levelly, "Let me tell you, John, if I get to where I want to get, I haven't sold out your membership. I think I know where your membership is. You've expressed that. If I have sold out, you guys will turn the fucking thing down and the strike will continue."

Phil Bennett said heavily, "That's right."

Rod Andrew and I went at it again by ourselves. I was convinced that General Motors would go for the wage increase at last, but at a price. What we finally got was a complicated formula that was purposely disguised not to appear to be an annual improvement factor. Added to the base hourly rate was an increase of 2.5 per cent an hour the first year, plus twenty-five cents more of a "special" Canadian increase, bringing it up to 3 per cent.

It was a major accomplishment. We had won on our principle of wage increases instead of lump-sum payments, but it wasn't the traditional 3 per cent AIF that the bargaining team wanted. I had to face the committee members with an offer I knew would raise hackles.

I asked Nick and Buzz to stand back. "Let me do this. It's not going to be easy."

I had underestimated how difficult it would be. The meeting lasted four hours and twenty-five minutes and was the toughest committee caucus I have ever been in in my life. Some oldtimers, who have been around collective bargaining longer than I, said it was the toughest they'd ever seen.

I started at the blackboard, laying out the deal with Sam Gindin. "I have no hesitation in saying to everybody in this room that you may not like the amounts, and we can fight about that, but there's no question that this is a major move in terms of the whole question of lump sums and whether or not we're going to get money in the workers' paycheques on an on-going basis."

I did most of the talking in the beginning. As I went through it I looked from one face to another of the twenty-five members of the GM bargaining team. Only three people were nodding approval. We then had a real, knock 'em down, old-fashioned trade-union discussion. It wasn't about personalities, but about where we were going as a union and what dangers were involved in continuing the strike.

I was really saying, "Look, we've won. We got rid of lump sum payments and we've got some money in the paycheque. We've improved pensions, we've done a number of things. This is a helluva good settlement. Let's get it done. Let's not put jobs in jeopardy here with a prolonged strike." Some were saying, "*It's not good enough.*"

"I don't believe it's their last offer," one caucus member said.

"Believe me," I said. "It is."

Another said. "I don't like to give up that three per cent. I've seen it for years and years and years, and I don't want my kid, or my sons-in-laws, or some other guy to give it up."

"I understand that," I said. "I understand how you feel about that. But if anybody asked me the question, is this GM's bottom line? Can you hang on and get three per cent, three per cent, and three per cent? My friends, the answer is no."

"I appreciate what you've done, Bob," said another. "But it's gotta be three and three and three all the way through. So my vote right now is no."

Another said, "I'm opposed to this. There's too much hanging out there."

John Clout snapped, "We're in one fuck of a box with this thing, I can tell you that. We're betraying the goddamned membership if we buy this. I don't know what's going on here. Sure are a lot of guys swimming the other way."

"Well let me say something, John," I told him. "You and I might as well get into it. It's one thing for you to tell me I didn't do good enough. But don't ever tell me that I'm betraying the membership with this proposal."

"I'm not talking of . . ."

"Yes you are. So's you know, so's you and I get it off on the right foot from day one, I came to this committee with this recommendation and I ain't betraying the membership in recommending it. Now you and I may disagree on what's in it, but don't ever accuse me of betraying the membership, my friend, because that's bullshit."

I took a breath. "Okay, let's start now. Now let's look at reality. Do you think you're not going to lose jobs if we keep out another month? You know the answer to that. You know it, John. Let's look at what Rod Andrew does tomorrow. He goes to the press and he says, Bob White said he wanted an agreement. What did he want? Up-front money? There's more money up front than there is in the U.S. agreements. No lump sums? There are no lump sums in this agreement. Cost of living protection? There's a new COLA, a Canadian COLA formula better than anything else in the Canadian industry. Seventy-four cents new goddamned money."

I was almost shouting. "If that's a betrayal of your membership John, I'll go with you to the membership meeting. It's a betrayal of the membership for us to keep them on strike for another month and then go back to them and say, you know what we did guys? We moved your increase up to three per cent. And that got you another fifteen cents. Man, we sure are tough."

"You want to tell the membership that they can't get what they had for thirty goddamned years, for Chrissake?" John roared back at me. "They can't get goddamned three per cent with the money this corporation's making after they've been on the street for a week? You might tell them that if they've been on the street for two months. You might even convince me of that. But you ain't convincing me that it ain't there within the goddamned week."

"I don't want to roll dice for another ten or twenty cents here, John, and lose some jobs," I said. "I want to say to the corporation that we fought you on a principle and we were right. We got some money. Let's go back to work and understand that this makes sense economically. And let's talk about the future."

Clout sat back. "Well, I ain't changed my mind on it."

Hours later Phil Bennett called for a vote. The committee approved the tentative economic proposal.

Final Offer showed some of that caucus discussion and demonstrated how tough it is for a union leader to sway a bargaining caucus. It was such a revelation of how open our bargaining tradition is to dissent that many of the public, accustomed to the view of us as all-powerful "union bosses," were astonished. I'm told the film has been shown in corporate boardrooms to educate directors on the realities of bargaining. Corporation heads don't have to face such confrontations and may have imagined that unions are run the way they run business, with little input allowed.

When I emerged from that meeting, I was absolutely drained. I'd been on my feet at the blackboard arguing steadily for four hours and twenty-five minutes and I was about ready to fall down.

The media had been waiting outside the caucus room listening to the sounds of shouting that came through the doors, trying to guess what was taking so long. I went straight into a press conference, my face showing the strain.

"What happened in there?" someone asked.

"Nothing," I replied evenly. "Just a nice little discussion within the UAW family. You know, these guys don't go to obedience school."

I added, "There is no question this is a fairly historic day." Our Canadian Region had refused to rubber-stamp the pattern agreement reached in the United States.

We still had some tricky pieces of the agreement to put together. The lowest paid workers were not getting enough. In the settlement, janitors had an increase of eight cents, plus the twenty-five cents. To bring them up to the 3 per cent increase, we needed another four cents for them. Minor assemblers were getting twelve cents and we needed another six for them.

I went back to Andrew with that news. "We've got to do this," I insisted. "It's not a lot of money and it will make it easier for us to get this thing ratified. The workers are right about this. The janitors and minor assemblers are coming up short. And we need more in the pensions."

"I can't do it," Andrew said.

I think I read him. His hands were tied. Bieber, I thought.

I called Owen.

"I think we're on our way," I told Bieber, "but I want to do something more with the bottom two classifications. Otherwise I don't think I can get ratification here. Two of the big units will oppose the agreement. I have got to get more money and I think I can get it."

"No goddamned way," Bieber said. "Someone wanted to do that in the Ford agreement and I wouldn't let them. There's no fucking way you're going to get any extra money than you've already got. I'll personally oppose it."

I talked about the money we wanted in the pensions. Pension costs are different in Canada, I explained, and we needed more in the pensions.

"No goddamned way," he roared. "You're not getting one mill more in pensions. If you take that issue on pensions I'll personally fly to Toronto and land on the goddamned Royal York Hotel. We can't stand this. It's going to give us all kinds of goddamned problems over here as it is, the way the settlement is coming out."

I went to Rod Andrew. "We can't get the settlement unless we get those extra pieces," I told him flatly. "We've got to have them." We argued back and forth and then I suggested that we put the extra pieces in the local agreements so they wouldn't appear in the brochure which is distributed nationally. That way American GM workers wouldn't know about them and it wouldn't cause Bieber political problems. Andrew wouldn't give anything on pensions, but he did allow four cents more for janitors and six cents more for minor assemblers.

We had to finesse the name of the general wage increase to avoid calling it AIF, which really it was. Instead we ended up calling the increase SCA, Special Canadian Adjustment. Bieber explained to his members that Canadian labour costs were less than in the States, so it was understandable that we would have a special adjustment that differed from their lump-sum payments.

Wilf List wrote in the *Globe and Mail* on October 26, 1984 that General Motors "appears to have backed away from its insistence on lump-sum payments in the second and third year of the contract as a substitute for annual increases in the basic wage rates."

That same day, with subcommittees working hard on health and safety issues, local work rules, benefits, and other non-economic issues, 12,300 more workers in American GM plants were laid off. Now, nine of GM's twenty-nine assembly plants were down and eighteen parts plants were either shut or operating with reduced shifts.

The settlement was reached at two o'clock Saturday afternoon, October 27, after a thirty-one-hour session that left us all grey with fatigue. I went before the media's cameras and microphones immediately to make the announcement, adding a comment that caught the attention of veteran labour reporters who suspected that I was having trouble with Bieber. I said, "An international union that wants to survive has to recognize clearly the collective bargaining realities of workers in both countries. If it fails to do that, it cannot survive as an entity. The days of rubber-stamping U.S. agreements are over."

We took what was being hailed as "the made-in-Canada settlement" to the Canadian GM membership and it was ratified by a vote of 87 per cent of production workers and 83 per cent of skilled trade workers. That was in contrast to the 57 per cent ratification of the agreement signed with General Motors in the States.

I attended the Oshawa ratification votes, for which our members packed the hockey arena three times. We were in the hotel while other GM plants were voting. The vote came in from St. Catharines, John Clout's Local 199 – 89.9 per cent of production workers in favour and 91.7 per cent of skilled trades.

I grinned, "And he thought I didn't understand his membership."

The twelve-day strike was over for 36,000 workers. At midnight on Monday, October 29, the Canadian GM assembly lines started to move again.

The agreement included some improvements in time off the job, pensions, and income security, and also, for the first time in a GM contract, dealt with such innovative benefits as child care, affirmative action programs for women and, something that caught a lot of public attention, a prepaid legal service to which General Motors contributed three cents an employee for every hour worked. GM workers, retirees, and their families now have free access to lawyers for such routine services as wills, real-estate transactions, and defending themselves in traffic courts. That was a major breakthrough for the labour movement in Canada, a first in any agreement, and we were proud of it. We knew the plan was a good idea, but we weren't prepared for the degree of enthusiasm it received from workers at the ratification meetings.

ON THE DAY GM WORKERS went back to work, Sam, Nick, Buzz, and I dragged ourselves to the Westbury Hotel to face a waiting and rested Ford bargaining team, where we announced an early strike deadline. That caught Ford's attention, and the corporation soon dropped whatever plans it had to demand that we follow the U.S. pattern. We insisted that Ford follow the pattern established in the Canadian agreement with GM.

A few hours before the strike deadline, Ford yielded. We had won our point that Canada and the United States aren't one country.

All through the struggle with GM I kept saying to Buzz, Nick, and Sam that I wasn't going through another collective bargaining with two adversaries across the table, the corporation and my own union. When Bieber became president, I had hoped that we would put behind us the conflicts that had developed with Doug Fraser during the Chrysler strike, but nothing had changed. If anything, the GM strike had been worse for the relationship between the Canadian Region and Solidarity House.

"We've got to be in charge of our own destiny," I said. "This international union of ours has got to recognize full Canadian autonomy."

On November 1, 1984, John Deverell had a bombshell story on the front page of the *Toronto Star*, saying that I was considering a move to lead the 120,000 members of the Canadian Region out of the international United Auto Workers.

Deverell wrote that there was "growing anger among Canadian UAW officials over recent attempts by U.S. counterparts to force workers at GM Canada to accept a contract patterned on the one in the United States."

He traced the history of the growing split, beginning in 1979, when the UAW accepted major concessions in the agreement with Chrysler. He noted that, in 1981, when the UAW accepted more concessions, Canadian Chrysler workers had protested. He made some shrewd guesses about the strains between me and Bieber during the GM strike just concluded, one of which was the rumour that Solidarity House had considered withholding strike pay for our workers.

"Bitterness," he wrote, "is running deep." He said it would surface when the Canadian Council of the UAW next met to take stock. Even while the bargaining with Ford was continuing, workers had begun to talk about leaving the UAW and Deverell talked to some of them. He quoted Gerry Michaud, president of Local 199 in St. Catharines and a long-time advocate of Canadian independence, who said, "There are good reasons to stay and good reasons to go, but I still want a Canadian union."

I was jolted. I wasn't contemplating setting up a Canadian union, as the story suggested. All I was thinking about was a change in the rules so that the Canadian Region would have autonomy and not be subjected to pressure from the international UAW, which for five years had made collective bargaining in Canada difficult.

I called a press conference and acknowledged that there were stresses within the union. I said we were not advocating a breakup but were looking at structural changes to give Canadians more flexibility.

Reporters went to Owen Bieber to ask what was going on. Bieber made some comment that I had an obligation to come to him and the International Executive Board first if I wanted to make changes in the structure.

He phoned our office in a fury about my statement. I was on my way to a meeting, so Buzz Hargrove tried to explain. "Bob just said he didn't want to talk about it now, but there would be talks in the future."

Bieber ranted and raved. He was offended that I hadn't kept the dispute in the club. But I wasn't feeling ready to open up the issue with Solidarity House. I was tired from the GM negotiations, we were trying to avoid a strike at Ford, and I needed time to think and consult.

Nevertheless, the ball was rolling. A few days later, Wilf List of the *Globe and Mail* wrote, "The UAW, North America's most innovative and pioneering union, is in a mid-life crisis. The team that grew up around Walter Reuther is gone. The UAW is now cautious, conciliatory and retreating from historic achievements while the Canadians are determined to push ahead. Robert White and Owen Bieber are on a collision course."

I let Bieber know that I wanted to introduce the matter of the relationship between the Canadians and the rest of the UAW at the December meeting of the International Executive Board, with a full discussion to take place at the following IEB meeting in March. Bieber replied frostily that media attention made it impossible to wait so long. He said we would "dispose" of the matter at the December meeting.

The Canadian Council met on December 1 in Toronto. I saved mention of our relations with the international union until the end. I began by tracing the simultaneous development of the UAW in the United States and Canada during the Walter Reuther years and the evolution of a measure of Canadian independence. Gradually but steadily, we were taking responsibility for our own destiny. We have to stop blaming the Americans for our problems, I said and "take responsibility for them ourselves."

I was frank about the difficulties with the international union that had emerged during the GM negotiations.

"So what can we do?" I asked. "Well, I guess we can take the grand step, say this relationship cannot continue and therefore we must discuss complete new structures independent of each other with close solidarity ties, but end the international union as we know it. Or we can, as I prefer to do at this stage of our development, change our structure internally to meet the new realities."

I paused. The room was absolutely still.

"But change we must," I continued. "My preference is to pursue the latter course and if that's not possible or acceptable, then a completely new structure must be formed. Either way, we must pursue this in a positive tone, in a mood of progressive, necessary change. We cannot be deterred by the faint-hearts in Canada who don't want the change because it means uncertainty or added responsibility. Nor can we be deterred by those in leadership positions of our international union who want the status quo to remain."

I asked that the Canadian Council give me a mandate going into the meeting of the IEB. I would propose a constitutional amendment to give Canada the right to pursue its own collective-bargaining strategy, independent of any U.S. strategy. Further, strike authorization would be automatic upon a request from the Canadian director, and when collective bargaining was being carried on in Canada with an employer whose head office is in the United States, the international UAW would not interfere except at the specific request of the Canadian director.

This would mean changes in administration so that all UAW staff working in Canada would be responsible to and paid by the Canadian office, including organizing staff, education staff, and some other departments currently on Solidarity House's payroll. Finally, I wanted the Canadian Region to have the right to pursue mergers with Canadian sections of other international unions.

"The discussion at the IEB is only a week or so away," I concluded. "It will not be an easy discussion and, because of the interest, there will be public statements and discussions. First, that discussion must commence here. Whatever we do, whatever direction we decide to go, we must be united. If we are, in my opinion our union and our members in both the United States and Canada will be better off in the future."

CHAPTER TWENTY

A Separate Union

MY DECISION to ask the Canadian Council to consider the alternatives of either more autonomy within the UAW or a separate union came after long consultations with my associates, primarily Bob Nickerson (Nick), Buzz Hargrove, and Sam Gindin. The difficulties we'd been having with the international union since 1979 had to end.

Buzz, Nick, Sam, and I make an excellent team. Nick is a detail man, a good analyst, a strong and thoughtful person. Buzz is more willing to take a chance, he's a gutsy, intelligent person. Sam has the data, and he's also very idealistic about the labour movement. We balance one another well, and there is a lot of respect and affection in the mix.

Faced with the crisis that had developed within the international union, we did what we always do when something important is in the wind. We talked it through, thought about it, talked it through again, got some sleep, talked it through five more times. From time to time, we pulled in a key staff member and asked him or her for an opinion. We concluded that to go to the Canadian Council with the single proposal to leave the UAW would tear the Council apart. We needed to present a good alternative, which was autonomy within the union.

The day before I went to the Council with that dramatic proposal, I did something I've never done before. I called all the staff together for a five- or six-hour discussion of what was happening. I still wasn't sure that I should present Bieber and the International Executive Board with an ultimatum. If we couldn't get full autonomy, what steps other than separation could we take?

I put that dilemma to the staff, opening up my heart about what happened during the GM bargaining. I asked them to tell me what they thought we should do.

"I need to know how you feel about this," I said, "because once we start down this road, we're all putting our paycheques on the line."

Some staff I hadn't counted on turned out to be stalwarts. They said, in effect, "We can't keep going through this. We've got to change. If we have to make a complete break, let's do it."

I left the staff meeting full of resolve, and that afternoon, I rewrote and toughened the proposal I would take to Council.

That night at eight o'clock the staff met again.

"We're all in this together now," I said quietly. "All the politics, all the boss-staff relationships are finished. If we don't get autonomy within the union, and there is a strong possibility we won't, that means we're charting a whole new course. It could mean that the international union will stop the paycheques of everybody in this room.

"All you have to do if you don't believe me is look what happened to the Canadian paperworkers when they tried to separate from their international unions."

That story is a labour-movement disgrace. The Canadian paperworkers voted to leave their international, expecting that the separation would leave them with a proportion of the union's funds to maintain their office and staff. Instead, the international convention voted to cut them off without a cent. A Canadian company took advantage of the situation right away and put the paperworkers into a long strike. The labour movement in Canada had to rally and help them out. To their great credit, the paperworkers survived, but it was an exhausting struggle.

"I'm in it for the long haul and I know what it means," I told the staff grimly. "This is no time for any shit in the system. If you haven't got the guts for it, just tell me right now."

The staff said unmistakably that they were with me, though it meant they were laying their futures on the line.

My Canadian Council report, which consisted of some twenty typewritten pages stapled together, usually is distributed in advance to the tables at which delegates sit. I changed the procedure this time because I didn't want announcement of the proposal to be released prematurely to the media who'd come to cover the meeting. We left the reports in boxes until I got up to speak, at which point the staff went through the room handing one to each delegate.

As I began to read the report, the tension in the room was palpable. Rumours had been running through the plants and offices, fanned by media speculation. Every delegate knew that UAW history would be made at this meeting. They listened intently, heads down, following the text as I read it. Every time I turned a page, three hundred pages turned in unison.

I came at the end to the current strife within the UAW. I outlined in detail the long evolution of Canadian independence and identity within the UAW and related how difficult the recent few years had been. With that framework in place, I read the options – autonomy within the UAW or autonomy, period.

When I got to the last line of my recommendation, the delegates leapt to their feet applauding and the room exploded into cheers. We hadn't been entirely sure what to expect, brickbats or bouquets, but the immediate enthusiasm was incredible. The thunderous standing ovation went on for minutes.

Then we opened up the debate. Some good people were opposed to splitting from the UAW. They made speeches about Walter Reuther and pleaded with fellow delegates to support the issue of more autonomy for Canadians but not to think of leaving the UAW. What about the internationalism that trade unionists had preached for years? they asked. Were we going to throw that dream away?

A few thought we should not proceed without a referendum vote of the entire membership. I couldn't let that happen. If we went out to the locals, opening the door for corporate interference and internal politics and personality clashes, by the time we counted the votes, the union would be split into pieces. The Council had to act as a true parliament, which it was. There were 300 delegates in the room, each one elected from the 115 locals in Canada to represent them responsibly and each one obliged to go back to our 120,000 members to report and be accountable for decisions made by the Council.

After a good debate, I insisted on a standing rather than voice vote. The vote was overwhelmingly in favour, with only three opposed.

I had a press conference at the noon recess. I decided to be frank about the situation because we could only benefit from improved understanding of what we were doing and why. I told the media exactly what was happening.

"I am an internationalist," I said, "but true internationalism requires us to be in control of our own destiny. If they say no in Detroit, if I get shut out, then I will call a special meeting of this Council to take the next step to independence."

I added, "The only thing an international president should do during collective bargaining negotiations in Canada is assist, not interfere."

I was asked if I thought the Canadian UAW could survive in its own. I replied, "We will not die on the vine. The corporations will not grind us into the ground."

The media reports made Bieber and others in Detroit absolutely furious, but I knew what I was doing. I wasn't going to Detroit for a nice closed-door discussion without having the Canadian UAW membership, and the public, fully aware of developments.

The Council met December 1 and 2, 1984, and the IEB meeting in Detroit followed on December 10. We discussed who should go with me, trying to anticipate what expertise would be needed. "Okay, I'll tell you who I want," I said finally. "Nick and Buzz, of course, Helen Kramzyk to handle telephone calls because we'll be on the phone a lot, and Wendy Cuthertson to take care of the media." I would have liked Sam Gindin to be included, but he was in Europe.

I sent Owen Bieber copies of my report to the Canadian Council, so he knew that the Canadian Council supported my proposal. I thought he would want to meet me before the meeting, but I heard no word. He refused to comment on the Canadian dissatisfaction except to say it would be handled at the IEB meeting.

We left Toronto on Sunday night and the next morning, I went to the officers' meeting with Buzz and Nick. I wanted them nearby in case the officers wanted a full-blown discussion and I needed to consult.

You could have cut the air in the meeting room with a knife. The faces turned toward us were cold.

Bieber frowned. "They're not staying for the officers' meeting!" he snapped, pointing a finger at Buzz and Nick.

"Of course not," I replied. "I thought we might need them nearby. Are we going to discuss my proposal at this meeting?"

Bieber said curtly, "No, we're not going to have two discussions about this. We'll put it first on the agenda at the executive meeting this afternoon and dispose of it."

Dispose was a curious word to choose, I thought. It suggested that the problem with the Canadians was a minor hiccup that could be suppressed in a few minutes.

"Okay, that's fine with me," I said. "There's no reason then for them to stay here."

Buzz and Nick went out and when the door closed behind them, I thought I'd better get one detail settled. I said, "I'd like to have Buzz and Nick with me at the board meeting."

As a rule, UAW officers could bring one administrative assistant to this meeting, but if someone brought two with him, nothing was said about it.

This time, however, Bieber wanted to make things as difficult for me as he could.

"You're not having two assistants at the board," he informed me sharply. "You can only have one."

"Goddamn it," I said. "They're entitled to be with me. You guys know how I operate. They ought to be part of the decision we're going to make here today."

Ray Majerus said, "Well, if we let you have two assistants then everybody will want two assistants."

"Everybody isn't talking about splitting up the union today," I said levelly. "I am. For you guys to deny me the right to take Buzz and Nick in to that meeting is unfair as hell. I need these guys. I don't want them to miss something that might be important in the process."

Bieber said, "It's not going to happen. You can take only one of them in."

I went out to tell Buzz and Nick.

"I've got some good news and some bad news, guys. The bad news is that only one of you can go in. I don't know how you're going to sort it out, but the good news is I'm not going to make a selection."

They are remarkable men. Neither wanted to miss this opportunity-of-a-lifetime, but each stepped back for the other.

Buzz immediately said, "You go in, Nick. You were with him in the GM thing."

"No, no. No goddamned way, buddy," Nick said. "We'll flip a coin."

Nick lost.

The meeting of UAW officers continued, dealing with only routine matters, while the media waited outside. When I left the room to go to the bathroom, I had to have security escort me through corridors packed with television crews, radio reporters with hand-held mikes, and print reporters. Other UAW officers, who went on the same errand, returned to make disparaging comments about "the bloodsuckers out there." They were worried that we would have to run a press gauntlet when the meeting adjourned.

"I don't have any trouble with that," Bieber said. "As far as I am concerned this is an internal matter. There's no reason to discuss it with the media."

That shot was meant for me, of course. From his point of view he was right, but I couldn't do what I'd come to do behind closed doors. The public was interested in what was happening, and the issue was too important to be confined to a private discussion in the club.

The officers' meeting concluded around noon and we moved to the IEB meeting room, wading through the media. Bieber refused to answer any of the questions thrown at him.

Bieber cleared the room of everyone but board members, his assistant, Ray Majerus's assistant, Buzz, and two court reporters who took the minutes.

Bieber nodded at me. "Go ahead Bob," he said briskly.

"In two months I will have been a member of the international union for thirty-four years," I began. "My roots are firmly entrenched in the international union. I am proposing that we make the union truly international – an equal partnership between Canada and the United States. My remarks will be candid, but they are not to be considered an attack on any individual's ability or integrity."

I had thirty-seven pages of handwritten notes, thirty-five of which were a historical account of the union beginning with Walter Reuther's days. I was trying to show how the changes were gradual and followed a logical pattern. The truth, I said, was that there had been a natural progression toward Canadian independence.

"We're ready for another step," I argued, "another major step."

My preference, as I made clear, was to have complete Canadian autonomy under the international union's umbrella.

After I spoke, Bieber took the floor for about twenty minutes. He chose to go over the events of the General Motors strike, saying who said what and when. His plan seemed to be to clear himself of blame. I thought his approach was somewhat irrelevant to the issue we were addressing, but I listened without expression. A couple of times I disputed his version of events. Once was when he referred to the GM strike authorization, which he declared he had given freely. I contradicted him.

"You threatened to take away our authorization," I reminded him.

"I never did," he retorted.

"You're saying to me that you never said you would call the board?" I asked.

"No, I didn't."

Bieber's version of the GM strike was that he had never interfered with me; further, the Canadian settlement was his work. He spoke of the helluva time he had with GM president Roger Smith and how he had to "bat it out of General Motors' brains."

After Bieber finished, the discussion opened up, and the debate lasted six hours. Some board members said they understood the necessity for Canadians to determine their own destiny, but they didn't see how we could do that under one organization. There couldn't be two presidents, they argued. We would be eroding the authority of the international president. If the Canadians did that, why wouldn't some other region like California want to do the same?

I murmured to Buzz, "They don't understand. It still hasn't penetrated that we're not another state in the United States, we're a different country."

I had two proposals. The first was the alternative of Canadian autonomy within the union, with details of how that might work. If that was rejected, the second proposal was to establish a structure to supervise the separation of Canadians from the international UAW.

The vote on the first proposal was twenty-four to one – my vote – against the proposition for Canadian autonomy. I immediately introduced the proposal that "we establish a committee to proceed with the separate restructuring of our union into an American UAW and a Canadian UAW with intelligent discussion as trade unionists recognizing the contribution each section of our union has made to this great organization and the entitlement and obligation to make sure each will be a viable institution in its own right in each country."

This was the obvious consequence of the defeat of the first motion, but the debate was unexpectedly sharp. Some people seemed to have misunderstood the implications of the first vote. They had voted against Canadian autonomy within the UAW in the belief that they were voting for the status quo. They said Canadians had no right to leave and treated us to some great oratory about "tearing this union apart."

To his credit, Bieber understood the situation. "Look, goddamn it," he said. "You can't reject on the one hand what the man's proposing and then tell him can't do the other either."

Many continued to argue that the question of Canadian autonomy had been dismissed. There was nothing more to discuss. I guess they thought that we should go home and calm down. Besides, as they pointed out, the UAW constitution did not permit a region to secede. What the Canadians wanted to do was illegal.

That certainly was true. Under the constitution, we didn't have the right to leave.

When our lawyers had told me, "You can't do this legally. It's in violation of your constitution," I'd responded. "I love you. You're great lawyers. Get me out of jail if I get thrown in, but don't tell me how to run the union."

We were ready to vote on the separation mechanism. I had a final word, saying it was important that the UAW to do this intelligently, with as little rancour as possible, and not have it end up in legal action and messy confrontation. Then we voted. My motion was supported by seventeen to seven. We sat silently for a few moments after the vote, each one of us troubled and saddened.

We decided to form an IEB committee to address the separation and work out the legal, financial, and constitutional details. Later, Bieber named the members: himself, me, Ray Majerus, and Joe Tomasi, a director from Toledo, an old stalwart on the board and a good person. I insisted that Buzz and Nick be allowed to attend, though they were not official members.

In a state of shock, we talked quietly about how we would handle the media outside. I offered to go first.

"Go ahead," Bieber said. "No problem."

I've never seen such a huge press conference in all my life, it was so immense it was scary. And it was only the first of many. Wendy Cuthbertson kept count, and in the next week I did 100 interviews.

I was mentally drained by the momentous decision we had made. I knew there would be criticism, and there was, but I was heartened by an unsolicited and welcome comment from Victor Reuther, Walter's only surviving brother and one of the founders of the UAW. He observed, "This move is a continuing expression of a strong nationalistic sentiment, and I say this in the best sense . . . I do not look upon this action as anti-UAW States-side. There does not have to be organic unity in order to have solidarity across international lines."

It was late in the day when we finished the press conference. We went to our room, a suite we had taken in the expectation we would need a good deal of space, and invited in some Canadian reporters who wanted more details. I ordered up some beer and sandwiches and we tried to relax, though we were all keyed up. I was on the phone much of the time, taking calls from all over, while Buzz, Nick, and Wendy tried to sort out the hubbub.

By a curious coincidence, Prime Minister Brian Mulroney was in New York that same night to make a speech announcing the dismantling of the Foreign Investment Review Agency. He was saying, in essence, that Canada was open for American business again, everyone welcome. Here we had the Canadian prime minister leading the country towards closer ties to the United States at the same moment that a Canadian labour leader was taking his union in the opposite direction.

Reporters caught the prime minister as he left the platform and asked for his views on the split in the UAW. He made a reasoned statement which we later used in our brochure. He said, "If they feel it is in their best interests as

Canadian workers to do this, then they ought to. Bob White is an outstanding labour leader showing remarkably sane leadership. He may be called upon to make that decision in the interests of his view of Canada and the national interests of his members."

We watched the CBC national news that night. The first item was a story on the split in the UAW and the second was the prime minister's statement about it.

That night I was too wound up to sleep. I kept going over and over in my mind the enormity of what we'd done. We were splitting the mighty UAW in two, tearing it apart along the borderline. I felt that I, too, was being torn apart, and I rolled over and wept.

I slept for a couple of hours and wearily got up to shower and dress for a seven o'clock feed to Canada AM, the CTV network's morning news show. As I rode in a taxi to the television studio, a wave of excitement hit me. My mind started to race with ideas of how the new UAW Canada could be structured.

The media reflected a general state of alarm about the upheaval within the UAW. Tom Miner, Chrysler's vice-president in charge of industrial relations, commented glumly that it was "one more complication in an already complicated business." The *Wall Street Journal* reported that the split was making corporate bigwigs uneasy. Alf Warren, vice-president of industrial relations for General Motors, said, "We can't afford to be held hostage by any union outside the U.S. . . . We've always had good relationships with the union in Canada, but those have been because of our relationship with the international UAW. I would hate to see us now finding ourselves dealing with a different union that perhaps wanted to go in a different direction."

My response was, "I didn't become the leader of the Workers' Revolutionary League overnight just because we are taking an autonomous or independent course. We are still the UAW with a serious obligation to our members and to the industry."

The *Toronto Sun* declared: WHEELS FALL OFF UAW.

The rest of the day in Detroit was occupied nonstop with media interviews. Our plan was to leave that night and take a plane back to Toronto.

Just before checkout time, we were all gathered in the suite. "Let's not go," I said suddenly. "Let's get a room service menu. We'll order up something to eat, and get hold of a blackboard and some chalk. Let's go into a session right now to decide what kind of a structure we're going to have in the Canadian UAW."

We argued for hours and hours that night, putting diagrams full of arrows on the blackboard and erasing them to draw different ones. We discussed the role of the Canadian Council and the Quebec Council and decided we couldn't scrap them, they were too valuable. The problem we faced was how to get rank-and-file input into the executive board without leaving the union vulnerable to some political group or unsavoury characters. How could we put in checks and balances to get the most worker participation and the least bureaucracy? We couldn't afford to be top-heavy because it would only serve to isolate the leadership from the members.

Our discussion lasted well into the early hours of the next morning, sometimes with us shouting and screaming at each other. What we finally decided on that blackboard is pretty much what we have today in the CAW. We decided on a twelve-member executive board with three fixed positions: a president elected by a national convention, a secretary-treasurer elected by a national convention, and the Quebec director, elected by the Quebec delegates and endorsed by the full national convention. Seven of the other nine members would be local union leaders elected by the Canadian Council or the Quebec Council, and the two others would be chosen directly at the national convention.

A constitutional convention would meet every three years, the Canadian Council and the Quebec Council would meet quarterly,

When we looked at the chart we'd made, it sunk in that we had created only one new staff position on the executive, that of secretary-treasurer. I had two administrative assistants, Buzz and Nick. Which one would get the new post?

The three of us had been as close as family since the day in 1978 when I was elected director.

"We have to settle this," I said to Buzz and Nick. "We've been through a lot together and you know I never show preference. But I have to make a choice."

I turned to Buzz. "You're a lot like me with money, my friend. You give it away, you spend it, you enjoy it, but you don't save it. Nick is a nit-picker. He knows how to manage finances, he's careful, he knows what's going on. I think there's no question that Nick should be the secretary-treasurer."

Buzz stood up and put out his hand to Nick. "Congratulations," he said with a smile.

As soon as we returned from Detroit we started to work on educational material to go out to all our Canadian members, explaining our decision and answering questions about the new organization, which we were calling UAW-Canada.

Dennis McDermott made a strongly supportive statement: "I applaud the decision," he said. "I think it is a positive move that takes into account the sharp differences between Canada and the U.S." Later, at the founding convention of UAW Canada, Dennis went even further. In a speech that was described as the most anti-American of his career, he said, "This union will be severely tested in the coming months, but as long as I have breath left in my body, this union will not die. If it takes the entire collective force of the labour movement to insure that, I pledge it here today."

Some reaction was unfavourable. One public figure described the Canadian UAW as a loose cannon on the deck that would destroy the auto industry. Mark L. Kahn, director of the master's degree industrial relations program at Wayne State University in Detroit, thought that the auto companies would be so concerned about facing an independent UAW in Canada that they would insure that their key production, or most of it, was moved to the States.

Several Canadian branches of American-based unions were alarmed and hostile. They said we were wrecking international unionism and now workers wouldn't support each other any more across national boundaries.

George Burt, the retired UAW director, said bluntly that I was crazy, that we were losing the bargaining skills of Solidarity House and that 36,000 Canadian GM workers couldn't get anything that U.S. GM workers couldn't get. I pointed out, as gently as I could, that George had lost track of events. In Canada 36,000 GM workers had just done exactly the opposite: they got a better contract than over 300,000 GM workers got in the States.

I called the special meeting of the Canadian Council for December 15, 1984, making it a joint meeting that included the Quebec Council as well. We set up simultaneous-translation booths in a conference room in the Royal York Hotel in Toronto.

Four hundred concerned delegates listened intently as I described what had happened at the International Executive Board meeting. Then I got to the matter of finances, knowing that thoughts of the paperworkers were in all our minds.

There were questions.

What will the corporations do? "The decision we made was not to set up the Workers Revolutionary Party in Canada or to circle the GM Oshawa plant with tanks. It was to move from an organic structure within one union to a looser arrangement between two unions."

Can we be financially sound? "The answer, of course, is we can – 120,000 UAW members in Canada pay an emormous amount of union dues into both the strike fund and the general administration of this union. We are entitled to expect our appropriate share when we set up our own organization – and we can and must be self-sustaining from then on. We should stop a lot of these silly rumours that somehow the international union will seize all the local union properties and call in all the mortgages. That's nonsense . . . Local unions are not going to lose financially because of this decision."

During the debate several delegates, including my good friend John Duff, president of Massey-Ferguson Local 439, a great supporter over the years, made impassioned speeches against the split. Once again, some people urged that we take this to the membership and hold a referendum vote.

"If it is necessary to have a referendum vote, we'll do that," I said. "However, our history in the UAW is the Canadian parliamentary tradition of leadership by elected delegates. The UAW constitution, in fact, does not provide for referendums. There are people inside and outside Canada, ranging from newspaper publishers to corporate executives, in political parties of all stripes, who would like to divide our union in Canada. A referendum would give them an opportunity to attempt to divide and weaken us."

If we had referendum debates and anti-split propaganda raging in the locals, the international union would be faced with a hopeless problem in sorting out its role in the transition. If two units of an amalgamated union wished to stay in the UAW and the others voted to split, how would that be resolved?

When the vote on the referendum question was called, all but about five people voted not to have a referendum.

With that out of the way, we set up a procedure to get the endorsement of our membership for the split. Delegates to the council went back to their locals and held meetings, at which the decision was ratified.

The Quebec Council was with us solidly. John DeFalco, president of the Quebec UAW Council, went to the floor microphones to say, "As a Quebecer and as a Canadian I think this is the greatest move our union has made in many, many years. We will be able to pursue our collective-bargaining goals with a freedom we never had before. We will be able to make our own decisions. We in Quebec are fully in favour of this and look forward to working with the rest of Canada in a Canadian union."

Kenny Gerard, president of the Canadian UAW Council, said much the same. "For years the international structure of our union worked well. But today, because of the differences in the cost-of-living, and because of the labour-cost difference, Canadians have to find their own route in collective bargaining. We can no longer say that what is appropriate for the U.S. is appropriate for Canada."

The big issue now was the financial settlement with the UAW. The international union had the power to give us nothing, to abandon us as the paperworkers had been, without a strike fund, or offices, or money to pay the staff. I wasn't sure what Bieber intended for us.

Sam Gindin worked feverishly to determine how much money we would need to operate a separate Canadian union. It wasn't a simple matter. Our finances were meshed with the international UAW's. We couldn't be sure of our overhead costs or even our potential income from dues. Local unions collected the dues, took out their share, and sent the rest to Detroit. We never saw the details of the income and expenses of the Canadian Region.

We had to figure out how many staff in Canada were on the Solidarity House payroll and how many were paid out of administrative funds allotted to me. Since the bookkeeping was done in Detroit, this was difficult. Canadian organizers, for instance, were charged to the international organizing department in Detroit. The education staff, the skilled trades staff, the communications staff, the auditing and strike administration, all were charged to the corresponding department in Detroit. Our figures, therefore, weren't exact, but we had a pretty good idea how much money we would need to administer a union when that staff was transferred to us. We were certain that with careful management we could be financially sound.

Two years later, in February 1987, Statistics Canada released the first figures on the returns from Canadian unions operating within international unions. It reported that Canada is more profitable for American unions than anyone had imagined. In 1984, the year the data was collected, the sixty U.S.-based unions with Canadian members collected $140 million in dues, interest, and dividends from their Canadian operations and spent less than $79 million in Canada, accumulating a surplus for themselves of $61.4 million.

Our record of responsible negotiations in 1982 and again in 1984 helped us in that vulnerable period. There was talk that corporations would move jobs out of Canada because the Canadian UAW was too militant, but little of it came from the Big Three or from the auto parts industry. We had earned a certain amount of trust and maybe even respect for knowing what we were doing, so they stood back and let us sort out our problems.

Sam Gindin and Wendy Cuthbertson prepared a first-rate document, *UAW-Canada: Building a New Union In Canada*, which laid out all the questions and provided succinct, reassuring answers. For example:

Why are we breaking away from the U.S. section of our union and creating a separate UAW in Canada?

"We have grown up . . ."

Why was this decision made so quickly?

"It wasn't really. The UAW in Canada has been striving for more independence for decades . . ."

Who made this decision?

"The decision ultimately lay with the Canadian UAW Council, the 350-strong mini-Parliament of the UAW in Canada . . ."

How will this affect our strike fund?

"The dividing up of the international strike fund is part of the IEB committee's work. Our position is that Canadians are entitled to our fair share of the strike funds. Year by year, we usually pay more into the strike fund than we draw out of it . . ."

What about jobs? Will the companies pull out their investments?

"The companies did not invest in Canada because we belonged to an international union. They invested in Canada because Canada is very profitable for them, because Canadians build a quality product, and because in the auto industry, our labour costs have been very competitive and are now close to $8-an-hour lower than in the U.S. . . ."

The material went out in a handsome, glossy book with a bright blue cover. UAW was printed in light blue over a yellow line with CANADA in red under it.

I waited for Bieber to call a meeting of the IEB committee to begin working on details of the separation. Silence. He was in no hurry. My anxiety grew, but I didn't call him.

The first meeting finally was scheduled for Wednesday, February 20, 1985, in Florida, where Bieber was attending the AFL-CIO executive meeting. I was eager to get the money issue settled because it was difficult for us to move ahead on restructuring and plan our founding convention with that anxiety hanging over the membership.

My proposal was that the UAW give us $60 million in Canadian funds, which I considered a fair amount based on the ratio of Canadian members in the international union. Canadians represented about 12 per cent of the international UAW membership and should, therefore, be entitled to about 12 per cent of UAW assets, which included more than $650 million U.S. in the strike fund.

Bieber and the others wanted to know why we didn't hold a referendum. They wanted to make a lot of the fact that opposition to the split had already surfaced in Local 251 in Wallaceburg. I assured them that Wallaceburg was an exception, there was no real division in the Canadian UAW locals.

Bieber listened to what I had to say and was noncommittal. The mood was tense and controlled. I had the impression that Bieber and the others were impatient to get everything settled as quickly as possible to get me out of their hair. We agreed we would meet again in a few weeks, March 11, in a restaurant in Detroit.

The Canadian membership was worried and I knew it. They were wondering what we would do, without a strike fund, if we had to take a strike. In public I was optimistic, but I was running on bravado, as worried as everyone else.

Bieber was ready with a counter-proposal when we met in Detroit. He made an offer which he said was "all-encompassing." The international UAW would give us $20 million Canadian, which would include UAW property in Canada valued at $1.2 million. Nick, Buzz, and I were devastated and furious. We could have lived with $20 million, but it would have severely limited our development and left us vulnerable. The corporations would know we didn't have the resources to take a long strike.

We set another date, March 19, this time in Chicago at Bieber's and Majerus's convenience.

Our lawyers assured us that there was nothing we could do about the mean-minded offer. Len MacLean had told us bluntly from day one that there was no legal precedent to support what we were doing. The only way to proceed legally would be to ask the next international convention of the UAW to change its constitution to permit a departure, something it was very unlikely to do.

We had absolutely no bargaining power. At one point I said facetiously to Buzz and Nick, "What'll we threaten them with? That we'll stay in?" That's about all we had. The UAW constitution didn't cover the possibility of a region leaving the union. If Bieber and the IEB wanted to, they could cut us off without a dime.

Our request for $60 million was modest, much less than we were entitled to expect if the assets were divided on a strict percentage basis. My objective was not to harm the international union. The last thing I wanted was a weak UAW in the United States, because its collective bargaining there would continue to influence what happened here.

I decided to put my pride in my pocket. I had to see Owen Bieber alone and appeal to him to put aside our past differences and deal with the separation as veteran trade unionists trying to resolve something fairly. Since the UAW had set so many standards within the labour movement, it was unbecoming that it should behave badly now.

I called him. He said he was flying to Chicago on the evening of Monday,

March 18, and could see me privately that night. I was addressing the Canadian Club at noon that day in Montreal. After the address, I caught a plane to Chicago and met him for dinner.

We sat down and looked at one another. "You may not like what we've done, Owen," I said evenly. "I don't want to get into a rehashing of all the reasons for it. Obviously there is a lot of tension between us personally. But the history of the UAW is much bigger than that."

I said, "We should do everything we can to avoid tarnishing the image of the UAW. We have a responsibility, the two of us, to make sure the UAW is above that. We two trade union leaders must come to a fair understanding on finances that will ensure that our union will remain strong in Canada and the UAW will remain strong in the United States."

I was appealing to Bieber's trade-union instincts. Let's get it done, I was saying, without it ending up in the courts and in open, and probably humiliating, confrontation.

I presented him with a new proposal: that the UAW give us $50 million Canadian, about 7.5 per cent of the UAW's strike funds, and that we work out an orderly transfer of those funds beginning immediately with $30 million. If the U.S. strike fund exceeded $550 million by the end of 1985, we would receive another $5 million. If the strike fund exceeded $550 million at the end of 1986, we would receive another $5 million. At the end of 1987, we would get a final payment of $10 million.

The international UAW could well afford to help the Canadian union when the strike fund reached $550 million.

"There's no goddamn way you're going to get $50 million," he told me flatly.

"It's less than ten per cent of your assets," I protested, "and you know we have more than ten per cent of the membership."

Bieber said attitudes on the split had hardened in the United States. Some IEB members where saying that even $20 million was too much to give the Canadians. We had made the decision to leave, so we weren't entitled to anything. He claimed that Canada had cost the UAW more than it earned. Doug Fraser, who was in Europe at the time the split was announced, made the comment that our leaving would be a financial plus for the American UAW. We knew that wasn't true. Our research indicated just the opposite, and it was later confirmed by Statistics Canada. Except for such years as when we had a 155-day strike, we put more money into the UAW than we took out.

Buzz and Nick arrived the next morning in preparation for the evening meeting of the full committee at eight o'clock. Owen called our room in the Airport Hilton.

"I haven't had a chance to go over this with Ray and Joe," He said. "Give us a little more time."

He summoned us at ten minutes past midnight.

We went downstairs to the meeting room. The faces of Bieber, Majerus, and Tomasi were grim. We sat at a square table, Nick and Buzz flanking me on one side. Ranged around the other three sides were Bieber, Tomasi, and Majerus, and Bieber's assistant, Dick Shoemaker, Majerus' assistant, Bob St. Pierre, and Red Fry from the UAW accounting department.

"This is our absolutely final position," Bieber said. "We will transfer to the new organization a total amount of $36 million dollars Canadian, including buildings, assets, and obligations." The buildings were the Toronto headquarters, the Windsor sub-regional office, which had been our old headquarters, and the former Local 195 union hall, which had been converted into an Unemployed Help Centre.

Bieber also agreed there would be no dispute about the assets owned by our Canadian locals, such as their union halls. The education centre in Port Elgin, for instance, had been bought by the Canadian Region with money raised from the sale of lottery tickets, although the deed was held by Solidarity House.

My guess is that the courts would not have recognized Canadian ownership of those properties. It was a matter of great relief to us all, especially to the locals, that Bieber did not contest that issue.

"Okay," we said. But the money wasn't fair. It represented only 5 per cent of assets, but it was better than the first offer. We had avoided something that made me sweat to think of it, that the UAW would dispute our right to keep our certification in the 520 Canadian plants where we had locals. If they had done that, we would have to start from scratch organizing on a plant-by-plant basis. It would have depleted our energy and resources for years.

Now the finances were settled, we could proceed to draw up a constitution and hold a founding meeting of UAW-Canada. Keeping $6 million in general revenue, we could set aside a strike fund of about $30 million, giving us the largest strike fund of any union in Canada. That put us out of danger. We could even survive an eight-week strike at General Motors.

Ray Majerus suggested that the international UAW begin separate accounting for Canada on April 1. Solidarity House would continue to collect dues and pay our bills but would show the Canadian income and expenditures in a separate ledger. He estimated that by May 1 we could untangle the two financial structures.

Peering at a recent financial statement, Bieber spotted an item, the cost of printing our booklet *Building A New Union In Canada*.

"Goddamn it," he said. "How come you billed us for that!"

I explained, "We had no choice. We don't have any money."

He was amused. "That's going to stop," he grinned. "It's like the Republican Party billing the Democrats for their campaign material."

He asked another question. "Have you started to look into the legal procedures?"

I said we had. It didn't seem overly complicated.

He looked doubtful. He said, "Get Len MacLean to talk to Jordon Rosen." Rosen was head of the UAW's legal department. "They should get their heads together right away."

Owen had to take the proposal to the International Executive Board meeting on March 27. I was entitled to be present, but decided not to go. I was persona non grata and nothing could be achieved by my presence.

In any case, I was busy with an economic summit in Ottawa called by Prime Minister Brian Mulroney, a media-saturated gathering of 130 delegates drawn from business, labour, women's groups, academics, anti-poverty organizations, churches, the unemployed, and so on. We were supposed to express our views on such matters as the economy, new technology, and competitiveness.

I used the time in Ottawa to talk to the executive of the Canadian Council and the president of the Quebec Council about the financial settlement we had reached and the details of the structure we would be proposing for the new Canadian UAW. I knew there was a lot of speculation about the structure, even rumours that White was going to run the new union with a bureaucracy of cronies, and I wanted to put that talk to rest.

At the meeting Sam Gindin put the financial settlement on the blackboard to allay any concerns that we wouldn't have adequate strike or operating funds. Then we drew a diagram of the structure. Far from being top-heavy with staff, the new organization would be dominated by members. Every one of the people in the room, the council executives, would be on the new National Executive Board.

The proposed structure was an unqualified success with the top rank-and-file leadership in the Canadian UAW. Everyone loved the checks and balances. They weren't losing authority, they were gaining. If it flew with them, and it did, we knew we had done it right.

The report on the financial split bothered some people. Kenny Gerard felt we had been screwed.

"You're right," I told him, "but we've got to move on. We'll be able to operate this union on what we've got, as long as we're careful. Besides, we don't have any choice."

We called a joint meeting of the Canadian and Quebec councils on March 30 and 31, 1985. Sam Gindin laid out the details of the financial settlement and we outlined how the new structure would look.

Initially, we hadn't been sure whether to unveil the plans at this council meeting or to wait for the founding convention, plans for which were already underway. Instead we decided to end the uncertainty and speculation by telling delegates frankly what we were hoping to do. Otherwise, we'd have gone into the founding convention with all kinds of political groups wanting representation. Retirees were talking about having a place on the executive, skilled trades thought they should have a spot, and so on.

We had a good discussion, after which the meeting endorsed in principle the structure we had proposed and accepted the financial settlement. We all felt that the UAW hadn't been fair, but the delegates understood that nothing more could be achieved.

Before adjourning, the councils made an important decision that was symbolic of our new independence. The UAW's strike fund had grown so huge that Solidarity House was sending 10 per cent of dues back to the locals – the amount that would normally go to the strike fund. The councils decided that this rebate should begin to flow directly into a new, separate Canadian strike fund. We were moving to self-sufficiency.

Majerus had been optimistic in thinking the separation would be completed cleanly by May 1 – it took another nineteen months. It was one thing to settle on the amount, but quite another to get the money. Bieber, Majerus, and the other directors did their best to make that as difficult for us as they possibly could. They gave their lawyers instructions to snarl the process by every means. The vote for separation had only stirred, not settled, the bitterness they felt at Solidarity House.

CHAPTER TWENTY-ONE

Strong, Independent, and Penniless

O NE OF THE BITS OF BUSINESS we concluded at the joint meeting of the Canadian and Quebec councils was to decide to hold the founding convention of UAW-Canada September 4 to 7, 1985, at the Sheraton Centre in Toronto. Next, we had to figure out how delegates to that founding convention should be selected. We decided to follow the formula of the UAW international conventions. Delegates would be elected by the locals and their voting power would be determined by the number of members they represented.

We were having fun talking to a designer about our new logo. I wanted the word Canada and the red maple leaf to be in the design. Wendy Cuthbertson worked with designer Ron Kaplansky on several versions each aiming at a fresh, confident, and completely new look. Meanwhile we used a simple UAW-CANADA.

My second motion at the International Executive Board meeting where we'd divided the union stated clearly that we were creating two unions, one of them the American UAW and the other the Canadian UAW. I put it that way because I didn't want us to lose the right to call ourselves the United Auto Workers. Ray Majerus had made me repeat the motion to make sure the correct wording was recorded, and no one had commented on the phrase "the Canadian UAW."

I therefore assumed there was no problem with the name. In the document we prepared for the membership about the decision to split I'd written, "We will always be the UAW. We will always preserve and cherish the proud traditions of our fifty years of history."

I also assumed after the March meeting in Chicago that the process of separation would get in gear quickly. We expected that we would get the cheque for $36 million right away and that Canadian dues would be diverted to Toronto in a month or two. The picture dancing in my head was of going to the founding convention waving that cheque, $36 million, plus whatever interest had accumulated since the agreement in Chicago.

At first we didn't notice the ominous lack of activity on our behalf in Detroit. Bills and salaries continued to be paid, but that was the only communication. We knew everything we spent was coming from our own account, but we didn't know exactly how much we were spending. We knew that our income was being tallied, but we had only a vague idea what that total was. We couldn't prepare a realistic budget for the founding convention.

We asked for figures and were told blandly that they weren't ready yet. That was nonsense; Solidarity House is completely computerized.

Kaplansky and Wendy came up with a smashing design for the logo. They dispensed with the venerable old UAW wheel, a ring of tiny workers holding hands around a wheel, which was hard to decipher. Instead, they came up with two lines of bold letters separated by a thin silver line on a deep blue background. The top line read UAW and TUA in white, separated by a red maple leaf, the one below read CANADA in silver. TUA, which stands for Travailleur Unis de l'Automobile, emphasized that we are a bilingual union.

They presented it to me beautifully framed on September 3, 1985, with the inscription, "Dear Bob – Hope this new symbol will stay with the UAW for many years."

We prepared blue backdrops and blue banners bearing the proud new logo for the founding convention. Wendy worked on the details for hours, and I was delighted with the results. I could imagine taking that logo to meetings abroad of the International Metalworkers Federation, picturing how it would stand out, instantly recognizable as the new Canadian UAW because the word CANADA and the red maple leaf were so prominent.

At the same time, a staff committee was working on the new constitution. We didn't want to make massive changes to the UAW constitution because it had served a very democratic union well, but we had to make a number of changes to adapt it to our new structure.

I had a lot to say during the drafting of the document. I wanted to make sure that the constitution protected and supported action on social and political issues and that we built a lot of flexibility into our founding documents. I knew that the new UAW would have to be flexible in order to cope with a major collapse of one sector as had occurred in the agricultural implements industry, where 80 per cent of our members were unemployed. I wanted the new constitution to give the Canadian UAW leader freedom to pursue new members, union mergers, and social activism.

Meanwhile, the silence from Solidarity House was unnerving. Nick, Buzz, Sam, and I were getting anxious about the transfer of funds. It was unnerving to be moving to a founding convention without funds and we knew staff morale was starting to unravel. Some urged me to telephone Owen and ask what was the delay, but I didn't want to do that.

"We're moving," I said, sounding as enthusiastic as I could. "We've got lots to do to get ready for that founding convention. Let's just keep going."

I didn't want to call because I didn't want to hear a "no." If Bieber was thinking of pulling out financial support, I didn't want to hear about it until I had to.

I turned fifty on April 28, 1985. That month the Sunday *New York Times* surprised a lot of people by running a long feature story about me written by William Serrin. The heading was startling: A SUPERSTAR FOR CANADIAN LABOR.

"When Robert White led a strike against General Motors of Canada last October," it read, "the American leaders of the UAW were as annoyed as the company executives. It was bad enough that the articulate and independent head of Canada's UAW had disregarded the pact already negotiated across the border. And worse, his strike stopped the important flow of parts from Canadian plants to the United States, forcing GM to lay off almost 15 per cent of its American work force ... And now, in a sharper blow, Mr. White's 123,000-member union is seceding entirely from its American parent."

We sent out a notice to the locals to hold elections of their delegates to the founding convention. Irregularities and misunderstandings are almost inevitable in such elections, so we notified the members to report their complaints to Toronto, rather than to Solidarity House as they were accustomed to doing. One member of Local 27 in London misread the instructions. On June 18, 1985, he sent a letter to Ray Majerus to complain about procedure, saying the election notices hadn't been properly posted.

Majerus could have handled it by forwarding the complaint to us. Instead, he passed the letter to Bieber. This is the reply that went from Bieber's office:

"Dear Brother: In reply to your letter of June 18, 1985, to secretary-treasurer Ray Majerus, there is no UAW founding convention scheduled for September 1985. The UAW was founded many years ago and since then has existed in Canada and the United States. We have no jurisdiction over the election you refer to because it does not involve the UAW. If you're interested in participating in that convention, your protest should be directed to the chairperson of the convention."

I had never given Bieber credit for a sense of humour, but I thought that was one of his better shots. I had quite a laugh over it.

Finally, that summer something started to happen. Bob Nickerson and our lawyer, Len MacLean, met with lawyers from Solidarity House and the two assistants to Majerus and Bieber. Nick reported to me that there was a serious problem with the timetable to hand over the money. Solidarity House was saying that the international union couldn't give us our own union dues until the next international convention, scheduled for June 1986, approved a constitutional change to allow the transfer.

I wrote Bieber on July 24, explaining that I thought the lawyers were being much too careful. I didn't want to get into a legal argument, however, so I offered a proposal to get around the problem. I suggested that immediately after the UAW-TUA Canada founding convention, the UAW could loan our new organization $25 million, interest free. This would really be our own money, an advance on the $36 million and interest we'd been promised, but we would wait for the final installment until after the international convention. Meanwhile, we could call it a loan.

I pointed out that there was ample precedent for one union making a loan to another union in a time of trouble. It's done all the time in the labour movement.

I continued that, in October 1985, all staff working in Canada would be transferred to the new UAW-TUA Canada payroll. In return, we would assume responsibility for servicing the collective agreements and paying strike benefits. We would take over the costs and rents of properties in Canada owned by the American union. Until their convention, dues would continue to be forwarded to Detroit, as the UAW constitution required, but they would be sent from Solidarity House to a bank account in Toronto in the name of the American UAW so, strictly speaking, they wouldn't be out of their control.

The $25 million would enable us to establish our accounting procedures and relationships with banking institutions. We could set a budget, fix the staff structure, and begin functioning independently with some sense of what our income and costs were.

"There will be a period of time," I explained, "in which we would have parallel organizations." During that period, I would carry on my dual responsibilities as Canadian director and international vice-president, while at the same time acting as president of the new UAW-TUA Canada. This relationship would end when their convention voted to change the constitution and confirm the arrangement reached in Chicago.

I asked for an immediate meeting with Bieber to discuss these suggestions around the impasse, but I got no response.

Some time early in August, I was returning from a meeting in Ottawa. As I got off the plane in Toronto, a woman tapped me on the arm.

"You don't know who I am," she said, "but I'm with a law firm that does work on patents. We've just sent you a letter that you can't use the name UAW. It's an infringement on the patent held by Solidarity House."

That letter, dated August 8, is priceless. It states in the pompous language that lawyers use that the firm had been retained by the international UAW to represent its interests. Their client, the letter went on to say, had the exclusive right to the trademark and name UAW. Any use of this by any other union was prohibited, especially the use of the phrase UAW Canada at a founding convention. Such use would make it impossible for people to distinguish between their client and the other union.

"We must accordingly demand that you do not adopt or use the words United Auto Workers or Auto Workers or the acronym UAW or AW, either alone or in combination with any other words or symbols or confusingly similar words or acronyms."

I tossed it into a file and decided to put it out of my mind.

I was more alarmed at the prospect of going into our founding convention in a few weeks with no money. I saw a real possibility that our vulnerability to the whims of Detroit would create deep confusion and fear in our ranks. We had to get the credibility that only money could give.

PLANS FOR THE FOUNDING CONVENTION were approaching the final stage. I decided the key committees should meet together the last weekend of August to go over the plans one more time and make sure we were all comfortable with what was going to happen. I wanted a relaxed, informal session so I decided to hold it at the education centre at Port Elgin. A constitution committee, a resolution committee, and a credentials committee were all working at top speed. Invitations went out to the top local union leaders.

We had heard from all of the speakers invited to speak at the convention except for Bieber. I knew Bieber probably would use the opportunity to imply some criticism of me, but I thought it was important that either he or Ray Majerus be there. By mid-August, neither had yet indicated whether he would attend.

There was still no word from Detroit about our money and we were growing frantic. I was urged to call Bieber, but I tried to seem unconcerned. "Beiber knows the date of the convention," I kept saying. "He'll be calling, don't worry. He's *got* to make the call. I'm not going to beg for a goddamned meeting. We'll be hearing from him."

I knew perfectly well that Bieber was capable of leaving me twisting in the wind, but I didn't want him to think he had me scared.

On Friday, just before the Port Elgin meeting, I finally had a call from Dick Shoemaker, Bieber's administrative assistant. Owen wanted to meet us August 27 in Detroit. I cursed silently. Bieber couldn't have cut it much finer, with the founding convention only a week later. To avoid taking too much time out, I arranged for a chartered plane to fly Buzz, Nick, and I from the airport at Kincardine, near Port Elgin, to Detroit.

At Port Elgin, I put the best face possible on the fact that we still didn't have any funds from the international union. "There's no question that we'll get the money," I said with assurance I didn't feel. "It's only a matter of when the legal difficulties get worked out. Our only problem is to think what this does to the mood of the founding convention and what we'll do about that."

I confided that I expected trouble from Bieber about the name. We turned that problem over a while, but could see no solution. Nevertheless, the meeting in Port Elgin went well. When I left for Kincardine to catch the plane to Detroit, we had started to hope that Bieber had summoned me to Solidarity House to present me with a cheque.

The meeting with Bieber was at noon in the boardroom of Solidarity House. The moment the meeting started, Bieber let loose with a tirade. He was furious about the National Film Board's documentary *Final Offer*. He learned he was in it when the producers approached him for permission to use his voice on the telephone calls I received from him during the General Motors negotiations. Owen had seen the film crew with me when we'd met in Solidarity House to discuss a target company for the 1984 bargaining, but apparently he hadn't realized that they would film the whole crisis, including his fights with me.

He ranted about how I'd violated a code of ethics. He and Majerus attacked me for exposing the private affairs of the UAW, contrary to the constitution. I reminded them that they had been informed that the crew would film the GM bargaining. I told Bieber I had their assurance that his voice wouldn't be used without his permission. What more could I do?

"Have you seen the film?" Owen demanded belligerently.

"No," I said, though I had seen a very rough rough-cut. "Owen, maybe the film is going to turn out more critical of me than it is of you. We don't know. It's just a film about what happened."

"You haven't heard the goddamned end of this," Bieber said, still enraged. "We're going to talk to our lawyers."

The National Film Board knew about the threat to take legal action and feared that Bieber would try for an injunction to prevent the showing of the film. To avoid that happening, they backed off. In *Final Offer*, Bieber's voice has been blurred.

Bieber continued to fume.

I observed, "Owen, this started out as an educational film about collective bargaining. They just happened to be there when things started to come apart and they've got the story. I'm not going to go back and tell them that they can't use the film. I don't care if it's bad for me or good for me; it's done."

After a while, he dropped the subject. He pulled out a piece of paper and said he had listed the five issues we would address: the question of the name, the transfer of funds, the strike funds, the property, and the contracts.

"We'll leave the number one to the end," he began, making a tick mark. "On the question of the transfer of funds, we won't transfer any funds until after the 1986 international convention."

"What about the loan?" I asked.

"There won't be a loan," he answered.

"I gave you a proposal on how to do it," I protested, "if you're worried about the legal implications."

"We're not going to do it," he said. "There's no difference in our opinion between a transfer of funds and a loan. That's the advice of our legal counsel. We're not turning anything over."

"Christ," I said. "If we had ever listened to legal counsel there never would have been a sit-down strike at Flint, we would never have had anything in the goddamned union. Why are we listening to legal counsel? Let's do the fucking thing."

"We can't do it," he repeated.

That was crap. A union can lend money to whomever it wants. The UAW helped out the rubberworkers when they were in trouble and the communication workers' union when it was on strike – it happens all the time. In 1986, the CAW made a loan of $1 million to the British Columbia woodworkers forty-eight hours after Jack Munroe phoned me to say they were out of money. I simply called the CAW board and said the woodworkers needed money, and it was done.

Bieber, however, pretended that it was impossible for the UAW to make a loan. He then inquired what constitution we would be operating under after the founding convention. I replied that obviously it would be the UAW constitution until the transfer had taken place.

He said, "You understand that under our constitition it is the president who has the right to discharge people."

"Yes," I said uneasily, wondering where this was going.

Then he said, almost idly, "Is Sam Gindin covered by collective agreement in Canada with your staff union?"

I saw what was in his mind, to fire Sam if he wasn't protected by the agreement, and I knew why. A few weeks before Sam had written a wildly funny poem, some cheeky doggerel about Bieber and the problems we were having with Solidarity House. Thinking it would help to lighten the mood at Port Elgin, I had read it to the meeting to the vast amusement of the group.

I know to this day which member of my staff was feeding such information to Bieber. Bieber himself let the identity of the mole slip while he was raging about *Final Offer*. That person is still with us.

Let them try to fire Sam, I thought. Just let them try it.

"Are you coming to the founding convention, Owen?" I asked, changing the subject.

He picked up his schedule and studied it, as if the suggestion was new to him. "No," he said, "I see I'm in Europe. I don't think I'll be back in time."

I looked at Majerus. Ray said he didn't think he could make it either, but he'd let me know.

The convention was eight days off. I made no comment.

That reminded Bieber that he didn't think much of the fact that we had invited Victor Reuther to speak at the founding convention.

I had given great thought to the speakers and special guests we'd invited. I wanted them to have the right effect on the delegates and to establish a proper sense of occasion. I'd considered a number of factors in making my choices: internationalism, Quebec, trade unionism, politics, traditions, and so on.

I'd selected Dennis McDermott, because he was president of the Canadian Labour Congress and I wanted to show that the Canadian labour movement was on side. I invited Jeff Rose, the recently elected head of the Canadian Union of Public Employees, to identify with public sector unions. Louis

Laberge, president of the Quebec Federation of Labour, was invited to represent Quebec's participation in the new union. Ed Broadbent, leader of the federal NDP, was coming to speak because of our ties to that party. Herman Rebhan, president of the International Metalworkers Federation, also would address the convention to strengthen our international links.

The choice of Victor Reuther was an obvious one because of the Reuthers' place in UAW history, and because he already had come out in support of us in the split.

Owen began to criticize Victor. That year, 1986, was the fiftieth anniversary of the UAW so Victor, as the only surviving Reuther, was much in demand on television and at union banquets. He was using the opportunity to take the leadership in Solidarity House to task for some of the recent settlements. At seventy-five-years old, he was still articulate and packed a punch with audiences, much to Bieber's annoyance. I found out that Bieber had been leaning on some local unions to cancel their invitations to have Victor speak.

I explained the two reasons we had asked Reuther to our founding convention: that he was a Reuther, and that he understood what we were doing.

"You may not agree with him, Owen," I said, "but Victor does have an understanding and sympathy for our situation that we appreciate."

Bieber grumbled that he didn't know what Victor would say at our convention.

"Look, I don't know what you're going to say, if you come. I don't write your speeches and I don't write his. And I promise you, Owen, that you won't get a hostile reception from our members."

We seemed to have exhausted that topic, so we returned to Owen's list. He made two more ticks. Nothing was going to happen about transferring properties or the contracts. That left the matter of the name.

"There's no goddamned way you're going to use the name of the UAW," Owen said.

"What are you doing here?" I said, my control slipping. "Again, this is a violation of what we agreed to."

"What the hell are you talking about? There was no agreement about the name."

"Look up the minutes of the International Executive Board meeting. You'll see in my second motion, the one that was passed, that the IEB agreed there would be two UAWs, an American UAW and a Canadian UAW."

He said no such thing had happened. "You can poll the board if you don't believe me," he said.

"Thanks, no," I told him coldly. "Do you think I believe I would get support from the board if I called them?"

I started to thump the table, glaring at him. "We've got our logo developed. We've got a convention on next week. And the UAW-CANADA logo is going to be on that platform."

Bieber took out a pencil and made another mark on his list. "That will be the first goddamned thing settled before there is any financial arrangement," he said. In other words, if we wanted the name, we couldn't have the money.

That left us in a fine spot. We were a week and a day from the founding convention with neither a name nor any money.

I was stunned. "This is unfair as hell, Owen. There is more to this than a simple falling out. You know our name isn't going to create any conflict with you. The logo is distinctly different. There will be no confusion in the States if auto workers in Canada are known as United Auto Workers. We have just as much right to that name as you have."

Owen shook his head emphatically then suddenly raised the question of strike authorization.

"You know that authorization of whether we strike Chrysler this year still rests with the president," he said.

"I'm aware of that," I nodded.

He gave me a hard look of warning.

It was Ray Majerus' turn. He had something to say about our building expansion. The two-storey headquarters in Toronto had been bursting at the seams for a number of years. The change in organization meant we'd be needing additional staff in accounting, payroll, and other areas. After consulting architects, we'd decided to add another storey and work had already begun.

Majerus said we had no right to do that without his permission. We would have to stop construction until the money matters were settled next June.

"We can't postpone that," I protested. "We have to do it. We need the room. Besides, the building costs are coming out of our funds."

There was nothing more to say. I got up to leave. Bieber said he would talk to the lawyers one more time about the loan, but I took no encouragement from that. It was clear nothing would change.

Bieber detained me as I was going out the door. He reminded me that the collective agreements with Chrysler were due to expire. We would be going into negotiations simultaneously in a few weeks. He wondered if we shouldn't meet first to go over our strategies. I agreed and a date was set, September 29.

That was interesting, I thought wryly. The public perception in both Canada and the United States was that the Canadians would be helpless without the wisdom and experience of the Americans. Here, at the first opportunity, was the president of the American UAW wanting to pick our brains.

I felt quite discouraged as I flew back to Port Elgin from that meeting, appalled at Bieber's behavior. The meeting had confirmed for me the correctness of our decision to leave the international union. I was depressed that there had been no effort to try to work the separation out in a cooperative spirit or any show of concern for the Canadian membership. Instead, Solidarity House was obsessed with protecting its political ass against criticism that it had let Canada go too easily.

I was saddened to see the leadership of the great UAW having such tunnel vision. Bieber and the others couldn't raise themselves above their offended feelings to recognize the broader issue. In future, our two fraternal organizations would need good communication. We needed to develop a way of consulting together in bargaining years with the Big Three. We should have been working on details of that collaboration, but there was nothing of that, nothing at all.

When the plane dropped us off at Kincardine, we drove back to Port Elgin. I was feeling so low that I didn't want to talk to anyone. I could see people sitting outside the cottages in the complex, waiting for me to call them together to give them the news, but I had no stomach for it.

I walked through the woods in the darkness and paced the beach. I wrestled with my mental attitude. It would help nothing for me to be angry or discouraged. It was a setback all right, but my responsibility was to pull myself together and give confident leadership to get us through it.

The next morning, I called a meeting of all the committees, which had been working in separate rooms on final details. I reported on the meeting with Bieber in the resolute spirit I had decided to adopt. I admitted we weren't getting the money right away as we had hoped, but I said that it definitely was coming. We had nothing to fear on that score. Bieber and Majerus had not indicated that they would renege, though they had the opportunity to do so. We could be confident our only problem was the delay. I didn't report the ultimatum on the name.

"I realized at yesterday's meeting that we did the right thing to leave the international UAW," I said. "We don't belong in that organization. It's too narrow in terms of its approach to change."

Still, I went on, we couldn't let our disappointment about the transfer of funds dampen the spirit of the convention. I reminded them of the excitement that had been generated across our membership. The elections for delegates to the founding convention had created a near-frenzy in the locals. Everyone, it seemed, wanted to be there to have something to brag about to the grandchildren. The room perked up. We were going to make history in another week, whether Solidarity House liked it or not.

They went back to their meetings in a great mood of elation, which left me curiously disturbed. I was scared by the confidence they had shown in me. I had said there was nothing to fear, and they accepted that without question. They were even reassuring me that everything was going to be great. These were the cream of the Canadian UAW, strong, tough people, who could take a very jaundiced view of something that didn't look perfectly feasible. Yet they went out of the room looking forward to the convention as if nothing had gone wrong or could go wrong.

We had made the arrangements for delegates at the founding convention but we also had to provide for hundreds of guests from the local unions – stewards and committee people who didn't want to miss the excitement. At almost the last minute, we set up a procedure to register guests so that we could keep some measure of control over the situation.

A day or two before the convention, I checked into the hotel, along with members of all the convention committees, who would be supervising the final details. I had my speech notes with me, written in the solitude of Port Elgin after the others had left. It was the single most important speech of my life.

My adrenalin was racing. I had put the problems of the name and the money behind me and was feeling something very close to joy. I went everywhere with a huge grin on my face.

The convention was a roaring success. The highlight was the great speech that Victor Reuther made at the closing banquet, when he held a thousand people in a stillness you could touch. I count it as a high point in my life and went home, as we all did, feeling that nothing could stop the Canadian UAW.

You learn fast in the labour movement that you don't get time to rest on your laurels for long. We were only weeks away from bargaining with Chrysler again. We had no strike fund, we had no money at all, we maybe didn't have a name, but after that convention we knew that we were a strong, free-standing Canadian union.

THE CHRYSLER BARGAINING was our first test. The agreements expired on October 15, 1985. Nick, Buzz, and I went to Detroit to meet with Bieber and some of his Chrysler department. We didn't waste time talking about getting the same settlement in both Chrysler U.S. and Chrysler Canada. In the States, Chrysler workers had a short way to go to reach parity with Ford and GM, while our richer settlement with Ford and GM in Canada in 1984 meant that our Chrysler workers were now farther behind. Parity meant a different adjustment in each country, but at least we were agreed that full and complete parity would be our common goal with Chrysler. We also agreed that we would try to get the Big Three back in sync by trying for a two-year agreement, bringing all three companies back to the bargaining table together in 1987.

The discussion was general and our manner impersonal and businesslike. Owen and I carefully avoided mention of the strike authorization. The UAW in Canada now had its own constitution, but because the separation was not complete, we were officially operating under the international UAW's constitution. Any strike at Chrysler Canada would require Bieber's approval.

The meeting took place over dinner, which was the only time Bieber could fit it into his schedule. As we were going into the restaurant, Owen asked me to stay behind when the meeting ended.

"I want a word with you privately," he said.

I thought, he wants to talk about *Final Offer*.

When we were alone, Bieber said, "I'd like to talk to you about the film *Final Offer*."

He had been worrying about what the film would say and how he would be portrayed. Since he had chosen to defend his role in the split within the union on the basis of his version of what happened during the GM strike of 1984, he obviously was uncomfortable that a documentary of the event would show his story at variance with the record.

"I haven't heard from the National Film Board lately," he said. "What's going on?"

"Call them up," I suggested. "I don't know what's going on. It's not my film."

"I hope they've got it right," he said, glowering at me. "That film shouldn't be shown to the public. It's union business."

"It's made by the National Film Board," I explained. "It's not mine. I'm not paying for it."

We started bargaining with Chrysler in the Westbury Hotel in Toronto. I advised Bill Fisher, who was heading the Chrysler Canada negotiations, that the strike deadline would be the day the agreement terminated, midnight on

October 15. Buzz, Nick, and Sam were with me along with Ken Gerard and the master bargaining team.

We made it clear from day one that we wanted full and complete parity with Ford and General Motors Canada on all issues. We also wanted some catch-up money in compensation for losses incurred by workers and retirees during the period of the concession agreements, and we wanted a two-year agreement in order to get all the Big Three negotiations back together again.

Negotiations moved along at a normal pace and three days before the strike deadline the company made us an offer that was close but just short of parity. It was missing some pieces, the most serious of which was the absence of the catch-up for active employees and retirees, who had been living on reduced pensions since the concessions.

The World Series was on, so we set up some television sets in the media room in the Westbury. We were watching the game around nine the night of October 15, confident that we were so close on the issues that we would have the settlement we wanted that night. We were waiting for another phone call from Fisher, who had been in constant communication all day. Abruptly, the calls stopped.

"What the hell's going on here?" I said to Buzz. "They know we're serious about the retirees and actives, but we aren't far apart. We just need a little bit of money here and we can get the thing done. What's going on!"

A Detroit labour reporter happened by. He said, "Have you heard what's happened? Some Chrysler U.S. workers have jumped the gun. They're out on a wildcat strike."

That explained why Chrysler had turned off the tap in bargaining. Now some of their U.S. plants were down, they had nothing to gain by meeting our terms.

"They're going to let us sit," I predicted bleakly.

I waited until about eleven-thirty that evening, but there was no word from Fisher. A half-hour before the deadline, I called him.

"My friend, what the hell is going on? We're drifting into a strike for no reason."

"There is a reason," he replied. "You want money for retirees and actives and we're not going to pay you."

"Bill, this doesn't make sense," I said, exasperated. "Come on, there's more here than meets the eye. I hear some of the plants in the United States have jumped the gun."

"Yes, they have," he said.

"Shit," I said. "I guess we're gone at midnight tonight."

He said unemotionally, "I guess we are."

It was an absolutely unnecessary strike for us in Canada but at midnight, Chrysler workers all over North America were on strike.

I called Fisher the next morning, and we arranged that the bargaining teams would meet around ten. The mood was lethargic, the momentum of the talks was gone. That happens right after a strike. Both parties usually work like hell up to the deadline and a strike takes the wind out of the sails.

We sat slouched in our chairs.

"I don't believe this," I said wearily. "We are so close."

He agreed, but had no solution. We gave up.

Kenny Gerard and others from Windsor, Ajax, and Etobicoke wondered if we shouldn't break off bargaining. Some wanted to get home, as nothing was happening in Toronto, and meet with their membership.

"Let's meet tomorrow and talk about it," I suggested.

I consulted with Sam, Buzz, and Nick. We were all puzzled. Something didn't feel right. We decided we would stay in the hotel over the weekend in case something broke.

"I don't know why, I can't tell you why," I said to the guys the next day, "but I want us to stick around the hotel this weekend. My sense is that we shouldn't walk away yet. If nothing happens by Monday, we'll go home and take a week off to meet the membership."

Most weren't happy about that. They had been in the hotel for five weeks, and they couldn't see the point in staying now that negotiations had stopped.

"Owen's *got* to settle in the United States," I said. "Christ, he's got seventy-thousand people on strike."

A meeting of the Chrysler Council in the States, the leadership of the Chrysler locals, had been scheduled for Saturday, in Huntsville, Alabama.

"He'll want a settlement to take to that leadership conference in Alabama," I predicted.

Later that Friday afternoon, I was working on some correspondence in our temporary offices in the Westbury, when Wendy Cuthbertson burst in.

"There's an announcement," she said breathlessly. "Owen Bieber has called a press conference at four o'clock this afternoon."

I figured he was going to notify the media that he was postponing the meeting in Alabama until Sunday because he was fully occupied with Chrysler negotiations.

"Make sure we have someone track that," I asked Wendy. "Let us know what he says."

316

She returned a short time later.

"Guess what?" she said. "Bieber has broken off negotiations. He says he has to be at the meeting in Alabama."

I was stunned. "Oh shit, here we go. Here we are with Chrysler on the edge of meeting our objectives, and now we're in another long strike like 1982. This is insane."

"What do we do now?" I asked Nick and Buzz.

We figured we'd wait through Saturday and maybe send the guys home on Sunday.

My phone rang about an hour later, not the special lines we had put in, but the hotel phone.

"Hello, Brother White," said a jovial voice, Tom Miner, Chrysler vice-president in charge of industrial relations. "How'ya doing?"

"Not worth a shit," I replied. "Listen my friend, you've got us on strike over here. There's no reason for it."

"You told us that if we gave you parity you didn't think there would be strike in Canada over local issues," he said. "We put parity on the table and now you've got us on strike. That's a breach of faith."

"Bullshit," I told him. "You haven't got parity on the table. We want some money for retirees and you're short on the actives on catch-up. You've known that from day one and it's still there today. We're on strike because you can't get your shit together over there. Why don't we settle this thing here and get it done?"

He seemed to be thinking that over.

"How're you doing in Detroit?" I asked.

"Not good. We can't find out what it takes to settle with Bieber. He's just postponed negotiations, and Iacocca is ranting and raving like a madman. He says he's going to the media to say what he thinks of you and Owen Bieber and the UAW. I told him, before you start going after White, maybe you'd better talk to him. Are you willing to talk to him?

"Sure, I'll talk to him, Tom, for Chrissakes," I said.

"Would you prefer to talk to him on the telephone or in person?" Miner asked.

"I prefer to talk to him in person."

"Then there's a problem," Miner said. "He's got to be in New York tomorrow. He's on his way there now. Would you be prepared to go to New York?"

"Sure," I said, knowing that Miner was remembering that the last time Iacocca and I had met, I had insisted that the Chrysler president come to Toronto. I'd made my point in 1982, I didn't have to do it again.

"I'll get back to you," Miner said.

I told Helen Kramczk to get reservations to New York for Buzz Hargrove and me either that night or as early as possible Saturday morning. I talked to Gerard, Nick, Buzz, Sam, and Jim O'Neil.

"Any doubts about it?" I asked. "Do you think I should go?"

"No doubt about it, you've got to go," they said. "Iacocca makes the decisions at Chrysler."

I waited for Miner to call back.

When he did, he said, "It's on. Meet Iacocca at nine o'clock tomorrow morning in our offices in the Pan-Am building. Let me know what flight you're on, and we'll have a driver meet you."

CHAPTER TWENTY-TWO

Final Offer

Most of the media had abandoned the watch on the stalled Chrysler negotiations. As I left the hotel that night to go home for a change of clothes, I was hailed by a lone reporter for the CBC's "The National," who was hanging around hoping something would break.

"Hey Bob," he called. "Where are you going, Highland Park?"

Chrysler's Detroit headquarters is in Highland Park

"No," I answered, thinking that if he put the question differently he would have a helluva story. "I'm going home."

Buzz and I were on a plane leaving Toronto at seven in the morning. In New York a driver was waiting at LaGuardia, holding up a sign that read CHRYSLER. He drove us in a stretch limousine to the Pan-Am building. The lobby was almost deserted except for some construction people and two security guards at a desk.

"Where's the Chrysler floor?" I asked.

From behind me someone shouted, "I'll take you up to the goddamned floor."

It was Lee Iacocca. He introduced his assistant and we shook hands all around. His offices were on the fifty-fourth floor.

"I've got Buzz here in case there are some technical questions," I explained. "Would you rather that you and I meet alone?"

"Yes, if that's all right with you and Buzz."

"We have no problem with that," I told Iacocca.

He ordered some coffee, and the two of us settled ourselves in some comfortable chairs for a talk.

"Shit, I don't know what's going on," he complained. "I can't believe what's happening in the U.S. Chrysler negotiations. I keep hearing two names – Bob White of the Canadian union and Roger Smith of GM. Neither of them are in the bargaining in Detroit, so I don't know what's going on. They're telling me that whatever I do in Canada, I gotta do it better in the States. And you're telling us in Canada that whatever we do in the United States we've got to plus in Canada."

"That's bullshit," I snapped. "I never said that and you know that's not true, my friend. I told the company from day one, parity plus catch-up in Canada. I don't care what you do with Bieber, whether you give him a three-year agreement that he wants or whatever else, more money or less money. It doesn't matter to me. We're operating separately in these negotiations. We know what our objectives are. When we get them, we'll get the goddamned strike settled."

We were asking $1,500 up front for retirees and widows of retirees, and the same amount for actives to make up for what they had lost in concessions.

"We've got to have more for retirees, Lee," I insisted.

"Shit, if I give you that it'll cost me forty-eight million dollars."

"No it won't. We don't have that many retirees. We've got twenty-nine hundred retirees and about six hundred and fifty widows."

"Whatever I do on the retirees in Canada," he said, "I have to do it in the United States."

"That's your problem. That ain't my problem," I told him.

He said disgustedly. "I guess it's only money. I guess I have to reach in the goddamned barrel and get it."

He chewed his cigar. "Maybe we can do this," he said. "Let me make a phone call. I've got to talk to Greenwald and Miner about this."

I could see his strategy. If he settled in Canada, it would get Bieber back to the table in a hurry. I was thinking, this is incredible. Here we are in our first negotiation as a new union and we were about to settle a major strike ahead of the Americans and set the pattern for the American agreement. That tasted sweet. Everyone, including a lot of academics who present themselves as authorities on the labour movement, had been saying that the new Canadian UAW would be toothless without the clout that Solidarity House provided. The corporations wouldn't talk seriously to a handful of Canadians, so they said.

Iacocca came back from the telephone call. "If we do this, how long will it take to put this goddamned thing together and settle that strike in Canada?" he asked.

"Twelve hours," I replied promptly.

We got down to negotiating. We would get the money for actives and retirees but not as much as we wanted, $1,000 instead of $1,500. I said I thought it would fly.

"I'm going to visit my mother tomorrow," he said. "Here's her phone number if you need to call me."

He saw me out, and waved genially at Buzz. I kept my composure until the elevator doors shut on us and then I let out a yell. "We've got it! Goddamn it Buzz, we've got it." The meeting had lasted little more than a hour and was described later in *Maclean's* magazine as a "one-cigar settlement."

The limousine took us back to the airport, where I immediately placed a call to Kenny Gerard. You don't get something into an agreement that the local leadership think their members won't ratify.

"Here's what he's prepared to do," I told Kenny, laying it out.

His response was, "Okay. Let's get at it."

"I'm on my way," I said.

I called Wendy Cuthbertson next.

"Wendy, get a press conference ready. Tell the media that I've just met with Lee Iacocca."

As soon as we got back to the Westbury, I called the bargaining committee together and went over the details of what Iacocca and I had discussed. A few people complained that the catch-up for actives and retirees wasn't good enough. Our guys are wonderful. They always want the best deal, not just a good one. You don't hear a lot of, "Congratulations Bob, another great job." What you get instead is, "Goddamn it, why didn't you get the whole $1,500?"

We went back into bargaining Saturday afternoon with a few money issues left to discuss as well as several non-economic matters. We pushed and pulled, hoping to get the package together in the twelve hours I had promised Iacocca.

Fisher was not helpful. He's a great bargainer and he had turned tough as hell. He wanted us to reduce the number of job classifications and we didn't want to do that. We wanted Chrysler to pay a penalty on excessive overtime, and he refused. We all hung in determinedly, keeping at it in sub-committee rooms all over the hotel as well as the main negotiating room in the basement.

At two in the morning, Fisher still wasn't giving us the little things that would make the package better for the members.

"Listen, goddamn it," I said at one point, "don't you think this strike's settled just because we got some catch-up from Iacocca. If you think we can settle this in twelve hours with you saying *no* to everything, forget it."

I banged the table disgustedly. "You're being tough because you think this strike is over, you don't have to give anything. It isn't over, my friend."

I was getting testy and so was he. We knew the media was waiting for an announcement, though the hour was close to three in the morning and we had long passed the twelve-hour deadline.

Fisher suddenly stood up and yelled, "I'm going to bed. I don't give a shit if we ever settle this thing."

In all the times I've negotiated with that man, he'd never behaved like that.

"Go to bed," I yelled back at him. "You're useless around here anyway. I'll call Iacocca and tell him that you screwed it up."

Of course I'd never do that, but we were tired and mad and frustrated.

Fisher left the room, red-faced with anger and almost snapped the head off a reporter outside who asked what was happening. Gerard and I stared at one another in horror. We had 10,000 workers out. The day had been cold and wet and we knew the strikers on picket lines were feeling miserable. A week into the strike, everyone was losing money – the workers, the corporation, and the communities. The strike was costing Chrysler $19 million a day, $7 million of that in Canada.

"Now what the hell do we do?" someone groaned.

We didn't go to bed. We talked a while, hoping he'd change his mind and return, but he didn't. "I'm going to call and get him out of bed," I announced after a few minutes. "We've got to settle this thing. This is nuts."

"What're doing, sleeping?" I asked Fisher when he picked up the phone.

"No, I'm not sleeping," he said.

"Get out of your pyjamas, get dressed and come down here. We gotta settle this thing."

He said to come up.

Kenny Gerard went with me. We sat down with Fisher and some other Chrysler guys and got the talks back on track. At one point I looked up and saw the sun rise.

Around eleven in the morning, twenty hours after we started, we got it settled. Chrysler gave in on the penalty on overtime, we gave in on additional wash-up time, and we both agreed to study the issue of fewer job classifications. I was especially pleased, however, that Chrysler accepted a legal services plan similar to the one at General Motors.

I called Iacocca at his mother's place.

"It took longer than I expected," I told him wearily, "but it's done."

"Good," he said. "I hope we'll be starting back soon in the United States."

With the news that Chrysler had reached an agreement in Canada, Bieber got back to the bargaining table the next day. Bargaining continued in the States over the three days it took for us to get the ratification vote, which were strongly in favour of the agreement.

I called it "an historic agreement for our union." For the first time in its forty-year history, Chrysler had settled with Canadian workers before the United States. "It's a recognition by Chrysler that the Canadian pattern is different." Bill Fisher observed, "I think it's historic in that it is the first major contract negotiated with the Canadian UAW."

Our Chrysler workers were back at work when an agreement was reached in the States about a week later. While our agreement in Canada was for two years, putting us back in line with the 1987 expiry dates of the GM and Ford agreements, Bieber asked for and got a three-year agreement. The American contract with Chrysler had more up-front money in it than we got, but it also had some profit sharing and a 3-per-cent increase in the third year. I was interested to see that Bieber was moving the American UAW back towards the traditional AIF wage increase of 3 per cent a year. He appeared to be reversing his policy of going for lump-sum payments instead of raises, the very issue we'd fought over in the GM negotiations.

Analysts got busy making comparisons to see who had the better agreement.

"Look," I said to our guys who were also playing that game. "Let's stop the comparisons. We had our objectives and we knew what we wanted to achieve. If the Americans had different objectives and achieved different conditions, that's fine with me. We've achieved what we set out to do."

I was pleased that we'd come through our first bath of fire so credibly. Iacocca hadn't settled first in Canada to do Bob White and the new Canadian union any favours. He's a very astute individual and he played it that way for his own good reasons. He had to find out first if it mattered to me what he settled for in the United States, and nailed down that it didn't. After that he was ready to settle us, only incidentally making us look good, because it would get Bieber's attention.

RIGHT AFTER THE CHRYSLER STRIKE was settled, the National Film Board and CBC were ready to preview their documentary, *Final Offer: Bob White and the Canadian Auto Workers Fight for Independence*. Buzz, Nick, Sam, and I had seen a three-hour rough cut in the NFB's Toronto offices. It jolted me to hear the language I'd used.

"This is going to change things for me," I predicted. I wasn't sure how –

for the better or for the worse. I speculated that Bieber might cut off our money after he saw it. I grinned, "This could be a thirty-six million dollar film."

Buzz said, "You've got a weird sense of humour, White."

The National Film Board and the CBC were nervous that *Final Offer* would not get on the air. They were expecting an injunction from either Bieber or General Motors. CBC lawyers were alarmed. I kept hearing, "this is dynamite." When it got on the air, in prime time on the CBC network, there was great jubilation.

I was asked about my language. "My mother will be shocked," I said. But she already had seen it, and she hadn't been shocked. Three weeks earlier, I sat with them and my sister Rachel in their apartment in London and watched it on their VCR.

When it was over, my mother said, "I think that's just great."

My father said, "It sure must be lonely making some of those decisions."

There wasn't a word of criticism of the language.

"Did you shut your ears to the bad parts?" I asked my mother. "I guess I did," she smiled.

My parents are in their eighties. Some years ago I gave them the present of a trip home to Ireland, which they loved. Unfortunately, my dad suffered a stroke while they were there. He has largely recovered but is partly paralysed. For a while he was very depressed and made life difficult for my mother. I wrote him a sharp letter telling him to pull up his socks. I said this was a hard blow to accept but he had to put it behind him and get on with his life.

The next time I saw him, he gave me a hug. "That was a tough letter Bob," he said. "But you're right."

When I told my mother I would be doing a book, her first comment was, "You're not going to put all that language that was in the film in a book, are you? You really do speak better English than that."

Calls of congratulations poured in the day after *Final Offer* was broadcast. Several callers opened the conversation in the spirit of the film by saying, "How the fuck are you?" Some commented that they'd always thought Dennis McDermott was the one who swore a lot, not me. When McDermott called, he said, "Now we know who does most of the swearing in the UAW."

I think the CBC had a lot of guts to show *Final Offer*. Though they'd broadcast a warning about the swearing, in some places the CBC switchboards lit up with complaints. My impression is that most Canadians who saw *Final Offer* appreciated that I was under considerable pressure and forgave me my language. I'm still approached in supermarkets and airports by strangers who tell me they liked the film. Just before Christmas 1986, when I was in Simpson's picking up some last-minute gifts, I was approached by two women who must have been close to seventy.

"Mr. White," they said, "we loved *Final Offer*."

"You weren't bothered by the language?"

"No, no, not a bit," they beamed.

Final Offer turned out to be a prize-winner. In September 1986, it won the Prix Italia for best documentary film in competition against films from twenty other countries, the first time a CBC TV show had ever won at Europe's most influential broadcasting awards. *Final Offer* won a Genie for best feature documentary in March 1986, the Gold Plaque at the Chicago International Festival in November 1986, and was co-winner of the Grand Prix and winner of the Rockie Award for the best political and social documentary at the Banff television festival in May 1986. The NFB hoped for a nomination for an Academy Award in 1987, but that didn't happen.

In the spring of 1986, as I was preparing for a meeting of the Canadian Council, I heard about some trouble in Oshawa. A petition asking for a referendum on the split with the international union was circulating in Local 222 and around 5,000 people had signed.

I thought it would kill me. It was bad enough that the 1,500 workers of Local 251 in Wallaceburg were against us leaving the international UAW, but it was considerably worse for the largest union local in Canada, operating in the largest manufacturing complex in North America and representing 13 per cent of the Canadian UAW membership, to express dissatisfaction with a Canadian UAW.

I sent a letter to the home of every member of Local 222, urging that they stay in the Canadian union. I called meetings with leaders of the local. Some key people came and were supportive, but others refused to attend. The background was that a number of prominent committee people were under investigation for "double-dipping," drawing pay for attending committee meetings while at the same time taking their company wages. To be fair, a lot of it was sloppy bookkeeping by the company, but we ordered a thorough audit and were waiting for the results.

The men under investigation decided the way to get back at me for the embarrassment was to stir up Local 222 to stay with the international UAW. Owen Bieber was delighted, of course, and was meeting and corresponding with John Sinclair, president of Local 222.

We were caught off guard because Oshawa GM workers had been very supportive of the split. Some influential members of that local had been advocating separation for years.

When I heard about the petition I was devastated. If the aggrieved members of 222 had been trying to get my attention, they certainly succeeded.

I read my Council report until I reached the part concerning Local 251 in Wallaceburg, which had just voted to stay with the American UAW. I stopped, put down my copy, and said I wanted to raise something that was much more serious to the wellbeing of our new organization than the opposition in Wallaceburg.

I went through the events since the unrest in Oshawa had begun and the serious ramifications of what was developing. "I'm not going to let local union politics tear us apart, not without a helluva fight," I said passionately. I was extremely emotional. Everything we had done to bring the Canadian UAW carefully into being could be destroyed. A decision by Local 222 to stay with the American UAW would rock the other locals. I knew Bieber was waiting for just this kind of significant dispute to develop. The damage that a handful of individuals with personal grievances could do to the union was beyond comprehension. We would be rendered almost helpless in the 1987 collective bargaining with GM if we represented only pieces of our membership.

It was one of the most difficult periods I've ever endured. I couldn't sleep. Buzz, Nick, Sam, and I talked of little else, but nothing we had tried so far had put out the fire. My appeal to the Council was our last hope.

The Wallaceburg situation differed in fundamental ways from what was unfolding in Oshawa. The seed of that revolt was planted early in 1982, when we were going through the difficult days of the fight against concessions. The president of Local 251 in the prosperous Eaton Automotive plant broke ranks on no-concessions. In spite of the best advice of our staff man there, Bill Zilio, and my office, he bargained a concession agreement with the company.

It weakened the united front we were trying to preserve in the auto-parts industry at that critical time and was a violation of the policy established by the Canadian Council. At the next Canadian Council meeting I took the Local 251 leadership to task. I couldn't allow other local leaders to get the idea that they could make concession agreements with impunity. The humiliation of that tongue-lashing enraged Local 251 leaders and created personal animosity, for which the CAW was to pay. When the split with the international UAW was announced, Local 251's president immediately said his members in fifteen Wallaceburg plants would not support it.

Bieber and other international UAW officers seized upon the Wallaceburg situation. "There probably are lots of other locals like Wallaceburg," they said to me. "What are we going to do about them?"

I said, "If a local union in Canada wants to stay in the international union, it has a democratic right to do so. I think Wallaceburg is an exception, but any local that wants to can make that choice."

My hope was to win over Wallaceburg, but it proved impossible. I still don't think the decision to stay in the American UAW really reflected the feelings of the membership. We had taken one of our toughest strikes in that amalgamated local, especially a messy one at Wallaceburg Plastics, and we'd worked hard on behalf of the local over the years. The leaders, however, were determined to be the odd men out.

Owen Bieber welcomed Wallaceburg back into the fold. Wallaceburg members, however, fought the move by circulating petitions asking for a vote. Reluctantly, the local president had to agree, though he stalled for as long as he could. Eventually he called two membership meetings, one to be addressed by me and one by Owen Bieber.

I went to Wallaceburg on a Sunday in the spring of 1986. My sense of the membership was that sentiments were fairly evenly split on the issue of affiliation. I saw in the crowd John Sinclair, president of Local 222 in Oshawa. Sinclair was there to give his encouragement to Local 251 to stick with Solidarity House. Solidarity House was reaping a good deal of benefit from the grudge fight in 222.

Owen Bieber came the next Sunday, his speech mainly devoted to going over his recollections of the events of the General Motors strike again and how supportive he had been of the Canadian negotiation. He seemed stuck in the conviction that the separation was over an argument between White and Bieber. He promised the members in Wallaceburg that if they stayed in the international UAW he would put a service representative in the local. Local 251 would become part of the Michigan Region of the UAW, and he, personally, would make sure the Wallaceburg members were well looked after.

We knew a referendum vote in Wallaceburg was planned but we couldn't find out when it would be held. We had scrutineers ready, but the vote was called so quickly they weren't able to participate. At some plants, the company barred our staff from the parking lots when we attempted to hand out leaflets. The vote count was held in the union hall, with the doors locked to keep us out.

The vote favoured the international union by sixty to forty. We could have made a strong case that the vote wasn't conducted in a fair and open manner, but I made a decision very quickly that we were not going to cry foul. I had sent a telegram of protest on the day of the vote because certain of our people were denied access to polling areas and vote-counting areas, but after the vote, I accepted the result as final. If we'd complained, we would be seen as being unable to accept an adverse decision.

Today, Wallaceburg is the only UAW local in Canada, the sole justification for Solidarity House calling the UAW an international union. Because of our no-raid agreement with the American UAW, we don't try to recruit Wallaceburg.

In 1987, the president who had led the campaign to keep Local 251 out of the Canadian union was defeated in the Local's elections. He was subsequently made assistant personnel manager at Eaton Automotive.

I reviewed all the events in Wallaceburg with the Canadian Council before launching into a description of what was happening in Local 222 Oshawa. I characterized the Oshawa situation as "very dangerous" and spoke with such intensity that the Council caught my alarm. I think people were shocked at the depth of my feelings and it put them on the move. My instinct to blow it wide open at the Council proved right. A lot of pressure, direct and indirect, was brought to bear on the trouble-makers by influential rank-and-file members. The petitions in the Oshawa plants simply vanished.

Months later, when we finally had the cheque from the UAW in our hands, staff people shared with me their feelings during that period of the crisis with Oshawa. They said that in the spring of 1986 they'd watched me. They'd imagined that my reaction could only have meant that I'd thought the international UAW would renege at the June convention and refuse to give us the money.

Naturally, the staff and our members were vulnerable to such doubts. We were totally dependent financially on Solidarity House. I kept up the fiction that there was nothing to worry about, but it was clear to everyone that we had no strike fund of our own, no administrative money of our own, not even a name.

To balance that, our membership trusted me. We had been through tough times together – the concession era, the success of the 1982 Chrysler strike, the good contract at GM, and so on. The faith that had developed in those crises saw us through the uncertainties of 1986.

In fact, the critical mail I received at that period didn't concern the split at all. Most of it complained of my support of Dr. Henry Morgentaler, when he was recharged for operating an abortion clinic in Toronto after an acquittal at a jury trial.

The legal preparations for the June convention of the international UAW were full of tedious detail. One of the most critical issues to be resolved was the transfer of bargaining rights to the Canadian union. We administer 526 collective agreements with 300 corporations in Canada, all of which were held in the name of the international UAW. Without that orderly transfer, we would have no agreements and, in a sense, no union.

Transfer of the agreements is such a complex and delicate matter that when it finally was done in 1986, it was necessary for us to go before the Ontario Labour Relations Board to establish that the procedure was proper and legal. We chose a test case, our Ford agreement, and presented it to the Board early in 1987. To our dismay, an old left-wing member from Windsor intervened on the application. He claimed that the Canadian union had no constitutional authority to exist, and he demanded that we hold a referendum in every local as proof that we had a mandate from the membership. To our relief, he later withdrew the objection and the board approved our position.

Meanwhile, we wrestled with the problem of a new name, a new logo, and the preparation of documents to send to the international UAW convention. The constitutional changes to free us, releasing our money and transferring bargaining rights, would be made there. We had a legal right to attend that convention because, according to Solidarity House, we were still the Canadian Region of the UAW, but we decided not to send delegates. The presence of Canadians could only inflame the situation.

Our lawyers were unhappy about the decision to be absent, fearing that the convention could turn on us. They saw the possibility of a repeat of the paperworkers convention when the Canadians were thrown out of the international union without a cent. They urged us to attend. But I insisted that our attendance wouldn't matter. If Bieber decided to change his commitment to us, there would be nothing we could do. My guess was that Bieber wouldn't get much opposition from UAW members if he decided to do that.

I think many American UAW locals were sorry about our departure. The Canadians were the voice of the union's more militant positions. However, the tone of the letter Bieber sent to each local was that the Canadians were spoiled children, who left because they couldn't get their own way.

To my surprise, the documents for the legal transfer were quite problematic. I had imagined a very simple proposal that would outline the constitutional change required to endorse the withdrawal of the Canadian region from the international and to endorse the recommendation of the International Executive Board on the division of assets. Another document would give the blueprint for transferring those assets.

Bob Nickerson, as our secretary-treasurer, headed our negotiating team, which included our chief lawyer, Len MacLean. The UAW sent several American lawyers, together with Canadian lawyers to advise them on Canadian law, though they knew MacLean was an expert, as he had worked for the international UAW in Canada for years. They hired one Canadian law firm to handle the dispute over the name and another to deal with the split.

Nick told me that at one meeting the UAW had four lawyers. Though Nick is a fairly patient man, he almost gave up a couple of times. The negotiations wore him down and were a real exercise in self restraint.

On April 9, 1986, the UAW presented Nick and MacLean with a thirty-page draft proposal of the document that would go to the international convention. Nick called me from Detroit, very concerned how this would hit me. The Oshawa local was still in a state of turmoil, and he knew that I wasn't in the best of shape.

"We'll have to talk about this," he opened. "We've seen the document."

I said quickly, "Is it bad?"

"It's, ah, got some problems," he allowed.

I went over it with Buzz, Nick, Sam, and our lawyers. We were incredulous. If we signed it, we would have no legal rights at all in Canada.

"It's so bad," I said, "they can't be serious. It's very simple. We're not signing this. There's no point in having a Canadian union if we're not masters in our own house."

I said later that if the UAW bargained with the corporations as tough as they bargained with us, the workers in the United States would have wonderful collective agreements.

It was full of conditions. One, of course, was that we didn't use the name UAW-TUA Canada. We had to terminate all advertising – direct and indirect – that stated we were auto workers. All local union signs with UAW and the UAW logo had to be removed. Letterhead had to be replaced.

The $36 million would come to us, the proposal said, in the form of a letter of credit that would run for ten years and could be revoked at the discretion of the international union at any time. Nick and I were to bear personal liability for any legal action resulting from the split.

It was designed to rub our nose in the ground. It was a lawyer's dream.

One of the worst clauses was Article 303, which opened: "Subject to the versions contained in Article 17 the UAW hereby agrees to pay Canada an amount of $36 million, called a donation, upon the following terms and conditions . . ." The terms and conditions which followed said that we could only collect the money, the "donation," on a pro rata basis after we had a vote in each local.

Bieber and I had discussed the question of a referendum vote and, at the time, he had fully agreed with my position not to hold one. I understood why. The matter of referendum votes is a sensitive one that comes up at every international UAW convention. Some members always speak in favour of it and the leadership always has to explain patiently that it isn't in the UAW tradition. Bieber couldn't insist on the Canadians having a referendum and then argue against a referendum vote at the convention. It seemed, however, that he had changed his mind and was prepared to live with the inconsistency.

The document also proposed that the UAW hold back $5 million of the $36 million in case we violated any part of the agreement. In addition, we would have to defend all challenges to the bargaining rights. The UAW would continue to hold the mortgage on our head office and other properties. We had to indemnify the UAW if there were any challenges in the States to the split. The document pledged us not to organize or accept for membership any UAW members in the United States or Canada, but was silent on the matter of the UAW raiding our locals.

They knew we couldn't accept it. Someone must have ordered the lawyers to put together the worst document imaginable just to shock us.

Nick and Len MacLean went back into a series of bargaining sessions with them. Some of the meetings were little more than raw confrontations, which put Nick on a ragged edge. The files of legal documents, legal interpretations of documents, and correspondence grew several inches thick. It wasn't until late on the night of May 28, 1986, only days before the convention in California, that we had a document we could sign.

The agreement still contained a lot that we didn't like, but we had removed the local-by-local vote, Nick's and my personal liability, a restrictive clause about the UAW controlling arbitration of disputes, and a few more of the most objectionable features. The insulting designation of the $36 million as "a donation" was removed, at our insistence. The $5 million holdout was reduced to $1 million.

The name was the thorniest issue of all. The name, United Auto Workers, had come to be a symbol of something deep in the psyche of Solidarity

House, and Bieber was unshakable in refusing to allow us to use it. Len MacLean, a loyal friend as well as our lawyer, used to drive Solidarity House nearly wild by wearing his UAW-TUA CANADA button to meetings.

I think Bieber and the other UAW leaders simply wanted to punish the Canadians. Nothing like that has happened in any other Canadian union that has split. The Communication Workers of Canada kept their name when they left the Communications Workers in the United States. The electrical workers, after they broke with the UEW, were known as the United Electrical Workers of Canada. The paperworkers are called the Canadian Paperworkers Union.

Canadian members of the UAW contributed as much as any other member toward the proud history of that union. I was convinced that we were seeing an exercise in good old American machismo, but there was nothing we could do about it.

Sam Gindin composed a humorous letter to Bieber in which he explained that we had asked for suggestions for a new name and received such ideas as "Reutherites," "Canadian Union of Men and Women Who Build Those Things-That-Drive-On-The-Road (the CUMAWWBTTTDOTR)," and "Canadian Otto Vorkers."

Sam said he was recommending an interim name, the Canadian Brewery and Salt Workers (CBASW). He pointed out, "It makes absolutely no sense and should therefore be readily acceptable to the IEB. And if we take out the BS – a slight problem for the IEB perhaps – we're left with the initials we'll eventually have [CAW]."

In a merry postscript, the letter reminded Bieber that he had not protested when the autoworkers union in Japan decided to call itself the Japanese Auto Workers. Since they were about to become the largest union of auto workers in the world, they might be considering a move to deprive the UAW of the use of their name. If that happened, I assured Bieber that he could count on the full support of his Canadian brothers and sisters. We never sent the letter.

But nothing about our name was funny any more. I thought that losing the name UAW would upset our members, but the feedback we were getting surprised me. Workers were saying they didn't mind the idea of a new name because it would fit with the new identity.

Late April or early May, I gave up fighting for the name UAW Canada. Nick had been saying for weeks, "Goddamn it, we're not going any place until you change the name. You know you're going to do it eventually, so when are you going to get at it?"

We started batting names around. I asked Nick, Sam, Buzz, and Wendy to think how our delegates identify themselves when they go to the microphone at a convention. They say, "I'm Joe Blow from Local 199, U-Ay-W." Very few people, Bob Nickerson being one of them, say the whole thing, United Auto Workers.

"What's the easiest transition for our delegates to make so they don't stumble all over the name?" I said. "I think it's CAW, Canadian Auto Workers."

That led to a big argument because CAW looks like the sound crows make. "They'll laugh us out of the convention," Buzz protested.

Nick, Buzz, and I then had a terrible argument about the acronym CAW. I decided to try it out on a couple of staff people to show that I was right. I called in, Pat Clancy, an old left-winger, and said we needed him to settle a dispute.

"Pat, what does C-Ay-W sound like?" I asked.

He said promptly, "It sounds like *caw*."

"Get the hell out of here," I told him. "I don't need your godammned advice."

We took the problem to the next meeting of the executive board. The reaction to CAW was mixed. People worried that it looked funny in print.

"No," I argued. "People will get used to it. Look at the Canadian Union of Public Employees, which is always called *kewpee*."

I insisted that we have Canada in our name. A counter-suggestion was "national." We looked at National Auto Workers, but that came out NAW and would be far too inviting for cartoonists. We went to the blackboard and wrote down all our ideas, some of which made us groan.

Nickerson was keen on Canadian Auto Workers. "The guys want to call themselves Canadian," he insisted.

"The Quebec guys too?" someone asked doubtfully.

We tested CAW around enough to get a feel that it was the best choice. One day I had enough.

"The decision's made," I said. "We're CAW. Get the designer up here. I want to call it CAW Canada. I know it sounds screwy, Canadian Auto Workers-Canada, but the logo is what's going to be up there."

I grinned. "Anyway, we're not really giving up the U in UAW. We're just turning it on its side."

We talked to Quebec and found that with using the French translation, making ourselves CAW-TCA Canada, they had no problem with the double mention of Canada. The full name is something else, the National Automobile, Aerospace and Agricultural Implement Workers Union of Canada –

Syndicat National des Travailleurs et Travailleuses de l'Automobile, de l'Aérospatiale et de l'Outillage Agricole du Canada.

I didn't think we'd have trouble with Bieber over keeping auto workers in the name. In fact, during one argument I had with him over UAW Canada he snapped, "You want to be Canadian Auto Workers, you should call yourselves the Canadian Auto Workers."

Ron Kaplansky designed a clear, sparkling logo and we started the expensive task of removing all signs of UAW from our buildings, letterheads, and documents.

Meanwhile, the document we had signed was ready to go to the international convention in California. We sent Len MacLean and some staff people as observers. Wallaceburg was represented in the Michigan Region, the only Canadians officially at the convention.

Some were worried about that. They thought that the Canadian Region might be removed from the UAW constitution and then put back in just for the Wallaceburg local. Then someone from Wallaceburg would be elected Canadian director and take over my office.

That was possible, so we had an emergency plan in place. We handpicked a group of delegates, still legal under the existing UAW constitution, who could fly to California at a moment's notice, form a Canadian caucus and outvote the Wallaceburg delegates.

I didn't take the possibility of a last-minute doublecross seriously. I felt we had reached the point where Solidarity House was fed up and wanted us gone.

The constitutional changes and the agreement on the terms of separation in the document were all passed at the California convention. People made speeches about how sad this occasion was, but the general tone of the convention wasn't against us. The breakaway of the Canadians was in competition with several hot issues, one of them criticism of the UAW leadership, so our departure didn't dominate the convention by any means.

According to our agreement with Solidarity House, the name change in Canada had to happen quickly. This required a constitutional change because all our founding documents were in the name UAW-TUA Canada. To avoid being in legal limbo, we had scheduled a special one-day convention in Toronto immediately after the Californian convention and were ready to go on June 10, 1986.

We considered how to introduce the new name. Brian Feil, president of Local 707 in Oakville, came up with the idea of having the logo on a fabric backdrop that would be raised when the vote to change our name in the constitution was completed. Wendy Cuthbertson was away so Peggy Nash, the other person in our communications department, worked on the logo. It's almost exactly the same as our original one, CAW-TCA in white letters on a deep blue background with a red maple leaf in the centre. When the delegates saw it unfurl, they loved it.

There was some regret about losing the UAW. I said, "It was a choice between the three letters 'UAW' and no money or 'CAW' and $36 million. But I have mixed feelings, too, about changing the name."

With only one dissenting vote, the three hundred delegates ratified the new name and the agreement on the transfer of property. The "friendly" divorce, which had begun eighteen months before, at last was final.

CHAPTER TWENTY-THREE

Planting the Flag
in Michelin

W E STILL DIDN'T GET our money from Solidarity House. Month after month, Solidarity House lawyers found ways to complicate negotiations or bring them to a dead halt. Every time one of them heard that a Canadian local still had a UAW sign out front, they tied up talks to complain at length that the agreement was being violated.

We had instructed every local to remove their UAW signs, but few had been able to act quickly. It's costly and time-consuming to get new signs. We printed all the stationery with the new letterhead ourselves and distributed it to the locals. But, despite our best efforts, there were union halls here and there with a faded UAW sign painted over the door, enough of them to give Detroit fits and delay the transfer of funds.

The switch to the new name wasn't easy. For a long time it took a conscious effort to say, "I'm Bob White of the CAW" after introducing myself for thirty-four years as "Bob White of the UAW." Sam Gindin, Wendy, all of us, still forget sometimes and say UAW when we mean CAW.

Amazingly, after all our concern, I've only heard us called *caw*, as in crow, three times. I said in a staff meeting right after we decided to go with CAW that I didn't want to hear anyone use *caw*, even in fun.

"If we don't start it, nobody will start it. Let's get it across that we're C-Ay-W."

Buzz Hargrove was talking to someone in Ray Majerus' office in Solidarity House in January 1987 and the American called us "*caw*." Buzz said he felt like crawling through the phone to get at him.

Nick was worn out dealing with Solidarity House's arguments over picky matters. Nothing, it appeared, was too small for the UAW lawyers to complain about for hours. Just when it seemed the last snag was resolved, some yo-yo would say that he'd been out for a spin around Windsor and saw a sign reading UAW. Solidarity House insisted we wouldn't get our money until every trace of UAW was wiped out in Canada.

On October 13, 1986, Nick was in Solidarity House with Len MacLean, going over final details. Incredibly, there were still hitches. He gave up, told the UAW to stick it, and went back to Windsor. He phoned me. I was sympathetic, but I told him to hang on. "We're at the end of the road, Nick. Just a little bit more," I said.

The next day he went back. On October 15, he and Len worked until midnight and finally the job was done. The document was ready for our signatures.

The next morning I was scheduled to tape a discussion on the Canadian political scene for Peter Gzowski's remarkable CBC radio show "Morningside." With Jim Coutts, former adviser to Pierre Trudeau, I was a member of what for a while was a weekly feature. As I was leaving, Coutts asked where I was going next.

I replied, "To pick up a cheque for $43 million dollars."

Bob Nickerson, Len MacLean, and I waited in the lobby of the Constellation Hotel on Toronto's airport strip for Solidarity House's lawyers to arrive with the documents. We greeted them and went into a small meeting room where we read the massive document through to make sure nothing had been changed. Nick wasn't in a good mood, and I appreciated that. He was glad that it was over, but the process had embittered him.

I was hoping the cheque would bear the signatures of Owen Bieber and Ramon Majerus but instead there was a bank draft with no signatures. We photocopied it anyway and had the picture framed.

Nick and I put our signatures on the document at nine forty-five in the morning on October 17, 1986. The lawyers from Solidarity House handed us the bank draft in the amount of $43,500,000.63, which represented our promised $36 million, the dues they'd collected since the split (minus expenses), and the interest that had accumulated. When we added in the value of our buildings, which had risen to more than $4 million, we were in very good shape. Secretary-treasurer Bob Nickerson reported at the next meeting of the CAW executive board that our strike fund was in excess of $40 million and our total assets in the neighbourhood of $57 million.

Solidarity House held back $1 million as a contingency fund against unforseen expenses. Bieber also insisted that we pay all UAW legal expenses incurred in the split, a considerable sum.

We had resources of our own. Right after the decision to split, to protect ourselves in case Solidarity House cut off our money, the Canadian Council voted on my recommendation that we put part of our dues into our own strike fund. As soon as the separation was made final at the UAW convention in California, Nick took an intelligent step that also helped. He ordered our locals to send their dues to Toronto instead of Detroit. Those two steps earned us about $7 million.

We should have rejoiced when the bank draft finally was in our hands that morning, but we felt curiously flat. After so much meanness and petty bickering, the presentation seemed anti-climactic. Wendy had arranged a press conference at eleven to announce the receipt of the money, but as we drove back to the office our mood was subdued.

Len MacLean turned up with bottles of champagne, which helped remind us that we had something to celebrate. "We've been waiting for so long, I think it hasn't yet sunk in that this is an important day," I commented to Nick.

We shut down the office and went into the board room to share the champagne with the office staff.

We'd just organized a small plant in Toronto and the staff member for the new local was in the office for a meeting with the local's newly elected committee. I invited them to join us for the champagne.

"By the way," I said to them, "there's a cheque for $43 million here. We do this about every other Friday, get $43 million, open up the champagne and celebrate. You've joined a great organization."

At the press conference I observed, "The union is well equipped to enter healthy bargaining, but this doesn't mean we want to strike."

We thought we'd hold on to the bank draft over the weekend and set up some more photo-sessions. The bank warned us it would cost $60,000 in lost interest, so we deposited it in a hurry.

The transition to managing our own financial affairs was smooth. Some months earlier, Nick had secured a $1 million advance from Solidarity House to help set up the necessary bookkeeping, accounting and other office procedures. Tom Saunders, who used to be with CALEA, the Canadian Air Line Employees' Association, passenger agents who merged with our union some years ago, worked with Nick to set up our new systems. He and Nick met with banks, trust companies, and financial advisers to establish the best possible banking system and the investment of our strike fund so it is available as needed.

We hadn't appreciated how much stress we'd been carrying since the split, but now it was over we all felt a new enthusiasm. We had plenty to do with our renewed energy. I was concerned that our union hadn't been energetic about getting new members. To remedy that neglect, I recommended to the National Executive Board that we add up to ten organizers to the payroll on a temporary basis – young, eager people who would have an opportunity to show what they could do.

WE TOOK ON one of the biggest organizing challenges in the country – the three plants of Michelin Tires (Canada) Limited in Nova Scotia. Michelin has a long history of anti-unionism. The French-based multinational company came to Canada in the 1970s with the help of millions of dollars in provincial and federal government subsidies and built two plants. Since then Michelin has resisted all efforts to organize its three thousand employees. The company even paid Canadian construction unions a penalty to allow it to build its plants with non-union labour brought from France.

The Operating Engineers were the first to take on Michelin with an attempt to organize the stationary engineers. That failed because the provincial government enacted some legislation to make the effort too difficult.

Then the United Rubber Workers conducted a campaign in the Granton plant, the most pro-union of the Michelin plants in Nova Scotia, and signed up the required 40 per cent of workers. Planning to organize the other Michelin plant in Bridgewater at a later date, they made an application for certification. The night before the hearing, an order-in-cabinet was passed, which is known informally as "the Michelin Bill." It requires unions to sign 40 per cent of workers in *both* Michelin plants, with the votes counted together. The application for certification therefore had insufficient numbers and collapsed.

Michelin then built a third Nova Scotian plant at Waterville in the Annapolis Valley. The Nova Scotia Labour Relations Board declared that the Waterville workers would be lumped in with the other two plants for the purposes of certification.

The legislation in Nova Scotia, designed specifically to keep unions out of Michelin, is unique in Canada. In Ontario, for instance, if there is a large plant in Guelph, another plant owned by the same people in Toronto, and another in Windsor, those three plants are organized one at a time, a feasible task. Under the rules of Nova Scotia, unions would have to organize all three simultaneously and get 40 per cent of the total number of workers in the plants.

Next the Canadian Labour Congress got involved. The CLC demonstrated that there was support for a union because they got a significant number of cards quite quickly. However, another condition in the Michelin Bill is that a union must apply for certification within four months. In Ontario, organizers are allowed a year. Though the CLC did very well in Michelin, it couldn't get the 40 per cent in time. It applied just before the deadline and the Nova Scotia Labour Relations Board found it was short of the required number.

Our staff member in Nova Scotia, Larry Wark, had talked to Michelin workers. He thought they could be organized, despite the record of failure. Wark asked Buzz to go to Nova Scotia to look it over. Buzz took with him a young man, Hemi Mitic, who we'd hired for Winnipeg three years earlier from a Kitchener local. I saw a lot of potential in Hemi, so I'd put him in charge of organizing earlier that year.

They reported back that Wark was right. We might be able to do it.

"There's no way," I argued. "Michelin is a hopeless situation. For twelve years we've watched unions try to organize Michelin."

"Bob, these guys are very impressed with the CAW," Wark insisted. "They've watched us with Chrysler, they watched us break away from the UAW. If anyone can do it, we can."

It was true that as soon as we had announced we were splitting from the UAW to form an all-Canadian union, there had been a sudden interest in us. We had calls asking us to send an organizer to non-union plants and calls from people in other unions who wanted to talk of switching.

I instructed my staff very clearly not to talk to people who wanted to switch unions. We hadn't set up a new organization in order to be cannibals in the Canadian labour movement.

I looked at the strategy the CLC had used in Michelin. The organizers had concentrated on Granton, where the union movement was strong, and did much less work in Bridgewater and Waterville. Maybe that was a flaw, I thought. Buzz, Nick, Hemi, and I talked it over. I still wasn't convinced, but Hemi made a good case. Maybe it would work, I conceded grudgingly.

Our guys figured that if I met the Michelin workers, I'd be sold. They called a meeting of key union sympathizers from the three Michelin plants for late July 1986. Buzz, Nick, and I booked a meeting room in a hotel close to the Halifax airport, and set up a session to begin with a reception Friday night and an all-day meeting Saturday.

I was touched as I listened to those Michelin workers. Some had been trying to get a union for ten, twelve years. They had gone through all the battles and in the process they had become seasoned trade unionists. They hadn't given up hope and they were willing to try one more time. They knew what it meant, that they would have no free time in the evenings or weekends for the next four months, but that didn't bother them. I decided we had to help.

I gave instructions to open offices in all three locations, not just Granton. I didn't want divisiveness. Three offices would mean three more staff people, but it was important that the workers in Waterville and Bridgewater felt as much a part of the campaign as the workers in Granton.

The Michelin workers urged us to start with a big splash.

"We're not going to do that," I said. "You'll have to trust us. We'll need your input, but we have to run this campaign and we have some expertise. We'll do it with you, but the final decisions on how to run this campaign will be ours."

A bad mistake had happened in the CLC campaign. The CLC had petitioned the courts against the Michelin Bill and someone in the CLC lawyer's office inadvertently included in the submission a list of all the Michelin workers in the Granton plant who had signed CLC cards. A copy of the submission was filed with Michelin's lawyers, so the company had the names of all union supporters in the Granton plant.

Word of the error spread immediately. The story was exaggerated to say that the company knew the names of people who had signed cards in the Bridgewater and Waterville plants as well. I talked to the senior lawyers in that firm, the best labour law firm in Nova Scotia, and I was convinced that it was an honest mistake.

I invited a senior lawyer from the firm to our meeting to explain the legislation. When the Michelin workers realized who he was, they tore his ass off. They told me they were dead against the CAW retaining that firm.

They were an excellent law firm and I wasn't prepared to throw them to the wolves, but my defence created quite a storm. I explained that most of our legal work was done inside the CAW, and I promised the membership list would never leave our hands. Finally, but not very happily, they agreed we could keep the firm.

Because many of the workers were taking August vacations and because our staff needed time to rent offices and get set up, we planned for the campaign to start September 1. Very satisfied, I went back to Toronto that Saturday afternoon.

Monday morning one of the Michelin workers called our organizing office to say the United Steelworkers had an organizer in Nova Scotia assigned to Michelin who was phoning workers to ask them to sign Steelworkers cards. He'd heard that the union had organized a meeting in Moncton for the following Saturday, at which it was reported that Lynn Williams, the Canadian who is the international president of the Steelworkers, would speak. Undoubtedly, an announcement of the Michelin campaign would be made at that time.

I couldn't believe my ears. I did some checking around and discovered that the Steelworkers indeed were planning to start organizing. I didn't see what basis the union had for going ahead. We had been meeting the key Michelin workers for weeks.

I called Gerry Docquier, national director of the Steelworkers in Canada. He wasn't in, but I left a message.

"He'll know what I'm calling about," I said to his secretary.

I called Buzz, Nick, Sam, Hemi, and Wendy.

"Guys, we have to shift gears. We've heard the Steelworkers are calling a meeting Saturday in Moncton. We can't let them make an announcement ahead of us. By the time we come out and say we're also campaigning, it'll look like *me too*."

"So what do we do?" Buzz asked.

"We're going to put a leaflet in those goddamned plants on Friday morning announcing that we're organizing, starting right now," I said.

"Our guys in Michelin will go crazy," Nick protested. "We've just finished telling them that we would start September 1."

"Can't help it," I said. "Let's get busy."

Later that day, Docquier returned my call.

"I want to talk to you about Michelin," I said. "We're down there, Gerry. We've been talking to the workers for a couple of months. We've had a good leadership meeting and we've got a campaign underway."

"So have we," he told me.

"No you haven't," I said. "We've got the leadership from the Rubber Workers campaign and the CLC campaign. There's no other leadership in those Michelin plants. It makes no sense for you and me to fight about this thing. Michelin is an auto-parts plant."

He said, "One plant makes steel."

"I don't know if one of us can organize Michelin," I told him. "But I sure as hell know that two of us can't. Why the hell don't you stay out of it and let us have a run at the goddamned thing?"

"I'm not going to do that," he said.

"Gerry, that makes no sense. We've just had a meeting of the leadership, thirty people. You haven't got those people. There's no goddamned way you can organize Michelin without those key people. All you can succeed in doing is splitting the vote."

He wouldn't change his mind.

"Okay," I said. "See you down the road some place."

I went home that night and wrote a leaflet. The next day, Wednesday, Wendy went over it and sent it to a printer, who had been told to stand by for an emergency. Buzz said, "Bob, you'll have to do this with a press conference."

"You're right," I groaned. "It will look crazy to the Michelin workers right after I finished telling them that it was a bad idea to start with a big splash, but we've got to do it. Wendy, set it up."

We put out the leaflets Friday morning, August 1, 1986, in the three Michelin plants, *An Invitation to Join the Canadian Auto Workers*, and had a press conference in Halifax at ten o'clock the same day. I was asked my opinion of the Michelin Bill.

"I don't like the Michelin Bill," I said, "but it is law in Nova Scotia. All I know is that we have to operate this organizing campaign under the rules of the Michelin Bill and I'm not going to waste a lot of time complaining about it, or going to the courts about it. We're going to try to organize despite the problems imposed by the Michelin Bill."

"What if you don't make it?"

"Our name will go on the Michelin tombstone with all the other unions that have tried it," I answered. "But I have a hunch we'll succeed.

"It's a challenge for our union, but it is one in which we don't have any hesitation in stepping up to. But, to be candid about it, Michelin employees will make the final decision here."

I was asked if I was going to be active in the campaign.

"If somehow my profile or my role in the labour movement can help get our union in Michelin, then I'm glad to be here and I hope to be here to lead the bargaining."

It went just great. Then I had to face our guys. I knew they would be mad because they had vacations planned, and I knew our staff would be caught with very little yet done. I had some tall explaining to do and I expected a rough time, which I got.

The success of the CAW, however, has depended to a great extent on our ability to be flexible and to move very quickly without a lot of bureaucratic hassle. We're fast off the mark. In labour organizing or collective bargaining, timing is vital. If we had spent three days debating what to do about the

Steelworkers, letting them have their meeting that weekend and make their announcement, we would never have picked ourselves up off the mat.

The next day the Steelworkers cancelled their meeting. We didn't hear from them again. But we faced a lot of division in the ranks for the first four weeks of the Michelin campaign.

Michelin was asked for a response. Ronald Musgnug, vice-president and general manager, replied, "I regret that Michelin employees are going to be subjected again to union promises and pressures and the disruptive environment which they were forced to put up with last year when they rejected the CLC."

Everyone told us it was hopeless it organize Michelin – our lawyer, Ray Larkin, the journalists we met, other trade unionists, people on the street, even Michelin workers in the plants. That made it extremely difficult to build morale and confidence.

We tried to figure how many cards we would need to get the 40 per cent, a difficult task since we couldn't get an accurate count of the number of employees in the three plants. I went to Nova Scotia several times and came back full of admiration for Hemi Mitic and the mostly young organizers we put on the job to help him. They had adjusted well from the shock of being thrown into the Michelin campaign on three-days' notice. They didn't stay in fancy motels. They lived right in the community so they could have meetings at night with key people.

The organizers had to drive miles every night to locate Michelin workers, who lived all over the countryside. They had to build up in-plant committees, starting with one or two workers and encouraging that nucleus to recruit others and turn over the names of potential sympathizers. They took in T-shirts with our new logo, which they tried to distribute. On a good day, you could spot maybe two people wearing them.

At one of the organizing meetings there was a discussion about how to advertise the CAW. One guy asked, "What do Nova Scotians like best? Caps!"

So we had caps made with the CAW logo, which went over like hotcakes. The campaign began to open up. Workers in the Michelin plants had been timid at first but they were taking heart. Guys started to wear the CAW-CANADA T-shirts in the plants. We had "T-shirt days" when we would give away dozens of them.

We had trouble renting office space in those small communities because of the level of fear about being associated with the union. After many rejections, we finally obtained locations in all three towns. We filled these offices with used furniture, put posters on the walls, and installed telephones. Spouses of workers who had signed cards came to help with typing and mailing in return for a little expense money, so it turned into a family effort.

Bridgewater, Granton, and Waterville people had never talked together before, but we brought them into Halifax for regular meetings to discuss the progress of the campaign.

I agonized over numbers. Since we could only guess how many people were in the plants, it was tricky to know how many cards were needed to make the 40 per cent requirement. We took mechanical counters to the plant gates, trying to get accurate figures. That meant we had to subtract from the total on the counters an estimate of the number of people who were management. Hemi Mitic pored over lists, culling out the names of people who had died or had left Michelin. The information was fed into computers and analysed, fed into computers a different way and analysed again.

I said we should assume there were 3,300 people in the three plants, but Mitic kept saying I was way out, there were fewer than 2,900. We later learned from the Labour Relations Board that his estimate was out by only six people.

I was keeping close to what was happening. Once or twice I made a circuit of the three towns and spoke to Michelin workers at well-attended meetings, though Waterville had the poorest turnout. Reporters asked me what stage I thought the campaign was at.

I always replied, "We've got a long way to go."

Some anti-union groups emerged in the plants. When asked about them, I said, "If workers don't want to have a union, they have the right to campaign against the union. If the company gets involved, that's different."

The company got involved. Michelin had group meetings inside the plants to talk against the union; they had private meetings with workers to ask them not to join the union; they had meetings in which they told workers that they knew who were the traitors who had joined the union. They indulged in just about every unfair and illegal labour practice there is, but we didn't protest to the Nova Scotia Labour Relations Board. There was no way that the board was going to certify a union in Michelin without a vote, regardless of what the company did.

The company's propaganda campaign was tremendous. They said that their workers didn't want a union and would be grateful when the harassment stopped. They tried to play on regional sensitivities. A new vice-president, fresh from France, complained that we brought in outside organizers from Ontario. I commented acidly that when I arrived at the Halifax airport, I hadn't noticed that I needed a passport.

I said, "I think it's strange that a vice-president from France would lecture us about organizers from Ontario, when we're all Canadians."

Michelin claimed my statements about the campaign revealed that it was a failure. "Even Mr. White says they have a long way to go," the company pointed out.

Our leadership got mad at me about that. "Don't you know what that's doing to us? We're trying to get cards and you're running around saying we've got a long way to go. It makes us sound like we're not going to make it."

At one meeting someone plaintively asked me, "Could you just take the word 'long' out of it?"

THE STAFF AND ORGANIZERS were exhausted and growing irritated. Michelin workers helping in the campaign were working all day in the plants and hitting the roads at night to talk to other workers, and that's difficult. Even a strong young person soon feels the strain, and not all those guys were young. Larry Wark was losing weight visibly and limping from a dog bite.

They asked me to make one more round of committee meetings at the three locations. Though I was keeping it to myself, we were almost certain we had the cards to apply for certification in ten days. After a careful count and study of the computer records, we thought we had the 40 per cent and a bit more for safety.

In Nova Scotia, the system works very quickly. On the day the application is made, the Labour Board freezes plant numbers. That prevents a company from hiring forty or fifty people right away to throw off the proportion. After a check to determine if the union cards represent 40 per cent of the employees, the board conducts a secret vote in the plants within seven days of the application, a very fast process. In Ontario the vote doesn't take place for three weeks or more.

We were worried about the timing. If the company learned the date of our application in advance, they could load new workers into the plants. I went to the three meetings, keeping the lid on. "You've got to get us more cards," I insisted. "We're still short."

The guys were upset. They were drained and discouraged by my negativism. In Waterville an in-plant organizer said, "Bob, I'm getting pissed off at you. Are we close or not?"

"Listen my friend," I said, "I've been at this too long. At a meeting like this, there is always somebody who is here because the company wants him here. You can be certain there's a pipeline to the company in this room. I'm not going to talk numbers here."

He looked unconvinced. "If you can't live with that," I told him, "and you want your card back, you can go ahead. I can understand how you feel. But I'm not giving out numbers. You have to trust me."

To meet the grumbling that was going on, I announced at every meeting that I would return to Nova Scotia within two weeks for another leadership meeting in Halifax at which I would tell them exactly where we were at.

Nick, Hemi, Buzz, Wendy, and I arrived in Halifax on Thursday morning, bringing with us the application for certification and the membership cards. We knew that the Nova Scotia Labour Relations Board closed at four-thirty. We advised our lawyers in Halifax that we wanted to meet with them again at two in the afternoon to go over the provisions in the legislation one more time. Wendy informed the media that we would have a press conference Friday morning to give an update on the Michelin campaign.

Nick, Hemi, and I, carrying bulging briefcases, met with Ray Larkin, our Halifax lawyer.

"How are you?" he asked.

"Fine," I said. "You know what we're going to do today? We're going to make an application for certification."

"You're kidding!" he said.

"We've got at least 40 per cent," I grinned. "There's no doubt of that. We've got the cards here."

The Nova Scotia Labour Relations Board is in the same building as CTV, so I couldn't show my face there. Our plan was that Larkin and Mitic would deliver the application and the cards at exactly four-fifteen. The Labour Board's offices closed at four-thirty.

Leaflets announcing the application were taken off the plane from Toronto that night. Wendy's idea had been to use the Michelin logo, the pneumatic, roly-poly man, on our leaflet, but dress him in a CAW Canada bib and cap. He looked great in his union togs. But Michelin's lawyers sent me a letter about it. For the first time in an organizing campaign, we were running ads on radio stations covering the issues involved – pensions, health and safety. I prepared one to announce the application, but we had to be careful that one of the local radio stations didn't leak to the company. The stations wanted twenty-four-hour advance notice to put them in, so we had to work around that problem.

At eight the next morning, Wendy called all the local media to say that my press conference would concern more than an update, that I had a very important announcement to make. When I got to the room we had reserved for the occasion, a lot of people had assembled.

The announcement caught Michelin completely by surprise. Our security measures had worked. In the plants the workers almost exploded with excitement. Because of my evasiveness, they had decided that the CAW campaign wasn't working. To them, putting in an application was a major victory, never mind that we still had to win the votes.

Our leadership meeting was scheduled for Saturday, starting with a reception in the hotel Friday night. More than a hundred ecstatic people showed up. We couldn't get them all into the room we had booked, so we had to get the hotel to find us a larger space off the lobby. The din of cheering and whistling was deafening.

We were advised by the Labour Board that the results of the check on our numbers would be ready late the next day. In preparation, I moved my office to a downtown Halifax hotel, the Citadel Inn. The board went to the Michelin plants to check employment records and promised to call us at six o'clock.

At six the phone didn't ring. My hotel room looked like a maternity ward full of expectant fathers pacing up and down. The call came at seven-thirty. Hemi Mitic took it. I heard him say, "We do, eh?" From the grin on his face we knew we had the 40 per cent and a yell went up you could have heard a mile away.

At the press conference November 14, 1986, I was cautious. "We haven't won yet," I said.

The next step was a vote of all Michelin employees, cardholders and non-cardholders alike. To be certified as the bargaining agent for the workers we had to get 50 per cent of all Michelin employees in the three plants, plus one more worker.

The vote for certification is secret, but it didn't look that way to Michelin workers. Their marked ballots went into a sealed envelope, which went inside another envelope on which a returning officer wrote the worker's name and clock number. They thought the company would be able to find out how they voted.

We agonized for hours how to convince the workers that no one would know how they voted. Finally we got the proper terminology. We distributed a leaflet which explained that the procedure was a safeguard for everyone, both the workers who were opposed and those who supported the union, and that the privacy of neither would be violated.

I had a gut feeling, and it isn't hindsight, that we didn't have the numbers to win the vote for certification. Experience has shown that a union can lose votes between the organizing period when people sign cards with nothing much at stake except two dollars to sign the card, and the time when workers get down to reality and vote. The organizers were buoyed up and confident we would win, but I wasn't optimistic. I saw that the company had recovered very quickly. The next day, Michelin had countered with radio ads asking workers to keep Michelin union-free.

The history of labour movement is far from being a series of unbroken successes, even for the often-victorious Canadian Auto Workers. People asked me why I had taken Michelin on if I felt so strongly that we couldn't do it. I explained simply that we had to try. It's my view that the CAW has an obligation to take on the tough fights, including those with a high probability of failure.

Voting in the Michelin plants would start on a Wednesday, November 19, at midnight. On the Monday before we were devastated to read in the one Halifax paper an interview with a professor of international business at one of the Halifax universities. He predicted that if the CAW was certified in Nova Scotia, the Michelin plants would close and leave the country. He said Michelin had just closed a plant in Belgium for that reason, moving the work to non-union plants elsewhere. There was too much capacity in the rubber industry, he explained, sounding knowledgeable, and plants had to close somewhere.

That front-page story was picked up by every radio and television station in the province and by the community newspapers who were hammering us anyway. The Waterville paper once ran a cartoon showing me standing in front of a locked and deserted Michelin plant with my foot on the bumper of a big car with an Ontario licence plate saying to workers, "But we still want your dues." Those papers ran headlines saying, PLANTS WILL CLOSE IF CAW SUCCESSFUL – EXPERT.

No question, that hurt us severely even though some responsible reporters were quick to point out this was only one academic's opinion. Municipal politicians declared the professor was right, the plants would close.

I considered getting into the debate but decided there was no point. The harm was done. The article played on the worst fears of workers in a province where unemployment is among the highest in Canada. One of our more active supporters told me his wife had tears in her eyes when she read the Halifax paper. "I told you!" she cried. "If the union gets in, you'll be out of work."

My only comment when the media asked me about the professor's warning was that the man should be more careful with his statements. I said there was no doubt in my mind that Michelin would not close. Production was good in those plants. Interestingly, Michelin never said it would close the plants, never. In the panic that ensued, however, it didn't matter that the company significantly was silent.

The voting concluded on November 21. The ballot boxes were sealed, but the Labour Board didn't schedule a hearing until January 14, 1987.

We took some issues to the January 14 hearing before the Nova Scotia Labour Relations Board. The board made its decision on these issues and then said it would need eight hours to count the ballots, starting on the next morning, January 15.

We weren't allowed scrutineers to watch the count. Ray Larkin, our lawyer, said the results would come to him and he'd call us immediately at the hotel. A young woman reporter for ATV in Halifax, thinking of the access I had given for the making of *Final Offer*, asked if her crew could film me receiving that call. I said sure.

I had work to do, but I couldn't get to it. I gave a long interview in my hotel bedroom to a reporter from *Businessweek*, a U.S. publication, and when I came out into sitting room I found it jammed with cameras and photographers who had heard about the arrangement with ATV. They also wanted to film me taking the call. I was already committed, so there was nothing to do but agree.

It was a time of raw emotion. Every time the telephone rang, we all jumped. To ease the tension, we went into the bedroom and played a game of tossing quarters against the wall. I tried to think what I would say if we won, what I would say if we lost. I can't do that, it would be phony if I did prepare myself that way, but I made a try.

About four-fifteen the phone rang again. Wendy said, "Just a minute Ray. He's right here."

The television camera people turned on the hard bright lights they use. I took the receiver from Wendy.

"Bob, you were right," Larkin said heavily. "We've lost it."

"We did, eh," I said.

I put down the phone and said, "We lost it," my voice choked. Buzz and Hemi, who had believed strongly that we would win, were shattered. Larry Wark, who had lost eighteen pounds during the hard four-month campaign, was in tears.

I walked a distance along a hall and down some stairs to the room we had reserved for a press conference, trying to compose myself. I had to push through reporters asking how I was feeling.

"Quite frankly," I said, "I feel very bad. But I always have to respect the wishes of the workers."

A CBC woman put a microphone under my nose and said, "Bob, you said when you launched the campaign that if you lost your name would go on the Michelin tombstone. What do you say now?"

I grinned at her. "It will be on that tombstone, but not forever."

I got myself a cup of coffee while I thought over what I would say. We had a lot to feel good about. We had broken through the Michelin Bill, a first, and we had given the workers their first opportunity ever to have a democratic vote for a union. I couldn't belittle those achievements by complaining.

In my statement to the media I said, "My staff will tell you that I was expecting this to happen, but still it's a shock. We put on the best campaign possible. There is nothing that I would have changed in the way we handled this. Regardless of how the vote went, we have planted the CAW flag in Michelin."

I added, "The question now is not if the Michelin workers will become members of the CAW, but when."

I was asked about the professor's remarks.

"Yes, they were damaging," I admitted. "Obviously, not everything turned on that, but when workers are worried about keeping their jobs, that concern becomes overriding. Any consideration about why they might want to have a union takes second place. When a family having breakfast together believes that a vote for the union might mean the job is gone, that's very likely to affect the way the worker votes."

I'm told I looked poised on television, but I was deeply shaken. Being a labour leader isn't all victory parades.

Michelin said after the vote that the company had learned from the CAW organizing campaign. Four days later, the company announced a number of changes to meet complaints that we had identified during the campaign. For instance there was a new relocation policy, a new policy for depositing pay cheques, more flexible hours for the day shifts, and the company started paying workers for travel and food expenses when they worked overtime. In a letter to employees, Michelin promised radical changes in management style, countering criticism of Michelin's intensely private way of doing business. Michelin said in future the company would make itself more open to employees and the public. So, even by losing, Michelin workers got some improvements in their work lives.

CHAPTER TWENTY-FOUR

Too High a Price to Pay

I N THE SUMMER OF 1985, the Canadian Airline Employees' Association, a spunky little union of 4,500 members spread over seven air lines, voted to join the CAW instead of fighting an increasingly uncertain industry on its own. Most CALEA members worked at the check-in counters and at reservation offices, but there were also flight attendants, mechanics, flight-kitchen workers, baggage handlers, and freight-forwarding agents.

CALEA was a small but strong union that had negotiated good collective agreements with the airline industry. They decided to merge with a bigger union because they saw concession contracts coming up in their troubled industry. At a special convention, they voted 82 per cent to merge with us.

That put us into unknown waters. We had to learn about a whole new industry in a hurry. In May 1985, I had helped the CALEA bargaining team settle their strike at Air Canada. Now, in November, we faced our first complete contract negotiation in the airline industry. I sent Buzz Hargrove to Vancouver to head the bargaining team opposite Pacific Western Airlines. PWA had two other collective agreements expiring at about the same time, one with CALFAA, the Canadian Air Line Flight Attendants' Association, and the other with the IAM, the International Association of Machinists and Aerospace Workers, which represented the baggage handlers and maintenance people. We agreed with CALFAA and the IAM to bargain simultaneously and present a common front.

In the United States deregulation had caused an upheaval in the airline industry, with some airlines disappearing altogether and others being absorbed. It was reminiscent of the worst days of the recession in the automotive industry. Airline operators were asking their employees in all three unions to take salary cuts and accept poorer working conditions or else the airline would fold.

We set a strike deadline for one minute after midnight, November 20, 1985, and got to work at the bargaining table, negotiating separately but simultaneously. The airline management continued to insist on concessions, and all three unions went on strike together. No one expected that PWA could function with three unions on strike, but it did. Service was reduced, but PWA continued to fly.

We had difficulties with our common front even before the strike. We discovered that the more established airline unions preferred a gentler bargaining style than we usually adopt. CAW people are quite willing to shout at management when we bargain if it's necessary. But even if we had adopted a milder tone, we couldn't get around the resentment of CAW as an outsider, the big boy on the block, and of me. In the west, where feelings about Toronto-based people aren't always charitable anyway, CAW's presence in the airline industry was resented by some.

It didn't seem to help that I had a personal connection in the industry through my wife, Marilyne, a national vice-president of CALFAA. In fact, as we were both to discover, our relationship only made matters more difficult.

I heard complaints from the rest of the bargaining team that Buzz's manner was too officious. Buzz isn't officious at all, but he can come across as sharp-tongued and will push hard to get decisions made.

The strike was dragging on. I grew impatient, as I often do. "This is nuts," I said. "We have to find out what is going on. I must talk to the top of this company."

A few days before Christmas, I announced that I was going to Calgary, where the PWA head office is located, to get involved in negotiations. A lot of media met me at the airport, which didn't endear me to the heads of the other unions. While they were slogging it out in meetings, my arrival drew a lot of attention.

I met with the top people at PWA, but I couldn't get them to be realistic. Because their planes were flying, their attitude about the strike was casual and almost disinterested. Hemi Mitic was our staff person assigned to PWA and, along with Buzz, was working hard to get the three bargaining committees to reconcile the differences between themselves as well as those with the company. We all knew we were going to have to give up some things in the contracts, but the disputes within our ranks centered on how much we could protect.

The strike was troubling. Our 800 airline members had been drawing strike pay of $100 a week for seven weeks in the middle of winter and over Christmas, a cruel time to be on strike.

In January, Buzz, Hemi, and the committee got a tentative settlement with PWA on our issues. We notified the company that we wouldn't go back to work, despite the tentative agreement, because we were in a common front with the other two unions. PWA would have to settle as well with the flight attendants and the machinists.

We met with the CAW local union airline leadership. They were pleased with the agreement but troubled to hear that we wouldn't allow a ratification vote to be taken until the other two unions had their agreements. Buzz, Hemi, and the committee went to membership meetings in Calgary, Vancouver, Edmonton, and Winnipeg to explain the position we were taking. In a couple of places, they got a rough reception. Members said they were paying dues to the CAW to get them a good agreement and end the strike. We had the good agreement and now they wanted to vote on it and get back to work.

We got little appreciation from CALFAA or IAM, who were furious that we had an agreement and they were still talking. "What the hell are they mad about?" I asked Buzz. "What's the point of cutting our ass? Our people are still out there on the picket lines." Buzz couldn't explain it.

We carried that strike seven weeks beyond the day we got a tentative settlement, a very bitter and difficult time for everyone. Buzz stayed in Calgary, keeping in touch with me by telephone, but negotiations with the other two unions appeared to be going nowhere. Suddenly, PWA tried another strategy. It gave CALFAA and IAM an insulting and incomplete offer and issued an ultimatum that if IAM and CALFAA didn't take the offer to their memberships at once for a vote, they would withdraw it. It was a curious move because the offer was one the membership was certain to reject.

Without consulting us, CALFAA and IAM ordered a vote. Our airline bargaining committee went wild. Here we were, holding off on voting for a decent settlement for seven weeks, and here they were rushing a bad offer to their membership without even telling us. On a Saturday morning I had a conference telephone call with members of our bargaining committee, spread from Winnipeg to Vancouver, to discuss what we should do about it.

The consensus was that if we didn't have the ratification vote on our own contract right away, we'd lose the union. The members couldn't stand any more delay after fourteen weeks on strike.

"Let's go," I said.

Our membership ratified the agreement by a majority of 90 per cent. As expected, the IAM and CALFAA members rejected their agreements. That left them still on strike, so we told PWA that we wouldn't work. We wouldn't cross the IAM and CALFAA picket lines.

PWA filed an unfair labour practice suit against us with the Canada Labour Relations Board. They claimed we were on an illegal strike because our membership had ratified an agreement, and PWA was absolutely right. The Labour Board declared the CAW strike illegal, and our members had no choice but to go through the CALFAA and IAM picket lines.

That went on for two weeks until finally the two unions got an acceptable settlement. During that unhappy period, their leadership made hard statements about CAW. They gave us no credit for keeping our people out for seven weeks after reaching a settlement, nor that we crossed their picket lines only because of the Canada Labour Board decision. They claimed we had violated the common front and held us up to ridicule and contempt as an organization of scabs.

I've never heard of a union keeping its membership out on strike for seven weeks without giving them an oportunity to vote on a valid temporary agreement, but no one was listening to our side of it.

CAW's baptism in the airline industry was a prelude to an involvement that got even messier. We found ourselves in the middle of the airline mergers caused by deregulation. In the summer of 1986, Canadian Pacific Air Lines announced the purchase of Nordair and, subsequently, Eastern Provincial Airways Ltd. Union jurisdiction was split all over the place. CAW had both the flight attendants and passenger agents at Eastern Provincial, but Nordair's flight attendants were with the airline division of CUPE, as a result of a recent merger between CALFAA and CUPE, and their passenger agents were with the IAM. Nordair's mechanics were also with the IAM. CP flight attendants were with the Canadian Union of Public Employees, the largest union in the country, and their passenger agents were with the Brotherhood of Railway and Airline Clerks, BRAC.

The Canada Labour Relations Board ordered two votes, one for the combined flight attendants, and another for the combined passenger agents, to decide which union they wanted to represent them in collective bargaining with CP.

CAW had the smallest number of workers affected of the four unions involved. There were about 1,700 flight attendants in CUPE's airline division and two hundred flight attendants with us. About 1,500 passenger agents belonged to BRAC and 220 with us. Obviously, we didn't have the numbers to win and I felt we should simply withdraw from the field.

Our members protested hotly. "We're members of the CAW," they told us, "and we want to stay in the CAW. You have to at least try."

Though I had serious misgivings, I agreed to put on a campaign. We conducted a low-key campaign which avoided running down the other three unions. The airline industry was changing, we said, and more mergers would take place. We had a good record of collective bargaining, and we had also shown that we believe in change internally in our own union. We had a fresh perspective to bring.

Our prediction that more mergers would take place was correct. A few short weeks later, PWA announced it had purchased CP Air. A new company was formed from the merger: Canadian Airlines International. Once again we were in a contest with BRAC and the IAM.

Jane Armstrong from our office, formerly with CALEA, was put in charge of the membership drive. In November 1986, she suggested I address a series of membership meetings across the country, starting in Vancouver and moving to Toronto, Montreal, and Halifax.

I couldn't believe the reception I got. The other unions went crazy. When I went before the invited membership in Vancouver, I saw some of the leadership of CALFAA and BRAC waiting with notepads, pencils, and hostile faces. I'd known those people in the labour movement for years. Some from CALFAA were people I'd met through my wife.

The same people grimly followed me to the Toronto meeting and to Montreal. Only a few went on to Halifax because we were very strong there. It didn't matter that we didn't have any choice but to try and support our members, the other unions were smearing us as a ruthless organization. A lot of the flak was falling on me.

Jane Armstrong had to defend me and tried to take the heat out of the situation. "He's part of the leadership and the profile, and we believe we have the resources, the experience and the leadership," she told the *Globe and Mail*. She refused to be drawn into a mud-slinging match with the other unions. "You have to respect people who are loyal to their own union," she said.

The IAM and some people in CALFAA sent letters to their members saying that if the CAW won the vote, the airline unions could never again have a common front because we couldn't be trusted. They gave a garbled account of the events in the PWA strike and said we had sold out. There was one funny touch. BRAC put out a button: BRAC NOT WHITE.

At every meeting of airline workers, I retraced the events of the PWA strike, explaining step by step how it happened that we were forced to go through those picket lines.

"You can criticize our decisions," I said to our detractors, "but don't tell us we don't practice solidarity."

The two votes were held in early January. Marilyne was put in a peculiar position as an executive of a competing union. Even though we made sure her integrity was intact by not discussing the dispute in private, her loyalty (never mine) was always suspect.

The first vote involving us was with the passenger agents, who decided to be represented by BRAC. On the same day in January 1987 we lost the Michelin vote, I got news of the second vote. The flight attendants, asked to choose between us or CUPE, voted to go with CUPE in large numbers. On CBC national news that night, labour reporter Alan Garr said, "This has not been a good day for Bob White."

Some people took satisfaction from that. They were saying, it's about goddamn time Bob White got knocked down.

THROUGHOUT THIS DIFFICULT PERIOD, I was spending as much time fighting free trade as I was fighting the corporations. I seem to have been one of the first to react to Prime Minister Mulroney's initiative. I had an uneasy feeling when I saw him at the Shamrock Summit in Quebec City in March 1985 singing Irish ballads with President Ronald Reagan and talking about free trade.

Talk of a free trade agreement began to build slowly. The prime minister was evasive when asked his intentions. Few were paying much attention, but I raised the alarm in my Canadian Council report in June 1985, only two months after the Shamrock Summit.

"I think there is something rather sinister going on regarding the important decisions to be made about a government trade policy," I said. "The government proponents for free trade with the United States are making a lot of public statements about the benefits to Canada in jobs, etc., and say they are consulting with various sectors. The consultations are taking place in small-group meetings such as CLC offices where opposition is expressed, but these are private meetings so this opposition does not get much publicity.

"The way the government is dealing with the Canadian people on this issue is like a person feeding a baby pablum. Give it a small spoonful at a time, and if it doesn't spit it out, feed it some more. It's difficult to get a debate going when the government is saying we're not sure, we want to have more dialogue, it seems like a good idea, the U.S. is our biggest market, etc. I think we must have more public debate and try and stop the government's momentum before it goes too far."

Shortly after our Council meeting, I attended a CLC executive meeting where I suggested that the CLC begin developing a national position and get the message out that free trade would damage Canada beyond recognition. The CLC executive met for a one-day special session to discuss the issue in July 1985. At the end, we unanimously adopted a strong position against free trade. As all regions of the country are represented in the CLC, we knew our resolution would make it much more difficult for the government to play one region off against another.

In the fall of 1985, the CLC rejected an invitation by the government to participate in a free-trade committee for the simple reason that the committee's mandate wasn't to determine whether Canada should pursue a free-trade policy but only how fast and how far. I started to make speeches from one end of the country to the other, saying about the same thing everywhere because the reasons for opposing free trade don't change.

I went back to the subject of free trade at the December 1985 meeting of the Canadian Council. "Bilateral free trade is about jobs and loss of jobs," I reported. "It is about our social programs and our ability to retain them or improve them. It is about retention of important cultural institutions, and it is not an overstatement to say it is about sovereignty – our ability as a nation to make independent political decisions, both domestic and international, with which the Americans may disagree.

"Free trade gets to the very roots of collective bargaining because it encourages the establishment of a society that is predicated on the survival of the fittest, on being the most competitive regardless of the costs to communities and workers. Free trade encourages deregulation as well as privatization of public services. It discourages economic planning, including regional expansion programs that encourage industry to relocate in areas of high unemployment."

The Mulroney government was saying that certain aspects of Canadian enterprise would not be on the table. I said it was extremely doubtful that Canada could control what was on the table and what was off once negotiations began; that in free-trade talks everything would be up for grabs. I've been in bargaining most of my life and I know that the other side puts things on the table whether you like it or not.

As early as the summer of 1985, I said that the Americans would not accept limits on what we were prepared to put on the table. This became clear when the governors of East Coast states told the premiers of Eastern provinces that summer that they thought the unemployment insurance paid to fishermen in the winter months was an unfair government subsidy.

In 1985 we had a $20-billion trade surplus with the United States. It is naive to suggest that under free trade we'll have an even greater surplus and more jobs in Canada. The Mulroney government and the Macdonald Commission weren't able to point to one single job that would be created in Canada under free trade. In fact, the reverse is true. Job losses would be felt immediately in manufacturing, especially in textiles, carpets, boots and shoes, appliances, brewing, food processing, computers, and boat-building.

Despite the protests that the Canada-U.S. Auto Pact isn't on the table, I firmly believe it is, and that if free trade talks proceed, either we'll be obliged to give up many of the safeguards in the Auto Pact or the penalties for failing to meet those safeguards will be amended. We have two car-assembly plants in Canada today that would have been wiped out during the recession but for the safeguards in the Auto Pact.

In January 1987, Peter Murphy, the outspoken American who is negotiating the free trade agreement for their side, said bluntly that he "couldn't imagine" the Auto Pact not being on the table. It accounts for one-third of all trade between Canada and the United States, amounting to $50 billion a year, and is the single most important reason that the U.S. trade deficit with Canada is that country's second largest, after Japan.

The prime minister may have thought the CAW would be quiet if he promised that the Auto Pact wouldn't be on the bargaining table. But the debate about free trade goes far beyond concern for preserving the Auto Pact I'm opposed to free trade because it will fundamentally change the kind of Canada we will have in the future – economically, socially, culturally, and politically.

It disturbed me that in 1985 the government's free trade initiative was met with apathy by most Canadians. Grant Devine, premier of Saskatchewan, criticized me angrily for speaking against free trade in his province, implying that an Eastern trade-union leader shouldn't speak on behalf of Saskatchewan farm families. I retorted that was nonsense. The issue of free trade isn't an east-versus-west matter. It is a national concern and I would continue to raise it on that basis.

The Mulroney government's brief honeymoon with Canadians ended at about the time that the implications of free trade began to sink in. I saw free trade as only one of a succession of steps that Mulroney already had made, though without much opposition, to integrate this country closer with the

Americans. It is highly unlikely that any Canadian government negotiator could agree with a U.S. proposal to drastically alter our important social programs such as medicare and unemployment insurance, because any such move would be politically unacceptable to most Canadians. But I firmly believe that a free-trade agreement would seriously hamper our government's ability to maintain and improve our social services in the future. Canadians should realize that many of the proponents of free trade disagree with the principle of universality that is fundamental to our social programs. They agree with the corporate sector that the costs of these programs make us uncompetitive and argue that the private sector should be allowed to provide these services for profit.

In many of my speeches about free trade, I have said that since Prime Minister Mulroney developed his special relationship with President Reagan, he has taken the teeth out of the Foreign Investment Review Agency, dismantled the National Energy Program, given up our Drug Patent legislation, accepted the 35-per-cent tariff the U.S. imposed on our shakes and shingles, and has self-imposed a 15-per-cent duty on softwood lumber in the face of U.S. threats. If that's what happens under a special relationship, my sincere hope is that we get back to a normal relationship quickly.

Over the years, Canada has developed into a reasonably caring society. We may think it isn't good enough, but when we compare our social programs to those in the United States, we're miles ahead of the Americans. That's a great credit to politicians of all political stripes. In the past there have been leaders in all parties who have had the guts to stand up and demand social justice. We have to make sure the cultural and social values we have in Canada will survive.

The strange apathy around free trade alarmed me. I felt if we could get a debate going, if Canadians learned the risks involved, the country would rouse itself against the talks. As a start, Wendy Cuthbertson and Sam Gindin worked on an excellent document, *Free Trade Could Cost Us Canada*, which was sent to every member of our union. A striking pamphlet printed with red and blue headings and highlights, it asked the questions Why? and Who supports this move? and provided answers, complete with graphs. We offered this alternative to free trade:

"We should be addressing the need to plan our trade and plan our economy and, rather than focusing on free trade, be asking: How can we build more of the machinery used to extract these resources? How do we develop a manufacturing base so that we have the skills and capacities to meet our needs and the flexibility to adapt to a changing world?

"Rather than free trade, Canada needs an independent industrial strategy to develop a strong economy, full employment, and adequate social programs. We want to emphasize our confidence in building a different, more progressive society north of the 49th parallel."

We sent that document to every member of our union.

The Ontario Federation of Labour under Cliff Pilkey's leadership was quick off the mark and conducted a first-rate campaign against free trade. The independent Coalition Against Free Trade put together a sensational night at Massey Hall in Toronto. A number of artists, among them the Royal Canadian Air Farce, Nancy White, and Erika Ritter, donated their time and considerable talents to a program of entertainment and speeches about the dangers of free trade.

I was about eighth in a roster of speakers that included Walter Gordon, Ursula Franklin, and Bishop Remi DeRoo, wondering what was left to say. I had scratched a few pages of notes, but they contained little in keeping with the euphoric mood that had seized the audience. Waiting my turn, I remembered that Prime Minister Mulroney was in Washington that night.

I opened with, "I've got some good news and some bad news. The good news is that the prime minister is out of the country. The bad news is that he's in Washington trying to give it away to the Americans."

I added, "How I wish he was down there telling them to get the hell out of Nicaragua instead." I obviously touched a chord, because it brought the house down.

The excuse the Mulroney government offered for seeking a bilateral free-trade agreement with the United States was that it would protect us from the spirit of protectionism that's growing in Washington. In my view, it's extremely naive to think as the free-traders do that being competitive automatically guarantees Canadians unlimited access to selling their goods in the U.S. market. The U.S. political system will never allow us to devastate certain sectors of their economy at the expense of thousands of U.S. jobs, free trade or no free trade.

We're already competitive in shakes and shingles, for instance, and that has meant that the States slapped on a 35 per cent tariff. We're competitive in basic steel, so we have voluntarily limited ourselves to 3 per cent of the U.S. market. We're so competitive in the auto industry that, going on labour costs alone, we average ten dollars an hour less than in the States but we're prevented from getting more auto production. We're so competitive in softwood lumber that we've agreed to put a 15 per cent duty on ourselves.

In the spring of 1987, a new lobby group in support of free trade was announced, the Canadian Alliance for Trade and Job Opportunities. Its members include the Chamber of Commerce, the Canadian Manufacturers' Association, the Business Council on National Issues, the Canadian Federation of Independent Business, and for some misguided reason, the Consumers' Association of Canada.

In many ways, except for the Consumers' Association, this grouping is quite predictable. Most of these organizations in the past have adopted the position that whatever is good for business and profit is good for the nation. They have opposed every important social gain we have made. If their point of view had prevailed over the years, we would have no medicare, no unemployment insurance, no indexed pensions, no minimum-wage legislation, no government commitment to equal pay for work of equal value, no prohibition on extra-billing by doctors. In short, we would have a very different Canada today – a country with no commitment to the poor, the disadvantaged, the elderly, the sick, or to working people. That tells me something about what sector of the economy free trade is intended to benefit.

In the beginning, we had a hard time convincing our own membership to come out against free trade. At first they believed that the Auto Pact was free trade. The Auto Pact worked to Canada's advantage, so why wouldn't total free trade? But the Auto Pact isn't free trade, it's managed trade. It's a negotiated bilateral trade agreement that said to the American auto companies that if they wanted to sell cars in Canada duty free they would have to make vehicles in Canada. They were forced to accept a 60 per cent Canadian content rule. Since there is no Canadian-owned auto company, there was no reason to impose a matching 60 per cent American content rule.

All sorts of odd alliances have formed between trade unionists and others in the country who feel the same alarm about free trade – computer experts, farmers, small businessmen, wine-makers, artists, broadcasters, academics, and women's groups. To my surprise, the New Democratic Party was a bit slow off the mark, but has been forceful of late.

I think the government is waiting for us to get tired fighting. It's true that I get sick myself of going over the same ground. I've talked to the Kiwanis, Canadian clubs, labour conventions, teachers, Rotary clubs, political conventions. My message on free trade hasn't changed in the years since this matter was first raised, and there a certain fatigue has set in from saying the same thing over and over.

Simon Reisman was hailed as a giant killer when he was appointed the Canadian government's chief negotiator for free trade. That gave me a chuckle. The idea was that our canny Simon Reisman was going to be too smart and too tough for the young American Peter Murphy, wet behind the ears. To put things in perspective, at the same time Washington was slapping a 35-per cent tariff on shakes and shingles without so much as the courtesy of a telephone call to the prime minister. To think that we dominate in those talks is ludicrous.

My experience in the international UAW helped me in this. I learned there that the Americans don't get out of bed in the morning and wonder what they can do for Canada today, nor should they. To make any impact on them, a Canadian has to keep making the case that Canada is not a northern state, it's a fundamentally different country. Given how the softwood lumber issue was bargained and how we accommodated the U.S. multinational drug manufacturers by changing Canada's drug-patent legislation, we should all be concerned about the Tory government's ability to deal with the Americans.

I don't underestimate the trade problems we're going to have with the States. They've already tried to get at our social and cultural programs and that pressure is only going to increase. Those are too high a price to pay. To protect ourselves, we've got to work on trade issues on an individual basis. Some we'll win and some we won't. My feeling is that we should be setting up a permanent bilateral trade commission, backed by a team of economists and research experts, to anticipate crises and to resolve trade disputes as they emerge. The opposites on the commission, like labour-management bargaining teams, would develop credentials with each other and build up expertise and trust that would enable them to minimize confrontations and quickly sort out the difficulties. Without such experienced people, we flounder from one mishandled collision to the next. We could set up this arrangement without totally integrating ourselves economically with the U.S. and risking our political sovereignty and our ability to plan our own economic directions for the future as we will through a free-trade agreement.

David Peterson, Ontario's premier, has been important to the free-trade debate, and I played a small part in helping him become premier. In the 1985 Ontario election, Frank Miller and his Tory party won the most seats, but far fewer than the NDP and Liberals combined. I was on a panel of people on Global television who were asked to comment as the returns were coming in. I said on the air that the Conservatives had lost their right to govern. Ian Deans, an NDP Hamilton member of parliament, who was also on the panel, argued with me after the show. He said they had the votes and they had a right to continue. I shook my head. "A significant majority of the people in

Ontario has said tonight that they didn't want Frank Miller to govern the province. I think we should pay attention to that. The Tories have governed too long. It's like a car after a winter. It needs a good wash."

I bumped into John Sewell, former mayor of Toronto, the next day. He said, "Do you really think there's a chance of getting rid of the Tories?"

I said, "I don't know. I've been thinking about it, but I don't know."

Later that day I saw a way. The NDP should not prop up the Tories in order to keep a tired government in power. If the NDP supported the Liberals, we could get a fresh perspective that would be good for the system.

Bob Rae, leader of the Ontario NDP, called me. "Would you be prepared to come to a meeting Sunday morning?" he asked. "A few of us are going to meet to talk about what we do as a result of the election."

"Where are you at?" I inquired.

He said, "I'm for trying to do something with the Liberals."

"So am I," I told him.

Ed Broadbent, Bob Rae, and some other prominent members of the NDP were at the meeting and we batted the subject around. Some worried, quite rightly, that if the party threw its support to the Liberals, Peterson's government would get all the credit for whatever good it did. Bob argued persuasively, and I did my best to help him, that we could get some good legislation out of it. The alternative certainly wasn't appealing. None of us wanted to see the Tories drag on under Frank Miller.

A few days later, Bob Rae consulted labour leaders on their views about the Ontario NDP working with the Liberals to unseat Miller. I couldn't attend that meeting because I had to be in Ottawa, but John Deverell of the *Toronto Star* caught wind of it. He caught me at the airport to ask what I thought the NDP should do.

I replied, "I think we should work something out with the Liberals and dump the Tories." That phrase, "dump the Tories," was a front-page headline in the Star.

I caught hell from other labour leaders for sticking my neck out ahead of the decision, but I think the NDP was wise to enable the Liberals to govern Ontario. The accord the Liberals and the NDP signed to support each other for two years produced some good, progressive legislation. One of the key moves they made was to introduce a bill prohibiting doctors from billing their patients more than the OHIP (the public health insurance plan) rate. Many doctors were outraged at the government's action and the Ontario Medical Association fought back with a variety of tactics including, ironically for an association which felt its professionalism was being threatened, organizing a strike. But the strike didn't win much support and public opinion was firmly behind the government. It was well worth the fight to protect Ontario patients from exhorbitant doctors' fees.

Other legislation included human rights, first-contract legislation, equal pay for work of equal value, and changes in severance pay. In other words, as a result of the accord, Ontario residents have benefitted from an active, reasonably progressive political agenda for change. The NDP has made Peterson look good, sure, but that has been healthy for the political process. The Tories are going through a wash, and they needed it.

CHAPTER TWENTY-FIVE

Controversy in
Labour's House

T OWARDS THE END OF 1986, we had trouble once again at McDonnell-Douglas Aerospace in Mississauga. McDonnell-Douglas has been a problem for us for years. In 1981, when the Canadian government decided to spend $5 billion on F-18 fighter planes, some of the work was supposed to be done at McDonnell-Douglas. That promise of more jobs proved empty. Instead, in 1981, 2,250 jobs were lost in the McDonnell-Douglas plant in Mississauga.

I went to the Ontario premier at that time, William Davis, to demand a full-scale independent inquiry. He wouldn't go that far, but he did assign a task force, which turned out to be a useless exercise. In October 1983 our contract with the company expired and McDonnell-Douglas came to us with a proposal for major concessions on seniority, job posting, pensions, and paid holidays, a deceptive wage increase for about half the workers, and a multi-tier wage system that would allow the company to pay new employees at a decreased rate for seven years.

The workers stayed on the job while we wrestled with our decision. In the middle of talks, the company shook us by laying off 500 more workers, justifying itself because of a strike in the States. We were getting nowhere with negotiations, so we set a strike deadline for March 21, 1984. As the deadline approached, our 2,400 workers were under a lot of stress. The Mississauga plant makes wings, floors, and tail sections for McDonnell-Douglas aircraft and had five months' supply of wings stockpiled. We were facing an exceedingly long strike.

The previous autumn the UAW had struck McDonnell-Douglas at its huge plants in Long Beach, California, Tulsa, Oklahoma, and Arkansas. Months into the strike, with Christmas approaching, the company dangled paid holidays and a 3 per cent bonus in front of strikers, who began to drift back to work through their own picket lines. The company invited laid-off employees to cross the picket lines until there were enough people inside to get the plants running. The strike was lost and workers got a miserable concession contract that gave them no wage increase and a tiered wage system.

The company was confident that Canadian workers, knowing what had happened in the States, would have no stomach for a strike. A few days before the strike deadline, I called two meetings of the membership, one with Local 1967, representing the hourly wage earners, and the other with Local 673, the office employees. As I arrived at the first meeting, a worker snarled, "You're the sonovabitch who's trying to take us out on strike. We're going to show you today."

I explained the reason we had to fight the tiered wage system before it spread into Canada. I called it "a cancer," and said it would erode the wage structure that had taken years for the union to gain. When we called for the votes, plant workers overwhelmingly declared that they were ready to strike. Office and technical workers also gave support.

We argued with management that Canadians couldn't follow the American pattern in the aerospace industry anymore than we could in the automotive industry. Because of the lower value of the Canadian dollar our labour costs were less by about six dollars an hour than their costs in the States. A company spokesman told me that he couldn't do anything to change the offer because it came from the chairman of his board. I told him that there was another chairman who once announced that the Canadians were going to have to eat concessions. His name, I said, was Lee Iacocca.

They came to their senses the day before the strike deadline and made us a money offer. The worst of the concession demands were withdrawn and, only ninety minutes before the workers were set to walk out, we hammered out a three-year agreement. Retroactive to October 1983, it saved the cost-of-living allowance, got immediate increases for more than 80 per cent of our workers, and eliminated the multi-tier wage proposal. We had to accept a modified version of the company's insistence on a lower hiring rate, but we were able to hold it to 85 per cent of the going wage, and the company agreed to eliminate the wage gap after eighteen months on the job. We did, however, have to accept lump-sum payments.

Less than two years later the company came back at us. In direct violation of the agreement, it was combining classifications. We protested but they went ahead anyway, in some cases combining as many as ten classifications into one. The workers observed a five-minute memorial silence inside the plant for the deceased classifications, which so infuriated McDonnell Douglas that they hauled us before the Ontario Labour Relations Board and charged us with conducting an illegal strike.

When the agreement ended in the summer of 1986, we took the position that the aerospace industry was recovering, and we didn't have to take any more concessions. By this time we were representing about 4,000 workers at McDonnell-Douglas, all of them determined to get wage increases, not the lump-sum payments of the previous contract.

Negotiations were awkward because McDonnell-Douglas had only one bargaining team for both Canada and the United States, which was tied up in Long Beach, where some 16,000 workers were facing the expiry of their contract but hadn't yet set a strike deadline. To accommodate the situation, we set a strike deadline for ten days after the California agreement was due to expire.

The company's proposal to the UAW in California was for lump-sum payments instead of wage increases in each of the three years of the contract. The McDonnell-Douglas workers rejected that proposal but still no strike vote was taken, so the company's bargaining team dropped negotiations there and moved to Canada.

Though I told them we were all through with lump-sum payments, each of the several proposals they made had at least one lump-sum payment in it. We made progress in a number of areas such as pensions and benefits but they wouldn't drop the lump-sum payment. Finally, at ten o'clock at night, twelve hours before the strike deadline, the company made a proposal which included an 8 per cent one-time catch-up – a lump-sum payment – in the first year instead of a wage increase, a 4 per cent wage increase in the second year, and 4 per cent in the third year. That meant about $2,300 as a lump-sum payment for most workers, maybe a little more for others and a little less for new employees.

Nick, Sam, Buzz, and I bounced their offer around, as we always do. "How do we take workers on strike when you've got them a lot more money? If we take the lump-sum payment this year, it will be behind us next year. We'll be through with lump-sum payments in the aerospace industry. We're back to wage increases in time for the 1987 round of aerospace negotiations and auto bargaining in 1987 with the Big Three. I know the workers want a wage increase in every year, but look what it will cost them to take a long strike."

As we all knew, McDonnell-Douglas is very tough in a strike. In fact, as the four-month U.S. strike in 1983 demonstrated, workers can go back with less than the contract proposal they rejected. Unions don't have much leverage in the aerospace industry with a short strike, because no one worries too much if a $40-million plane is a few months late for delivery.

So I recommended to the Local 1967 and Local 673 bargaining committees that we accept the offer. The committees were troubled by the lump-sum payment in the first year, but it was a significant amount of money, and the other pieces of the contract were good. We would be rid of lump-sum payments in the second year. If the agreement had been in the reverse order, they would never have accepted it.

At around seven in the morning, three hours before strike deadline, we called off the strike and scheduled ratification vote meetings for later that week in the International Trade Centre in Mississauga, across the road from the plant.

Chairs were set up for 3,500 workers. The voting would be done in waves, starting at ten in the morning with production and maintenance workers. Buzz, Nick, Sam, and I arrived about a quarter to ten. As soon as I entered the room, I could feel the hostility. One of the workers fell in beside me and said in a low voice, "White, I've heard you're a helluva speaker, but you've got your work cut out for you today. This crowd is goddamned mad."

"What about?" I asked.

"Fucking lump-sum payment," he snapped. "They want a dollar an hour catch-up, not the lump sum."

Certainly they were entitled to that, but the question was, could they get it? And what sacrifices would they have to make to get it? I was convinced that it would be too big a gamble for me to recommend a strike. Now I was going to have to argue that position with the members.

When I got up to speak all hell broke loose. Though we had an excellent sound system – that's essential at a ratification meeting – I couldn't be heard above the roar of boos and the chants of BULLSHIT! and SELL OUT! SELL OUT! accompanied by stomping feet. Two guys paraded in front of me with a hand-painted banner BETTER RED THAN WHITE. Everyone was standing, giving me the thumb-down gesture and the finger-up one, too.

"Look guys," I shouted above the din, "I'm going to speak here today." The room was no quieter. "If you want to vote against the agreement," I went on, "you've got a right to do that. But I'm the president of the union, I'm the elected president of this union, and I've been in the bargaining. I have some obligations to tell you what happened and why I'm recommending this agreement and we're going to be here until I do it. The more booing you do, the longer it'll take, but I'm going to stay here."

The boos only increased. A group on the right side of the room organized the BULLSHIT! chorus and had it going at commendable volume.

"Let's try it one more time," I shouted. "At least I'm entitled to make my points. Those of you who are against the agreement can make your points, but first let me make mine."

After about five minutes or so, it started to quiet down. Five minutes is a long, long time to stand in front of 3,000 people yelling. I was looking for people who weren't yelling. There weren't many.

But eventually people got tired or hoarse. I explained how the negotiations had gone, what had happened in California, and how this was the first time we had reached an agreement in the aerospace industry ahead of the Americans. I told them my rationale for recommending that we take the one-time lump-sum payment, our success in getting back to wage increases in the final two years of the contract, and the major improvements we won in pensions, dental care, and health care.

I couldn't get any place. The explanation was punctuated throughout with boos and catcalls and more chants.

I had one sure-fire victory to tell them about. This concerned the treatment of foremen who had once been members of the bargaining unit. The practice during layoffs had been, instead of being laid off, the foreman went back to the bargaining unit and bumped someone working on the shop floor out on the street. We had put a stop to that. McDonnell-Douglas had agreed that after a certain time, a foreman would lose his seniority in the bargaining unit, although he would, of course, keep his service for pensions, vacations, and other company benefits. Any time we got that in a contract, workers always cheered because they love to get back at foremen. I told Local 1967 the good news, there wasn't a ripple of applause.

It took me twenty minutes to finish my explanation because of the interruptions. At the end I said, "I am not prepared to recommend a strike on the basis of this proposal. If you tell me that you don't want it, and you're prepared to strike McDonnell-Douglas, and go on strike for as long as it takes to change the agreement, I'm with you. I'll go back to the bargaining and I'll do my best to get what you want."

"You won't," a hundred people yelled. "You won't fight for it. You'll sell us out."

"I've spent my life in the labour movement," I said. "I don't sell people out. You may question my judgment but I don't sell people out."

When Munir Kahlid, head of their bargaining team, got up to speak, they gave him just as hard a time, especially over the changes in classifications. Reduction in the number of classifications admittedly is hard to take, but there are a reality in the aerospace industry and there isn't much a union can do about it. When it was Nick's turn, he didn't do any better than I did. The members stood and booed the benefits, a good package, just as loudly as they had the lump-sum payments and the reduced classifications.

Every one of the six floor mikes had line-ups of ten, fifteen furious people waiting impatiently for the speeches to end so they could attack us. I think there were only two poor souls who meekly suggested that the meeting should ratify the agreement. They were booed to the rafters.

At least part of the workers' anger was over the way they were treated by McDonnell-Douglas, a rage that had been building for years. At contract times, anger against the company is often taken out on the union. Workers need a chance to vent their frustrations, and the president of their union and their bargaining team are the only available targets they've got. Almost no one was yelling at McDonnell-Douglas for insisting on lump-sum payments and cutting classifications. Instead they shouted that they were going to vote out the entire bargaining team and me, too.

They argued against the agreement from contradictory perspectives. One member declared that because we got the big lump sum, the company would start laying workers off. I said it was just the opposite, the industry was in an upswing and would be hiring. Another worker, an older man whose face was livid, said if that was true why didn't we go after the company for the one buck an hour raise? I said bargaining was the art of the possible, and that wasn't possible.

We stayed on the platform and fielded the complaints and jeers for about three hours. During the interludes of shouting, I took a poll of the platform to see how people thought the vote would go. We couldn't be sure. Nick didn't think we had it, but if we did it would be a squeaker. By now the meeting was in complete confusion because the office and technical workers, whose ratifications meeting was scheduled for one o'clock, had started to arrive.

The floor was littered with shredded paper – torn copies of the agreement and ballots many of them had thrown away to express their disgust. Somehow we got it calmed down enough to conduct a vote. Of the plant workers,

52.6 per cent were in favour of the agreement. With the office workers, who found their agreement a little less objectionable, the overall vote to ratify the agreement was 54 per cent.

When it was over, I said to Nick, "It was a good lesson for us. It keeps us in touch with workers' problems." He nodded, knowing what I meant. It was the toughest membership meeting of my life, and I've been in rough ones. The McDonnell-Douglas workers couldn't have cared less about the Bob White the public sees, the one who meets with Lee Iacocca, the one on Peter Gzowski's show and on "The Journal," the man whose picture is on magazine covers, the one who led the Canadians out of the UAW. They saw me as what I was – the man who'd negotiated a settlement they didn't like. They wanted my hide, and they had the right to go after it. They pay the dues that provide my salary. It's called democracy.

I said to Nick, "I wish the media had been here to see how the trade-union leadership leads its members around by the nose."

I LEAD A LOT OF NEGOTIATED SETTLEMENTS for our members, but I'm convinced I also have to be active on behalf of the CAW, not just in the labour movement but in the community. I spoke out against the doctors' strike in Ontario and got letters from several wives of doctors telling me that overbilling was none of my business. I wrote them back that our union has been involved in fighting for better health care for a long time. We were one of the driving forces behind universal access to health care and overbilling *is* our business.

The test of a good union is whether it gets involved in such matters. When people look at my term as leader of this union, I want them to see that we were active and outspoken on more than collective-bargaining matters, that we also took responsibility in such areas as human rights, free trade, and international affairs.

A key task for the labour movement at this point is organizing working women. Most women's jobs are in the service industry, which has been very difficult to organize. I'm proud of the way we fought for the Fleck women and the women at Blue Cross. We supported the Wholesale, Retail, and Department Store Workers when they tried to organize Eaton's, and we also were active in the small, significant strike by women against the Bank of Commerce.

This happened in the VISA department where some 300 women, many of them single parents, many of them immigrant women, were working in a basement for desperately poor wages under conditions that would never be tolerated in industry. The Canadian Labour Congress established a Union of Bank Workers and hired some organizers. The women signed cards in good numbers.

Dennis McDermott called. "We don't have the expertise," he said. "Can you lend me a good staff person to help us with the collective bargaining?"

I sent Jim O'Neil, one of our best. As always happens with us, he talked to Wendy, Sam, Buzz, and me, so, before long, about half our staff was involved. It was obvious that the bank was determined that there would be no contract. The lawyers they brought to the bargaining table were laying out their terms in a language that belonged in labour-history museums.

The women were frightened. They hadn't joined the union to have a strike, they'd joined to get better wages and conditions. Their demands were modest, but still we were getting absolutely nowhere. So we set a strike deadline, moving along very carefully. Ultimately we called a meeting, late in 1985, to pull the women together. Just as happened in the Fleck strike, the women had time to get to know one another and real solidarity was developing.

We wanted to take the bank by surprise, draw some media attention and public sympathy. We decided that the women would stage a sit-in, but we didn't want them to be alone. We wanted O'Neil in there to give support. Bank security, however, had been tightened. No one, not even customers, could get in without being identified. The solution was simple. Someone had forgotten to watch the back door. O'Neil got inside and we announced that the strike had begun.

It began one evening and stayed through the night. Husbands came to pick up their wives and found that they were staying the night. We hadn't contemplated the special difficulty women strikers face because of child care. We learned that the women couldn't hold the sit-in for long because they had to get home to their children. When men strike they don't have to worry, usually, about getting the kids fed or off to school.

The sit-in lasted until the next day and then the women came out and formed a picket line. The CLC announced that it would pay $200 a week strike pay, close to their normal wages, to protect the women from being starved back to work. That created some hostility in the labour movement. There are always bureaucrats who think everything should be done the same way, no matter what other factors are involved. If labour leaders in the early days had thought like that, we wouldn't have unions today.

The strike went on for almost nine months. On the second day of our founding convention, the women marched into our conference room, where we cheered them. After that, the entire convention went to the lavish Bank of

Commerce centre at Bay and King in Toronto and demonstrated against the bank.

The CAW was criticized for taking such a major role in that strike. We were accused of trying to take over unionizing the banks. All we were doing was putting money and time into an issue that should matter to everyone – the lousy wages and conditions that most working women face.

Finally, I got a meeting with the president of the Bank of Commerce. It was totally unproductive. His paternalistic line was right out of the dark ages. The bank wanted to wait a year and then ask that the union be decertified. In January 1986, the Canada Labour Board began hearings into suggestions that the bank was bargaining in bad faith. Jimmy O'Neil's value at those hearings was beyond measure. He keeps copious notes, and I think he was on the witness stand for two and a half days. The Board ordered the implementation of a first agreement and got the women back to work. Early in 1987, they got their second contract, without a strike, and they got raises.

The bank knew what it was doing. Even though the women won, they kept them out for long enough to discourage other bank workers, even other workers in the public and service sectors, from trying to organize.

Our alliance with the goals of the women's movement is not unlike our support of the New Democratic Party. There is no question that the NDP is becoming a significant political force in Canada. We share the continent with a giant which views socialism and social democracy as not much different than communism, and some of that attitude has spilled across the border. But the NDP has been able to build a base of integrity despite the pressure of that kind of thinking. The party has been able to articulate a policy that is distinct from those of the other two major parties in this country.

Beginning with the CCF, the social democrats have been a major influence, well beyond their numbers, in the development of such social programs as pensions, medicare, and mother's allowances. When the NDP was founded, the labour movement was there because we identify with those social issues. We're directly involved with the party today. I've been a vice-president of the NDP since 1981. Around the world, every social democratic party has a strong labour foundation.

Our participation in politics used to be questioned. There used to be talk that the NDP was "tainted" by strikes, but that's changing. During the NDP's 1986 convention in Montreal there were more labour people taking part in discussions and debates than I've ever seen before, and the media took no note of it. It's becoming accepted that we belong with the NDP.

Our CAW members don't vote NDP because I say so. Lots of them vote for

374

the other parties, though I can't understand why. The NDP's issues are a natural extension of our concerns. You can't separate the bread box and the ballot box. We can solve a good many things around a collective bargaining table, but we can't do anything there about a rise in price of prescription drugs, or the lack of support for day care, or the damage that free trade will bring.

EARLY IN MARCH 1987, I got a call from Richard Cashin, leader of the Newfoundland fishermen's Local 1252 of the United Food and Commercial Workers, an international union with a history of treating dissidents in its ranks quite roughly. Cashin, who in the late sixties organized the Newfoundland fishermen into an independent union, the Newfoundland Fishermen's Union, which later joined the UFCW, told me that his union wanted out.

That fishermen's union is more than another union: it's a social force in the Atlantic provinces. Its members are spread over Newfoundland, Prince Edward Island, and Nova Scotia, and they're an independent-minded group of people. They were in a struggle with the international union for more autonomy and they weren't getting anywhere. They wanted to get free of that union but they had reason to be wary. In British Columbia where another local of the UFCW disagreed with the international leadership, the international union simply moved in and imposed a trusteeship without a semblance of democratic process.

At a special convention in January, the delegates to Region 18 UFCW voted for more autonomy, a motion that was rejected by the international union. That's when Dick Cashin asked for a meeting with me. He came to Toronto on Monday, February 23, 1987. He told me the fishermen had decided to get out of the UFCW. They had two choices, going back to being an independent union of some 23,000 people or joining another big union. They had decided on the latter. They weren't shopping around, they had decided they wanted to be in the CAW.

Under the rules of the Canadian Labour Congress, a local which leaves a union can't apply to be recognized as a new union within the CLC. There are reasons for this rule, but it was never intended to mean that a local would put itself out the Canadian labour movement because it was seeking more Canadian identity. The fishermen are a culture unto themselves; they belong in the Canadian labour movement.

It is true that they could have followed a different procedure, but it was one which would have left them exposed to the kinds of reprisals that the other UFCW local suffered in British Columbia.

We spent a day talking it through, at the end of which I invited Cashin and other leaders of the Fishermen's Union to attend the meeting the next week of our Executive Board. Cashin came with two of his colleagues, secretary-treasurer, Earle McCurdy, and the director of their industrial union department, Reg Anstey. Cashin spoke at length, outlining the history of the union, the mergers that led them into the UFCW, the real concern they had for their members as a result of discussions with the international on the role of Canadian directors, Canadian autonomy, and trusteeships. He gave a picture of a union that practised goon-like tactics, that lacked any sense of the need for Canadian autonomy, and was becoming less democratic and less involved in the fight for social change. Cashin wound up by saying that he had spent too much of his life helping to build the Fishermen's Union to see it destroyed.

It was an impassioned presentation from a man who, along with Father Des McGrath and others, had built the union from a small meeting of sixty-nine people in a church basement to the strongest union in Newfoundland in less than twenty years. Their union had been more than a simple union of fishermen, it has been a vehicle for social, political, and economic change in Newfoundland, and, to a lesser extent, in Prince Edward Island and Nova Scotia.

Cashin repeated what he had told me earlier. They were leaving the UFCW and were prepared to be no more than their own organization, but their preference was to become part of the CAW. They saw the CAW as a union that was receptive to change, that had a high profile which would help them in the political struggle ahead, that was open and democratic, and that was founded on the same social philosophy as the Fishermen's Union.

After a long discussion, I asked Cashin and his group to leave the room. I then recommended that we try and find a way to make the Fishermen's Union a part of the CAW. I said I knew that what the fishermen wanted to do would be controversial in the labour movement and that we would be attacked if we accepted their proposal. But I also said that the CAW could not and should not turn its back on the fishermen at a time when they were fighting to remain true to their principles and continue as a vibrant organization within Newfoundland and within Canada. This was not just another disgruntled local union, this was an organization whose leadership today includes many who built it in the early seventies. This leadership has been in the forefront of all their strikes for recognition, for economic progress, for political and social change, and they don't want what they've built to be demolished by an international union insensitive to the fishermen's roots.

376

The National Executive Board voted unanimously to pursue discussions with the fishermen. Unfortunately, word got around and we had to move quickly to save the fishermen from having their assets seized by the UFCW. I flew to Newfoundland on March 11 and met with the fishermen's executive board the next morning. Some 130 leaders of the union had met the day before and had decided officially to withdraw from the UFCW and join the CAW. When I met them they were excited and happy as hell.

On March 25, the UFCW asked the Canadian Labour Congress to expel the CAW. This was interesting because the CAW pays its full per-capita tax of around 48 cents per member each month to the CLC, while the UFCW has never paid its per-capita tax on more than half its membership. They show a membership of about 145,000 and consistently pay dues to the CLC on less than 60,000 members.

Some leaders of other unions were publicly critical. Gerry Docquier, head of the Steelworkers in Canada, led the attack with the CLC, describing my behaviour as "predatory." He said, "If this isn't a raid, I don't know what is."

A week later, the top officials of about ten unions gathered in Toronto to figure out their strategy. Bill Wynn, international president of the UFCW, vowed that he would do everything in his power, "offensively and defensively," as UFCW lawyers prepared actions against Cashin, me, and the CAW in various courts. On April 9, the UFCW sued me, the CAW, Richard Cashin, and others for $43 million in damages, declaring that I was guilty of a "flagrant, cynical and high-handed breach of duty." Ten million of that is personal damages against me.

My comment was, "I think the whole image of a union going to court to stop its members from leaving points out why the members want to leave more than anything else."

The UFCW also filed raiding charges against us at the Canadian Labour Congress, and a hearing was held before veteran labour arbitrator Senator Carl Goldenberg in Montreal. The UFCW obviously hadn't done much research because the CLC constitution clearly states that an affiliate cannot pursue an action within the Congress against another union while it is also engaged in an action against them in the courts – and Senator Goldenberg so ruled.

The UFCW, through their court actions, were trying to limit Cashin's and the other local leaders' access to their members. But they refused to be intimidated. On April 21, Cashin and the entire twenty-four-member executive board resigned. They announced courageously and confidently that they would start from scratch. They would go out and rebuild the union completely, getting their members to sign cards for a new union which could then freely merge with the CAW.

It was a gutsy move. Many staff people gave up pensions and other benefits with the UFCW. They turned over their cars, their offices, and started all over again to sign up 23,000 fishermen and allied workers in Newfoundland, P.E.I., and Nova Scotia. This decision, made just days before our CAW collective-bargaining convention in May 1987, caught the UFCW off guard.

When Cashin addressed our convention, his speech brought 500 cheering delegates to their feet. He said he was especially disturbed by a number of stories in the Toronto media criticizing the Fishermen's Union's decision.

"What the hell do people think we are in Newfoundland?" he cried. "Goddamn it, we were a separate country. We created our own union . . . This is not a legal battle, it's a political struggle. The workers want a union that represents a value system, and if some people have differences with that, they can go to hell."

After Cashin finished speaking, I joked that we should change our constitution to make sure he couldn't run for president of the CAW.

Cashin and his colleagues quickly ran out of money because the UFCW had tied up all their funds. But our National Executive Board authorized Bob Nickerson to advance sufficient funds to the new union until they have cleared all legal hurdles and start receiving dues from their members. We will then work out an arrangement to reimburse us for these expenses.

Two weeks after our convention in Toronto, the fishermen held the founding convention of their new union in St. John's. Even then, the UFCW tried to make the new union's life difficult by telling the hotel booked for the occasion that the union had no funds to pay for the convention. The hotel was on the point of cancelling when Nick heard what had happened and phoned to assure them that the CAW would pay the bills directly.

I spoke to the delegates on the second morning of the convention and received a rousing reception. The atmosphere reminded me of our founding convention in June 1985. The delegates were excited and were debating the issues before them clearly. They made changes in their constitution to make the new union even more democratic than the last.

I told the delegates what I had told our members at our convention in Toronto, that a lot of people were asking us about what benefits the fishermen would receive by being part of the CAW. My answer was to talk about how the CAW will benefit from joining with the Fishermen's Union. They bring to us the dynamics, the enthusiasm, the commitment, and the expertise of working people whose roots are planted deep in hundreds of communities in a part of Canada where we haven't many members. It is good for us to learn about the problems of fishermen, fish-plant workers, and others in this new union. It is good for us to see our union grow beyond the urban, manufacturing industries we current represent. I know the fishermen will help ensure that the CAW stays close to our roots with working people. I assured the convention that we would support them throughout the difficult period ahead – financially, organizationally, and publicly.

I've been told this was one of my better speeches, and as I left the microphone, Cashin said jokingly that he would be including a provision in their constitution to prohibit me from running for president of the Fishermen's Union.

Later that day, the delegates unanimously passed a resolution stating that once the new union completes its reorganization, it will merge with the CAW. Delegate after delegate went to the mikes and spoke of how proud they felt that soon they would be a part of the CAW. It was a very emotional time for me. If men and women like this wanted to join us in the CAW, then I knew we were and will be a dynamic force for change in Canada – a union that not only protects but advances workers' rights. I, too, felt proud of my association with this fine union.

The decision to respond to the Fishermen's Union's request has been the most controversial inside the labour movement in many years. The UFCW is using every legal trick in the book to keep the workers in their union. As I finish this book, I still don't know where that struggle will end. My hope is that it will lead to some changes within the CLC so that if another union finds itself in a similar situation, there is a procedure within the CLC to help members determine their own destiny and protect them from the heavy-handed tactics of their international union.

Because of the many and varied issues I have been involved in since leading this great union, I am constantly asked by journalists and others, What are you going to do next? Are you going into politics? My answer is that I really don't know. I've never been one to sit and contemplate my personal future. I never could have predicted that one day I would be president of a Canadian auto workers' union. It's a long way from my days on the shop floor of Hay & Co. Some of the distance I've come has been based on hard work, some based on good luck, but all of it has been a challenge, all of it exciting.

I do know for sure that I won't stay in this position until I reach the compulsory retirement age of sixty-five. For one thing, I couldn't keep up the pace and, for another, it would not be healthy for the CAW. If the CAW is to remain a dynamic organization, it needs periodic changes in leadership. It needs new, younger people to take over: men and women who have their own style, their own teams, and their own directions. The CAW is full of people with leadership potential and talent both on staff and in local unions.

I'll be moving on some day, but where to, I don't know. I honestly don't know.

Index